Horace Greeley is now remembered only for his famous slogan, "Go West, young man," yet once he was a candidate for immortal fame as an American president. The people turned him down. Irving Stone writes a fascinating history of the "also rans," right up to the latest defeated presidential candidates.

What tragedies were averted when the public turned down the self-seeking Stephen Douglas and Henry Clay; the silver-tongued, empty-headed William Jennings Bryan? What opportunities were lost when a genius like James Cox was whipped by a nonentity like Warren G. Harding, when Judge Alton B. Parker and explorer John C. Fremont were defeated?

As he questions the course of history, Irving Stone exposes the reasonings and recreates the realities of American politics. As in all the other biographical works by this great writer, *THEY ALSO RAN* plucks figures from the pages of history and presents them as living human beings. Here are the men who had a try at glory, and lost by the ballot box.

Other SIGNET Books by Irving Stone

☐ **THE AGONY AND THE ECSTASY.** The magnificent biographical novel of Michelangelo which topped the bestseller lists and was produced as a motion picture. (#Y2800—$1.25)

☐ **THE PRESIDENT'S LADY.** The tumultuous love story of Rachel and Andrew Jackson. (#Q3373—95¢)

☐ **THOSE WHO LOVE.** The bestselling love story of Abigail and John Adams, two people whose devotion to each other was equalled only by their patriotic passion for freedom.

☐ **I, MICHELANGELO, SCULPTOR edited by Irving and Jean Stone.** Spanning 67 years of Michelangelo's life, and including more than 400 letters and poems, this is the first full chronological edition in English of the great artist's personal writings. An astonishingly vivid portrait of the man and his times. (#T2462—75¢)

They Also Ran

THE STORY OF THE MEN WHO WERE
DEFEATED FOR THE PRESIDENCY

By Irving Stone

A SIGNET BOOK
Published by The New American Library

SIGNET TRADEMARK REG. U.S. PAT. OFF. AND FOREIGN COUNTRIES
REGISTERED TRADEMARK—MARCA REGISTRADA
HECHO EN CHICAGO, U.S.A.

SIGNET BOOKS are published by
The New American Library, Inc.,
1301 Avenue of the Americas, New York, New York 10019

FIRST PRINTING, SEPTEMBER, 1968

PRINTED IN THE UNITED STATES OF AMERICA

TO JEAN

(who works miracles)

Prologue

THIS IS THE STORY of the twenty-three men who enjoyed, or suffered, an identical fate: they were all defeated for the presidency of the United States. The stories are not told in their chronological order but are grouped according to those analogies which give history a fascinating plot structure.

The truth can sometimes be seen more accurately at an oblique angle than head on: the lives of the presidents too often have been sweetened to salve nationalistic pride; no one has thought it necessary to whitewash the defeated candidates. Their lives provide a high-powered and amusing lens with which to judge the standards of their times, the qualities of their victorious opponents and the political wisdom of the electorate.

How often were the voters discerning, how often dumb? How frequently were they fooled, and how frequently did they go unerringly to the better man? How often did they elect the apparently superior candidate, only to find that the presidency was the one job in the nation that he could not handle? How often did they choose the man who was more capable of solving the existing problems, only to have a radical change in the course of history render his particular qualities useless and make the defeated one the ideal executive to handle the new situations? What is the box score on democratic elections since 1800? Are the voters getting smarter all the time, making fewer and fewer mistakes, or are they repeating the identical errors they made a hundred years ago? What is our percentage of wins, loses and draws?

I have attempted to extract the vital essence of each man rather than to tell his full life story; in this sense the sketches are biographical line drawings rather than portraits in oil. However, the protagonist of the book is not merely the revelatory human pattern, but the inner design which led this group to its peculiar end: for men who share a common fate rarely do so by accident. What were the inherent traits in the characters of such disparate individuals as Wendell Willkie and Henry Clay, Alfred E. Smith and Horace Greeley, Charles Evans Hughes and William Jennings Bryan, Alf Landon and John C. Fremont, which led them all to the same sacrificial block?

This book does not include those who served one term in the White House and were then defeated, such as Herbert Hoover, nor those who were defeated first and subsequently elected, such as William Harrison; nor does it include the men who were defeated before modern popular elections came into existence. C. C. Pinckney cannot rightfully be declared to have been defeated in 1804, nor Rufus King in 1816, for neither man was nominated, neither agreed to run, neither canvassed or had anything to do with the election. De Witt Clinton wangled a nomination from the Federalists in 1812, but there was so little interest in the election, because of the War of 1812, that even the political journals did not mention the contest. This book deals solely with those whose paths led them, sometimes by dramatic and circuitous routes, to the very door of the Executive Mansion, only to have it closed peremptorily in their faces.

What kind of a people would we be now if the men in this book had been elected to the presidency, instead of defeated? Would we still have a democracy, or would we have slipped into a dictatorship or one of the numerous isms that have arisen since 1800? Would we Americans have become a more intelligent nation, or would we have reverted to a state of barbarism? How might the defeated ones have changed the course of our history?

The reader will not find all the answers in this book, but he will find a number of cogent questions which will enable him to play the guessing game of "Might Have Been."

They Also Ran took me a year and a half to write. During the first nine months my wife, Jean, produced a son; during the second nine she produced a coherent book out of a thousand rambunctious pages of manuscript. Following the pattern of literary acknowledgment, it behooves me to remark at this point that any weaknesses to be found in either my son or my book are my responsibility; any virtues to be found were contributed by my wife.

IRVING STONE

Encino, California
January 6, 1943

All source notes, quotations and references are credited at the back of the book and may easily be found by chapter and page citation.

Source notes on Adlai E. Stevenson, Richard M. Nixon and Barry M. Goldwater will be added when these preliminary studies have been expanded into full chapters.

June 6, 1966

Year	FEDERALIST	DEMOCRATIC	WHIG	REPUBLICAN
1788	George Washington			
1792	George Washington			
1796	John Adams	Thomas Jefferson		
1800	John Adams	Thomas Jefferson		
1804	C. C. Pinckney	Thomas Jefferson		
1808	C. C. Pinckney	James Madison		
1812	De Witt Clinton	James Madison		
1816	Rufus B. King	James Monroe		
1820		James Monroe		
1824		John Quincy Adams	*Henry Clay	
1828		Andrew Jackson	John Quincy Adams	
1832		Andrew Jackson	*Henry Clay	
1836		Martin Van Buren	William H. Harrison	
1840		Martin Van Buren	William H. Harrison	
1844		James K. Polk	*Henry Clay	
1848		*Lewis Cass	Zachary Taylor	
1852		Franklin Pierce	*Winfield Scott	
1856		James Buchanan		*John C. Fremont
1860		*Stephen A. Douglas		Abraham Lincoln
1864		*George B. McClellan		Abraham Lincoln
1868		*Horatio Seymour		Ulysses S. Grant
1872		*Horace Greeley		Ulysses S. Grant
1876		*Samuel J. Tilden		Rutherford B. Hayes
1880		*Winfield Scott Hancock		James A. Garfield
1884		Grover Cleveland		*James G. Blaine

Year	Democratic	Year		Year	Republican	Year
1888	Grover Cleveland	1888		1888	Benjamin Harrison	1888
1892	Grover Cleveland	1892		1892	Benjamin Harrison	1892
1896	*William Jennings Bryan	1896		1896	William McKinley	1896
1900	*William Jennings Bryan	1900		1900	William McKinley	1900
1904	*Alton B. Parker	1904		1904	Theodore Roosevelt	1904
1908	*William Jennings Bryan	1908		1908	William Howard Taft	1908
1912	Woodrow Wilson	1912		1912	William Howard Taft	1912
1916	Woodrow Wilson	1916		1916	*Charles Evans Hughes	1916
1920	*James M. Cox	1920		1920	Warren G. Harding	1920
1924	*John W. Davis	1924		1924	Calvin Coolidge	1924
1928	*Alfred E. Smith	1928		1928	Herbert Hoover	1928
1932	Franklin D. Roosevelt	1932		1932	Herbert Hoover	1932
1936	Franklin D. Roosevelt	1936		1936	*Alfred M. Landon	1936
1940	Franklin D. Roosevelt	1940		1940	*Wendell L. Willkie	1940
1944	Franklin D. Roosevelt	1944		1944	*Thomas E. Dewey	1944
1948	Harry S. Truman	1948		1948	*Thomas E. Dewey	1948
1952	Adlai E. Stevenson	1952		1952	Dwight D. Eisenhower	1952
1956	Adlai E. Stevenson	1956		1956	Dwight D. Eisenhower	1956
1960	John F. Kennedy	1960		1960	Richard M. Nixon	1960
1964	Lyndon B. Johnson	1964		1964	Barry M. Goldwater	1964

On this chart the losers are printed in bold type; the heroes of the story are starred.

BOX SCORE

	win	lose	%
Democratic	24	18	.571
Republican	15	12	.556
Whig	2	3	.400
Federalist	3	5	.375

Cast of Characters

(THOUGH NOT IN ORDER OF THEIR APPEARANCE)

1. **Henry Clay** — Defeated in 1824 by J. Q. Adams and Jackson; in 1832 by Jackson; in 1844 by Polk.
2. **Lewis Cass** — Defeated in 1848 by Taylor.
3. **Winfield Scott** — Defeated in 1852 by Pierce.
4. **John Charles Fremont** — Defeated in 1856 by Buchanan.
5. **Stephen A. Douglas** — Defeated in 1860 by Lincoln.
6. **George B. McClellan** — Defeated in 1864 by Lincoln.
7. **Horatio Seymour** — Defeated in 1868 by Grant.
8. **Horace Greeley** — Defeated in 1872 by Grant.
9. **Samuel J. Tilden** — Disputed election with Hayes, 1876.
10. **Winfield Scott Hancock** — Defeated in 1880 by Garfield.
11. **James G. Blaine** — Defeated in 1884 by Cleveland.
12. **William Jennings Bryan** — Defeated in 1896 and 1900 by McKinley; in 1908 by Taft.
13. **Alton B. Parker** — Defeated in 1904 by T. Roosevelt.
14. **Charles Evans Hughes** — Defeated in 1916 by Wilson.
15. **James Middleton Cox** — Defeated in 1920 by Harding.
16. **John W. Davis** — Defeated in 1924 by Coolidge.
17. **Alfred E. Smith** — Defeated in 1928 by Hoover.
18. **Alfred M. Landon** — Defeated in 1936 by F. D. Roosevelt.
19. **Wendell L. Willkie** — Defeated in 1940 by F. D. Roosevelt.
20. **Thomas E. Dewey** — Defeated in 1944 by F. D. Roosevelt; in 1948 by Harry S. Truman.
21. **Adlai E. Stevenson** — Defeated in 1952 and 1956 by Dwight D. Eisenhower.
22. **Richard M. Nixon** — Defeated in 1960 by John F. Kennedy.
23. **Barry M. Goldwater** — Defeated in 1964 by Lyndon B. Johnson.

Table of Contents

BOOK ONE

The Press Pass

I: HORACE GREELEY
II: JAMES MIDDLETON COX

Horace Greeley was the first journalist to be nominated for the presidency. James M. Cox was the last. What kind of president would a newspaperman make?

———— ◆ ————

CHAPTER ONE

Horace Greeley

WHILE THERE ARE DOUBTS as to my fitness for president," observed Horace Greeley dryly, "nobody seems to deny that I would make a capital beaten candidate."

Until the advent of Abraham Lincoln, for whose nomination he was partly responsible in 1860, Greeley was the most widely known and heatedly discussed figure on the American landscape; from his pen poured a torrent of articles, essays and books, from his lips an almost equal torrent of words; for three decades, from 1840 to 1872, he exercised one of the strongest influences on the mind and motive of the nation.

"Having loved and devoured newspapers," he writes in his *Autobiography*, "I early resolved to be a printer if I could."

He could never have become anything else: he had printer's ink in his veins. By the age of twenty-one he was a known and respected printer in New York City, having set up a press and started his first paper; at twenty-three he had founded a literary weekly, and been invited by James Gordon Bennett to become a partner in the founding of the New

York *Herald;* at twenty-seven he was commissioned by the political boss of New York State to publish a political paper, at twenty-nine began a second political paper, which dominated the Log Cabin and Hard Cider Campaign of 1840; at thirty he founded the New York *Tribune,* revolutionized the conception of a newspaper, its manner, form and content, and singlehanded created modern journalism.

"He chased rascals, not dollars."

He chased ideas even more ardently, and caught up with them—rascals, dollars, ideas, all three. The man who was too frightened to play baseball because of the speed with which the ball was thrown at him took his life in his hands to go bail for Confederate President Jefferson Davis after the Civil War, walking unafraid on the streets of New York with frenzied crowds around him singing:

"We'll hang Horace Greeley to a sour apple tree!"

He had the weirdest appearance in any professional circle, making Lincoln seem debonair: tall, skinny, angular, neither his head, torso nor limbs seemed to bear much relation to each other, as though all three had been sired by different parents and stuck together with mucilage. His head was as round as the baseball he feared, with a bulging forehead; his skin was a dead though not unhealthy white; his hair was colorless, his pale blue eyes almost expressionless. He wore his long hair around his face and under his chin until the advancing years had enabled him to achieve neck whiskers. He rarely went abroad without high boots, one trouser leg stuffed inside, the other hanging out. The rest of his getup consisted of a string necktie which generally hung over one shoulder, a white linen suit, a tall white hat and a bulging umbrella.

He appeared to be a mild, ugly, absent-minded and innocuous schoolmaster; actually the strange body, bulging head and fantastic garb housed one of the most powerful and penetrating spirits to which the United States had given birth.

As a child he had been all brain and little body; he could read at three, had finished the Bible by the age of five and devoured everything the countryside had to offer, from the *Arabian Nights* to the *Pilgrim's Progress.*

"His mind was a marvelous storehouse of facts, dates and events. He was a political encyclopedia, of the best revised edition, and entirely trustworthy."

He consumed such quantities of print that he became nearsighted; he read with his nose so constantly and so deep in a book that the book appeared to be a part of him, another organ of perception, such as an eye or an ear. He would sit in his little cubbyhole of an office at the *Tribune,* surrounded by a welter of newspapers, magazines, reports and scrawled

14

copy, "his nose nearly touching the paper on which he was writing" furiously and uninterruptedly. His pen was an appendage without which he could not have lived: a third arm, an inky lung.

Next to Henry Ward Beecher he was also the most popular lecturer of his day. Few walked out on him; a listener might say after the first sentence of his unattractive voice, "Two minutes of this is all I shall be able to stand." Two hours later he still would be hanging on intently.

Horace Greeley had little to go on: no important family or connections, no charm, no physical attractiveness, no social graces, no money, no friends. All he had was a brain, integrity and passion.

They took him a long way.

2

"I am drifting into a fight with Grant," he said in 1872. "I hate it. I know how many friends I shall alienate by it, and how it will injure the _Tribune_, of which so little is my own property, that I dread to wreck it. Yet I should despise myself if I pretended to acquiesce in his re-election. I may yet have to support him, but I would rather quit editing newspapers forever."

He had a good reason to dislike the idea of fighting Grant. Greeley had been one of the founders of the Republican party in 1856, had waged a stout campaign for Fremont against Buchanan, had fought a superb journalistic battle for Lincoln in 1860. Though he had not been enthusiastic about General Grant he had supported him in 1868. Now he loathed the thought of doing injury to the party he had helped found, yet he knew that, just as Lincoln and the Republican party had contrived to win the war, Grant and the Republicans were contriving to lose the peace.

There was no thought in his mind when he said, "I am drifting into a fight with Grant," that Horace Greeley would be the candidate of the opposition. For thirty years he had been an office maker, not an office seeker. There had been a time, eighteen years before, when he would have liked to be governor of New York. He had reasoned that he could do a better job than most of the men whom he saw elected; in addition he had felt that the party which he served in election after election, without reward or compensation, owed him a gesture just once, a sort of loving cup bestowed publicly in token of his services. He had not wanted to be an office-holder for very long; he had never wanted to be anything but an editor; but he would have enjoyed successfully carrying an

15

election, proving that he could be a first-rate public executive.

His ambition had been thwarted by politicians Weed and Seward, the men for whom he had founded his first political paper. In retaliation he had gone to Chicago in 1860, when it was certain that Seward would receive the nomination for the presidency, and by a shrewd campaign swung the nomination to Abraham Lincoln. Seward, in turn, prevented Greeley from being named for the United States Senate by the New York legislature.

Only once had he been elected to office—as a Whig congressman from New York City in 1848. A highly trained and astute political economist who believed that the well-being of a nation depended upon the humane and orderly functioning of its economic pattern, he had been for most of the right causes for the right reasons. He tried to limit the granting of public lands to actual homesteaders; he fought a congressional grab in the form of a proposed bonus; he killed a bill which would have raided the Treasury for the private printing of debates; he headed a movement to abolish flogging in the United States Navy.

His most colorful contribution, and one which brought down upon him the wrath of his confreres, was an exposure of the means by which congressmen were mulcting the public funds by drawing traveling expenses on the longest and most circuitous routes from their homes to Washington. He drew up charts showing how much each congressman could save by utilizing the newest and fastest routes of travel. The congressmen used them from that time on; he had left them no choice.

His record in the House had been as good as his position had been awkward; for he had felt obliged to use his job as editor of the *Tribune* to expose everything he found in his job as congressman. This infuriated the House, which promptly created the precedent that acting members of Congress might not use their inside information for the edification of their newspapers back home.

The year 1872 was not very old before Greeley realized that he would have to oppose the re-election of Grant in spite of the shattering injuries it might do to the Republican party and to the *Tribune*. He was not alone in his determination, for by now most of the outstanding editors of the land—Joseph Medill, Joseph Pulitzer, Carl Schurz, William Cullen Bryant and a host of others—had joined him in exposing the devastating list of crimes, corruptions, usurpations and incompetencies for which Grant had to be held responsible.

As soon as he announced in his *Tribune* that Grant must be defeated, his fellow Republicans assumed that he was waging his fight for selfish reasons, that his driving force was a desire to replace Grant in the White House. They set out to expose him to the country as a seeker of the presidency, doing such a good job that they sold the idea to Horace Greeley, the new Liberal Republican party, the Democrats and the country at large. He is the only one among the Also Rans who was in effect nominated by the opposition.

What kind of campaign would an editor be able to make? If he were elected would he set the precedent for a long line of newspapermen in the White House?

Eighteen years before, Greeley had said, "I am a beaten, broken-down, used-up politician and have the soreness of many defeats in my bones."

Nominated to the presidency at the age of sixty-one, he promptly forgot about the soreness in his bones, stumping the country in the most vigorous campaign since Henry Clay had tried to defeat Polk in 1844. From the first moment he was confident that he and the Liberal Republicans would win. For him to imagine that he could be defeated would have been a violation of the character of the boy who had been born on a rocky and mortgaged New Hampshire farm at the beginning of the century, February 3, 1811, and whose astonishing rise in the world formed a perfect model for the Horatio Alger stories which were to adorn the end of the century.

3

Young Horace was admitted to the public school in Bedford even though his parents did not pay taxes there, the board ruling that "No pupils shall be received from any other town, except Horace Greeley alone." In later years presidents, cabinet members, senators, all manner of public figures would amend this to read, "I wouldn't take that from anybody but Horace Greeley!"

He was such an outstanding student that a wealthy neighbor offered to send him to Phillips Exeter Academy and then through college. Horace's father, about to flee to Vermont to keep out of debtor's prison, refused on the grounds that a Greeley did not accept charity.

The Greeley family, which included four children besides Horace, went through years of rural poverty in New Hampshire and Vermont. At one time their total equipage consisted of two milk pans, the five children eating their mush out of one, the parents out of the other. Zaccheus Greeley was the third of that name, the first having arrived from England in 1640; he was a good man, cheerful and intelligent, but an unsuccessful farmer. Mary Woodburn Greeley was a woman of fine intellectual perceptions but a harum-scarum housekeeper; Horace's wife was to prove an even worse housekeeper than his mother. From his mother he acquired his love of poetry; she encouraged him to sit in a corner and read Byron and Shakespeare instead of going outside to play with other children.

The boy made his first attempt to become a printer at the age of eleven, walking to the neighboring town of Whitehall to apply for a job. The publisher took one look at the frail, white-faced youngster, another at the heavy hand presses, and sent the lad back home. At fifteen he tried again, this time successfully binding himself over to a printer at Poultney for his board, clothing and forty dollars a year.

He stayed four years at Poultney, working long hours in the print shop and loving it, reading widely in his spare time, learning the newspaper business. For another year he wandered on foot over Pennsylvania and upper New York State as an itinerant printer, ending in New York City in August of 1831 with ten dollars in his pocket, the clothes on his back, and not an acquaintance within a hundred miles.

Turned down by city newspapers because he looked like a country yokel, he set type for a Bible publisher, secured work on fly-by-night weeklies, became acquainted with other printers. He saved a few dollars, then formed a partnership with a friend and went into the printing business. Knowing that the best way to insure work for one's presses was to have a paper of one's own, Greeley started the *Bank Note Reporter*, which became successful as an organ of the lottery business. Other printing contracts came in; the firm began to make money.

When he was twenty-three he founded the *New Yorker*, a literary and political weekly which started with twelve subscribers and rose to seventy-five hundred. In the *New Yorker* Greeley cut his eyeteeth on editorial writing, encouraged such poets as Edgar Allan Poe, raised the tone of American journalism by imbuing the paper with a high quality of literary excellence. Within a year he had become known as one of the most competent editors in New York City. He married, set up a home, was well on his way to success, though a visitor to New York called him "the greenest specimen of an editor I ever looked at."

When the panic of 1837 hit New York, Greeley wrote an increasing number of the articles himself, set them in type, made up the pages. He found a sixteen- or eighteen-hour day in his office and print shop highly enjoyable. His rapidly whirling brain did not permit him to sleep much, perhaps five hours a night; when he grew tired during the day he would fall into a semicoma: he would hear everything that went on, but his body would be asleep.

At the invitation of Thurlow Weed, he set up the *Jeffersonian* to help the local Whig campaign in 1838, winning acclaim for his political articles. Two years later he introduced the *Log Cabin* to the country with an eighty thousand circulation and a new Whig campaign song with every weekly issue, starting a campaign-song custom that remained until the end of the century. Harrison defeated Van Buren, and Greeley became known nationally; however, the venture proved to be as costly to his purse as it was profitable to his reputation.

Being broke at thirty did not frighten him: he borrowed a thousand dollars from a friend, threw in the circulation of the *New Yorker* with what was left of the *Log Cabin* after the campaign, and started the New York *Tribune*. His timing was perfect: the *Tribune* was a success from the first issue that hit the streets.

4

"Newspapers are, or ought to be, printed for the information and entertainment of the whole community," announced Greeley in his revolutionary credo. "When they are mere advocates of petty or even of ponderous private interests, the advertisers of personal schemes, and puffers of men who have a large amount of axes to grind, they must lose all independence, manliness and substantial patronage."

His success as a publisher of the first modern newspaper came from the boldness of his mind and the daring of his imagination. There was little he could find to approve in the journalism of his day: he rejected the unreadability of the print, the unattractive appearance of the page, the illiteracy and grossness of the writing, the dullness of the content, the emphasis on crime news, the repetition of gossip instead of fresh and authentic news, the shallowness of the thinking and the partisanship of the opinions. He was not a man to be tied down by existing forms or bound by precedent: he invented a modern newspaper, whole, in much the same way that Edison invented the light bulb.

Above all it was Greeley's mind that dominated the paper and gave it flavor; his thinking was sharp, incisive, his writing utterly lucid, colorful, full of drama and dry humor, spiked with delicious phrases, writing that tickled or excited or soothed according to the need of the issue on hand.

"His paper bristled with important news, much of it as provocative as the editorials. The *Tribune* was a model of

19

compactness and good editing, and extremely well printed. He possessed an equipment for the metropolitan newspaper field not duplicated in that day or this."

If he merely had been a good editor and journalistic innovator, his importance would have been limited; he was above all a great polemicist, a scientist at dissecting the economic and industrial forces at work behind society and government. He was a crusader and reformer because he burned to see mankind live in a just and orderly world, because mass suffering seemed to him to be not only brutal but suicidal. He spared no one and played no favorites; his was a powerful voice of liberalism trumpeting its calls in a social wilderness, always a half-century ahead of his times, sometimes a full century.

"For forty years Horace Greeley was the busiest and boldest editor in America. He pried under and tipped over with pitiless pertinacity. No rival journalist ever created an influence that penetrated so deeply. The New York *Tribune* was Horace Greeley. Far and wide men and women followed his guidance in great causes. No matter of moment escaped him, no fears ever made him pause. He gave neither himself nor the nation rest."

He was a trust buster sixty years before Theodore Roosevelt wielded his stick. "All combinations or bargains to raise prices," he wrote, "are exceptionable and contrary to law." He fought for the need of workmen to form trade unions only two decades after laborers were being arrested, convicted and imprisoned for attempting collective bargaining. "We believe that unregulated, unrestricted competition, the free-trade principle of every man for himself and buy where you can the cheapest, tends everywhere and necessarily to the depression of wages and the concentration of wealth. Capital can wait, labor cannot; it must earn or famish. Without organization, concert and mutual support among those who live by selling their labor, its price will get lower and lower as naturally as water runs downhill. We are in favor of trade unions or regular associations of workers for the establishment and maintenance of fair and just rates of wages."

He became the first president of the Printers' Union, bringing respectability and force to the movement. He worked for the distribution of public lands to the poor and needy, particularly those crowded into the slums of the cities. He was one of the first men in the United States to insist that, since the government was the agency of the whole people, it was up to that government to rescue its members in times of crisis, depression and poverty, not to allow whole segments of the population to decay. His program for the alleviation of the

20

suffering caused by the depression of 1837 was similar in nature and detail to the program of the New Deal in the depression of 1937.

He was the first public figure of importance to sanction the cause of Fourierism, onto which his opponents tacked the label "Socialism," a new word designed to destroy the *Tribune* and Mr. Greeley with it. Greeley did not take flight; he devoted considerable space in his paper to educating the people on the principles of the new socialism.

"When I took up this cause," he said, "I knew that I went in the teeth of many of my patrons, in the teeth of the prejudices of the great mass, in the teeth of religious prejudice. But in the face of all this, I went on."

He gave money to certain of the experimental colonies, in particular five thousand dollars to Brook Farm; he was the vice-president of their association and the strongest voice in their behalf. But he was also their flagellating critic: "A serious obstacle to the success of any socialistic experiment . . . is the kind of person who is naturally attracted to it. Along with many noble and lofty souls who are willing to labor and suffer reproach for any cause that promises to benefit mankind, there throng the conceited, the crotchety, the selfish, the headstrong, the pugnacious, the unappreciated, the played out, the idle and the good for nothing generally who, finding themselves utterly out of place and at a discount in the world as it is, rashly conclude that they are exactly fitted for the world as it ought to be."

Tireless, incorruptible, sensitive, on the side of the angels, every day of the week he was a mighty force for good. Circulation of the *Tribune* soared until it reached three hundred thousand, the paper literally sweeping the country, for Greeley published a weekly edition which was mailed to every hamlet of the land.

People everywhere began to ask, "What does Horace Greeley think about this?" They saw him make mistakes, but they were positive of his integrity, certain that he would state the truth that was in him at all costs, that he followed principle rather than master, that he was hard to fool, that he had the gift of analysis and clear, forceful statement; above all, that he would use his gifts for the common people and not for the spoilers, political or economic.

He refused to make a fortune out of the *Tribune*. The best young writing talent of the nation beat its way to the door of the *Tribune,* and its editor spared himself no cost to make his paper the finest news collector and disseminator in the world. Yet Greeley could have become a wealthy man in a very few years, as had Bennett from the *Herald*. Instead, he took in a

21

partner to handle the business end of the *Tribune*, and to this partner he consigned the tremendous profits. He paid himself a liberal wage, in consonance with the job he was doing, but would accept no profits as such, gradually selling off his shares at a modest figure. To preserve his integrity and full courage he must have only what his efforts earned; if he began thinking about how much profit he could make out of the *Tribune* he soon would be trimming his sails, placating, mollifying, hesitating to fight for fear of alienating subscribers or advertisers. A sure touch for every individual and every cause that held out a hand, he never would utter a sentence for the sole purpose of making money.

"The darkest day in any man's earthly career," he said, "is that in which he first fancies that there is some easier way of gaining a dollar than by squarely earning it. He has lost his way through the moral labyrinth and henceforth must wander as chance may dictate."

Horace Greeley was not a wandering man.

His fear of unearned money was his chief but by no means his lone peccadillo. So fiercely did he concentrate on a specific problem that he took no notice of what went on about him. When introduced to a roomful of people he would nod abruptly without interrupting the flow of his harangue. When at dinner he would fasten onto some one plate, eat it clean, never thinking that somebody else might like a bit of cheese or a doughnut. Then he would touch nothing else. It was not safe to pass him a communal pitcher of milk or cream, for he would down it to the bottom. He was a vegetarian, did not drink or smoke, and crusaded against women's corsets as vehemently as against their equal rights or suffrage. Though he had many devoted friends among the women intellectuals, such as Margaret Fuller, Susan B. Anthony, Harriet Beecher Stowe, he had a low estimate of their capabilities, a state of mind encouraged by the growing misfortune of his marriage.

He met his first and only love at a boardinghouse conducted by Dr. Graham; though neither Dr. Graham's crackers nor his cracked diet did young Horace any appreciable harm, it brought him untold confusion in the form of a wife. Mary Cheney was a schoolteacher, "slight, exquisite, dressed in clouds of white muslin, cut low, her neck and shoulders covered by massive dark curls." Margaret Fuller called her "a typical Yankee schoolmaster, crazy for learning," while a long-suffering family friend described her as "a female crank, born so, who could not help doing as she did."

For the first five years the Greeleys were happy, entertaining in their home and mixing in the best literary circles. Mary Greeley idolized her first-born, a son, refusing to allow him to associate with other children, cooking him special, eccentric foods, working for hours every day over his complexion and his long silken hair, making him a hothouse flower of beauty and delicacy.

When the boy died of cholera at the age of five, his mother's mind was permanently affected. Though she bore six more children, four of whom lived, none was able to replace her idol. With the passage of the years she became increasingly psychotic, making Greeley's life a hell. At his home on Nineteenth Street, their farm at Chappaqua or their home in Turtle Bay he could find no comfort and no moment of peace. When she grew angry at his preoccupation she would seize the manuscript on which he was working and fling it into the fire. Nothing pleased her: she harped and criticized until the stricken husband would flee to a hotel for a few days to get his work done.

For the latter half of his life, as Greeley has said, he had no home. He had taken a wife with the same name as his mother, and with the same housekeeping proclivities. His wife had a fixation on cleanliness, scrubbing everything in much the same manner as she had scrubbed her first-born, but this was her solitary domestic virtue. She cared nothing about her home, which was always a boar's nest of confusion and discomfort. She cared nothing about food, and it was impossible for him to bring friends home.

In spite of his burdens, Horace loved his Mary; he was unfailingly kind and sympathetic; he took no women in her place. Yet no man ever had greater need of a sensible wife, one who would have given him a comfortable home, seen that he had a balanced diet, stuck both trouser legs in his boots when he left for the office in the morning, laughed him out of his foibles and eccentricities. His effervescent mind needed a governor; and who better to provide it than a wife?

Thus he went his way, a tall, angular, absent-minded man in spectacles and a high white hat, carrying a whalebone umbrella; a Jeremiah of the inkpots, a faddist whose open mind would try any experiment to see if good might come of it; a pamphleteer in the tradition of Thomas Paine, a blood brother of Upton Sinclair, his twentieth-century counterpart.

5

As far back as his *New Yorker* days Greeley had been writing treatises to the effect that slavery was ruining the south economically, aside from the morals in the case. By the fifties he was taking a militant stand against further appeasement of the south, maintaining that it could keep its institution of slavery if it wanted, but that slavery must not be extended to one more free mile of American earth.

"It would be better to see the Union a thousand times shivered," he cried in the *Tribune,* "than to allow slavery to be planted on Free Soil."

He was no abolitionist, but he castigated the Fugitive Slave Law, waged a blistering campaign against Stephen Douglas for reopening, in his Kansas-Nebraska Bill, the possibility of extending slavery to the new territories. When a civil war in miniature broke out in Kansas, Greeley fought the slavers in such fulminating terms that twenty-two thousand dollars came by mail to the *Tribune* with which to buy rifles, jocularly referred to as Beecher Bibles, to be shipped into Kansas in shoe boxes. When John Brown raided Harpers Ferry, perhaps with some of the *Tribune's* Beecher Bibles, feeling throughout the country turned against Greeley as an incendiary.

Because of his telling blows, the anger and bitterness of the south concentrated on his paper. Any southerner daring to subscribe to the weekly *Tribune* would have been mobbed at his post office; the *Tribune's* reporters and agents had to travel under assumed names and conceal the nature of their business. Yet Horace Greeley was one of the strongest voices in the land for letting the southern states go, "providing they go peacefully," when they wanted to secede. Though he realized the dangerous possibility of an alliance between the south and England, or other European countries, of a Confederate-South American bloc aimed at the heart of the north, he was convinced on the basis of economic necessity that the south would sue for a return to the Union within a very few years.

"The cotton states are meditating a withdrawal from the Union because of Lincoln's election," he wrote in an editorial that went into three hundred thousand homes scattered through the farm belt, the northwest, and as far away as California. "We again avow our deliberate conviction that whenever six or eight contiguous states shall have formally seceded from the Union, and avowed the unanimous and earnest resolve of the people to stay out, it will not be found practicable to coerce them into subjugation; and we doubt if any Congress can be found to provide for such coercion."

But when the south fired on Fort Sumter, the *Tribune* fired a broadside at the south: "Fort Sumter is lost, but freedom is saved. There is no more thought of bribing or coaxing the traitors who have dared aim their cannon balls at the flag of the nation." In both attitudes the *Tribune* was voicing the sentiments of millions in the north.

War was no sooner declared than Greeley began to harass President Lincoln to strike immediately and in full force against the rebels. Lincoln listened not only because he knew that Greeley had helped to secure him the presidency, but because of the enormous weight and breadth of his influence.

When the battle of Bull Run was lost, and the north plunged into despair, contumely was poured upon Greeley for forcing the army into premature action. At each of the northern defeats Greeley suffered as only Lincoln must have suffered. Nevertheless he kept prodding and pushing for faster and greater action. He pounded at the president, lashed at the cabinet, hounded the Congress and flailed at the generals in a paroxysm of determination that the north fight, that it win, that it redeem its honor and preserve the Union. When the Draft Act was passed in 1863, mobs stormed the *Tribune,* threatening to burn down the building. Its editor sat unperturbed in his little wire cage, writing more incendiary editorials while the mob howled for his life. At the abyss of the northern defeats he suffered an attack of brain fever, in the course of which he asked if it might not be better to declare an armistice, to let the south go. He also participated in one mysterious peace conference.

Next to his determination that the north must throw its full resources into the war and win quickly, Greeley was most set upon an immediate emancipation of all slaves to assure the people that the ghost of slavery would never rise again. President Lincoln wrote to him frantically, "What I am trying to do is save the Union, not free the slaves!" When the Emancipation Proclamation finally came, at the earliest moment that Lincoln thought it safe for the war effort, Greeley was acknowledged to have been the spearhead of the drive.

Sometimes he had talked idealism without the men or guns to back up his words, but always he was a fighter who knew that there could be but one end to the conflict. If there is any truth in the charge that he was partly responsible for the war, then it is equally true that he was partly responsible for the victory.

6

He was an idealist and a humanist in the early New England tradition. Instantly upon the cessation of hostilities his mind turned to the binding up of all wounds. "We plead against the passions certain to be fierce and intolerant," he wrote only a few hours after Lee's surrender; "we plead for a restoration of the Union, against a policy which would afford a momentary gratification at the cost of years of perilous hate and bitterness."

Coupled with President Lincoln's determination that the south should not be bled or despoiled, the powerful voice of the *Tribune*, reaching families in every corner of the land, continued to carry Greeley's beautiful pleas for forgiveness, for brotherhood, for the restoration of the south to its full powers that endless misery and tragedy might be averted, generations of misunderstanding and hatred avoided, a unified nation made strong in a spirit of compassion.

But Abraham Lincoln was assassinated. The voice of Horace Greeley was drowned in the cry for blood. Convinced that the further incarceraton of Jefferson Davis was a destructive act of vengeance which kept the south embittered, Greeley traveled to Richmond where, with Commodore Vanderbilt and several other northerners, he signed a hundred-thousand-dollar bond for the release of Davis.

He had spent a lifetime in the midst of frenzied battles, but all that had gone before was a gentle zephyr compared to the tornado that rocked him for this effort. The quarter of a million circulation of the *Tribune Weekly* fell off to fifty thousand, with post offices turning back the issues by the tens of thousands. The second volume of his history of the war, *The American Conflict*, after the first volume had been a tremendous success, was almost entirely canceled at the moment of its issue. He was hanged in effigy. He stood alone, his paper failing beneath his eyes, his name and character reviled. He became the most execrated man in the United States.

"At last a man has turned up who is more unpopular than Jefferson Davis, and that is Horace Greeley. I think if Greeley could be hung now, they would be content to let Davis go."

The Union League Club, which he had joined for patriotic reasons at the close of the war, decided to try him in Star Chamber for treason. Greeley wrote a two-column reply in the *Tribune* which should go down in history as one of the great cries of defense made by an authentic martyr. Only then did the feeling against him soften. He had few of the external appurtenances of a proper martyr, but then, martyrs so seldom look the part.

It was with misgivings that Greeley had supported General Ulysses S. Grant, the Republican nominee, against Horatio Seymour in 1868. He was grateful to Grant for bringing the war to a close, but he knew that the presidency, particularly in as difficult a period as the nation had ever faced, should not be handed out as a reward. He did not feel that a military man was the proper one to bring peace and harmony to a war-ravaged country; from what little he knew of Grant he felt pretty certain that the general could not handle the job.

It did not take him or the other penetrating minds of the country very long to see what Grant had let them in for: the incompetence and scandal stank to the high heavens. With other independent editors who held the interests of their country above the interests of their party, he rained criticism upon Grant, hoping to clean up some of the infected areas. President Grant turned from his critics with annoyance and distaste. After three years of intolerable conditions Greeley broke from the Republicans in power as dishonest perverters of the real aims of the party.

The recalcitrants called themselves Liberal Republicans. They assembled in convention at Cincinnati on May 1, 1872, drawing up a platform which contained a sizzling indictment of Grant and his followers that is almost word for word the indictment levied against Warren Harding half a century later. The strongest candidate of the convention was Charles Francis Adams, whose family already had provided two presidents for the United States. Greeley was the second choice, having been jockeyed into this position by the overzealous opposition. Adams started out strongly on the first ballot, but when it was realized that he would never be accepted by the Democrats of the south, with whom the Liberal Republicans were hoping to form an alliance, Greeley's strength increased. He was nominated on the sixth ballot.

In his *History of the Presidency* Stanwood comments, "The work of the convention was received by the Republicans throughout the country with a shout of derision. Greatly as Mr. Greeley was esteemed for his sincerity and respected for his ability, he had always been regarded as an erratic man, and there were few persons who credited him with the cool judgment and tact needed in a president."

When in 1868 honest, kindly, confused and politically unborn General Ulysses S. Grant had been asked if he wanted to become president, he had replied sagely, "No, I am a military man, not a statesman. I would just like to be mayor of Galena long enough to build a sidewalk from my house to the station." If he had stuck to that determination Grant might have saved the country from a holocaust as tragic in its social and economic implications as the war itself. Grant's conception of a statesman was one who could build a sidewalk from his home to the station; upon his induction he had loaded the government payrolls with so many relatives that Washington observed it had never seen anyone get in a family way so fast.

Grant's relatives proved to be the best of his appointments;

27

his friends turned out to be the worst set of rascals the country had yet experienced, not to be equaled in viciousness until the advent of Warren Harding's inner circle in 1921. Seizing power in most states of the Union through the distribution of patronage, they not only kept the south prostrate and despoiled but outraged every function they could absorb in Washington, gouged the people of millions, perverted the machinery of government for their own purpose, weakening with every gesture the fabric of democratic civilization.

Even this graft and corruption did not accomplish as much fundamental damage as the fact that Grant had not the faintest conception of what a president should do, of what his duties or obligations were, of how much control he should exercise, of what the division of power should be between the three branches of the government. Like Harding, who, when faced with a complicated problem of national importance, would run a hand over his glazed eyes and murmur, "The hell with it, I can't make out what this is all about," Grant gazed with the mind of a child at the affairs of state, blinked uncomprehendingly, and turned them over to his friends to be kicked around.

The Republican press, while flailing Greeley, omitted any discussion of whether Ulysses S. Grant had displayed cool judgment, tact, or any one single quality that would have entitled him to be re-elected.

"I accept your nomination," said Greeley, "in the confident trust that the masses of our countrymen, north and south, are eager to clasp hands across the bloody chasm which has so long divided them, forgetting that they have been enemies in the joyous consciousness that they are, and must henceforth remain, brethren."

The Democratic party, but a shadow of its former strength, confirmed Greeley's nomination. Once again the Republicans hooted; they did not want to clasp hands with the south; they wanted to wave the bloody shirt of war, win elections and remain in power.

At the age of forty-three Greeley had complained, "I have the soreness of many defeats in my bones." At sixty-one those bones gathered up their strength for one final effort, giving as robust a performance as ever had been witnessed on the American landscape.

"I never saw a happier face than that of Greeley," said Colonel McClure of the Philadelphia *Times*. "He was entirely confident of his success, and in a facetious way reminded me that I had underestimated his strength with the people."

Greeley was not depending on any backlog of popularity or vague memories of his stands. He resigned as editor of the

Tribune and jumped into the campaign with an energy and intentness that was worthy of two other Also Rans, William Jennings Bryan and Wendell Willkie. He opened his campaign in Portland, Maine, in the middle of August and fought hard every hour of the way, stumping the country and speaking in every important city. Tremendous crowds and great cheering greeted his appearance, with gigantic parades of men dressed in raincoats and hats to catch the dripping tallow from the candles held aloft in the night.

He was careful to document his speeches and think everything out beforehand so that, "I would not throw my chances away by any blunder." His attitude on the stump was marked by spirit and breadth of view; one Democrat from Indiana observed that, "for elevation of thought, for broad philanthropy and for Christian statesmanship, the speeches of Mr. Greeley have no parallel in American history."

President Grant said nothing.

The *Tribune* supported Greeley with great vigor, but the *Sun*, now edited by Dana, whom Greeley had trained on the *Tribune*, opposed him, as did his old friend Henry Ward Beecher, who abandoned him on the grounds that the Republican party must not be broken up, no matter how bad Grant was. The independent press, stroked by the brilliant pens of Schurz, Medill, Pulitzer and Bryant, did intelligent and constant campaigning for Greeley.

He enjoyed the canvass, except for the fact that his daughters sometimes had as many as four hundred to feed at Chappaqua of a Saturday afternoon; that the photographers were forcing him to assume ludicrous poses, in the manner of glacial Calvin Coolidge being photographed in an Indian hat and feathers. Through September and October he continued his fervid speeches, quoting figures, stripping bare the Grant malfeasance, uttering some of the profoundest sentiments for unity and peaceful reconstruction that the country had heard. He remained confident long after his supporters saw how the wind was blowing: that the soldier vote would be cast pretty solidly for its own general, and against the south; that vast sections of the country would be voting neither for Grant nor against Greeley, but for the Republican party which they had brought into existence; that there was no possibility of getting a fair comparison of Greeley and Grant before the electorate because the people were too tired and beaten to think; that the country was weary: weary of bloodshed, of wrangling, of accusation, of change.

"Grant may be kinda bad, like they say he is, but Greeley might be worse, who knows? Let's go along as we are for another spell."

Ballots were cast quietly and without tension, for there could be no doubt that Horace Greeley was beaten before he started. Grant received three quarters of a million more votes, the final score standing at 3,597,132 for Grant against 2,834,125 for Greeley.

7

What kind of president would Horace Greeley have made? How would he have stacked up against Ulysses S. Grant?

Many charges were made against Greeley during the campaign: he was a faddist; he was hotheaded; he was rash and tactless and flew into political rages; he was unpolished and had no manners; he was "a self-made man who worshiped his Creator"; he was dictatorial, refused to take orders, to work with the boys; he had failed as an experimental farmer; his attitudes were not always consistent; he had suffered from brain fever; he didn't look like a president; he was "unlike anybody else, including himself."

The charges fade into the background when one realizes the importance and the extent of his work for the nation, the depth and vigor of his brain, his grasp of political economy, his insight and understanding of the workings of government, his undisputed honesty and integrity and courage, the heroic and unflagging wars he had waged for the people, for efficient government, for liberal reform, for tolerance, for an economy based on justice and order. He was running against a man whose four years as president revealed him to be what he had been before the Civil War: a failure at everything he tried, unread, unthinking, with no understanding of the forces that were at play in the world, or any wish to understand them. "Grant's innocence of the nature of American government was as astounding as was his ineptitude. Blind to the great emergency confronting him, and incapable of dealing with it even if he could have seen it, Grant became little more than the political puppet of his flatterers, and consequently he stands today in our history as the most pathetic figure that ever occupied the office of the President of the United States."

In his one political office, that of congressman, Horace Greeley had done good work; as the founder and director of national newspapers he had a brilliant record not only of success, but of raising the tone of journalism and public thinking. He was already old and tired, he would have been better in the office fifteen years before, but deep fires still burned in his soul, fires to right the wrongs of Reconstruction, to bring the south back to health, to take government out of the hands of the incompetents and swindlers, to make the government an efficient agent for the whole people.

One of Grant's contemporaries said that Grant missed the greatest opportunity since the inauguration of George Washington. Horace Greeley would have done something with that opportunity. He would have made mistakes, he would have made enemies, he would have made blunders in proportion to the enormity of the task, but it would always have been on the side of trying to do too much for the nation and its people rather than too little. With the opportunity to accomplish great things, the training, the intelligence, the courage and the will to essay them, he might have been, in spite of his shortcomings, one of America's most valuable presidents.

"A fussy old man in a white hat and a linen duster," says one of Grant's biographers in describing Greeley; "it was hard to think of him as president."

It was true. But the fussy little man in the white hat who burned to do good, to serve humanity and help to release it from its chains of ignorance and poverty, whose head under that tall white hat was bloody and scarred from doing battle for humanity and liberty and truth, might have turned in a job of which Thomas Jefferson, Andrew Jackson and Abraham Lincoln would have been proud.

Mary Greeley died just five days before the election. It was a bitter blow to Horace, who watched over her and nursed her during her last hours. After his defeat, tired, discouraged, ill with weariness, he resumed the editorship of the *Tribune*, only to learn that a strong movement was under way to oust him from the paper he had founded. Under this blow he became more ill, feeling himself now to have no place and no purpose. He spent feverish days and sleepless night, and died only three weeks after the election.

"While there are doubts as to my fitness for president," he had said, "nobody seems to deny that I would make a capital beaten candidate."

They were wrong; the defeat killed him.

With his death all animosity and criticism stopped at once; his loss was more deeply felt than any since Lincoln's. Greeley would have enjoyed reading his obituary notices, though doubtless he would have done a little editing here and there, written a series of articles on the lessons of his life.

The "obits" came too late, too late for him to receive the loving cup across the chasm, too late to save the nation from another four years of corrupt and fratricidal government under Grant.

It was "thirty" for Horace Greeley, one of the most fantastic, lovable and valuable creatures ever produced on the soil

31

of North America. All that would be remembered of him was that he once said, "Go west, young man!"

What he had meant by west was Erie County, Pennsylvania.

CHAPTER TWO

James Middleton Cox

HE IS ONE of the clearest cases in all American history of the best man having been defeated. He was the right candidate running at the wrong time.

When James Middleton Cox was asked what he thought might be the most important quality in a president, he replied:

"The power to take a situation by the nape of the neck and the seat of the trousers and shake a result out of it."

He was a hustler, a driver, a go-getter; he had ants in the pants. He loved a knock-em-down-and-drag-em-out fight, with no holds barred. Like his confrere, Horace Greeley, he was a Horatio Alger hero in the best American tradition, working his way up from a thirty-five-cent-a-week janitor to a two-hundred-thousand-dollar-a-year newspaper owner, with millions in resources.

"When he goes fishing he wants to catch all the fish in the creek; when he goes hunting he never quits until he has his legal limit; when he starts to make money he wants to make every nickel the enterprise affords."

He relished activity and enjoyed a contest so greatly that he would not relinquish until he had squeezed them dry of excitement and conquest, until he could murmur triumphantly to himself, "Boy, I sure wrapped that one up."

James Cox was short and stocky, looking a trifle like Napoleon or Theodore Roosevelt. He had pictures of them hanging on his walls, and leaned on their legends. His associates in Dayton, Ohio, where he was the leading citizen, looked at him with "the same sort of admiration they have for a cash register or a motorcar or an independent lighting system for which their community was celebrated."

Everyone labeled him a self-made man; he had pulled himself up by his bootstraps. "He was forever reaching out and upward," commented the *Outlook*, "attempting what seemed impossible to other men, relying solely on himself to get there, usually doing it." Like most self-made men, he lacked personal warmth; he was too determined, too intent, driving

33

too hard to have a large circle of friends or time for the amenities.

Just before the Democratic convention in San Francisco in 1920 he said, "My friends are urging me to open up a vigorous campaign. But I prefer to wait. If, when the convention opens, they finally turn to Ohio, all right. We either have an ace in the hole, or we haven't. If we have an ace concealed, we win; if we haven't, no amount of bluffing and advertising can do much good."

Once he had been nominated it was a different story. A delegate who opposed him at the convention remarked, "I never talked to a more practical-minded politician. There isn't a prejudice or a hypocrisy in him. He is frankly out to win. He has no hesitation of false dignity; he does not compel you to beat about the bush. He makes me think of one of those twelve-cylinder cars that can turn around in its own length: no lost motion."

A journalist observed that Cox was "coldly and absolutely confident that he will be elected president. He is as concretely analytical as an engineer, but he never thinks of failure, never prepares for it, never believes in it."

Prepared or not, he got whopped. His opponent, Warren Gamaliel Harding, was the most feeble and incompetent nonentity ever nominated by a cynical and power-mad machine; in no previous election except that of Greeley versus Grant had the differences in the qualifications between two men been so enormous or so recognizable. Yet he received the worst drubbing ever administered to an Also Ran, practically being left at the post.

2

Both the man and his career were short, swift, stocky, staccato. *Collier's* characterized him as "a serious-minded man of peculiar intentness, dynamic, but with no superficial sparks." A self-trained man, he had consumed large quantities of books, become enamored in the first flush of his learning with high-sounding words; it had been with pride that he had dragged out a five-syllable word to fit an occasion to which the word was tangential. As a cub reporter he had found so many things "Astounding!" that he had become known as Astounding Cox. For the next twenty years he lived up to his nickname with great zest.

He was born at Jacksonburg, Ohio, on March 31, 1870, the youngest of seven children, in a clay-brick house which his grandfather, who had come west in a prairie schooner from New Jersey, had built with his own hands. His father, like Greeley's father, though a good man in other respects, was not successful at farming; the family was never affluent. The boy's earliest ambition was to become a shopkeeper in Middleton, the little town to which he occasionally was taken in the wagon by his father. He never developed any appetite for the family vocation of farming; in a sense he did become a Middleton storekeeper.

The strongest influence in his life, as in Greeley's, was his mother, a devout Methodist who sat up nights with her youngest son, after the rest of the family had gone to sleep, reading to him *The Pilgrim's Progress*. She was a woman of strong character and unflagging devotion to the simple Christian virtues; from her the boy derived his courage, his determination to rise in the world, a rigorous sense of ethical values.

Young Jimmy helped with the chores around the farm. Needing money to get on in the world he became the janitor of his little red schoolhouse for thirty-five cents a week, which he faithfully deposited in his savings bank, and janitor of his church at the rate of one dollar a month. There was a legend that young Jimmy put the dollar in the collection box as soon as he received it, but this was probably campaign apocrypha; he was no sentimentalist, he knew that in order to own a store in Middleton a chap had to save his hard-earned money and not squander it, even on the Lord.

"I can never remember the time when I did not have a little money ahead," proudly announced the bourgeois Mr. Cox.

When he was fifteen he went to live with his married sister in Middleton so that he could attend the advanced school. His brother-in-law owned the weekly newspaper, and after school and on Saturdays the boy worked in the shop as a printer's devil. Young Cox got his first smell of printer's ink; he was to remain a newspaperman all his days.

He was not fond of boning in school, but had only to read or hear a thing once to know it for keeps. At seventeen he had qualified to be a teacher. With his characteristic energy he taught day school two miles out of Middleton, night school in Middleton, and on Saturdays and other spare hours worked on his brother-in-law's paper. After three years of teaching he gave up what was for him too sedentary a career to work full time on the family paper. The twenty-year-old boy became its lone reporter, rewrite man, proofreader, city editor, make-up man, printer, circulation manager and bookkeeper. It is not likely that, having sired the paper from rumor to printed sheet, he would abandon his efforts until he had personally placed a copy on every front porch in Middleton.

Among his minor duties was that of Middleton correspondent for the Cincinnati *Enquirer*. One night there was a railroad wreck close by. Cox sprinted to the scene, secured his first information, then ran at top speed to the telegraph office, where he handed the operator an old newspaper and ordered him to keep the wires jammed with this useless material until he could return with the full story. Other reporters tearing up to the telegraph office with their stories found the operator sewed up by Cox. The following morning the *Enquirer's* front page carried an exclusive story of the wreck.

It is doubtful whether Mrs. Cox would have thought her son's smart trick of journalism in accordance with the simple Christian virtues, but it earned young Cox a job on the *Enquirer*. He arrived in Cincinnati a gawky, sunburned country boy with dark brown hair, friendly brown eyes, glasses, and high collars that cut into his neck. His chief asset as a cub reporter was that he pursued stories relentlessly, never resting until he had secured his information.

"Jimmy Cox was about the best reporter and the worst writer in southern Ohio. There was not a week that he did not turn in a sensational scoop, and seldom were his facts wrong. He never spared himself in any effort to get firsthand, exclusive information; his only vanity was in being first, his only pride in beating all rivals. But when it came to writing, his copy usually had to be done over in the office."

When he had taught school at Middleton, Cox had caught the attention of Paul Sorg, a millionaire tobacco man who was serving on the Board of Education. Several years later Sorg was elected to Congress; he offered Jimmy the job of private secretary. Cox went to Washington with Democratic Congressman Sorg, and there had his first taste of politics.

When he was twenty-eight, and Sorg's term had expired, Cox borrowed money from his employer to buy the Democratic Dayton *News,* which was rapidly failing; the paper had lost almost its entire circulation, its advertising had disappeared. He had no money to go on, could not afford a staff; often on Saturday nights he had to borrow from friends to pay the printers he did employ. Once again he tried to put out a one-man newspaper. He discarded the standard boiler plate used by small papers and put Associated Press stories in its place; he uncovered inside stories that gave him constant scoops, wrote flaming editorials in white heat and tortured English against the political frauds and financial manipulations of his district. Like Horace Greeley, his reformer's zeal pursued any group that enriched itself at the expense of the community; there was never a time when his paper was free from libel suits. He was no yellow journalist; his main beat was political and industrial dishonesty. When a group of eastern financiers came into Dayton to consolidate its banks and take over the utilities, Cox investigated in his bulldog fashion, became convinced that the Daytonians were going to be left holding the bag, and exposed the deal. They promptly sued him for a hundred thousand dollars, the sheriff locking up the *News* on an attachment. Five minutes after a rival paper had reached the streets with the announcement that the *News* had been closed down, James Middleton Cox's paper came rolling off the press: he had raised the hundred-thousand-dollar bond. At one time the *News,* whose total assets could perhaps be stretched to five thousand dollars, had a total of half a million dollars in suits against it! They were mostly scare suits, designed to frighten Cox and stop his exposures. They never went to court, and no one ever collected a dime.

He was a dynamo of energy, working night and day, instilling a fighting spirit into the paper which gave the businessmen of Dayton confidence that his venture would last. The people of Dayton enjoyed the vigor and dash of the *News;* his circulation mounted, and with it his advertising. As money came in he invested it in a crack staff and was soon turning out an entirely modern and successful newspaper.

Dayton began to thrive as an industrial center, and the *News* grew prosperous along with its community. As was the custom, industries settling in Dayton presented the paper with blocks of stock in order to insure publicity and friendliness. Cox would have refused the stocks had he thought they were being proffered as a bribe against the public interest, but what he would have done had any of the industries in which he had been presented with stock begun to operate dishonestly is an open question.

By the time he was thirty-five James Cox was an influential man in his neighborhood. He had bought the Springfield *Press-Republican* and turned it into a Democratic paper. He was modestly wealthy, widely, albeit scatteringly, read, had delved into history and biography to give himself an understanding of the world in which he lived.

"The story of James M. Cox is that of the agile, energetic, intuitively brilliant and hard-hitting man who has forged his way from the bottom to the top by the sheer force of indomitable will, who seeks the limelight and never hesitates to make enemies. Cox doesn't wait for things to come to him; he goes after them and gets them."

Though his efforts had earned him many vehement opponents, he had few personal enemies. He was credited with the ability to bind up the wounds of those he had defeated, no mean accomplishment.

3

In 1908 he decided that the time had arrived to begin his political career. His first step was to run for Congress on the Democratic ticket. His Republican opponent obligingly involved himself in a scandal by getting wrecked on a joy ride, and Cox won hands down. Folks began to talk about "Cox luck."

His four years in Congress were mediocre. Appointed to the important Committee of Appropriations during his second term, he did reliable bread-and-butter work, but made no noteworthy contributions. In his one interesting venture, when the committee was being asked for more money with which to feed the animals in the Washington Zoo, Cox made an investigation, learned that the government was spending more money per head to feed its animals and its prisoners than to feed its war veterans in the national homes. He saw to it that the veterans' food budget was increased. Of the eight hundred bills he introduced into Congress, more than seven hundred were to secure pensions for war veterans.

At the end of his second term an observer would have been justified in saying, "Back to your newspaper, Jimmy Cox, you have no place in politics." Yet elected to the governorship of Ohio in 1912 he proved to be one of the ablest and most constructive governors the state had known. His period in Congress had been one of quiet but intense observation; he had not wanted to go off half-Coxed. That he had been learning a great deal, and of an important nature, is evidenced by his immediate record as governor.

There had seemed only small likelihood that he would be elected: he was a poor public speaker; his record in Congress was nothing to brag about publicly; he had made enemies during his exposures; even his home town of Dayton sometimes accused him of being a wrecker instead of a builder. Yet he gathered twice as many votes as either of his opponents. His victory was in part an extension of the Cox luck: Theodore Roosevelt had split the Republican party in his bolt from Taft, and even in Ohio the Progressives took half of the regular Republican support. But over and above the luck was sound judgment; Cox had seen what Roosevelt was going to do to the Republican forces and reasoned that a Democratic regime was about to begin; he also had the opportunity to campaign on the basis of proposed progressive amendments to the state constitution.

During his campaign he told Ohioans that "Progressive government means keeping government geared up to modern requirements." He lauded the work being done by La Follette in Wisconsin and promised an equally forward-looking administration. As governor he drove fifty-six separate laws through a critical legislature to get the amendments into work. That Cox was able to do this without conflict or injured feelings proved his abilities as a public executive.

One of the permanent interests of his life was the public-school system. He appointed an investigating committee and, when their report was ready, named a School Survey Day in which all of Ohio participated. A special session of the legislature, working under his guidance, then enacted a school code which made more funds available for educative purposes, replaced the little red schoolhouses with modern, centrally located schools, raised teachers' salaries and improved the normal schools so that Ohio could train more and better educators.

He had pledged himself to provide a businessman's budget for the government, though few states had such a scientific approach in 1912. Leaning on his experience with the congressional Committee of Appropriations, he set up a system under which all monies were paid into the state treasury, and not one dollar could be spent until it had been recommended by a department, appropriated by the legislature, its use checked by the governor and the auditor. Grafting and inefficiency were considerably reduced. In spite of the fact that his reforms cost millions, the new budget system saved much of the additional money that was being spent.

He was a good and sympathetic governor for labor. The workers of Ohio still were staggering under the "fellow servants" doctrine; no workingman who was injured in any accident caused directly or indirectly by a fellow worker could collect damages, or his widow receive compensation. Cox put into effect compulsory workmen's compensation, under which employers paid into a state insurance fund, the state investigated accidents and claims and paid out benefits; a transition from a medieval industrialism, saving endless suffering and tragedy for the people of Ohio. Coupled with workmen's compensation, he created an insurance fund to cover widows' pensions. In a period of considerable unrest, during which strikes were common, Cox never once called out the state militia to police a strike; never was blood shed on the soil of Ohio. In the neighboring state of Pennsylvania, during the steel strike, state troopers were riding down workers and women; when the meetings moved across the line into Ohio they were peaceable and no one was hurt.

He had come up through poverty and labor; he believed that the government belonged to the people, not to the few who had gained control of the mills and the millions. His reforms were consistently aimed to protect the public: a strengthening of the civil service, passage of restrictive laws to protect against fraudulent stock issues, the initiative and referendum for state laws, the direct nominating primary. He was not the originator of these advances in modern government, for he did not have an original or creative mind. He was an eclectic: he could discern the progressive legislation and scientific methods of government being tried in various parts of the country and weave them together into a workable pattern. He insisted upon putting experts into governmental jobs, refusing to make hidden deals, swaps or bargains, carrying on the business of state in the open, without secrecy or befuddlement.

His opponents labeled him a radical and defeated him on this basis in 1914—then did not attempt to repeal a single one of his reform measures! The defeat roused Cox's fighting blood. He was re-elected in 1916 and again in 1918, against heavy odds, when the Republicans carried everything else in the state as well as the Congress. Only Rutherford Hayes before him had been elected three times to head the state, and never before had this honor befallen a Democrat.

At fifty he was as strong and vigorous as he had been in his youth, a gamecock of a man, a steam engine that never ran down. His success had developed in him no symptom of pretension or pose. He had remarried in 1917, after having been divorced. The first Mrs. Cox had kept the youngest boy, the two older children had stayed with their father. No scandal or unfriendliness attended the divorce; it had been a case of incompatibility, the couple having parted on amiable terms.

Cox, his second wife and seven-months-old baby now lived in a beautiful home outside of Dayton, called Trailsend, set on a hilltop amidst trees and flowers and shaded walks. He had many associates but few friends, for he was still a lone wolf, preferring a walk in the woods to an Elks' clambake. He had a hunting and fishing camp in Michigan, liked hunting big game in Labrador, enjoyed cooking venison and trout over a campfire. Trailsend had a well-stocked library which he used constantly. "I can never remember the time when I did not have a little money ahead," he had said. Now he had several millions ahead, lived comfortably though not ostentatiously. He cared little for the social graces, rarely went into society, entertained only for his intimates, never became a habitué of the theater, opera or concert hall.

On his newspapers he was a benevolent autocrat; his men were well treated and well paid, taken care of in times of hardship, retired on pensions; unlike Horace Greeley with his *Tribune*, no one was allowed to own stock in the business. The men on his staff spoke their minds freely and had their way when they could convince him he was wrong; a hard man to turn aside from a course of action once he had determined upon it, his men sometimes outargued him. But James Cox shared responsibility and power with no one. When he was doing a job there were few amenities in him; he was hard-boiled and serious, even grim. He could not relax when there was work to be done; he had never learned to soldier, to take it easy. Work had been his means of rising in the world, and he could not treat it debonairly. He was a plain and informal man who asked folks to call him Jimmy, and liked to hear a funny story, but no one ever had occasion to say, "Jimmy, you're a card!"

The charge that Cox was a radical had evaporated with the years and with the efficacy of his reforms. "I sympathize with Jefferson's view that that is the best government that governs least—but in this age I consider that also the best government is the one that concerns itself most with the betterment of its people. Government must be a great living organism devoted to pushing the masses up the grade."

This was James Middleton Cox, just rounding out his third term in the governor's office. This was James Cox in the hour when the Democratic convention, confused, divided and uncertain, met in San Francisco. Would the Cox luck hold?

4

His ace in the hole proved to be the Republican nomination of Warren Gamaliel Harding on June 12 in Chicago. Harding was an Ohio man, and who was better able to defeat an Ohio man than another Ohio man? The Republicans had had two powerful candidates to choose between: first, Leonard Wood, who as governor general of Cuba had supervised the purging of yellow fever, a chief of staff of the United States Army, whom Harding's biographer calls, "a man of sturdy intellect, unimpeachable principles, ardent patriotism and spotless record." The second was Frank O. Lowden, former governor and congressman from Illinois, in both of which positions he had done good work.

Neither of these experienced and competent executives was able to secure the nomination because their managers had declared a war to the death on each other. Wallowing in trickery, chicanery and shady dealings, overlaid with the passage of large sums of money, the Republican convention was symptomatic of the regime it put into power. After hours of conniving, while the delegates suffered from the intense heat and purposelessness, a small group of professional politicians and senatorial bosses met in a smoke-filled hotel room at two o'clock in the morning and selected a man who would follow their orders and let them run the national government: Warren Harding of the beautiful face, who had sat like a dummy in the United States Senate, who was liked for his convivial habits of drinking and gambling and regarded as a high-grade moron in affairs of state.

If Warren Harding had not been nominated at Chicago, James Cox might not have been nominated at San Francisco. Thus he would have missed what he considered the climax of his life; he also would have missed his greatest drubbing, and might not have passed from public life at the early age of fifty.

There were sixteen potential candidates besides himself when the Democrats convened in San Francisco. Woodrow Wilson was too ill to lead his party; there was considerable revolt against him in any event. William G. McAdoo, son-in-law of President Wilson, had the largest support, with A. Mitchell Palmer, who was later responsible for the outrages in the so-called Red Hunt, running second. James Cox was third in strength on the first ballot, followed by Alfred E. Smith of New York. By the tenth ballot Smith had disappeared from the list and Cox had passed Palmer. For the next thirty-three ballots it was Cox versus McAdoo, with neither man able to secure the two-thirds majority.

Cox gained strength constantly, for very evident reasons: though he had backed the Wilson administration, he had not been identified with it and could not be held responsible for its conduct; he had played no part in the quarrels over the League of Nations, and hence he accumulated no enemies on that score; he was wet enough to assure the anti-prohibition forces but not sufficiently wet to antagonize the drys; he had a progressive record, had proved his ability to carry on the Democratic ideal of liberalism and government for the people.

On the night of the nomination Cox, his wife and friends waited for the results in his office at the newspaper. Cox had just filled his pipe and was about to stroll out for a smoke when a group of his employees rushed in with the news, hoisting him to their shoulders. Mrs. Cox kissed her husband, and there were happy tears shed. The first thing the following morning he visited his mother's grave.

James Middleton Cox was nominated on the forty-fourth

ballot. Mark Sullivan commented, "While it is true that Cox was named by the bosses, they did it in the open. There were no conferences in closed rooms." Harding's biographer observes that there was an undercurrent of pessimism at the Democratic convention, that the delegates thought it did not matter much who was nominated because he was going to be badly beaten, "that a change of party was inevitable."

The Democrats did their best to rally around Cox; the New York *World* reported that, "President Wilson and every administration leader in Washington are greatly pleased with the nomination of Governor Cox." Joseph Tumulty, secretary to President Wilson, said, "The leaders of the party have never been so optimistic of success before an election as they are today as a result of the nomination of Governor Cox."

His reception by the press was mixed. The independent New York *Globe* called him a "man of mediocre ability and unimpeachable party regularity," while the independent San Francisco *Bulletin* commented, "Cox is a candidate of presidential quality, a man of the people; he has risen to his present position by hard work and superior abilities." The independent Syracuse *Herald* saw the two candidates "as alike as two peas," but the New York *World* observed that "the San Francisco convention has given its party a leader well versed in the principles of democracy, a man who in high office has demonstrated the capacity to legislate and to govern." The Republican papers were courteous, saying that "the Governor is a fine fellow and a formidable campaigner, but he is tied up with a hopeless cause."

Nearly every journal in the land joined in congratulating the Democratic party on their selection of a candidate for the vice-presidency: Franklin Delano Roosevelt of Hyde Park, New York; the New York *Globe* reporting that "if the Democratic ticket is elected, even Republicans will be glad to have Roosevelt in Washington." The truth of this prophecy did not run out until some years later.

Cox had his shortcomings, but there was only one front on which he validly could be criticized. In 1916, when he had been running for re-election to the governorship, he had courted the hyphen vote: the German-Americans were a considerable bloc of voters who might turn victory into defeat. After the *Lusitania* had been sunk by a German submarine, with loss of American life, Cox's paper observed that, "the U-boats have committed no crime against us." Cox had not written the editorial himself; once war was declared he became a vigorous war administrator; yet the responsibility of pandering to a group of native Germans who could not understand their American citizenship must be laid at his door.

The only other charge standing against him after ten years of public service was that while he was governor, at the time of the Dayton flood, he had loaded an old printing press onto a boxcar in Columbus, attached it to a relief train, and had the *News* printed on the outskirts of the flood area. It was in character for Cox to send in a press to get papers to the stranded Daytonians, but if, as was charged against him by the editor of the *Journal-Herald,* he did not extend courtesy to the rival Dayton papers to use the press, then he took an unethical advantage of his office. His mother would not have approved of opportunism.

5

Cox or Harding, Harding or Cox?
You tell us, populi, you got the vox.

Shortly after their nomination Cox and Roosevelt made a pilgrimage to Woodrow Wilson, the dying warrior in the White House. Wilson spoke with tears in his eyes of the League of Nations and its opportunity to create a permanent world peace. When the candidates left the White House they determined to campaign on the issue of the League, though they knew it was not a popular cause. Cox took to the stump, touring the country and telling the people that he believed wholeheartedly in American participation in the League of Nations, with the League having the power to enforce its decrees for peace, even to the extent of going to war.

In one of the most articulate statements of his campaign Cox set forth his philosophy of government. "It is a bitter disgrace to our civilization that there is seventeen per cent illiteracy in the United States, that in the midst of plenty there is ofttimes lack of the necessities of life, that one man starves while another wastes, that the mountains are full of coal and the bins empty, that with no end of work to be done there should be workless men. I don't believe in socialism, and I do deeply believe in individual self-reliance and initiative, but government is merely a committee for mass action, and through government we can teach, inspire, and set the example; and I say today that no government is worth its salt that is not supremely concerned with the betterment of its people."

He told his audiences, "I have no doubt that the thought of the country is predominantly and decisively progressive. I think that progressive votes will be intelligently cast where they will do the most good. There is a positive drift away from reaction. The prevailing feeling of the country is progressive."

It was his first sizable error in political judgment, big enough to break the proverbial Cox luck: he misjudged the mind of the people.

While Cox was canvassing the country enunciating his beliefs, speaking to large crowds in every important city, the Republican Senate cabal decided that Harding had better stay at home and keep his mouth shut, even as Grant had remained silent against Greeley. Puppet Harding, who wasn't sure he wanted to become president, sat on his front porch in Marion, Ohio, receiving delegations, smiling his beautiful smile, shaking hands warmly with everyone who came to see him, and saying absolutely nothing. When it was imperative for him to make a statement, his backers wrote it for him and gave it to the press.

It was a polite and well-bred campaign, the only sinister aspect of the canvass being the spreading of the rumor that Harding had Negro blood, a tactic which was repudiated by the Democratic leaders. They also knew about Harding's liaison with Nan Britton, and of his illegitimate child, but did not make campaign fodder of the scandal. Nor did the Republicans bring up the matter of Cox's divorce, the emphasizing of which could have been expected to alienate the Catholic vote.

The two candidates uttered only pleasantries about each other. This was Cox's second mistake. Instead of treating Harding with the jovial affection of a brother publisher, he should have laid bare the record of a congenital incompetent who had bungled every job he ever held, who had accepted a senator's pay without attending the Senate; one who could not understand the simplest connotations of the world problems which the regime would face. Perhaps James Cox realized that these disclosures would do no good, that they would not divert sufficient votes to make worth while the muddying of the waters. He fought clean, on the issues, on the differences between the Republican conception of government in America and the Democratic conception, trying to rouse the people to an enthusiasm for the League and for progressivism as an ideal of co-operation.

But the people were tired: tired from the war, tired from the suffering and bloodshed, tired from hysteria, tired from being geared to the breaking point, tired from the vast expenditures of money and morale and man power, tired from eight years of idealism, tired from personal government, tired from internecine wars in Washington. For just a little while they wanted to be let alone, to sleep in the sun, to recoup their energies and their enthusiasm. Even the progressive *New Republic* was able to say, "Harding stands for a kind of candid and unpretentious reaction that anyone can respect, and that a great many people momentarily desire."

Harding had been the nominee of exhaustion at the convention in Chicago. He was now the victor of exhaustion at the election. There was no score on which Cox did not put up a better fight, wage a more intelligent campaign, state a more articulate and timely conception of government, in which he did not show a greater grasp of existing problems or prove by his record that he could provide the people with executive government that could be honest, alert, efficient, modern, scientific. He waged a campaign that would have been difficult to surpass and which entitled him to the decision.

But the American people only yawned. They said to James Middleton Cox, as they had said to Horace Greeley, "You may be right, but we're just not interested. Go away and leave us alone."

Sixteen million people, including women, who were voting for the first time, cast their ballots for Harding. Only nine million voted for Cox, an almost two-to-one decision, unprecedented in American elections. In voting for Harding the people did not appear to be voting against Cox, but against war and death and mutilation and suffering; against Germany, the Kaiser and militarism; against Europe in general; against Wilson, the Democratic party, liberalism and strong personal government.

Thus the American people achieved the feat of electing the worst president in their entire history by the largest majority in their entire history.

6

It is an amazing plot coincidence that the only two journalists to be defeated for the presidency, Greeley and Cox, should have run against the two admittedly least eligible presidents in the history of the United States, Grant and Harding, who were the worst in identically the same manner and for exactly the same reasons; that the two candidates who understood the most about the fundamental nature of democratic government and who made important contributions to its development should have been defeated by the two men who understood its inner processes the least; that two of the most liberal and progressive candidates should have been defeated by two of the most reactionary; that they both should have been defeated in the lethargy following major wars.

Will this same lethargy follow World War II?

Greeley was the more complex man living in a simpler world; Cox was the more simple man living in a more complex world. Greeley was the more brilliant and visionary, Cox the more emotionally balanced, yet James Cox is the lineal descendant of Horace Greeley, just as William Jennings Bryan was the lineal descendant of Henry Clay, his stablemate.

In comparing the qualities of Cox and Harding as potential presidents one has the choice of sardonic laughter or scalding tears. There is no single point in the entire range of personality, character, abilities, intelligence or past performance, with the single exception of looks, in which Cox was not incomparably superior. He was a constructive liberal whom not even his enemies called a radical, whereas Harding was a standpatter because he did not have sufficient brain power to understand the changing needs of the times. Cox had been an able governor who had given Ohio three terms of vigorous leadership, whereas Harding had been a glad-handing conciliator whom the politicians of Ohio had pushed around for their own purposes, first in the state legislature, then in the United States Senate, a man whose record in the Senate was *in vacuo,* not only because, as his colleagues soon discovered, he could not understand the debates on the floor, but because he preferred to rendezvous in the apartments of friends or in New York hotels, to play poker or golf or any other pleasant game when he should have been sitting in the Senate and participating in the government of his country. Where Cox was a successful newspaper publisher, Harding was the handshaker for the village paper which his wife managed successfully. Where Cox studied constantly to improve himself and to gain a better grasp of international problems, Harding admitted that he had never read a serious book in his life, and could hardly summon the concentration to read a newspaper. Where Cox was courageous, willing to fight on any issue he believed right, regardless of the consequences, Harding was willing to play any man's game to get himself re-elected in order to draw his pay as a time-server. Where Cox had an interest, an understanding and a sympathy for the ordinary people and the working people, Harding couldn't be annoyed with their problems: he knew where the big money and the power lay, and he played ball where the turf was the greenest.

If the country had set out on a treasure hunt to find the worst possible candidate for the office of the presidency, it is hardly conceivable that they could have done better than Warren G. Harding. President Harding took no pains to con-

47

ceal that he was breaking any and all laws that interfered with his pleasures, enabled a gang of rogues to bilk the government and make a mockery of government agencies by selling pardons, licenses and concessions, to riddle government services with graft and corruption until even the Republicans held their nose at the stench of what William Allen White called, "the debris of decency of the Harding Administration."

If Cox had been elected in 1920 he would have saved the nation from its most wrecking scandals since the administration of Grant. If Cox had been elected there would have been no sabotage of the League of Nations; the chance of avoiding World War II might have been greatly increased. During the hysteria following the Russian revolution Cox took a sane stand; if he had been elected president he would have prevented the beatings, imprisonments, killings and wanton destruction of civil liberties that took place under Harding's attorney general.

"There is some hysteria over active elements in this country that are menacing to government," stated Cox. "There is no danger in the situation, though it might be aggravated if the government policy of restraint and common sense that has endured through the years were to become one of force and terrorism. If the alien, ignorant of our laws and customs, cowers in fear of our government, he is very apt to believe that things are much the same the world over, and he may become an easy convert to the doctrine of resistance or rebellion."

The governor of Ohio who had passed a law in 1912 controlling stock issues would not have permitted the nation to lose its savings in an orgy of uncontrolled stock speculation. If the crash and ensuing depression could have been averted, or even cut in half, how different the history of the United States, and the world, might have been!

Cox was never subtle; he cared little for the art of indirection; he was literal-minded; he had no sense of humor; his greatest pleasure was to carry on two full-time jobs at once. During his occupancy the White House would not have been a center of cultivated salons and soirees, but the walls would have shaken with a tornado of activity. He would have been a salutary reaction to Wilson for those who needed an antidote after eight years of theory; he would have provided the antidote without wrecking the government and popular faith in the democratic form.

But the people wanted Harding, and they did not want Cox. If ever a nation made a valiant attempt to commit suicide, the United States did in the year of 1920.

The fault of the defeat is not Cox's; it must be laid at the door of the voters. Yet the fault of electing Warren Harding lies more squarely in the lap of the senatorial clique which gave them a Republican nominee who would be weak and amenable in the White House because they wanted to run the country to suit themselves. Until nominating conventions are mended to make impossible such cabals, a Warren Harding can be nominated and elected, and bring the Federal government down over his head; a James Cox, unwilling to seek a minor office after having run for the major one, will withdraw from public life at the age of fifty and be lost to his country.

What the sixteen millions who voted against Cox thought of the record of public scandals, thefts, wreckage and destruction which unrolled itself under their eyes, most of which was predictable in 1920 when they cast their ballots, would make an interesting commentary on the functioning of popular government.

James Middleton Cox would not have gone down in history as one of the United States' more brilliant presidents because history would have had no way of divining the Harding calamities he would have averted.

BOOK TWO

Three-Time Losers!

I: HENRY CLAY

II: WILLIAM JENNINGS BRYAN

Clay and Bryan made a career of running for the presidency. They are as alike as father and son, these two fanatical pursuers of the Golden Fleece. In spite of the Baumes Law, each strove for a fourth nomination.

———⟩⟩◆⟨⟨———

CHAPTER ONE

Henry Clay

HENRY CLAY SAID, "I would rather be right than be president."

This was the sourest grape since Aesop originated his fable.

He sat in his bedroom of the boardinghouse on Ninth Street in Washington, a quizzical smile at the corner of his mouth. He had reason to smile: defeated soundly in the presidential election of 1824 by Andrew Jackson and John Quincy Adams, and by a narrow margin by William H. Crawford, the kind fates had jockeyed him into position to dictate to the United States who their next chief executive was to be. An adroit maneuverer, Clay's task of deciding America's president was salve to his wounded spirit: he reasoned that a man who could make a president surely could be made president himself.

He was over six feet tall, lithely built, with a face that was homely in repose but fascinating in action; he rarely let anyone see him in repose. He wore his prematurely white tousled hair in the French Republican style; his forehead was high, his gray eyes small, his crooked nose bony, his skin pallid. He was not overly strong, but the fire that burned in him for fame and power never allowed him a moment's respite, and made him stronger than the men around him.

The campaign in which he had just been defeated had been the first in which a president was to be elected by popular vote. Perhaps for this reason it had been the first dirty campaign in the life of the young nation. He had played a considerable part in making it dirty by heaping abuse upon his rival candidates instead of criticizing the issues for which they stood. He was one of the progenitors of personal politics. When it came to heaping abuse, he was the master of his age; for a full century no one was to surpass him.

Sitting alone in his boardinghouse room, overlooking the shacks and muddy streets of Washington, he decided that he had ample reason to feel aggrieved. The election laws said that the candidate receiving a majority of all votes cast would be elected, but if no one received a majority, the House of Representatives would select the president from among the three highest contenders. Clay was not only the Speaker of the House, but its master as well. He had been certain that he would be among the three highest candidates, that he then could bully, cajole and persuade the House to name him the sixth president of the United States.

His reasoning had been good: his 47,217 votes had stood third to Jackson's 152,901 and Adams' 114,023. However, because of the distribution of the votes among the states, William Crawford had received four more electoral votes than Clay and thrown him out of the contest. To make the situation the more bitter for Clay, Crawford, a six-foot-two giant, was put out of the running because of a paralytic stroke brought on by a prescription given him by his physician. The contest now was between Jackson and Adams, and it was Clay who had to give away the job by swinging his votes to a man he hated—for he hated both of them—the job he wanted more than anything in life and which he was to pursue relentlessly through thirty-two years and seven campaigns.

The eyes of the twenty-four states were upon him. Every newspaper carried long articles on his coming decision. Wherever men met they talked of Henry Clay and wondered what he would do. At the age of forty-six he thus had achieved the first half of his ambition, to become the most important public figure in America. He had the center of the national stage; he was warmed and thrilled by the floodlights upon him; an actor of superb histrionic talents, he had no intention of giving up the role of leading man until the final curtain of his drama had to be rung down.

Which candidate would he choose? In the mushrooming capital, where every slight rumor circulated instantly, he would give no hint of his final reasoning. Mail flooded in upon him, speeches were directed at him from every section of the country, pressure groups dogged his footsteps. He only smiled enigmatically. If he let it be known which candidate was going to be president, attention would shift to the chosen man and Clay once again would be relegated to the wings. From the beginning of December until the end of January he kept the nation on tenterhooks, a considerable portion of business and politics being suspended because of uncertainty, while he fed his tapeworm ego.

To which candidate would he give his benediction? If he chose rightly he himself would be president in four years, or eight at the most. If he chose wrongly it might prove to be as catastrophic a blunder as Aaron Burr's fight to take the presidency away from Thomas Jefferson. Which man would he choose, the one who had received the most votes and hence was wanted by the largest single group? The one who had recieved a majority in the largest number of states? The one whose policies and social philosophy were more closely aligned with his own? The one who would do the greatest amount of good for the country? Or the one who would do the greatest amount of good for Henry Clay?

The answer could emerge only from the character of the Cock of Kentucky.

It was the closest he was ever to come to being president; he enjoyed hugely his moment in the sun, never suspecting that it was the climax of his career, a climax from which the remainder of his long passionate life would be a falling away.

2

He delighted in telling people about his humble background, that he had been "an orphan boy brought up in the midst of poverty and ignorance." This was another of his poses, designed to bring in the votes of the rough-and-ready west, for he had been born in a comfortable story-and-a-half frame house near Richmond, Virginia, on his father's prosperous four-hundred-and-sixty-acre farm which was worked by the eighteen Negro slaves owned by the family. Born on April 12, 1777, he was the seventh of his mother's twenty children, nine of whom were sired by his father, eleven by his even more prosperous stepfather. His mother was a cultivated woman who believed in education and books, while his father was a well-read preacher who sent young Henry to the district school for three years, all the public education available in the 1780s. In his youth Henry's father had been a dancing master, an art which Henry extended to include contortionism.

The first ambition of the boy's life was to become an orator. By the time he was eleven he was going to the courthouse at Richmond to hear John Marshall, James Madison, James Monroe and Patrick Henry debate the desirability of Virginia's ratifying the Constitution and becoming a member of the United States. For him the greatest of these was Patrick Henry because Patrick Henry was the outstanding orator of his day. He decided that he too would become an orator, and spent many hours alone in the barn or walking in the cornfields or woods, practicing the art of speaking.

When he was fifteen his family moved to Kentucky, leaving him behind to clerk in a grocery store. A year later his stepfather secured him a job in the High Court of Chancery in Richmond. It was his first piece of good luck. The second followed almost immediately, for he was made amanuensis to seventy-year-old George Wythe, Chancellor of the Court, Virginia's ablest legal mind and teacher of such men as Jefferson, Monroe, Marshall and Breckinridge. Chancellor Wythe took a liking to the lanky lad, trained him in legal procedure, and advised him to go into the law. This was the equivalent of advising a bird to fly, but young Henry was too smart to tell his benefactor so. Wythe tried to awaken in the boy a love of books and literature, but Henry's was an oral rather than visual type of mind: his brains lay in his ears and his vocal cords; he could not concentrate on books or study from them but there was no limit to the extent to which he could learn from what the fine minds around him were saying. He attended court constantly, listened to the lawyers wrangle and the judges rule, spent his evenings at the Richmond Debating Club practicing his two crafts of listening and orating.

"I never studied half enough," he was to write to one of his sons; "I always relied too much upon the resources of my genius."

He was admitted to the bar before he was twenty-one, then left for Kentucky to join his family. Although the great reaches of the state were occupied by rifle-toting pioneers who were felling trees, clearing fields and building log cabins, Lexington already was beginning to call itself the Athens of the west, was reading the best books from England and Europe, had a good newspaper in the *Gazette,* and several vigorous debating clubs. For a tall, spindly, gawky, beardless boy with a flame of ambition it was rich and fertile country. In cultivated Richmond, mother of some of the greatest legal brains of the new world, Henry's oral pyrotechnics might not have carried him far. In Kentucky, particularly in the backwoods country, it was as good a knowledge as any other kind, for oratory was the favorite means of communication.

"It is the art of all arts," he later proclaimed; "to it I am indebted for the primary and leading impulses that stimulated my progress and have shaped my entire destiny."

In this sentence lay the key to his life. He was always more interested in how he said a thing than in what he had to say; more interested in the emotional effect he had upon his listeners, his ability to bend them to his will, to achieve his desired ends than in the nature of the material he was presenting, its validity or usefulness. As a result his mind became a swift-flowing, shallow mountain torrent.

Starting out on a career which would keep him a force in national politics for half a century, young Henry had a number of assets: he was as fast and light as a cat in thinking on his feet; he had the courage to argue with anyone on any subject; he remembered all the ringing phrases he had ever heard and developed the facility of whacking out some pippins of his own; he could instill fear into people which made them do his bidding; he had a slashing sense of humor, satire and ridicule with which he cut his opponent to shreds; he was a jolly good fellow who would drink, gamble, carouse and swap yarns until the cocks crowed; above all he had a magnificent voice which he had been developing for a full decade.

"It was like some superb instrument, it could be pitched at will to majestic denunciation, withering scorn, light pleasantry, deep or tender emotion. It was the voice of an actor; the expressive face and emotional temperament of this man who could move others to tears belonged to the footlights."

Clay touched greatness twice in his long and stormy career: at the beginning, when he was twenty-one, and at the end, when he was seventy-two and fought for the preservation of the Union. In between lies a veritable jungle of opportunism, conceit and power politics. He was a stripling when he reached Kentucky, yet he plunged at once into the stormiest battle in the state's history, advocating a gradual emancipation of the slaves, popular election of the governor and senators, flinging his arguments heedlessly into the teeth of established attorneys and businessmen of the state.

It was audacious, but it was also smart: the entrenched gentlemen had no need for him; as a tag-along he could have been little but a mascot. But as a voice of the weak and unorganized opposition, pouring forth highly impassioned appeals and moving his audiences to outbursts of emotion; as a fighting liberal and advocate of Jeffersonian democracy against the still predominant and autocratic Federalists, he became known at once, like a shot. His battle for democratic reforms won him friends among the plain people and the frontiersmen.

His success as a lawyer was also immediate and phenomenal; within five years he was known in every hamlet of the state, was called one of Kentucky's best lawyers, and had accumulated a modest fortune. He was the Clarence Darrow of his day, defending a long line of murderers and losing no one to the gallows. His powers were peculiarly fitted to a frontier country where technical law played second fiddle to forensics. He bulldozed judges, put on shows for the juries, played tricks on the court which might have earned him disbarment in Richmond, Philadelphia or New York.

He had a magnificent time riding circuit with the other lawyers, galloping at breakneck speed through the forest trails to play a new town each day, spending his nights drinking and gambling and roistering at the taverns. Court quarrels were plentiful; the whole countryside gathered to drink and fight and witness the legal brawls which took the place of the theater. Since Henry Clay put on the best show of all with his alternate arrogance and humor, his boldness, adroitness and manipulation, his emotional debauches which confused the jury and obscured the law, he won cases that made him a legend while he was still in his mid-twenties.

"He fulfilled the popular conception of the great trial lawyer—dominating, hypnotic, ingratiating, with a church-organ voice and unlimited command over tears and laughter; one who could shrivel up witnesses with a flash of the eye, convince jurors that black was white, and elevate a petty case into a drama of such intense human interest that it was worth coming miles to see."

When he was still in his twenties he married into one of the wealthiest and most important families in Lexington, adding to his extensive criminal practice the lucrative business practice of his wife's family and friends. He had become known as the defender of the poor, the downtrodden and the unfortunate, and so he was when he could make a great show of it in a public courtroom; but on the business side of his practice he served the money interests. He fought for the right of owners to employ women and children in the early factories on the sophistry that, "Constant occupation is the best security for innocence and virtue, and idleness is the parent of vice and crime." He opposed all control of labor exploitation on the grounds that exploitation arose out of the nature of man, and was inescapable. He defended the salt monopoly in Congress, accusing its opponents of being revolutionary.

At the age of twenty-one he had preached the gradual emancipation of the slaves; a very few years later he was buying and selling slaves, helping to enforce the Fugitive Slave Law by returning runaways to their masters, answering hecklers who demanded why he did not free his own slaves with brilliant but entirely specious arguments that if he freed them now, the old ones and the children would starve. Before many more years he would be fighting for the right of slavery to be extended to the newly acquired states. He had won his early campaigns by denouncing monopoly in finance and business, yet when an insurance company in which his father-in-law was a heavy stockholder began banking illegally and monopolistically, he fought for the renewal of their charter in the state legislature, forcing his will upon that legislature by an unscrupulous maneuver. Perceiving a campaign issue in 1811, only seven years after this successful furthering of monopoly, he heatedly opposed the chartering of the Bank of the United States which was exercising the identical monopoly and restraint. Five years later he doubled back on his tracks when he became employed by the same Bank of the United States and pushed through the House of Representatives a bill authorizing the bank to perpetuate its monopoly by recharter.

From 1810 to 1812 he was one of the most fiery leaders of the War party, helping to force the country into a war with Great Britain which neither the president nor the Congress nor the people wanted, and for which they were ill prepared. In 1823, when it appeared as though the hero of Mr. Clay's war of 1812 might secure his place in the presidential race, he denounced General Andrew Jackson for his conduct of the war, heartily condemning the war and its leaders. In 1812 he had promoted a war to promote himself; in 1823, further to promote himself, it was necessary to slander the men who had fought the war. Such minor contradictions did not embarrass Clay's oratories.

He was a chameleon: he could turn any color that might be useful to him. To read of his career one must have corkscrew eyes.

3

He leapt as agilely as a mountain goat from law to politics, serving six consecutive terms in the state legislature and being elected Speaker on his seventh. Though he engaged in his share of logrolling and special pleading, he also did good work for the one cause he served most consistently: nationalism, the strengthening of internal resources, the building of roads and canals, the pushing out of the frontiers.

In 1810 he was appointed to the Senate, arriving in Washington with three thousand dollars of advance payment for pleading certain business cases before the Supreme Court. He announced that he intended the session to be a tour of pleasure, fulfilling this promise to himself by "becoming a favorite with the ladies, being in all parties of pleasure, out almost every night, gambling much, reading little." His first service to the nation epitomized his career: he plumped for a central government strong enough to pay out money for internal improvements which would benefit the states, but not strong enough to take away any of the states' rights; he fought against a strong army and navy in the fear that they might be used against the states, then cried for "resistance by the sword" in the country's international disputes.

In 1811, after only one year in the Senate, he stood for the House because he "preferred the accustomed turbulence of a lower House to the solemn stillness of the Senate." His eloquating had packed the ladies' gallery of the Senate whenever it had been announced that he would speak, but he had made little impression on his confreres. His success in the House, where speechmaking was the chief weapon, was as immediate as his success in the law in Kentucky. He was elected Speaker and became the party leader, for he exerted a powerful influence over large groups of men. They felt in him the qualities of the Leader, following him faithfully, sometimes through affection, sometimes through respect, sometimes through fear.

His tongue had no equal in Washington; as his powers as a spellbinder increased, his egomania knew no bounds. He could spill a flow of words into any subject and the next day spill an equal number into the opposite stand. He could argue logically if his immediate purposes could stand logic; if his cause were spurious he could argue with daring illogic. He convinced people that he was forthright and sincere because he believed himself to be forthright and sincere on every swing of the cycle. No American lawyer had made so much noise in a courtroom or legislator in a Congress; he was known as "the noisy Mr. Clay," yet into the noise went some of the best oratory of the day, some of the most sparkling wit and daring forays.

"In March, 1824, Clay espoused a bill in the greatest protectionist speech in American history. Much that was native to Mr. Clay's character adorned the address: a warm and brilliant imagination, fervid felicity of phrase, shallow but showy research, half knowledge dexterously disguised. Yet the effort constitutes a model for protectionist orators to this day."

He had skyrocketed too young, too fast. With his first taste of power he lost balance, became arrogant, contemptuous of the abilities and rights of others. He ruled the House proceedings with an iron hand, murmuring, "I dislike being a dictator in any sense."

One day a representative replied, "You do it so well, you ought to like it!" whereupon other members cried, "That's fair!"

Since he had succeeded without work he came to think of himself as a native genius, one whose belief in an idea or thesis made it right by that very fact. His powers as an orator took precedence over the powers of other legislators to reason, to research, to think, to feel. He lashed opposition into line, controverted inescapable evidence, mesmerized his listeners by his histrionic abilities; carried them on an upsurge of emotion to do the thing he wanted. It was hard not to like him; he had superb poise, he was ever charming, gracious, entertaining. His gambling and drinking made him popular; since he never intruded politics into his social life he was a jolly companion, good fun, full of jokes and laughter. Though John Quincy Adams had a very low opinion of his companion on the Ghent Commission, calling him a "gamester in politics as well as cards," all doors opened to him, he was lionized, the Madisons and the Monroes championed him.

He held his power over the House and a large portion of the electorate because he projected a physical emanation: electrical, chemical, X-ray: a substance that left his body and entered the body of his listener, sent his audiences away with such a heady emotion that after the issues had passed, the memory of what Henry Clay had done to them remained fresh and vivid. Literally, he seduced his audiences; as often as not it was pure rape. Once that bit of emanated Henry Clay entered the body and blood stream of a listener the virus was impossible to wipe out. When General Glascock of Georgia was asked, upon taking his seat in Congress, if he would like to be introduced to Clay, the general replied, "No sir, I am his adversary, and choose not to subject myself to his fascination."

The only antidote was a cold and objective review of Mr. Clay's mind, which rarely stood still long enough to be reviewed. He was a popular idol of his day, with a popularity so solidly entrenched that no manner of defeat could wipe it out, no reversals on the stands that had endeared him to the public could discredit him, no manifestation of opportunism, viciousness or self-interest dethrone him.

He was a consummate wielder of the dagger: he would dine at a man's house one night, eat and drink with his host, embrace him upon leaving, cry, "God bless you!" and the next morning surreptitiously go to the president to urge that "that damned fellow" not be appointed. When it suited his purpose he split his own party, just as Bryan would split his in 1904 to serve his own ambition. No one knew better than the Cock of Kentucky which side his bread was buttered on: and he liked butter. A considerable portion of his public life was spent in trying to find butter for both sides of the slice.

Hotheaded, impulsive, he belched bombast—some part of which was helpful to his state and to the nation. From the standpoint of Kentucky and its people, he served them well. As Speaker of the House, as leader of his party, as a three-time presidential candidate, he brought recognition and honor to Kentucky, a frontier state which otherwise might not have earned so large a share of the news. Kentucky was grateful even when Clay was wrong, just as Idaho was to become perennially grateful to Borah for making a small state seem so important. He had an astute nose for issues, and served many worth-while causes in the process of serving himself: the Monroe Doctrine, co-operation with South America, a stiff foreign policy, America as a place of refuge, the central government's backing of internal improvements. He had one great vision, that of a gigantic and powerful nation extending all the way to the Pacific Ocean. Out of the profusion of words that he uttered, these few show him at his best and illustrate his basic philosophy of "An American System."

"We are not legislating for this moment only, or for the present generation, or for the present populated limits of these states. Our acts must embrace wider scope, reaching northwestwardly to the Pacific, and more southwardly to the River Del Norte. Imagine this extent of territory covered with sixty, seventy, or an hundred millions of people!"

He broke up organized groups, scattered logic like tumbleweed in a Texas typhoon, shouted so long and so loud that all over America people listened. When the interests of his country and his career happened to coincide, the United States had a gallant and fearless champion.

4

During the years of 1812 to 1816, when James Monroe

had been secretary of state under President Madison, Clay had been Monroe's warm friend and admirer, had called him Dear Colonel, and had followed his advice and guidance. Since from the time of Washington the line of ascendancy had been from secretary of state to president, it was universally accepted that Monroe would be the next president. Clay felt with equal certainty that he would be President Monroe's secretary of state, that after Monroe had served two terms Crown Prince Henry would be elevated to the throne. But President Monroe appointed as his secretary of state John Quincy Adams, the ablest statesman on the scene.

Clay's outrage and bitterness were epic in their proportions. It was the first time the young man had been crossed. He would not become reconciled, refused to serve as secretary of war or ambassador to England, preferring his independent position as Speaker of the House: from this position he could wreck Monroe's administration, so completely discredit Secretary Adams that the line of ascendancy would be broken and Clay then would become president in 1824, instead of Adams.

His first move was to spoil Monroe's inauguration. Since he was the master of the House he assumed the chamber to be his private castle, refusing to surrender control of it to the Senate committee in charge of the inaugural ceremonies, denying them permission to bring in the fine red Senate chairs on the ground that "the plain democratic chairs of the House were more becoming." In the end he succeeded in keeping Monroe out of the House altogether: the president was sworn in on a temporary platform erected outside the Congress. He added affront to the office of the presidency by refusing to attend the ceremonies.

Thus did the Cock of Kentucky declare war against his former friend, benefactor and chief executive. For the next eight years his every wile, artifice and trick was used to discredit the president and his regime; his incessant insults, obstructionism and destructive criticism almost drove President Monroe out of his mind. He condemned Monroe's message to Congress as devoid of reason; those who defended the president he denounced as sycophants and parasites; nothing won his support. He sabotaged not only necessary and beneficial government action, but sweated mightily to destroy the very policies for which he had worked hard between 1812 and 1816 when he had imagined himself the Crown Prince. President Monroe hobbled along with the dead weight of the Speaker and his subdued House tied around his waist.

As Binkley points out in *The Powers of the President,* Clay used the Speaker's Chair to smash the powers of the president by refusing to let the House co-operate; by killing the chief executive's bills; by throttling his influence even with his own party members; by milking from the office urgently needed functions that had been painstakingly built up by Washington, John Adams, Jefferson and Madison, powers which a frightened electorate had given up grudgingly because of their fear of such dictators as King George III. When in an attempt to justify his conduct he ordered the House not to show abject submission to the executive pleasure, a brave southern representative drawled, "Since when is it the Speaker's exclusive right to assume the character of the champion of liberty?"

He was not intent upon smashing presidential control because he thought it dangerous to the freedom of the people; once he had eased himself into the office he would have done another of his about-faces and set out to wrest all power from the Congress. He would have been America's first elected tyrant; in his quest for absolute mastery he would have gone a long way toward wrecking co-operative government.

If his rage against Monroe was intense, it was the mildest breeze compared to his determination to destroy John Quincy Adams, the man immediately in his way. He worked indefatigably to break down Adams' foreign policy, ridiculed his patience with Spain in a delicate situation, insinuated that he was under foreign influence, heaped scorn upon him for his attempts to accomplish solidarity with South America, surreptitiously tried to discredit the secretary of state with the nations with whom Adams had to deal. It made no difference to Clay that he was weakening his own nation, increasing the contempt expressed for democracy among the monarchies of Europe, an attitude against which he had helped thrust the nation into war. He was going to be the next president if he had to destroy the nation in the process!

John Quincy Adams was not as disturbed as President Monroe. He went about his tasks quietly, doing a statesmanlike job, commenting about Clay, "His opposition to Monroe and myself arises out of a disappointed ambition, a determination to run down the administration and become president by hook or crook in 1824."

It was entirely in character that he should be the first to get himself nominated for the election of 1824. For three full years he had been promoting his candidacy by a hailstorm of letters to every part of the nation, arguing, pleading, asserting, cajoling, threatening, outlining all the reasons why he should be supported, why all other candidates were unacceptable, why he was positive to be elected. At the same time he tried to cover his palpitance by such demure statements as, "If an idea were taken up that the office were sought by me, it could not fail to be injurious to me. It would be said to display a most inordinate desire for office, which I certainly am not conscious of feeling." In the heat of the campaign he coyly would ask his campaign manager, "When have I shown an avidity for office?" He interpreted everything that happened as a good sign; he was superbly confident not only that he would win, but that in his winning, virtue, justice and truth would triumph. Again in the 1832 campaign against Jackson he would write to one of his campaign managers, "I think we are authorized, from all that is before us, to anticipate confidently General Jackson's defeat. If we fail, it will be because the power of corruption is superior to the power of truth."

Since it was before the advent of the convention, Clay was named in November of 1822 as a presidential nominee by the Kentucky legislature. The Federalists having passed from the political scene, there was no opposition: Clay and his opponents, Adams, Jackson, Crawford, Calhoun, Clinton belonged to the same Democratic party that had been founded by Jefferson. Up to this time the presidential nominee had been selected by a caucus of party leaders. Since the party caucus wanted Crawford to succeed Monroe, Clay and the other candidates took the fight directly to the people, demanding the popular selection of candidates. They fought so brilliantly that they won, and the caucus gave way to the people's primary. As all six of the candidates were Democrats there was little to choose between them on the question of issues.

Henry Clay, out of the raw west, had to convince New England, New York, the middle states and the south that he was for them all. Since geographic antagonisms were universal and economic interests irreconcilable, he brought to this task his great gifts of phrasemaking, evasion, wangling, energy and unwaning confidence; maintained a straddling act which made him America's first nominee for the definition of a mugwump: a man who sits on a fence with his mug on one side and his wump on the other.

In his local campaigns he had been able to take to the stump to reach his electorate. In a national election it was considered neither dignified nor proper for a candidate to take to the road. Though this restriction seriously cramped Clay's style, it would have been an impossible task even for him, the only means of travel through large portions of the country being horseback. He was limited to making a few speeches at barbecues where the amount of roast beef consumed was exceeded only by the amount of oratory; to writing articles for those newspapers which were supporting him; to attempting to reach by correspondence as large a percentage of the voters as Franklin D. Roosevelt would chat with over the radio.

It was no pastime for a fainthearted man; two months would elapse before all the returns reached Washington and a candidate could know whether he was to spend his next four years in the White House. Clay passed the anxious weeks at his palatial hundred-acre estate on the Richmond road, called Ashland, where he raised corn and hemp, Hereford cattle which he imported from England, sheep and champion race horses. Here with his wife and their seven children he lived as beautiful a life as could be found anywhere in America, for Henry appeared to be devoted to his family's welfare. Lucretia Hart Clay was said to be "neither beautiful nor intellectual, but a woman of good sense, discreet and kind, a good manager and mother." Yet in her picture she shows a lovely face: strong, clear-eyed, rich in character. She went in as little as possible for society while in Washington, preferring to spend her time with her children; she was a sensible counselor for her husband, comforted him in his dark hours, nursed him through nervous illnesses: an intrepid voyager who stood resolutely by his side from the moment she married him, at the age of eighteen, until his death fifty-three years later.

The balloting began on October 17, 1824. In spite of the fact that this was the first time the people would choose between men whom they themselves had nominated instead of those thrust upon them by the party machine, less than five per cent voted. The politicians had been frightened by the possibility of a "revolutionary rising of the masses," but the masses forgot to rise, casting less than four hundred thousand votes, giving no one man a majority.

"As ballots were counted postriders, river steamers, coastwise vessels, indeed every traveler bore the news piecemeal, to and fro." The nation was crisscrossed by flowing streams of rumor, gossip, invention, fragmentary truths. Clay kept up his courage until the last possible moment; by mid-December he had to admit that he Also Ran.

The fourth horse runs out of the money, but then, the fourth horse is rarely Mr. Henry Clay!

When the election results became known crowds poured into Washington: and with them Prince Hal. While the excitement mounted, Clay surveyed the field. There were many reasons why he should throw his votes to General Andrew Jackson: the Kentucky legislature had passed a resolution asking him to do so; the two Kentucky senators in Washington urged him to make Jackson the president. Jackson had received a third more popular votes than Adams, had carried eleven states to Adams' seven; most of the men who had voted for Clay unquestionably would want Jackson as their second choice. Jackson was a western man who would carry out his program for the development of the frontier, a people's man who would fight for the forward movements Clay had espoused in his youth. Clay had spent eight years hamstringing Adams' every effort, had never wasted an opportunity to tell the country what an impossible president Adams would make.

Adams had had more experience as an administrator, was a statesman, cultured, levelheaded, a man who enjoyed working in harness with his fellows for the furthering of the democratic principle. Adams too had sponsored many of the causes for which Clay had ballyhooed, so that he would not be putting in a man with whose policies he disagreed for anything more than immediate political purposes.

He despised Adams for having been appointed secretary of state by Monroe, but he also hated Jackson for his popularity. Never before had a westerner risen to national power, and now two of them had arisen at the identical moment! He reasoned that Jackson had stolen his votes: if Jackson had not run, Clay would have been elected. And if he selected Jackson to be president it would be a very long time before another westerner would succeed to the office. Adams had no personal following or warm friends, and he, Clay, could control the administration, take over the party machine which would back him at the next election. Jackson was so popular that he would be re-elected and then dictate his successor . . . and it wouldn't be H. Clay!

But the most important factor in his reckoning was that he had to be secretary of state in order to be in line for the presidency. By a circuitous route his friends propositioned General Jackson, who administered a hearty rebuff. After delicate negotiations, during which Adams observed in his diary that he was walking over fires, Clay and Adams met in Adams' home on January 8, 1825, agreed to forget their differences and stand together. Adams did not promise Clay that he would be made secretary of state in return for his votes, but certainly Clay knew that the office would be offered to him.

Though he was the wiliest and most astute politician on the American scene, he was unprepared for the storm that descended upon his head when he came out for Adams. With a roar of indignation he was branded a traitor, a turncoat, a conniver, a defeater of the public will. It was only a short time before Adams had to announce his selection for secretary of state. When it was learned that none other than Henry

64

Clay had been offered the post, the cry of "corrupt bargain" sprang up everywhere.

Clay was convinced that the road to the presidency ran straight through the office of secretary of state, and he was determined to have the office at all costs. He hesitated for a full week while the tumult swirled about him. When he accepted the offer he became the most universally loathed public figure since Aaron Burr, a detestation which was not to be equaled until Horace Greeley went bail for Jefferson Davis. He was declared to be a dead man politically. A maneuverer of Machiavellian resourcefulness, he always succeeded magnificently right up to the immediate objective, then made a blunder which brought his entire structure down over his head.

Had he rejected the offer, remained Speaker of the House, he might have achieved his life goal.

He loved the presidency not wisely, but too well. In politics as in romance a soupçon of reluctance aids in the conquest.

5

Having broken his political neck to get the job, Clay neither liked nor enjoyed it. To whom was he going to make impassioned speeches in the cool, quiet office of secretary of state? How was he going to wield power over a living, fighting body of men? But he had made a bargain, and he would stick to it, work hard and conscientiously, give up his drinking and gambling, behave like a model citizen so that the country would realize that he had been the right man for the job, and elect him to the presidency.

He was given a severe dose of his own medicine. He who had kicked and screamed and sworn and blocked everything Monroe and Adams had tried to accomplish between 1816 and 1824 now found the majorities in both Houses, allegedly outraged at the "corrupt bargain," kicking, screaming and blocking everything that he and Adams tried to accomplish for the good of the country between 1824 and 1828. When he tried to promote a conference with South America, whose results could only be beneficial, an avalanche of opposition arose on the most nefarious grounds. No matter what he attempted, no matter how wise or unselfish or farseeing, he was denounced. In the solitary grandeur of his office he could console himself for being the most heartily disliked and impotent secretary of state the country ever had had by remembering that it was he who had taught the opposition most of its tricks.

He had reasoned that Adams would be re-elected in 1828 and that it would be his turn in 1832. Though he was positive right up to election day that he would be secretary of state for four years more, the majority of the American electorate made the choice of which he had robbed them four years before, and sent Andrew Jackson to the White House with 647,-276 votes against 508,064 votes for Adams.

Mr. Clay was out in the cold. An expert figurer who always worked out the percentages, his figuring somewhere, somehow, had gone wrong.

He retired to Ashland where for two years he repaired his mill, erected an icehouse, increased his livestock and built fences not only around his farm but around his political party as well. He had left Washington determined to run against Jackson in 1832. As groundwork he attacked Jackson's policies before the nation, pointing out how much better he could have done the job. But Henry Clay knew that he would have to get into the limelight, that he could not secure a national audience by making occasional gratuitous speeches and crying, "Down with Jackson!" In 1831 he managed by a slim margin to have the legislature of Kentucky send him back, twenty years after his first appointment, to the Senate.

Once again he was the fiery and brilliant Cock of Kentucky, the greatest speaker and politician of his day. He waged a hard fight for a high tariff to please New England; came out for the sale of public lands, albeit at a high price so that cheap labor would be plentiful for the east, thus keeping New York business pleased; he insisted that the revenue from the sale of land be used for internal improvements, which delighted the west. Never had one man been so well represented in Congress! Passions ran high, the debates were electrifying, the press played up the battles. Clay gathered strength from the indigenous American habit of making a hero of any man whose name appears constantly in the news. His cry for an "American System" caught on; within a year he was entirely repatriated. He was now the number-two man of the nation. All he needed was an issue to defeat Jackson.

There being no legitimate issue on the horizon, he created one. Andrew Jackson was hostile to the Bank of the United States; although the bank was used by the government for its official business, it was privately owned by Nicholas Biddle and a group of his associates who controlled most of the finance of the country. They were sound money adherents who had stabilized the wildcat currencies of the country, but also had created the greatest monopoly to be known in America until the 1890s. Jackson believed them to be a threat to the independence of the government and to the freedom of individual business; he was determined not to renew their charter.

Clay was an attorney for the Bank of the United States. Prior to his appointment to the Senate he had advised Biddle against applying for recharter before the next election because he had felt it unwise to force Jackson's hand. Now that he needed a campaign issue he persuaded his client to apply for his recharter at once, telling Biddle that Jackson would not dare to refuse. He was certain that Jackson would veto the bank over the votes of the Senate; he planned to defeat him for the presidency on this tactical error.

Just as in 1828 Clay's and Adams' enemies had combined to elect Jackson, so now Jackson's enemies combined in the National Republican party. The National Republicans met in convention and nominated Clay unanimously on the first ballot. Apprehensive lest the country suspect steam-roller methods, he had written the convention a letter asking them "to weigh him with every man available for the nomination solely on the basis of fitness for such a position." How much he meant this letter is indicated by his outburst four years later, when he learned that the following convention had not renominated him.

"My friends," he cried, "are not worth the powder and shot it would take to kill them!"

Revolutionary change is made by the outs. The National Republican convention was the most interesting that had yet taken place: in it Clay's name was presented to the nation in the first nominating speech in history; its chairman made the first party keynote speech; the delegates voted for Clay in the first oral roll call; the first notification committee was sent to advise him of his nomination. All this caused discussion, gave to Clay's candidacy important news value.

Clay's client, Biddle, wrote to his attorney, "As to Jackson's veto measure, I am delighted with it. It is really a manifesto of anarchy such as Marat or Robespierre might have issued to the mob of Faubourg St. Antoine, and my hope is that it will contribute to relieve the country from the domination of these miserable people. You are destined to be the instrument of that deliverance." To back up his words Biddle contributed forty-two thousand dollars to Clay's campaign, the equivalent of a million dollars in 1940.

Clay set out to convince the country of what a great thing Biddle's Bank of the United States had been for them. So certain was he that the voters would agree with him that he ordered thousands of copies of Jackson's veto message printed —at the bank's expense—and distributed throughout the states. A class-war campaign developed, with Clay and Biddle screaming, "Anarchism! Revolution!" the Jacksonians replying, "Monopoly! Financial dictatorship! Oppression!" One of the astute observers of the day commented, "Attachment to a large monied corporation is not a popular attribute. The feeling of common minds is against Mr. Clay." The common minds were perhaps apprehensive of what would happen to their government if the bank's employee were elected on the bank's campaign funds.

Clay did not know that the bank was unpopular with the mass of Americans; he would believe not a word of this. He was certain that he would whip Jackson decisively, that the people would not again vote for that demagogue, that revolutionist; that the solid citizens would rise in their might in favor of the respectable Mr. Clay. He fought a vigorous, loud, unrelenting fight, and the harder he struggled, the more people he reached, the more votes he lost.

It was his class war, for he had created it. He who had started out at twenty-one as the friend of the pioneer, the common man, the poor, the oppressed, was now fighting for the financial interests as only Alexander Hamilton had fought before him. In his consuming passion for the Golden Fleece he had abandoned his own section of the country, his own philosophy, had thrown in his lot with big business and the oligarchy. Because Harry of the West had become Prince Hal, arrogant, dictatorial, superior, blind to everything but his own preening ambition, indifferent to the wishes of the common people from whom he had sprung and who had started him on his career, he was given a thumping. He carried only six states, received but forty-nine electoral votes against two hundred and nineteen for Jackson. The people had crushed him in the most effective way they knew how.

One historian of the period comments, "The cause of Clay's failure was his ingrained contempt for democratic processes."

Henry Clay understood politicians perfectly, simple voters not so well.

6

Twelve years would go by before he would get another chance at the presidency. In the Senate he resumed his policies of 1816–24, opposing everything Jackson proposed, calling him a tyrant, an evildoer, a wrecker. In his fury he went so far as to deliver a three-day tirade against the president, demanding a Senate condemnation of Jackson and his regime. "We are in the midst of a revolution," he cried, "hitherto bloodless, but rapidly tending towards a total change of the pure republican form of government, and to the concentration of the power in the hands of one man." For three months he waged his excoriation of Jackson, whipping into line enough backers to have the condemnation resolution passed. The storms he caused were so violent that if any new form of government had been available, he might have wrecked democracy.

His defeat left him genuinely baffled. Concluding that he had been bested by party organization rather than by the will of the people, he became instrumental in forming a new party, the Whigs, who he was positive could elect a president; and this time he was right. The Whigs were composed of the National Republicans, the Antimasons, the advocates of the Bank of the United States, Jackson's personal enemies, and all those who opposed the regime for any reason whatsoever. The harmony of the Whigs, many of whose groups hated each other as bitterly as they hated "King Andrew," is best illustrated by the story of the man who sat in the parlor every night holding his wife's hand: if he ever let go, she would kill him. The only policy on which they could agree was that they wanted Andrew Jackson and his party out of power.

As the leader of the Whigs he had confidence he would receive their nomination in 1836 and be able to whip Van Buren, whom Jackson had named as his successor. Once again he worked indefatigably for two years to insure the nomination; at the last moment other party leaders, discouraged by his former defeats, gave the place to William Harrison.

Clay had a mind that moved in four-year cycles. "At the very beginning of Van Buren's administration, Clay pictured himself as the Little Magician's opponent in 1840. A yearning for the nomination manifested itself in letters to his friends, and as the summer of 1837 wore on, he discovered prospects of being 'again forced into the presidential arena,'" the exact words to be used by William Jennings Bryan sixty years later.

As the Van Buren administration ran into trouble Clay tightened his hold on the Whig party, for it was clear by 1838 that the Whigs could elect whomever they nominated. Informed that the legislatures of Kentucky, Maryland and Rhode Island had come out for him, he wrote to his son, "If I am to judge from information which daily, almost hourly, reaches me, there is everywhere an irresistible current setting in towards me." For once this was not sheer ego-posturing: he was the strong man among the Whigs, and the Whigs had become the strongest party in the country. At last Clay breathed

69

easy; after twenty-four years of unrelenting pursuit he had caught up with his life ambition: he would be president.

The news that his enemies had defeated him at the convention and again nominated Harrison was brought to him while he was in his cups. It was then he had exclaimed, "My friends are not worth the powder and shot it would take to kill them!" adding lachrymosely, "I am the most unfortunate man in the history of parties, always run by my friends when sure to be defeated, and now betrayed for a nomination when I, or anyone, would be sure of an election. If there were two Henry Clays, one of them would make the other President of the United States!"

When the convention offered him the vice-presidency he rejected it disdainfully; if he had accepted he would have been president only one month after the inauguration. Harrison died, and Tyler came into office.

In his one short month of tenure Harrison had found it necessary to order Clay out of the White House, saying, "Mr. Clay, you forget that I am the president." Clay is reputed to have exulted, "Tyler will not dare resist. I will drive him before me!" He proceeded to push Tyler around. Once again he had a serious problem on hand: should Tyler prove to be a good and strong president he would receive the Whig nomination in 1844. Clay's solution grew out of his political pattern: he would have to destroy Tyler! He thereupon hatched a plan which makes him a nominee for the title of one of the most consistent and effectual saboteurs of popular government: he would renew the bitter struggles over the Bank of the United States, for the recharter of which the Whigs had campaigned, but he would set up the recharter bill in such a fashion that Tyler would be forced to veto it. Thus Tyler would lose the support of the Whigs.

As admiring a biographer as Poage says, "Clay was far more concerned with the political implications of the Bank bill than he was with the actual setting of the Bank in operation. He had defeated the plan of the moderates, sown the seeds of distrust between President and Cabinet, laid the basis of a revival of the 'Executive Usurpation' issue, and goaded Tyler into compromising counsels. Everything had gone well with his plans for eliminating all rivals and securing an uncontested nomination in 1884."

Just as he had double-crossed Biddle in 1832 to secure a campaign issue with which to beleaguer Jackson, so now he betrayed his own party, broke up the administration, kept the Senate wrangling for months when there was important work to be done. When Tyler felt impelled to veto Clay's insidious

Bank Bill his entire cabinet resigned, branding him before the nation as a renegade.

Clay's ruse had worked. The regime was rendered impotent, Tyler so completely discredited that his party abandoned him; and Henry Clay again stood forth as the leader of the Whigs. The ruse worked rather too well: in destroying Tyler and his administration he inevitably had crippled the Whig party.

His three-year campaign for the nomination was crowned in 1844 by a unanimous vote on the first ballot and a shout which shook the building. He was pleased when the Democrats nominated as his opponent the first dark horse, James K. Polk, for everywhere he heard people asking satirically, "Who is James K. Polk?" He openly despised his adversary as a nobody whom he could defeat with his left hand. But Polk's very anonymity proved an asset: if no one knew anything for him, neither did anyone know anything against him.

It was a dirty campaign, as dirty as those in 1824 and 1832, for wherever Clay appeared as a candidate the worst manifestations of the popular election shot to the surface. In his two previous runnings it had been Clay who had administered the beating; this time he took it. Stories of his gambling and drinking and loose talk were published; he was accused of killing Andrew Jackson's beloved wife Rachel by spreading a vile slander about her; he was accused of causing a man to be killed in a duel, of forcing duels with members of Congress over politics. Men paraded the city streets with banners reading: "No gambler! No duelist!"

He was called a dictator, a tyrant, a martinet, an obstructionist who had perverted the purposes of Congress to secure himself the nomination, an employee of the Bank of the United States whose purpose it was to control the government; a trickster, an intriguer, a congenital straddler, an enemy of the poor and the humble, a malicious gossiper, a revenger, a hypocrite, an enemy of democracy. The astonishing history of his inconsistencies was reviewed as men sang the ditty:

> He wires in and wires out,
> And leaves the people still in doubt,
> Whether the snake that made the track
> Was going South or coming back.

Nor was the opposition content to rest its case upon the truth; a German paper accused him of threatening to hang every Dutchman who insisted upon voting, or planning to marry every German to a Negro wife; handbills were spread among the Catholics claiming that Clay had congratulated the anti-Catholics for burning churches in Philadelphia; the opposition newspapers were used as poison sheets to spread any scurrilous story that could be invented by a hysterical journalist. The Whigs did their best to blacken Polk in turn, but Polk had lived a quiet and strait-laced life; up against Clay he looked a paragon of virtue.

The election turned not upon slander, however, but upon slavery, for here in 1844 was the first national outcropping of the quarrel which was to split the nation sixteen years later. In 1837 Clay had prevented the Senate from passing pro-slavery resolutions by introducing compromise measures which enabled both sides to save face. He could be a wrecker, but he also could be a sweet singer of harmony when it was harmony he needed to further his purposes. As is pointed out in *America's Silver Age*, "Clay's resolutions were seized with joy by a grateful Senate and rushed through. Yet they lost something of their effect by reason of the suspicion that they were intended to further his political ambition. Clay was in quest of the Golden Fleece, and everyone knew it, so it was widely assumed that the resolutions represented, not his sincere convictions, but an effort to collect votes on both sides."

If this magnificent stamina and singleness of purpose could have been utilized for his people and his country, what noble deeds Henry Clay might have wrought! Clever, yet too clever; smart, yet not quite smart enough; a *génie manqué*, a genius lacking perhaps a conscience or a soul. A man so good he should have been better, and if he had been better he would have been great. It is difficult to distinguish between a man's love of his cause and his love of self, between his desire to do good and to do himself some good. Utterly egoless men are rare and perhaps without value; need for self-expression has as often served the social weal as the social woe. But Henry Clay always put himself first.

Once again by his cleverness he thwarted himself. The annexation of Texas was the immediate issue; the south wanted Texas admitted to the Union because she believed that slavery could be extended there; the north was against annexation for the same reason. Clay had always had a great interest in Texas, had been determined that the territory should one day be part of the United States. Now he straddled the issue, held a conference with Van Buren, who was certain he was to receive the Democratic nomination, after which they simultaneously issued letters declaring that annexation at that time was dangerous to the integrity of the Union. By this evasion Clay antagonized both sides and was accused

72

of another corrupt bargain. Had he taken an honest stand he might have achieved his Holy Grail.

Already seventy, Clay staged the most spectacular campaign of his career. Now known as the Old Prince, he addressed mass meetings of as many as a hundred thousand followers, "visiting all the important cities like a general riding along the line, giving instructions and encouragement to the subordinate commanders, and stirring the rank and file with his inspiring presence. His progress was conducted in grand style, with no end of enthusiastic ovations and speechmaking."

He was attending a wedding party when a paper was handed to him announcing the result of the election. He had lost by a scant 37,000 votes out of a total of 2,700,000 ballots cast! So close was the election in every sector of the country that in only four states did Polk receive a majority of 10,000, while in three states he received a majority of less than 1,000. A shifting of 7,918 votes in the proper states would have given Clay the election.

"As he read the death knell of his political hope and life-long ambition," records an observer, "I saw a distinct blue shade begin at the roots of his hair, pass slowly over his face like a cloud, and then disappear. He stood for a moment as if frozen. He laid down the paper, and turning to a table, filled a glass with wine, and raising it to his lips with a pleasant smile, said, 'I drink to the health and happiness of everyone here.'"

When he and Mrs. Clay were at last alone they wept in each other's arms.

The suspense had been agonizing; people had refused to go to bed watching by day and night for the mails. "When the Whigs learned they had lost, they broke out in a wail of agony all over the land. Tears flowed from the eyes of men and women. Business places were deserted."

Clay interred his last campaign with his typical reaction:

"The late blow that has fallen upon our country is very heavy. I hope that she may recover from it, but I confess that the prospect ahead is dark and discouraging."

He blamed his defeat on fraud, foreigners, Catholics, abolitionists, Tyler-ites, renegade Whigs—on everything except the life, career and character of Henry Clay.

7

What kind of president would Henry Clay have made? There would have been differences of degree if he had been elected in 1824 or 1832 or 1844; he might have been milder in the early years, the attainment of his ultimate goal might

73

have slaked his thirst a trifle, made it unnecessary for him to scheme so hard; though surely he would have had to indulge in all his subterfuges during the first term in order to assure his re-election. It is likely that he would have attempted to perpetuate his personal power, running a third and a fourth time, annihilating whoever attempted to get in his way.

At no time in his life would the man who had turned state-craft into witchcraft have made a constructive president. He would have ruled his party with a heavy hand, subjugated his cabinet, crushed the Congress and turned it into a den of snarling antagonists by playing man against man and faction against faction. A hummingbird politician who could reverse himself without first stopping his forward movement, who could stand perfectly still in mid-air while making tremendous body motions, he would have kept the country in a state of befuddlement, never knowing whether it was coming or going, nor why. No greater potential enemy to the co-operative form of government ever wielded power for his own purposes; the careers of few lifelong public servants add up to so much skulduggery, to so little constructive work for the nation. It is part of the blind genius of a democracy that it can three times defeat a Clay and save itself from catastrophe.

Under the mantle of three political parties, the Democrats, the National Republicans and the Whigs, Clay had run for the presidency. Three men had defeated him: John Quincy Adams, who secured the office in 1824, stands as one of America's statesmen: wise and cultivated; unselfish, grimly ethical, incorruptible; revering the nation and its form of government. Andrew Jackson, who had defeated Clay in 1832, extended the conception of democracy to include the poor man and the common man. Polk, edging out Clay in 1844, proved to be an able executive who "strengthened the fibers of his office without attempt at tyranny or subterfuge."

For Clay to have replaced any of these three men would have been a tragedy. Henry Clay would have come first; the financial and business interests would have come second. For the rest of the American people it would have been a case of They Also Ran!

CHAPTER TWO

William Jennings Bryan

HE WAS A GALVANIC SPEECHMAKER, the greatest of his age. His voice had the power to anesthetize masses of people and bring their emotions to a boil.

He was the closest the United States ever came to having a clergyman for a president.

His speeches were crammed with bombast and Bible. His campaigns were gigantic revival meetings. Of the five and a half millions who voted for him in the campaign of 1896, a sizable portion rushed for the polls on election day with the ardency of a sinner bolting up the tabernacle aisle to the mourner's bench: in voting for William Jennings Bryan they were registering a vote for the Good Book.

His mind was like a soup dish, wide and shallow; it could hold a small amount of nearly anything, but the slightest jarring spilled the soup into somebody's lap.

Yet it need not have been so, for as a young man he was a good student, energetic in pursuit of facts. When he was only twenty-three and had first hung out his shingle in Jacksonville, Illinois, he spent several clientless years devouring books on politics and the history of the Democratic party. His greatest interest was in election campaigns and the biographies of public men. He subscribed to the New York *World* and to the Atlanta *Constitution* as the strongest voices of the Democratic party, followed the *Congressional Record* for the debates on the coinage of gold and silver.

Moving to Lincoln, Nebraska, because the competition in Jacksonville had been too stiff, and the only money he could earn was as a bill collector, he founded a Round Table where interested folks gathered to discuss the current problems: the tariff, monopoly, railroad legislation, agriculture. He was a leader in these discussions not only because of his warm and lovable personality but because he had studied more and could express himself better than his neighbors. They elected him to Congress at the age of thirty, where he instantly plunged into a debate on the tariff which was so solidly founded and adroitly presented that he routed his adversaries, Republicans who had been in the House for years. He received his first praise in the nation's press: the New York *World* commented that no new member had received such an ovation in years, while the New York *Times* observed that Representative Bryan "jumped at once into the position of the best tariff speaker in ten years."

This was the peak of Bryan's performance as a scientific thinker. For the next forty years he would become less and less interested in facts unless they served his purpose; as the religious impulses grew stronger in him he began substituting a jelled content of thought for a fluid laboratory method of thinking.

When he set out for the Chicago convention in 1896, taking his wife with him so that she might have the pleasure of seeing him nominated, he said to himself, "God is with me." When he, who had few supporters outside the Nebraska delegation, secured the nomination in the wildest acclaim in history, he amended his sentiment to read, "God is for me." When six million people across the breadth of the land thronged to hear him, gazing up at him idolatrously, drinking in his words as though they were divinely dispensed wisdom, he said, "God is in me." When he saw his face plastered on the front page of every day's newspaper, watching his slightest word and gesture being reported and read avidly by the nation, he decided, "God is me; I am God."

He had gone Hollywood.

As God, there was no longer any reason for William Jennings Bryan to study, burrow for facts, organize his material, think straight and hard and clear, accept the dictates of cold logic. Whatever wandered into his mind had to be right because he was God. To one of his political lieutenants who showed him facts and figures which proved that his stand had been wrong, Bryan replied calmly:

"I am always right."

The truly abstemious man is abstemious in all phases of his life; Bryan was a glutton for self-righteousness, power and applause. Applause was like strong drink to him, he wallowed in it, could not keep away from its intoxication; time and again he wrecked his party's chances rather than share power with anyone else. He was abstemious only in the moral concepts that had become lodged in his head early in his youth: drinking, swearing, smoking, minor vices compared to the major vices which he carried to repletion.

A psychograph of his life indicates that he shares the distinction with General George B. McClellan, who ran against Lincoln in 1864, of being the only psychopathic cases to be defeated for the presidency.

He came by his religious fanaticism legitimately. He was

born on March 19, 1860, at Salem, Illinois, of English and Irish stock. His mother had been his father's pupil at school; both were religious by nature. Bryan's father became a lawyer, a state senator of Illinois, a circuit-court judge. The Bryan children were raised in a house which Silas Bryan had built with his own two hands; Silas also added a spare room for visiting clergymen, who abounded. When Silas Bryan was informed that he was dying of pneumonia he promised God that he would pray three times a day as long as he lived, if only he could live. Recovering, the judge paid a usurious interest on his debt, falling on his knees in court to ask divine guidance before rendering a decision. Unhappily, Judge Bryan and his confreres prayed to divergent divinities, for the state Supreme Court reversed him more often than it sustained him. After six consecutive reversals Judge Bryan set precedent for his son by commenting publicly:

"The Supreme Court is wrong."

This fanaticism fell on fertile soil, yet William would not have become so ostentatiously religious if he had not discovered, when he took to public lecturing after being defeated for the Senate in 1894, that the language and imagery of the Bible were so magnificently suited to his mellifluous voice. It was a marriage made in heaven.

The first ambition of his childhood had been to become a Baptist preacher. He imagined that he had abandoned this pursuit in favor of law and politics, but in both spirit and performance he remained a Baptist preacher to the end of his days.

2

There was little William Jennings Bryan did not know about the craft of politics; he knew everything about elections except how to win them. Yet in his first start, running for Congress, he showed acumen and skill. He won over such hopeless odds that his neighbors felt no hesitancy in predicting that he would sweep the world before him in all elections to come. He very nearly did.

By the time he was thirty Bryan had succeeded in earning almost two thousand dollars in one year from his law work. This again was one of the peaks of his youth; two years later his income had dwindled to twelve hundred dollars; he was slowly working himself into bankruptcy. He badly needed to win the election of 1890, for it was becoming obvious that he would never be any great shakes as a lawyer. He was devoid of business sense; he had no executive skill which would render him valuable to a corporation; in all forms of the law where logical thinking within the premise of a legal code was imperative he was lost. He could have achieved some success pleading before juries, choking up the jurors' emotions so that they sometimes would have brought in the verdict Bryan demanded, regardless of facts. Left to his own devices as a small-town lawyer, he might have become moderately successful because of his honesty and sympathetic personality, worked himself up to a five-thousand-dollar-a-year income, and never been heard of outside of Lincoln, Nebraska; all that his talents entitled him to.

But Bryan had no intention of remaining a small-town lawyer; he hungered for fame and power. Politics was the only open gateway. Nebraska was a solidly Republican state, no Democrat ever having been elected to Congress. No one wanted the Democratic nomination, for defeat was certain. No one, except William Jennings Bryan, who knew that even if he were defeated the campaign would gain him publicity throughout the district. It took courage to be a Democrat in a Republican stronghold, but it also was clear to him that it would take twenty years to get anywhere in the Republican party. Even as Henry Clay had moved from Richmond to Lexington, so Bryan had moved from Jacksonville to Lincoln because he did not wish to spend the years trying to compete with older and more firmly established hands. Bryan too was looking for short cuts. He could not afford to wait. He needed success right now.

Starting out on his first campaign, he was one of the most attractive men ever to stand before an American electorate. He was a big fellow, tall, broad, stout-beamed, massive without being fat, the kind of body that awes smaller folk. His head was enormous, with a high forehead, strong, flashing eyes, wide mouth, a forceful, jutting nose, a monumental chin: the face and body of a giant, a fighter, a leader. He projected an engulfing energy, a warming and endearing ray. Shaking hands with him was like touching a metal doorknob after having walked across a carpet: a shock ran through one's body. His voice, deep, musical, sonorous, vibrant, carried the full burden of his tremendous sexual charm.

Since he had little law work on hand he spent his days and nights scouring the countryside, talking: talking to individuals, families, groups small or large, wherever he could get them assembled. He spent nothing but energy—his entire campaign cost him thirty-four dollars—but of this physical coin he had an unlimited supply. He loved to talk; every rolling phrase brought him intense pleasure; when talking he was living to the fullest and at the height of his powers, for his genius lay in his larynx.

78

His first campaign was a prototype of his future campaigns: he demonstrated that his sympathies were in the right place by assuring the people over and over that he was for them, for the poor and the downtrodden, though he had no concrete social program for their betterment. He manifested his courage and daring by attacking Wall Street, trusts and monopolies, but without presenting detailed and incontrovertible evidence which could have been used against them. He abandoned his natty clothes for the alpaca coat, shoestring necktie and sombrero of the professional politico: he played his voice consciously and artistically as though it were a church organ to arouse the emotions of his listeners; he quoted heavily from the Bible to make his own mind appear noble and sacrosanct. He gazed lovingly into the eyes of each voter, clasped his hand and gave him a beautiful smile, for it was his belief that no man upon whom he smiled could ever abandon him.

The Democrat whom everybody except William Jennings Bryan was positive would be left at the post won by a length. Thus was a demagogue born. A demagogue whose function it would be to lift people to such a pitch of fever and fury that they would rush out to . . . vote for him!

His love for the people was genuine, for his emotional capacity was deeper than his brainpan. It was the spiritual love of an old, white-haired preacher for his flock, the love which a patriarch feels for humanity. But with Bryan pity and sympathy for downtrodden mankind were abstract, a gaseous feeling about the heart, based on nothing solid. He liked to call himself the Commoner, but this was pure posturing, an aping of Abraham Lincoln, in whose footsteps he believed he was treading.

He knew nothing about the common people, except that they occasionally provided him with an audience to whom he might profess his undying devotion. He had never worked with them or lived with them or rejoiced or suffered with them. He had never done an hour of manual labor, except for chores on his father's farm; had never seen the inside of a coal mine, a smelter, a sweatshop. He was no man of the people; his family always had been comfortable; they had put him through Illinois College and Union Law College, sent him money when he could not eke out a living at the law. He had led an entirely sheltered life, had neither seen nor experienced misery or degradation; human suffering was something he read about in a book or magazine. He never understood the working people because he had only an amorphous idea of what it meant to work an eighty-hour week, to live with marginal wages, to be unemployed. The stories he read aroused his sincere indignation, for he had the sensitive and kindly nature of the fuzzy-minded humanist, yet his fights to alleviate the hardships of the people were always in terms of vote catching, campaigns, the retention of his own political power.

Bryan loved the common people—but he was anti-Negro! He disapproved when Theodore Roosevelt invited the Negro leader, Booker T. Washington, to the White House for luncheon. One can scan his speeches endlessly without finding a word about the betterment of the colored people. Were not they too God's children? Did he ignore them because their skins were black? Or could the fact that the Negroes voted solidly for the Republican party have caused his indifference?

The strongest and most consistent drive behind William Jennings Bryan was his lust for power. He was a publicity seeker of infinite resourcefulness. To the end of his days he tried to dominate every movement and organization with which he was connected, political, economic or religious; he never had any inkling of what it meant to compromise, arbitrate, adjust. Wherever his personal power was challenged or a program was put through with which he did not agree, he sabotaged his comrades, worked not only for their defeat but their destruction; if they would not play according to his rules, he broke up the game. Like Clay, he paraphrased Louis XV's, "After me, the deluge," to read, "Without me, the deluge."

On his one opportunity to demonstrate the quality of his action, as Woodrow Wilson's secretary of state in 1912, he made a shambles of his high office. The appointment, a reward for swinging the Democratic nomination to Wilson, was the greatest tragedy that ever befell him, for it gave evidence to the people of what would have happened had they elected him president. The most bountiful gift he ever received was that he was three times saved from exposing himself.

3

Re-elected to Congress in 1892 he made a stinging speech in favor of the income tax, which was opposed by the Republicans as radicalism. He also made the welkin ring for the coinage of silver at a sixteen-to-one ratio to gold, a panacea he believed would dissipate hard times, rescue the debtors from the grip of the eastern capitalists and bring prosperity to the farmers and workers. This speech was as unmitigated a piece of vocal nonsense as had been heard in Congress for many a moon: he dragged in Charles Martel at Tours, Napoleon at Marengo, the Islamic Wars, the Punic Wars, the

80

American Revolution, the Liberty Bell, Carthage, Hannibal, hundreds of historical characters and events which had no possible connection with bimetalism.

In 1894 he was defeated for the Senate, but a more insidious bug had already bitten him. Taking the job of editor of the Omaha *World-Herald,* he utilized the following two years in writing long articles on free silver, agriculture, public utilities, the tariff, sending marked copies of his paper to every Democratic politician, newspaper and magazine in the country. He reprinted excerpts from Democratic papers, then sent their editors articles which they had to print as a return courtesy. He assiduously pursued party leaders, editors, clergymen, educators, everyone who could do him good; he went out on self-arranged lecture tours, even hiring the halls and distributing the announcements. He went into states and towns uninvited; often he lectured to a handful of people in a cold, empty hall. But nothing discouraged him, nothing deterred him. He spent every dollar he could lay his hands on to get his name before the public, his face before the politicians. Finally he secured the lists of the delegates to the coming convention in Chicago, bombarded them with articles, letters. He sought friendly letters in return, so that somewhere in the brain of every delegate might be lodged the name of William Jennings Bryan, to be extricated at the climactic moment.

He pursued the coming nomination for the presidency with the eager-eyed ardency of a Harpo Marx chasing blondes.

It was a crafty, workmanlike plot, but for a moment it looked as though he had been wasting his time. Although he was selected to serve as a free-silver delegate from Nebraska, the state also sent a gold-standard delegation, Bryan to be relegated to the press box if the gold delegation was to be seated. The Democratic convention went free silver and Bryan was in. He immediately went about buttonholing delegates, trying to cadge votes in the manner of a barfly trying to cadge drinks. Governor John P. Altgeld, the brains behind the party, exasperatedly told him to go home and stop annoying the convention.

The most promising Democratic candidate was "Silver Dick" Bland, party leader of the House, who had sponsored the free-silver bill in Congress and had succeeded in getting it past both Houses over the president's veto. Had Bryan's primary interest been the election of a bimetalism advocate who would rescue the farmers and small merchants from the eastern gold bugs, he would have backed "Silver Dick" Bland to the last ditch. Bland was the most likely to be nominated; an experienced officeholder with a good reputation, he had the best prospect of any Democrat to be elected; because of the depression and current discontent, he had a better than even chance of becoming president. But Bryan was interested in neither the election of a Democrat nor the free coinage of silver. He was interested in William Jennings Bryan. If he could have been given the choice of Bland nominated and elected or Bryan nominated and defeated, he still would have worked torrentially for his own nomination: only thus could he be pulled up out of his obscurity, become boss of his party.

Bryan knew two things for sure: if he did not get a chance to address the convention he would not even receive the backing of his own Nebraska delegation; that if he once started talking, the heavens would fall before he stopped. For two years he had been rehearsing a convention speech, rewriting and adjusting according to the reactions of his audiences, determining the most effective timing, sharpening his "cross of gold and crown of thorns" hyperbole because:

"I recognized its fitness for the conclusion of a climax, and laid it away for a proper occasion."

The occasion had arrived—but how was he to get to sing his madrigal? Then came the break which proved that although not quite anybody can be elected president, anybody can be nominated. The chairman, remembering all the lecturing and writing Bryan had done about free silver, invited him to take charge of the discussion on the platform. William Jennings Bryan's hour had struck.

That night in his hotel room he put the finishing touches to the speech for which he had been preparing for two years. The following morning two senators and a governor spoke on the merits of a gold economy, attempting to convince the convention that bad money drives out good, that no act of Congress could force a gold-based world to accept silver at one sixteenth its equivalent in gold. These men labored not only under the disadvantage of talking hard, unromantic facts, they were in the bargain mediocre speakers; only a portion of the thousands jammed into the gigantic hall could hear them.

When Bryan rose to conclude the debate his Wagnerian voice filled every nook and cranny of the auditorium. It beat inescapably in wave upon wave on the ears and innards of the convention. He reached out a mighty vocal hand, clutched his listeners by the throat and heart, gathered them to his spacious bosom in what remained the outstanding instance of mass hypnotism until the advent of Adolf Hitler.

"They were like a trained choir," gloated Bryan.

Men who heard this speech declared it the greatest single emotional experience of their lives. It was like hearing at one and the same time, Melchior sing, Heifetz play the violin, Rachmaninoff play the piano, Irving do Macbeth, and the Zacchini Brothers fired out of a circus cannon. He was the greatest living practitioner of the art of oratory; his oratory, and his oratory alone, rocketed the convention, for he said nothing that had not been said by other Democrats in speech and press a thousand times. He essayed no economically valid refutations of the sound-money men, proposed no new social legislation, no startling methods by means of which his party could be unified, victory achieved, or the country's perplexing problems be solved.

"Ah, my friends," orated Bryan, "we say not one word against those who live upon the Atlantic coast, but the hardy pioneers who have braved all the dangers of the wilderness, who have made the desert bloom as the rose, the pioneers away out there who rear their children near to nature's heart, where they mingle their voices with the voices of the birds—out there where they have erected schoolhouses for the education of their young, churches where they praise their Creator, and cemeteries where rest the ashes of their dead—these people, we say, are as deserving of the consideration of our party as any people in this country. We have petitioned and our petitions have been scorned; we have entreated and our entreaties have been disregarded; we have begged, and they have mocked when our calamity came. We beg no longer; we entreat no more. We defy them!"

All this had very little to do with the price of eggs, but he received thunderous applause. Then, the consummate actor, he concluded with his immaculately staged, "Having behind us the producing masses of this nation and the world, supported by the toilers everywhere, we will answer to their demand for a gold standard by saying to them: You shall not press down upon the brow of labor this crown of thorns, you shall not crucify mankind upon a cross of gold."

The convention, almost to a man, went out of its mind. Farmer delegates who never had known they possessed tears wept openly; quiet men yelled deliriously; rival delegates embraced each other, others jumped over desks, raced for the platform to grab their new leader, raise him to their shoulders and carry him around the roaring hall. The Messiah had come. No such scene of bedlam has been witnessed in a convention before or since.

The next day the Bland cohorts managed to keep their leader ahead for two ballots. On the fourth ballot Bryan passed him, and on the fifth he was nominated in a maelstrom of charging, parading, shrieking madmen who kept chanting, "Bryan! Bryan! No crown of thorns, no cross of gold!"

An orator was now the head of the Democratic party, a biblical phrase not only its slogan, but its platform.

What manner of man was this who had set out single-handed to make himself president of the United States?

4

He had many stalwart virtues. He was completely honest in money and business matters. He was generous with his earned money, giving liberally to worthy causes, paying high wages to the hired hands on his little farm outside of Lincoln, treating the men as part of his family. He was a clean fighter and a good loser, had stamina and the courage of his convictions, conducted his life in accordance with the strictest moral standards. He was a good family man and husband, a fine father to his children, a co-operative and friendly neighbor. He had an amiable sense of humor: when he was asked to ascend a manure spreader to address a crowd assembled in a field, he cracked, "This is the first time I have ever spoken from a Republican platform." When it was feared that he had offended the Japanese admiral by refusing to join in a champagne toast, he extricated himself from the painful position by quipping, "The Admiral has won his victories on water, and so I shall drink to him with water; when the Admiral wins his victories on champagne, I shall drink to him with champagne." He had enormous physical vitality and concentration; except by his own convoluted mental processes he was incorruptible.

He was a liberal with an eagle eye for the depredations of the industrial oligarchy and a tongue of flame with which to denounce them. A doughnut dunker in the coffee of other men's ideas, he orated continuously for the income tax, public ownership of utilities, including the railroads; for the arbitration of labor disputes, the curbing of the injunction against strikers and the recognition of the unions; for the regulation and control of Wall Street, stock issues and gigantic corporations; the protection of farmers, small merchants and debtors against the usuries of the credit banks; for governmental insurance of bank deposits so that small depositors could not be wiped out; for the popular election of senators, the taking of government out of the hands of the trusts.

Never did he come forth with an original social idea of his own; he was not even an eclectic, a weaver of men's ideas into a consistent fabric. He simply winnowed other men's thoughts, clothed them in the purple language of the Bible,

Goldsmith, Robert Burns, Gibbon or Carlyle, and sent them forth, piecemeal and fragmentary, but shimmering in the diffusions of his matchless voice. Yet if he could not originate, neither could the originators popularize. He was the greatest popularizer of his age. He put into words, for a long-suffering and inarticulate public, their grievances, their case against rapist-capitalism. He gave them the strength to protest, to organize, to demand social improvement; he gave them sorely needed leadership. So effectively did he light the way for social amelioration that the Republican party was forced to advocate certain of his reforms in order to hold a majority of the voters.

Small wonder that millions of simple and humble folk loved him. He was for them, he was fighting their cause, trying to improve their lot, rescue them from the boot of the oppressors. So few men had been for them! So few had been willing to fight their battle! So few could reach them with the message of deliverance, make it intelligible, illuminate the way to freedom!

How could the people know, gazing up into his benign face during mass meetings, reading his speeches as they were reported in the press, that this man was for them because he wanted their votes, because he wanted to wield the power which their backing could give him? How could they know that an opportunist is dangerous even when he uses liberalism as his ladder, that it is his opportunism which will prevail, and not his liberalism? How could they tell that this man was fifty-one per cent for himself and only forty-nine per cent for them, when Bryan himself did not know it, when his motivations were buried so deep in his unconscious that he believed himself an authentic Messiah?

Bryan had serious, perhaps fatal liabilities. His mind was fuzzy, his mechanics of thinking sleazy and tangential; rarely did he flush a straight line. His mind was closed to all voices except his own; he would take no counsel, no advice, no influence, no reason. In the arts, cultures and sciences he was astonishingly ignorant; he knew absolutely nothing of music, painting, sculpture, literature, architecture, the drama, and cared less for them, unless they illuminated a religious precept. A militant crusader of the kind that destroys men's minds instead of their bodies, he spent years trying to prevent the teaching of the sciences in American schools. He was a glutton: for food, for publicity, for power, for exhibitionism; at the same time he was a religious reformer trying to keep the people from enjoying those pleasures in which he was not interested. He was a saboteur; if he sabotaged the Democratic party in 1904 when the convention named Judge Alton B.

Parker instead of the man he himself wanted, how much would it have taken to make him sabotage the nation, the people?

5

If pure display of physical energy could have elected a president, Bryan would have come in on a landslide. Though Henry Clay had broken the precedent of the office seeking the man, up to 1896 it still was not considered dignified or in good taste for a candidate to rush out and actively solicit votes. But Bryan had sensed from the beginning that he had nothing to gain from convention. Never before, and not until Wendell Willkie was to galvanize the nation in 1940 by his geographic acrobatics, would the nation witness such a dumfounding performance.

Bryan achieved the miracle of addressing five million people in a little more than three months. From his ball-bearing lips rolled between sixty and a hundred thousand words a day! He traveled eighteen thousand miles on slow-moving trains, addressing crowds at every station; insisted upon being wakened at two in the morning if anyone had gathered along the tracks, often standing on the back platform in an icy gale to address a dozen farmers. No water-tank stop was too small, no gathering too insignificant, no village hall or community barn too mean for him to whip out his trusty voice and go to work. He existed on three hours' sleep a night, was up at five in the morning, either wrote, talked or gave interviews for the next twenty hours. Trying to catch a little sleep between meetings he would be disturbed by dreams of people crying out: "Bryan, let us see you! You will lose a hundred votes if you don't!"

He created a world's record by speaking nineteen times in one day, and not one of the speeches was short. In the 1900 campaign he would raise his own mark to twenty-one, in the 1908 campaign create an all-time record by speaking thirty-six times within twenty-four hours. He ate six meals a day, slept in his seat for ten minutes between talks, and at night rubbed down his body with gin to obliterate the perspiration. He was saddened when his exhortations failed to keep the newspapermen traveling with him from trying to eradicate the perspiration from their brain by applying the gin internally.

As with Wendell Willkie, many of the reporters who had been contemptuous and hostile when they started slowly came to find themselves respecting the man for his staggering physical vigor, the unrelenting drive which forced him out of a one-hour bed to address a handful of shivering cattlemen on a Montana prairie. They urged him not to exhaust himself, not to risk a breakdown before election day; what they did not grasp was that Bryan was living at the height of his powers, that campaigning and public speaking were air and food and ecstasy to him.

Of the six million words that gushed from his mouth in three and a half months, how many of them made sense? Is it possible for a man to talk sense for a hundred thousand words a day? Is there that much sense in the world? If it had been a contest for Christianity, Bryan would have won hands down: in this one campaign he quoted from the Bible more than had been quoted before or since in all elections put together. The residue consisted of one quarter arguments in favor of a cheap money, one quarter parables and poem reciting, one quarter flag waving, one quarter humorous stories, for Bryan tried to imitate Lincoln by telling homely little jokes and anecdotes to make his point. Great as was Lincoln's genius for telling a story that was right on the nose, exploding the opposition's pretension like a shot, equally great was Bryan's genius for the tangential, for stories that missed the point anywhere from a hairsbreadth to a mile. These yarns got to be a fixation, he could not think without them; in defending himself he said, "I try to tell stories that will illustrate a serious point, and the people forget the funny part in remembering the point." The direct opposite was true: people remembered the joke, forgot the point. Bryan had fizzled it, driven it out of their minds.

All this time the Republican nominee, William McKinley, was taking what amounted to an unfair advantage. He never uttered a word either to the public or the press that he had not thoughtfully written beforehand. When visiting groups came to Canton, McKinley made their chairmen write out the speeches with which they were to introduce him, edited them himself, then dug up material which would enable him to answer with facts and figures. He was stacking the cards: how solid and sensible he sounded in comparison to Bryan!

The capture of the Democratic party by Bryan was both a boon and a body blow to the liberals of the country, for the leaders among them soon came to the conclusion that he was a voice without a brain. They were in a difficult and anomalous position: they were elated that Bryan, because of his theatrical personality and mesmerizing voice, would be able to reach millions of hitherto inaccessible people with the message of economic democracy; but they knew that in America a liberal had to be solidly based in fact, fastidious in his thinking, conservative in his manner of speaking, that the combination of a radical advocate and a radical idea often proved fatal to the idea; that an irresponsible liberal was worse than no liberal at all. Every morning they scanned the papers with trepidation, walking on sociological eggshells for fear the Boy Orator of the Platte would expose their movement to ridicule and contempt.

Those who without thought of self-aggrandizement had worked for years for social democracy feared Bryan to be a false prophet who never could fulfill his campaign rhetoric, an untrained man, unqualified to hold a job that required organization and hard practical thinking. Would it not be better, they asked themselves, to wait until a genuine leader appeared? If this incompetent one were elected, would not the people lose confidence in their judgment; would not the conservatives be able to say, "Perhaps we do not give you quite as much of the national income as you imagine you deserve or need, but neither do we make you false or flabby promises"? Might Bryan not do so much damage that the cause of the common people would be injured for decades to come?

Because of their years of loyalty to their party, because of their determination to show that a party of the people could stand unified and sweep the country, the intellectual Democrats voted for Bryan. But their hearts were quaking at the thought of what might happen if he were elected!

6

The Democrats, with a candidate who could do palpable harm to the country and the office of the presidency, fought a comparatively clean fight. Their campaign fund was small, consisting for the most part of voluntary donations from enthusiasts, with no force exerted in the gathering. Little mud was flung, and no excrement; they made few attempts to engender mob hysteria or to propagate conscious lies; no injury was done to the system of free elections. When the election was over Bryan congratulated his opponent, told his followers to go quietly about their business.

The Republicans, on the other hand, who had in William McKinley a candidate who could do no possible harm to either his country or his office, achieved through their campaign methods a greater sum of injury to the democratic form of government than could possibly have been accomplished by a bumbling Bryan in four years of office. The clergy used their pulpits to vilify Bryan: Thomas Dixon, Jr., of the People's Church of New York, told his congregation that Bryan was "a mouthing, slobbering demagogue whose patriotism was all in his jawbone." The Reverend Charles H.

Parkhurst said to his flock that Bryan's attempt to become president on a free-silver platform, "I dare, in God's pulpit, to brand as cursed and treasonable." The Reverend Cortland Myers of the Baptist Temple in Brooklyn cried, "I must be heard and will be heard against all dishonesty and anarchy and kindred evil. I love every stripe and every star of Old Glory, and it is at this moment in danger. I must speak every Sunday from now until November. I shall denounce the Chicago platform; that platform was made in hell."

Thus a country in which church and state allegedly were separated was treated to the spectacle of the spokesmen of Christ, who founded a religion for the common man, the poor and the oppressed, using that religion to desecrate one who was pleading the cause of the common man, the poor and the oppressed.

The same pressure that had been exerted upon the church was exerted upon the schools. The president of Brown University, who had commended Bryan on his stand on free silver, was reproved by his board. At Yale the students so jeered Bryan he had to give up his attempt to speak, a display of college spirit which was approved by the president of Yale and hilariously acclaimed by the Republican press. The newspapers were festered, running sores; the greater portion of the campaign material in the press did not deal with the issues but was concerned solely with defiling Bryan as a person and a citizen. He was called a traitor, likened to Benedict Arnold, Aaron Burr, Jefferson Davis. He was called insane, a degenerate; every kind of lie and malignant fiction was invented to cover him with muck.

Democracy never comes so close to destroying itself as when it is attempting to perpetuate itself by free elections.

It was a class-war election, one of the strongest since the Clay election of 1832, and the most clearly defined until the election of 1940. Manufacturers called their employees together to tell them that if Bryan were elected the plants would never open again; depositors were told that their banks would fail, policyholders warned that insurance companies would no longer be able to pay, stock and bond holders informed that their investments would be worthless. Contracts were made contingent on the election of McKinley; insurance agents were instructed to tell their farmers that if McKinley were elected they could have a renewal of their loans at low interest rates.

The genius behind the campaign was Mark Hanna, promoter of McKinley and business manager of the Republican party. He was a successful businessman out of Cleveland, a square shooter who had accumulated millions in the coal and

89

iron business, a traction company, a newspaper and an opera house. Hanna was enormously shrewd, but honest and ethical withal, a man who kept his contracts even when they cost him money, who arbitrated his labor differences peacefully, who was respected by those who had dealings with him. William McKinley was the great admiration of Hanna's life; Hanna secured him the nomination in 1896, then set out to elect him in the same manner that he had set out to accumulate millions: by turning politics into a hardheaded, practical business. He said, in effect, "There is no such thing as politics; politics are one form of business, and must be treated strictly as a business." Up to this time the collection of campaign funds had been haphazard and voluntary; Hanna turned the Republican party into a gigantic corporation whose purpose it was to manufacture and sell a commodity in every hamlet of the land.

Bryan was on the upward surge; the Republicans were frightened. Hanna opened books, assessed the banks at one quarter of a per cent of their total capital, other corporations in similar proportion; banks, insurance companies, stockbrokers, manufacturers came through with the largest checks ever contributed to a campaign, the Standard Oil Company alone handing over a quarter of a million dollars. Estimates of the amount of money collected by Hanna range between the sum of three millions, stated by his official biographer, and sixteen millions, figured by a clerk in Congress. If he had wanted twice this amount or twenty times this amount, Hanna would have collected it, for he said to business, to industry, to the financial interests, "The Republican party is your party."

With unlimited resources at hand Hanna started his gigantic manufacturing and distributing plant: one hundred million pieces of campaign literature were mailed out of the Chicago office alone! Fourteen hundred speakers were hired to swarm over the nation like an army of ants. In a campaign of total propaganda Hanna swamped the country with arguments, pleaders, books, pamphlets, buttons, signs, newspaper and magazine articles. He took no chances: his money, men and material went not only into the doubtful states but into every state in the Union; a small fortune was spent in getting voters to the polls, in paying farmers and workmen for the time spent away from their jobs. Hanna neither collected nor spent his money illegally, yet his all-out attack made it appear that the entrenched interests were buying the election.

Was it necessary to use such socially destructive methods to get McKinley elected? Is it so difficult for the best man to win an election that the issues have to be obscured and poisoned? Did the Republicans blast out a victory, not over the

Democrat, but over democratic methods? Does not a democracy lose under such circumstances though it gets the better man?

Bryan, who didn't know beans about business, with a fund of less than half a million dollars, found himself up against the cleverest organizer in the history of American politics. The more millions Hanna spent, the wider Bryan traveled and the faster he talked; the harder Bryan fought, the more millions Hanna spent in counterattack. It was hardly a fair fight, one man against the interlocking billions, but Bryan put up a magnificent show. Where most of McKinley's votes were accumulated by Hanna, Bryan earned most of the Democratic votes by his own efforts. He had a great heart; if his brain had been the equal of his heart he would have been a political genius, just as Clay would have been if he had had a conscience.

For several days before the election gigantic mass meetings were held, the Republicans wearing gold bugs, gold hats, sheaves of wheat; in New York City a hundred thousand men made up of delegations from every industrial and financial interest marched in parade, wearing chrysanthemums and carrying golden oranges. Feeling ran high and bitter. On the day before election Bryan spoke twenty-seven times, then went to bed in a state of collapse. He had fought to the limit of his capacity.

McKinley received a little more than seven million votes, Bryan a little less than six and a half million. The vote was so close that any one of a dozen factors could have changed the result: if the Gold Democrats had not abandoned Bryan; if he had talked less and stuck to sound issues; if the church and the school had been kept out of politics, a legal limit set on the amount of libel and abuse in the press, a legal limit on the extent of campaign expenditures; if the Republicans had had some less thorough and scientific campaign manager.

There is almost no phase in which McKinley was not superior to Bryan as a public administrator. Where Bryan was egocentric, McKinley was modest; where Bryan was noisy and talkative, McKinley was quiet, unassuming; where Bryan was a narrow and intolerant reformer, McKinley went to church on Sunday and minded his own business; where Bryan was a moralist, McKinley believed in letting every man settle his own destiny. Bryan accepted counsel only from God; McKinley sought the best skill to assist him. Bryan made countless enemies; McKinley made only friends. Bryan was befuddled; McKinley was clear and concise. His was no giant intellect, but he had been a successful lawyer, a successful congressman and governor of Ohio. He was a good middle-of-the-roader, like Taft and Cleveland: solid, conscientious, ethical, honorable; he could be relied upon not to go off on tangents, not to make a fool of himself or his office, to get lost in extraneous issues or flounder in the swamps of moralism.

The better man was elected, by the worst possible methods.

7

The only respect in which Bryan would have made a better president than McKinley was in Mrs. Bryan, who had by far the better mind and more balanced nature of the family. By the time she reached the White House Mrs. McKinley was too physically and mentally ill to be of help to her husband or her country, but Mary Baird Bryan would have been a creative figure in Washington. A woman of superb vigor, courage and intelligence, she would have given incentive to the feminist movement, expedited women's suffrage, the flow of women into business, the professions, the arts, the breaking of taboos which were not dissipated until the close of the first World War. Like Lucretia Hart Clay, she was her husband's superior; in many ways she would have compensated for Mr. Bryan.

After the election Bryan answered some sixty thousand personal letters that had accumulated during the campaign, while he recouped his finances by earning a thousand dollars apiece for lectures and magazine articles. In the four-year interval until he again could lead his party he kept plugging for the income tax, Federal licensing of trusts and corporations, with publication of their expenses and earnings, laws against the watering of stock. He traveled the country crushing opposition to his leadership wherever it arose, maintaining his organization in full flower for his nomination in 1900. In 1898 when war with Spain broke out he joined the army. At the end of the war, to create a political issue on which to fight the campaign of 1900, he urged the Democratic senators to ratify the peace treaty.

For all his unflagging efforts, the passage of events was unkind to the political career of William Jennings Bryan. Gold was discovered in plentiful quantities in Alaska, Australia and Africa, loosening credit and making silver unnecessary as a sound money companion to gold. The war with Spain brought on a wave of prosperity, farm prices were high, the farmers were able to buy machinery and goods; unemployment was wiped out, wages were rising and, along with them, the standard of living. McKinley's administration had been honest and able; the Republicans had fulfilled their pledge of being the official party of prosperity. Their 1900 campaign slogan of "A Full Dinner Pail!" was almost unbeatable; class wars can be waged only in times of depression.

Now that the need for silver not only had been obviated but apparently been proven specious, Bryan was left without a major campaign issue. The 1900 convention pleaded with him to ignore the silver question. Bryan defied the majority of his party, cried, "You will declare for sixteen-to-one coinage of silver, or I will not be a candidate!"

The Democrats had no one else who could collect six million votes. They declared for silver.

As passionate, exciting and bitter as had been the campaign of 1896, just as placid and uneventful was the campaign of 1900. Having plotted for the ratification of the treaty with Spain, Bryan now attacked the administration as imperialistic for having ratified it, based his campaign on the slogan, "Immediate Freedom for the Philippines!" The western states opposed him on the grounds that the defenseless Philippines would be seized by Japan and used as a base of aggression against the Pacific coast; but mostly Bryan was out of season. The American people, beginning the new century, were thinking that it would be nice for the United States to become a great world power, as powerful and rich as England, France or Germany; they had no desire to conquer peaceful and defenseless peoples, but they did want their place in the sun. "No Imperialism" was a negative slogan, something spiritual and abstract compared to the "Full Dinner Pail."

The nation already had heard Bryan orate; it was not possible for him to weave a knockout spell the second time. His remarkable accomplishment of covering the country, speaking to millions, was being duplicated by Theodore Roosevelt, Republican nominee for vice-president, who was doing McKinley's active campaigning for him and doing it exceedingly well.

Fate had stolen Bryan's thunder.

He collected 6,358,071 votes, a remarkable showing for the opposition when the country was enjoying prosperity and an amiable administration. McKinley greatly increased his majority over 1896, receiving almost a million more votes than Bryan.

Like Henry Clay, Bryan's mind ran in four-year cycles. Filling in the dull and unimportant years between conventions he published a weekly magazine called the *Commoner,* lectured on the Chautauqua circuit, kept up his vast political acquaintanceship. He refused to believe that he was through as the leader of his party.

He did not attempt to get the nomination in 1904, though this out-of-character abstinence was pure craftiness. He felt that Theodore Roosevelt, who had become president after McKinley's assassination, was certain to be elected; he reasoned that it would be wise to let someone else take the drubbing: when Teddy had run his course and the Democratic party had seen how weak they were without him, Bryan, they again would nominate him to defeat a new Republican. Though he was able to keep a gold plank out of the Democratic platform when free silver was as dead an issue as slavery, the eastern Gold Democrats secured the nomination of Alton B. Parker, a solid, able and reputable judge from New York. Judge Parker promptly announced that he would fight the campaign on a gold standard.

This gave William Jennings Bryan the excuse for which he had been looking. He subtly sabotaged Parker, ostensibly campaigning in his favor, but making sure that not too many people voted for him: Parker had to receive a sound beating if Bryan were to remain in control. In his *Memoirs* Bryan gloats over how little enthusiasm he was able to arouse for Parker, while in the *Commoner* he repudiated his party, announcing his intention of reorganizing it right after the election. Both his prediction and his scheme were fulfilled: Parker received only five million votes against more than seven and a half million for Theodore Roosevelt.

After the election Bryan and his wife toured the world, Bryan sending back syndicated articles about the trivia of his travels. No great Democratic leader having arisen meanwhile, he was given a noisy welcome on his return. By 1907 he started out to reorganize his electors in every state.

He was still amazingly popular with the people. Wherever his voice was lifted he was able to form a new organization, crush the opposition, hold the majority of the delegates. After having carried his party twice to defeat, he received the third nomination with a tremendous uproar.

The Democratic platform demanded that no campaign contributions be allowed from corporations, that the source of all contributions be published before the election. Though William Howard Taft, Theodore Roosevelt's first lieutenant whom he had named to succeed him, was a middle-of-the-roader, he was backed by a formidable array of tycoons, Morgan, Carnegie, Rockefeller, who contributed lavishly in the names of their corporations. Taft agreed with the Democrat's radical departure in political ethics, but under Roosevelt's prodding insisted that the contributions should not be made public until after the election—when it could not make any difference. Both Bryan and Taft stated they would not stump, but by August Bryan was on his way, covering thousands of miles; Taft soon followed suit.

A radical idea is always more potent and effective in the hands of a conservative; it was useless for Bryan to cry out in mortal agony, "Taft and Roosevelt have stolen my credo and my platform." The inescapable truth was that President Roosevelt had been a vigorous if opportunistic progressive, had secured the enactment of liberal legislation, was prosecuting illegal combinations in industry; that Taft also was pledged to continue the trust busting. Unlike his stablemate Henry Clay, Bryan could not reverse himself, for a reversal would have been an admission of error.

Even so, Bryan enjoyed himself thoroughly. Win, lose or draw, there was nothing that he loved so much as being one of the two most important men in his country. He was no longer the beautiful man of the 1896 campaign: he had grown fat, lost his hair; his mouth had become a thin, taut line; his brain had congealed; his voice had lost its power to consummate mass orgasms. He willfully created a religious issue by telling the American people that Taft was a Unitarian who did not believe in either the immaculate conception or the divinity of Christ; taking their cue from their leader many Democratic clergymen, particularly the Fundamentalists of the south, attacked Taft on the grounds that "he looked upon Our Saviour as a common bastard and low, cunning impostor," started a whispering campaign that brought their church to as low a point as the Republicans had brought theirs in the campaign of 1896.

Though he built up the Democratic vote by bringing back into the fold those liberals who had deserted to Roosevelt in 1904, Bryan received the worst licking of his three campaigns, trailing Taft by a million and a quarter votes. Thus in politics as in his practice of the law Bryan reached his climax at the beginning of his career, steadily working himself downhill.

After his third defeat he looked, in his own words, for "a revolutionary change in the political situation which would justify a fourth nomination."

8

What kind of president would Bryan have made?

In his one opportunity to display his administrative ability, as Woodrow Wilson's secretary of state, he was able to expose the "dollar diplomacy" of big business, made some very Christian but impractical attempts at international peace treaties. For the rest, he was probably the worst secretary of state

95

the nation had had. The man who had been crying for honest politics promptly brought in the spoils system by appointing what he called "deserving Democrats" to important positions. This was not only a kick in the groin to the struggling civil service, but served to paralyze the diplomatic service by sending deserving Democrats to countries and jobs about which they did not know the first rudiment. His own diplomats coming to him for orders were staggered by his ignorance of international affairs. He spent a large portion of his time at his desk sending out temperance cards, another considerable portion of his office hours at Chautauqua meetings lecturing on "The Prince of Peace."

He would have been the most vocally religious president ever to sit in the White House, started a movement of revivalism unparalleled in American history. He would have deluged the country with blue laws: anti-smoking, anti-drinking, anti-pleasure on Sunday, anti-nude painting, anti-realism in literature, imposed a strong censorship upon every form of American life and communication, with standards set by his Fundamentalist religion. The man who, as secretary of state, refused to appoint a Unitarian as ambassador to China on the grounds that only a Christian should be sent among the heathens, would have discharged from the governmental service every Unitarian, Universalist, Congregationalist, free thinker, agnostic and atheist.

By his pitiable ignorance he would have created in the minds of the educated and cultivated people of the land a contempt for the office of the presidency. His dogmatism, his belief that he was always right, his unwillingness to listen to counsel, his inability to think in a straight line, his reluctance to adjust or compromise would have atrophied the government. Most dangerous of all, as demonstrated by his attempt to win the presidential nomination in 1924 on an anti-evolution platform, he would have hamstrung all institutions of free education by making them teach according to the precepts of revealed religion, let loose upon the land a spirit of bigotry and fanaticism which would have been a serious drag upon the spirit of scientific investigation just awakening in the country.

By way of rebuttal, Bryan would have quickened certain liberal movements, the regulation of industry and curbing of monopolies, the eight-hour day for labor, the insurance of bank deposits, the income tax. Fanatics can accomplish great good if they happen to fasten upon socially helpful causes; if not, they are a scourge. It all depends upon luck, and luck is a mighty hazardous determinant for a democracy.

Because of McKinley's assassination Bryan has to be compared with three opponents: McKinley, Theodore Roosevelt and Taft. Along with his progenitor, Henry Clay, he enjoys the unique role of having been less desirable than all three of his opponents.

William Jennings Bryan is the greatest enigma in American political history, enough like Henry Clay to be his blood brother. It is no mere coincidence that these men alone ran three times for the presidency: the pursuit arose from the identical needs and twistings of their character, drove them both to seek a fourth nomination. They were accomplished actors, hypnotic orators, had two of the largest mouths in history, Clay's being so large that he had trouble controlling it when he wanted to spit, Bryan's being so large he was alleged to be able to tickle the lobes of his ears with his tongue. They shared the greatest lust for the presidency, as well as two of the most flashy, shallow and undisciplined minds of the nineteenth century.

They were prisoners in the steel cages of their own egos, unscrupulous opportunists parading in the guise of patriots, impotent when they could not employ their sound boxes. Both were resourceful manipulators of men and ideas; both were demagogues with large and blind followings; both controlled through animal magnetism rather than integrity, vision or constructive program; both were wreckers, Clay wrecking the Whig party in 1840, Bryan the Democratic party in 1904. They were equally well signified by their titles: Clay, known as the Cock of Kentucky, who liked to strut and crow and laud it over the barnyard; Bryan as the Boy Orator of the Platte. Photographs of the interior of their minds would resemble nothing so much as a surrealist painting. The numerous biographers of both men find it difficult to begin a paragraph of praise without ending it on a note of criticism, to begin a paragraph of censure without finding a phrase of admiration creeping in.

William Jennings Bryan had a large portrait of Henry Clay hanging in the living room of his home. Nor was this still another coincidence: Clay was Bryan's idol; Bryan was Clay's lineal descendant.

If the character of Bryan is a dilemma, his political significance is a more confounding riddle. It is an inherent tragedy of self-government that an ignorant, narrow-minded demagogue can rise to power; at the same time it is one of the strengths of self-government that a man fighting for the common people can gather a following. It is a powerful indictment of democracy that a rabble rouser can control a major party for sixteen years, but at the same time it is a vindication of self-government that such a candidate can three times be defeated, albeit, as in 1896, by undemocratic methods.

William Jennings Bryan wrote his own epitaph:

"If events prove that my defeats have been good for my country, I shall rejoice over them myself. It is better for me that my political opponents should bring good to my country than that I should, by any mistake of mine, bring evil."

The brain with which he first entered Congress in 1890 gave promise of contributing ideas, service and movements of social value to the American democracy. The brain with which he died in 1925, after spending the last years of his life in an attempt to prevent the teaching of sciences in the high schools and universities, was one of the most corrosively dangerous under which the American people had labored.

BOOK THREE

"Judge Not!"

I: ALTON B. PARKER
II: CHARLES EVANS HUGHES

Should the Bench be raided for political officers?
Parker and Hughes, the only two high-court justices
to be nominated for the presidency, said, "No!"

CHAPTER ONE

Alton B. Parker

HE IS THE FORGOTTEN MAN among the forgotten men who
Also Ran.

Of all the unsuccessful candidates for the presidency of the
United States no longer living, he alone has had no biography
written about him.

This is something less than justice: there have been periods
in American history when the country could have used him
to excellent advantage as president.

No public officer ever had been asked to give up more to
run for the presidency.

As chief justice of the New York Court of Appeals, Alton
B. Parker held one of the highest judicial positions in the
land; he enjoyed his work, enjoyed the protected seclusion of
the court; he was making his contribution to the functioning
of democracy. He knew that his sense of duty would oblige
him to resign his position as chief justice, and that it would
be difficult if not impossible for him to get back into the
pleasant routine of his life if he were defeated. Campaigning
was not native to his temperament: that was why he had re-

fused to run as Democratic nominee for the offices of governor of New York and of United States senator when his chances of being elected had been robust. He preferred the cool quiet life of the specialist who could follow legal reasoning to its ultimate implication, outside the whirlpool and cesspool of partisanship.

He had the feeling that the Bench should not be raided for executive officers, that the men of the judiciary should remain at their highly technical jobs. Neither he nor the thinking public favored the idea of judges being able to use the Bench as a steppingstone to more lucrative or powerful positions; its personnel might be invaded by schemers who would render decisions with an eye to their political implications.

He was living a busy, happy life and was contented with his lot. While the Court of Appeals was in session he lived in a suite of rooms in the Ten Eyck Hotel in Albany, rising early for an hour's horseback ride through the suburbs, in the morning conferring with the other justices, holding court until six in the afternoon, dressing for dinner, lingering for a pleasant half-hour over his cigar with friends in the lobby, then going upstairs to read authorities, study briefs and write decisions. There was no recess for him as chief judge; he worked all the time, and when he went home to Rosemount for the week end with his family, his brief case bulged in the manner peculiar to legal brief cases.

At Rosemount he rose at six-thirty every morning, walked down the grassy slope of his farm to the Hudson River and dove from his dock for a swim. Then came an hour's ride on his big, high-spirited horse, in winter snowstorms as well as summer heat, through his fields and vineyards and orchards. After breakfast he began his day's work, which generally did not terminate until midnight. The summers he spent on his farm near Kingston, rising at dawn to work with his hired man taking in the hay or feeding the livestock before retiring to his library to work on his written opinions. Sunday mornings he and Mrs. Parker took their little boat to Kingston to worship at the Episcopal church, whose rector was their son-in-law; on Sunday afternoons he romped with his two grandchildren; there were usually friends to be taken around the farm with great pride and shown the crops and prize bulls. Over the dinner table there was lively conversation.

He thrived on work for he was broad-beamed, hard-muscled, indefatigable, weighing two hundred pounds of solid flesh and standing up six feet, in unfailing health and good spirits. The journalists of the day called him a great ruddy engine of vitality. Now only fifty-two years old, he was that most fortunate of all human beings, a perfectly co-ordinated structure, as devoid of phobias as a show dog of fleas.

Alton Brooks Parker had been the only redhead in the county school near Cortland, where he had to wage many a fist fight before he could persuade the other boys to stop calling him Red Top. He had a big symmetrical head and a full face, with an aquiline nose, big white teeth and large brown eyes, kindly, sincere and direct in their gaze. His jaw was large and curved; he wore a generous-sized tawny mustache. His skin was fresh and unwrinkled. Everything about him gave the impression of bigness: his strong body, his easy, straightforward manner, his moral courage. Because he was fair-minded, courteous to his opponents, a man who tried always to see things whole, he radiated confidence. When a bank of which he was a trustee was reported to be in danger Parker thrust his way through the crowd that had collected to demand its money, jumped up on a counter and exclaimed:

"The bank will meet its demands. If you wish your money, come and get it. But you will be wiser if you let it stay."

"How do we know we'll get our money?" someone cried.

"I pledge you my word," replied Parker.

The depositors took his word; the run was averted. Parker served as president of the bank, without pay, until the institution was on its feet. Having fulfilled his pledge, he resigned.

Elected surrogate of Ulster County, New York, at the age of twenty-five, he did such a good job that the Republicans of the county refused to run a candidate against him in the following election, setting a precedent that would be climaxed when he received the backing of Republican leaders in his Democratic contest for the presidency.

He had been successful very young, and solely on his own efforts, for his family had been in straitened circumstances; young Alton had had to give up his ambition to attend Cornell University and take to teaching in a country school to help out. His success had not spoiled him: he was friendly, without ostentation or pose, neither aggressive nor self-conscious, though he was firm in spirit and carried himself with dignity. He sometimes had political opponents, but few enemies; he was loyal to his own friends, and gentle in his judgment of others. On one occasion when he was holding a reception at Rosemount for the prominent people of the community, Mrs. Parker saw the name of a certain man on the list drawn up by the judge's secretary.

"I hope you are not going to have that individual in the house?" asked Mrs. Parker. "Surely you haven't forgotten how he tried to injure you?"

"Well now, it did escape my memory when I was glancing

101

over the list. But he doubtless thought he was right. Let him come, if he wants to. It would seem as if I were harboring resentment if we didn't invite him."

In only one phase of his life was he an iconoclast and revolutionary: with his pigs. He maintained that the intelligence of pigs was superior to that of the other domestic animals, deriving pleasure from training them to answer to the sound of their names, to come to him whenever he might be on the farm, to play certain games which he had taught them. He believed that pigs have "an instinctive preference for cleanliness," and had modern conveniences built for them. In spite of these heresies, and the fact that he was perforce a week-end farmer, his hundred-and-forty-acre farm was self-supporting; the Albany freight steamer frequently stopped at his little pier to carry his crops into New York City, and his apples, which he preserved in his own cold-storage bins, were famous in a modest way—even as he was.

He had the bluff geniality of the big man, was easy to talk to provided one did not try to extract political commitments which would involve his court. *World's Work* published a colorful portrait of the judge on the Bench: "As he develops his thought in ready speech, colored by a magnetic, resonant voice, his eyes narrow, wrinkling at the corners, and he shoots an incisive, level gaze at his auditor. But as he rounds a sentence or reaches a climax, his powerful chin begins to project, and the last word bitten off is emphasized with a grim, decisive locking of the jaw. This, with the utmost courtesy. There is no egotism in the manner, and no lack of restraint. But there is concentration, driving power, and the air of persistence."

He was doing no more than a hundred conscientious and well-trained judges throughout the land, nor was he any better known to the general public than the other ninety-nine. But among lawyers and judges his work already had penetrated; he was admired as a jurist for his straight thinking and the soundness of his decisions. At one time his own court decided against him by a five-to-two decision, the majority maintaining that a New York law compelling the city to see that contractors paid their workmen the prevailing rate of wages was unconstitutional. For two years Judge Parker used every spare hour to collect decisions on the constitutionality of statutes. When a similar case was brought before the court he had a great wealth of material to sustain his opinion. This time his court voted with him; and the United States Supreme Court, deciding a like case appealed from Kansas, followed Judge Parker's reasoning. Thus he had rendered a double service to the people: he had helped to release the legislature, which makes statutes, from its bondage to the courts, had helped large groups of workingmen to get higher rates of pay.

He believed that the legislature, elected by the popular vote of the people, had the right to pass laws for the betterment of society. He persistently fought what he called "judge-made law," maintaining that the legislature alone had this right. The greatest mass of his work was aimed at limiting the right of his own or any court to usurp the powers of the people's legislature!

His decisions had been uniformly progressive and humanitarian. Not even in the heat of the political campaign were his opponents able to unearth decisions in which he had acted against the interests of the people. He decided in favor of the constitutionality of the eight-hour law, upheld the right of a union workman to strike or to threaten to strike, maintained that government interference on the side of either capital or labor resulted in the abridgment of the rights of one or the other. He upheld the right of the legislature to impose franchise taxes on corporations. In 1896 he handed down an opinion in a trust case that it was immaterial whether a combination in restraint of trade was reasonable or unreasonable, that the right to restrain trade was forbidden by the common law.

Judge Parker was called a friend of labor, a friend of the trust busters, but actually he never took sides. He was a friend of the legal codes and the Constitution. The *Independent* described him as a judge "presenting an average of eminent fairness." *Harper's Weekly* said, "There is no trick or warp in his mind. He is normal in all things."

His basic philosophy of government for America was bound up in his statement that "whatever government interference in the life or business of a community is needed should be authorized by the people's legislators who are responsible, at short intervals, to the people themselves."

He liked being a judge. He had no great desire to be president. He had no desire whatever to go through a presidential campaign.

Why then did he consent to run?

2

At the back of his mind there was of course the excitement of the thought that he might be selected the chief executive of his land. Also he believed that Bryan's hold on the Democratic party had to be broken if the party were to survive. His associates persuaded him that he had the best chance of

103

restoring harmony to the party to which he was devoted. But all this would not have been sufficient to tear him from the life and work he loved if he had not been convinced that no man who adheres to representative government has a right to refuse the candidacy. He went back to Andrew Jackson for his attitude: "The presidency cannot properly be sought nor declined." He was guilty of only one inconsistency: if he had thought that he would be able to refuse the call to the presidency, then he should not have refused the call to the governorship of his state or to represent the people in the United States Senate. But just as Governor Charles Evans Hughes, who was appointed to the United States Supreme Court and thus was able to extricate himself from New York politics, exclaimed, "Thank God!" so Judge Parker had kept saying to himself silently, "Thank God I don't have to be governor!"

"A judge who seeks a political office insults his robes," said Andrew Jackson, and Parker stuck to this principle so rigidly that it nearly cost him the presidential nomination. When it became evident that he was the outstanding possibility among the Democrats he was asked to express his opinion on the tariff, on imperialism, on the gold standard, on trust busting, on labor. Judge Parker refused to express his opinion on anything.

"I am a judge of the Court of Appeals," he said. "I shall neither embarrass the court by my opinions nor use the dignity of the court to give weight to them. I shall do nothing and say nothing to advance my candidacy. If I should receive the nomination, I shall then resign from the Bench and state my views as a private citizen."

He could find no one to sympathize with this stand, not even his most loyal supporters. They told him that he now had the ear of the nation, that since he was unknown outside of New York it was his obligation, if he were going to permit himself to be drafted as the Democratic presidential candidate, to utilize the opportunity to discuss public affairs and earn himself nationwide publicity. They told him that only by stating his political views could he make friends and secure backers; that only by criticizing the Roosevelt regime could he weaken its hold on the electorate.

Alton Parker stood firm. The only opinions he expressed during the critical months were contained in his legal decisions.

He was accused publicly of being a coward. He was charged in the press with being afraid to express himself for fear he would lose the nomination. He was goaded as being a weakling, a kept politician, a nincompoop without any opinions to express. The newspapers that had been advocating his nomination grew faint, some of them dropped away. The Parker boom was collapsing fast. The judge knew it. He continued his heavy schedule of court work, refusing to make speeches or give newspaper interviews.

The New York *World,* strongest voice in his behalf, ran a series of sizzling articles, demanding that he speak out because his silence was destroying him as a candidate. A reporter friend on the *World* wrote to him outlining the gravity of the case. Parker replied from Albany, on June 17, 1904, "You may be right in thinking that an expression of my views is necessary to secure the nomination. If so, let the nomination go. I took the position that I have maintained—first, because I deemed it my duty to the court; second, because I do not think the nomination for such an office should be sought. I still believe that I am right, and therefore expect to remain steadfast."

That was the last word out of him on the subject. He showed courage and integrity in this stand, a stand which was the forerunner of a bold stroke a month later when he would come to grips with William Bryan, titular head of the Democratic party.

The struggle inside the Democratic party over the nomination was to prove as exciting as the election itself. Though he had been out of active politics for twenty years, had neither enemies nor errors to make him unavailable, a bitter battle was waged against Parker by the more radical wing of the party in the months before the convention. Despite the fact that he had supported Bryan in 1896 and 1900, Bryan hated him for being a Gold Democrat. Bryan wanted the weakest man nominated, one who could not take the control of the party away from him; he denounced Parker as a tool of Wall Street. Parker's strongest opponent was William Randolph Hearst, who owned eight newspapers, all of them friendly to labor, vigorous in their trust-busting activities, fighting the cause of the people who worked for a living. Because of this liberalism Hearst had the Illinois delegation pledged to him, and the promise of several other states. The prospect of having Hearst for a candidate so frightened the conservative Democrats that they renewed their efforts to get Parker nominated on the first ballot.

Seeing that Parker was coming into power, Bryan committed a clever piece of chicanery. Though the majority of Democrats wanted to cleanse themselves of the free-silver virus of the past two elections, and the subcommittee had inserted a strong gold plank in the platform, he waged such a skillful fight that the plank was omitted. Surely Parker would not run on a platform which did not wear a gold wedding band to make it respectable?

The Democratic convention that met in St. Louis on July 6, 1904, has been called "one of the most exciting and sensational in the history of the Democratic party." A thousand tiny campaigns had taken place in the months before the election, enemies had been placated, opponents reconciled, facts had been reviewed and weighed. The Republican party had nominated Roosevelt to succeed himself; the Democrats knew that he was colorful and popular with the people; it was felt that only a good man could defeat a good man. With the exception of the Bryan and Hearst backers, everyone called for Parker. So great was the feeling of unanimity that he received 658 votes on the first roll call, nine short of the necessary two thirds. Before the result could be announced, twenty more votes were transferred to Parker; the nomination was his.

Only Bryan was sour, announcing that as soon as the election was over he would reorganize the party, get it back into true hands. But even in his sourness he wore a little smile, for he had kicked out the gold clause, made it appear that the Democrats still were loyal to the carcass of free silver.

Parker had spent the day of the balloting plowing in his hayfields, gathering wild flowers for Mrs. Parker, working in his library. A friend telephoned at midnight to tell him the result. Where before he had refused to speak out, he now sprang into action, promptly dispatching a telegram to the convention. It read, "I regard the gold standard as firmly and irrevocably established and shall act accordingly if the action of the convention today shall be ratified by the people. As the platform is silent on the subject, my view should be made known to the convention, and if it is proved to be unsatisfactory to the majority, I request you to decline the nomination for me at once, so that another may be nominated before adjournment."

William Jennings Bryan had reckoned without Alton Brooks Parker.

It was the first time a candidate had made such a move. It was an act of daring that might have lost him the nomination, made him an outcast from the party he had served and believed in all his life.

What forces had bred such stamina and integrity?

3

Alton Brooks Parker's great-grandfather was a farmer of Worcester, Massachusetts, who had fought under General

Washington during the Revolution of 1776. His grandfather had moved to Cortland, New York, in 1808, where he bought a farm and prospered moderately. Here Alton's father was born, and Alton after him on May 14, 1852; the father was known throughout the countryside as a lover of books and knowledge, but somehow he wasn't very successful as a farmer, and the family had just enough to go on. Alton's mother was a devout and intelligent woman. The boy grew up in an atmosphere of books and learning. He was a sturdy and pleasant-tempered youth who helped with the chores on the farm, went to the village school, Cortland Academy and the normal school. When he was a small boy his father had taken him into court to watch a day's proceedings. On the way home the boy said quietly:

"Father, one day I'm going to be a lawyer."

He never deviated from the ambition. During his academy years he planned to go to Cornell, recently opened at Ithaca, then to law college. By the time he was eighteen his family not only could not help him, but needed his assistance. One day he set out for the village of Virgil where he had heard there was a teaching position open. When he returned home that night he told his father that he had been accepted for the job.

"Why," said his father, "I had a better offer than that for you today."

"I'll give up the place at Virgil and take the other," replied Alton.

"No," said his father. "You made a contract; it is your duty to uphold it."

He taught for one season at Virgil, then accepted a better-paying position at the school in Accord. Legend has it that he promptly established discipline by thrashing the school bully, but then, the bully was probably giving away too much weight. At the height of his career as schoolmaster Parker earned three dollars a day. He next secured a job as clerk in the law office of Schoonmaker and Hardenbergh in Kingston. Since he had become acquainted with Schoonmaker's daughter while teaching at Accord, his entering of this particular office does not appear to have been altogether accidental. After a year with Schoonmaker and Hardenbergh he had saved enough money to enter a law college in Albany. He was a good if not spectacular student. Upon graduation he married Miss Schoonmaker, returned for a short time to his father-in-law's office, then took a young partner and started out for himself.

His practice was general and modest; his assets were his thoroughness, honesty and common sense. The first year he

107

was back in Kingston he fell into politics: his father-in-law had been a judge but had been defeated for re-election. He had taken the defeat pretty hard, believing it to be the work of his personal enemies. Parker, only twenty-four, thought it imperative that the judge be re-elected to restore his health and confidence. He persuaded his father-in-law by saying: "You must run again and win. I will manage your campaign," then went out to stump Ulster County. He made it his business to meet and become friendly with every Democratic voter and many Republicans. He stated his case so well that his father-in-law was restored to the Bench. A short time later, in 1877, a new surrogate was needed for the county. Having made such a favorable impression, Parker was nominated for the position by the Democrats and elected by a comfortable margin. He now combined his private practice with the surrogate's duties and salary of three thousand a year. A Kingston lawyer reports:

"Surrogate Parker won an important case for the town. Twenty years after I still believe that I, as the opposing counsel, had the better case. But Parker had set out to win, and he won."

He was re-elected almost unanimously, the Republicans refusing to put a candidate in the field against him.

Once having entered politics, there was no escape; nor did he want one. He became the Democratic party leader of Ulster County, which had frequently gone Republican but now returned Democratic majorities with what the Kingston Republicans called "distressing regularity." He called himself simply an adviser, leaving the title of party leader to someone else, but his work brought him to the attention of Tilden, Democratic leader of the state. He attended the Democratic convention of 1880, helping to secure Hancock's nomination, and in 1884 brought in his county for Cleveland. President Cleveland offered him the position of first assistant postmaster general. Parker, now only thirty-two years old, made the journey to Washington to decline the honor. While he was talking to the president Postmaster Vilas walked in. Vilas had wanted somebody else for the job.

"Parker says he doesn't want the place, Colonel Vilas," said President Cleveland.

"May I inquire why?" asked Vilas.

"I cannot afford to give up a five-thousand-dollar-a-year position," replied Surrogate Parker, "to take a three-thousand-dollar position."

"But I gave up a ten-thousand-dollar practice to take an eight-thousand-dollar position," said Vilas.

"Well, Colonel Vilas," answered Parker, "if I had been

making ten thousand a year for ten or twelve years, I too might afford to accept the president's offer."

Cleveland chuckled; twenty years later, in recommending Parker to the nation, he recalled the incident.

In 1885 David B. Hill was nominated by the Democrats of New York to run for governor. Despite the fact that young Parker was not a member of the state committee and had never campaigned outside of Ulster County, Hill asked him to become his campaign manager. Parker tackled the state in much the same manner he had set out to conquer Ulster County for his father-in-law. He visited every tiny sector, made countless friends, established harmony, inspired confidence by his simple and genuine manner, and brought in a clean victory for Hill. From that point forward he could have gone anywhere as a political manager or boss; but that was not what he wanted.

A few months after the election one of the justices of the New York Supreme Court died. Governor Hill appointed Parker to serve for the balance of the term. Parker was thirty-three, an extremely young age for a state Supreme Court judge. Since it was a political appointment it might have caused an outcry, but Parker was so well respected that the appointment was approved throughout the state. When the term ran out, in 1886, he was elected to succeed himself; he did so without electioneering. Once again the Republicans, who could not understand why he insisted upon calling himself a Democrat, paid him the honor of running no one against him.

In 1888 he was transferred to the Court of Appeals, and in 1897 was elected by a majority of sixty thousand to be its chief judge. This victory so impressed the state Democratic leaders that they offered him the nomination for the governorship. He refused to say he would be a candidate. What would have happened if the party had drafted him, as they were to draft him in 1904, is conjectural.

As a judge, Parker became known for "the temperate language of his judicial decisions, the absence of literary preachments, political *obiter dicta* or self-conscious virtue."

Chief Judge Parker had only one further ambition, and this he kept secret: he hoped someday to become a justice of the Supreme Court of the United States; he had every reason to hope that this honor might befall him. For twenty years he kept out of partisan politics, earned a good salary, managed his father's old farm, his wife's farm, and the new one he bought near Esopus. His property and savings together totaled about thirty thousand dollars. So entirely available was he as a candidate that he was offered the nomination for every high office of the state; upon one occasion the leaders of the party met in Albany, studied the situation and informed him that it was the consensus of opinion that he must be the candidate for the United States Senate. Judge Parker asked if he might consider the proposition, left the room, and returned in a few minutes. His jaw was set.

"Gentlemen," he said, "I have no wish to be a candidate. I beg you to choose another. My ambition is to serve my state and my profession on the bench of the court. And it is not seemly that a judge of that court should be a candidate for a political office."

He meant it. Everyone in the room knew he meant it.

And so he passed twenty years on the Bench, twenty years of being elected by the people without electioneering, twenty years of handing down objective, logical and forward-looking decisions which helped his country to function legally and constitutionally, with the right of all persons, big or little, upheld. Everyone liked him and respected him; he was no genius, he only sometimes was brilliant, but he was one of the broad beams upon which his society was built. He was on his way to becoming an outstanding jurist; if a United States Supreme Court justice should happen to retire or die during a Democratic regime, there was reason to believe that Alton B. Parker would be appointed to the highest court in the land.

That is probably what would have happened to him—if he had not felt that no member of a co-operative government can refuse to heed the call to the presidency. That sense of duty upset his applecart.

4

It was a cockeyed election.

The radicals in the Democratic party denounced Parker as a conservative; the conservatives in the Republican party denounced Theodore Roosevelt as a radical. Conservative Republicans voted for Parker though he belonged to a party they feared. Radical Democrats voted for Roosevelt though he belonged to a party they detested. Folks were heard to mutter that Parker should have been the Republican nominee, Roosevelt the Democratic nominee! The election of Parker was urged on the grounds that he was a guarantor of government according to the written constitution and the written laws, as against the personal policies which controlled the Republican administration: a complete reversal of both parties' attitudes. The electorate was treated to the delicious spectacle of having Wall Street financiers such as August Belmont and the directors of the Standard Oil Company turn to Parker to save them from the radicalism of Theodore Roosevelt, a Republican! Theodore Roosevelt had been a trust buster, a renegade, a traitor to his party and class? Very well, two could play at that game! They too would throw their weight to the opposition. They would fight and bleed—their treasury—for Parker, set up a tradition of chastisement for any Republican who dared to step out of line. They knew that it was a dangerous experiment, that they could not come out into the open and condemn Roosevelt, combat him by crying, "Radical!" for that might be a boomerang. Nor could they easily approve a Democrat, for then the voters might get into the habit of voting for them.

In spite of the dangers they took the gamble; they were not too frightened because they knew from his political philosophy that Parker would remain within the constitutional confines of the presidency, not try to take over the legislature and the judiciary, as Roosevelt was doing. They knew too how much greater chance reform had to succeed when it came from the conservative party. When a Republican exerted himself for economic reform surely the electorate could be expected to say, "Since the conservatives are suggesting these reforms they must be sound and beneficial, and we should work for them." No, better to elect Parker; Parker could not do them too much harm, but Roosevelt might ruin them.

After having had the Republican party cast its eye on him throughout his career, Parker enjoyed the honor of being the only Democratic candidate whom Wall Street yearned to see in the White House; for up to this time it had been their opinion that the worst Republican was better than the best Democrat.

Harper's Weekly declared, "There will be no outpouring of money such as Mr. Hanna reveled in in 1896. With two such candidates as Roosevelt and Parker, fear cannot be created, prediction of panic and destruction of values can produce no more than a shrug of the shoulders. Therefore it will not be a money campaign." This pretty well represented the viewpoint of the nation, for it only rarely happened that the people had the opportunity to choose between two excellent men.

"Only stupid people will assail either candidate," observed the *Review of Reviews*.

There was not much anyone could find to say against Parker. Certain journals, such as the *Arena,* charged that he must be friendly to the trusts in spite of his consistent rulings against them, else how could Wall Street prefer him? The *Nation* criticized him for ducking the question of Negro suf-

111

frage while addressing the Georgia Bar Association, a charge having some truth to it, for Democratic candidates since the Civil War had found themselves embarrassed by the Negro problem. The *Independent* carped that "he would not gratuitously go in search of trouble by doing an unwise thing in response to a mere impulse of chivalry," and the *Review of Reviews* said mildly that "he speaks as a judge rather than a statesman." Several other papers pointed out that Parker had had no experience as an administrator.

That was the sum total of criticism that could be levied against him. Most people knew that Grover Cleveland was speaking the truth when he wrote, "I do not believe that closest scrutiny of Judge Parker's entire course will develop a single instance of cowardice or surrender of conscientious conviction."

Nor was there a great deal that honestly could be charged against Roosevelt's regime: in the one scandal occurring in the post office and land office, it was Roosevelt himself who demanded the investigation, publicized the results against the advice of his party leaders, and cleaned out the thieves. He was inclined to be dictatorial and martial, he sometimes overstepped the bounds of his powers, as when he forced the coal operators and unions to arbitrate their differences, and he was hell-bent to break up the trusts, which the big operators did not enjoy; but no one could assail his integrity, his intelligence, his vigor, his interest in the welfare of the country.

So close together were the two parties that few differences could be detected in their platforms. Both were for the gold standard; though the Democrats were more outspokenly against imperialism, both believed in fair treatment for the Filipinos and eventual liberation; both believed that labor unions had the same rights as individuals before the courts; both believed in Federal protection of the buying public against unscrupulous manipulators; neither proclaimed the necessity of an income tax. Latané says that "as the campaign developed the trust question became the most important question, and was handled with unusual bitterness on both sides." This feeling of bitterness was confined to the professional politician and financier; it did not extend to the electorate. The people knew that both men were against monopoly, that neither of them could do much against the combined billions with the existing laws and machinery of enforcement.

Of the three great campaign crusades of the Democrats, free silver, anti-imperialism and trust busting, the first two had been absorbed by the flow of history, the third had been absorbed by their rivals.

Except for his plea for a lower tariff to help give the work-

112

ing people more of the creature comforts, Judge Parker had no weapon with which to fight. Nor, for that matter, had he intended to fight: only to box. He had covered Ulster County for his father-in-law, the state of New York for Governor Hill, but for himself he refused to go on a campaign tour, make speeches, stir up extraneous excitement. "If the people of this country want me to be president," he said calmly, "they will elect me." Like McKinley, he waited on the front porch of Rosemount for delegations to come to him. Not many did. With an administration that had been blundering, dishonest or ineffective, or an American people aware of shortcomings in its government, Judge Parker might have swept the country. His very matter-of-factness and refusal to campaign would have been tremendous assets; the people would have seen in him an honest and able man who would give them a clean and competent administration. His quiet, incorruptible manner, his radiation of confidence would have fired them with the reformer's zeal. But the times were against him; good a man as he was, the people could find no valid reason for turning Roosevelt and the Republicans out of office. For eight years under McKinley and Roosevelt they had been prosperous and contented.

In addition, the Democratic convention had tied an eighty-one-year-old candidate for the vice-presidency around Parker's neck, a dead weight to be carried through the campaign. Henry G. Davis had received the nomination because he had a lot of friends in West Virginia, and it was believed he could swing the state. Davis had had an honorable career in politics, was also a millionaire mineowner, railroad magnate and banker. In addition to the fact that the voters did not like to contemplate the possibility of an eighty-one-year-old man succeeding to the presidency in the event of Parker's death, it was a double indiscretion to nominate a millionaire at the particular moment when the party's nominee was being charged with conservatism. The party should have nominated a young and vigorous radical to run with Parker, to stump the country for him the way Roosevelt had stumped for McKinley in 1900.

It was a well-bred election coming at a time when the nation was in sore need of a dullish and well-bred election: for the elections of 1896 and 1900 had disgorged hate and vilification. The poison pens were silent, truth and decency were not outraged, the excrement of the body politic was not exposed to public view. Though the excitement mounted somewhat as election day drew close, the affair was pervaded by good will. It went a long way toward mending the damage done by the previous class-war elections.

113

The Democrats were disappointed when Judge Parker, whom they had expected to make a vigorous and colorful campaign, refused to campaign at all. His associates convinced him that he must make some key speeches. He was a strong and clear speaker, but no rabble rouser, no man to strike emotion in the breast of his listener. As one journal commented, "His mind is legal rather than forensic." He would have made a good president, but he was modest in telling the nation about it. He believed that elections should be quiet, dignified, truthful, that they should do only good to the technique of democracy. In this he made as important a contribution to the continued working of his government as any he might have made as president.

His speeches had little effect on the ground swell toward the Republicans.

During the last weeks of the campaign, irked by the omnipresent signs of defeat, Judge Parker flung two criticisms at Roosevelt: first, that his treatment of the Filipinos had been unjust; second, that in appointing George B. Cortelyou as his campaign manager, Roosevelt had purposely used his former secretary of commerce because Cortelyou, knowing the secrets of the corporations, could extract large contributions from them. The charge created quite a stir, for it was the first to be issued by Judge Parker. A few days before the election President Roosevelt replied, "The statements made by Mr. Parker are unqualifiedly and atrociously false. As Mr. Cortelyou has said to me more than once during the campaign, if elected I shall go into the presidency unhampered by any pledge, promise or understanding of any kind."

Parker's charge of unjust handling of the Filipinos was found to be exaggerated; for once the judge had handed down a decision without sufficient facts to justify it. His inference against Cortelyou, however, had been sound. In 1907 it was disclosed that the insurance companies had contributed rather too heavily to the Roosevelt campaign; that Roosevelt himself, only a week before the election, had called E. H. Harriman, the railroad king, to Washington to ask him to raise funds to carry New York State. To this extent Judge Parker had been right, but his charges marred an otherwise flawless performance.

The mildness of the election is best illustrated by the fact that almost a half million fewer people voted in 1904 than in 1900, despite the increase in population. The Republicans gained four hundred thousand votes over their total in 1900, while the Democrats lost a million and a half, a serious beating. The final result, 7,628,785 votes for Roosevelt against

5,084,442 for Parker, was an overwhelming defeat for the Democrats.

Alton Brooks Parker had waged a fight he really had not wanted to wage, in a manner which most of his colleagues disapproved. He had done things the way he thought they ought to have been done; for all this he could have no reward except the inner satisfaction of having followed his convictions. He was now a man without a job, his life plan rudely shattered. For him the election was a tragedy. On July 6, 1904, he was a happy man, doing an important job and doing it well; on November 8 he was broken out of his career, somehow unable to return to the Bench, obliged to return to the private practice of law, for which he had no appetite, in which he had no chance to continue his public contribution. Like James M. Cox, he could not aspire to a minor office after having been defeated for the major one. More than any other Also Ran he sacrificed his happiness for the sake of the two-party system, coming out of the melee a casualty.

All he had ever wanted was to become a justice of the United States Supreme Court. He probably would have become one, too, if he had not listened to the siren song of duty. If he had any regrets, he did not express them.

5

What kind of president would Parker have made? He gave a good idea of his attitude toward the office in his memorial speech for President McKinley:

"His mind was judicial, and would not be drawn from a patient search for the evidence that would show in which direction truth and justice lay by the clamor of those who insistently demanded that the President should always lead the people instead of working their will. He submitted without a murmur to undeserved criticism, and kept his counsel when unjustly assailed, apparently content that his deeds should in the end speak for themselves."

Parker and Roosevelt were as similar candidates as Clay and Bryan, Greeley and Cox were different from the men who had defeated them. Both were powerfully built champions of "the vigorous life"; both had the intestinal fortitude to stand by their convictions; both were practicing liberals, had alert, penetrating brains, the same kind of social conscience. Both commanded the respect of their country and their confreres. Both were dynamos of energy for work and play. Though Theodore Roosevelt appeared to be the more dashing figure in the eyes of the people, Alton Brooks Parker would have achieved the same results with less fanfare, less

115

spectacular means: instead of crying "Charge!" at San Juan Hill, he would have said quietly to his troops, "Gentlemen, shall we proceed?"

Since there were no major incidents to cope with during the years of Roosevelt's tenure, since it was a quiet period in American development, there would have been little demonstrable difference between the regimes of President Roosevelt and President Parker. The differences might have appeared later: without Roosevelt's backing and his four years of high touting as secretary of war, William Howard Taft might not have been elected in 1908. If there had been no Taft, there would have been no split in the Republican party by Roosevelt in 1912, breaking the sixteen-year Republican reign, turning over the government to Woodrow Wilson and the Democrats. The results of the first World War might have been vastly different; the postwar reaction would have been against a Republican incumbent; Cox might have been elected in 1920 instead of Harding.

Those few Americans who remember Alton Brooks Parker think of him as something of a stuffed shirt, a bit on the dullish side. This is true in the sense that Parker's big-bosomed shirt was stuffed full of manly virtues and solid citizenship, the desire to live quietly and pleasantly with his family, and do his job. This kind of life does not make hot copy for the press, and so Alton B. Parker will never be known as a colorful or dramatic figure.

He will never, alas! have a biography written about him.

CHAPTER TWO

Charles Evans Hughes

THAT IS the strangest man I ever met," said a notorious Albany politician about Charles Evans Hughes. "You can't make any sort of trade with him; you can't approach him on the side of personal advantage; you can't seem to touch his political ambition. He is beyond me; the fool simply does right the whole time!"

On the night of the gubernatorial election in 1906, when his fellow Republican candidates on the state ticket were seen to have been defeated, Hughes turned to his wife and said:

"My dear, I congratulate you. You have escaped two years of genteel poverty at Albany."

Because of his reddish, luxuriant whiskers he had been called by William Randolph Hearst, who was attempting to defeat him by ridicule, an animated feather duster. The name stuck; voters like the idea of an animated feather duster sweeping grafters and manipulators and incompetents out of office. The following morning, thanks in part to Hearst's genius for name calling, Hughes found himself elected by a squeak, the lone Republican to survive.

After giving New York four years of good governorship he was appointed a United States Supreme Court justice by President Taft. He told a friend that he had been intending to return to private life but that President Taft's offer opened a field for which he felt himself trained, and a life which he knew would be most congenial.

"It also removes me definitely as a presidential candidate," concluded the governor happily.

"Don't be too sure of that," replied the friend.

Hughes, greatly upset, cried, "You mustn't say that!"

For six years he enjoyed his life as a justice in Washington, the completely happy and adjusted figure, like Alton B. Parker, a magnificent specimen of human efficiency, of nervous and mental adjustment. Now, in 1916, with every Republican in the land except the political bosses demanding his nomination, he announced:

"I hope that, as a justice of the Supreme Court, I am rendering a public service and may continue to do so for many years; but the Supreme Court must not be dragged into politics, and no man is as essential to his country's well-being as the sustained integrity of the courts."

Nor was it believed that the justice was being coy. His friends insisted that his declination was made "without mental reservation; that what he most desires is to continue his services on the Supreme Court bench." The New York *World* maintained that the politicians in Washington were disposed to consider it as final; the New York *Sun* reported that Justice Hughes and Chief Justice White had discussed the nomination and that the chief justice spoke for Hughes when he said, "One who has accepted a seat on the Supreme Court has closed behind him the door of political ambition. It is such a man's duty to refuse any proposal to serve in the presidency, and no patriotic citizen would urge him to cast off the judicial ermine in order to enter the political arena."

Justice Hughes did not want to run; he was firmly resolved not to run; he is the only man on record who threatened to bring suit against a state for nominating him for the presidency.

The Republican bosses were delighted; the last man they wanted in control of their party was this animated feather duster who would strike no bargains, who made appointments on the basis of talent, who leaned over backwards to say no to his friends for fear he might be doing them a favor at the public's expense.

The Republican voters felt differently. Just as Henry Clay had defeated himself by his panting avidity for the position, so Hughes's reluctance only whetted their appetite. After Bryan, Mark Hanna (who ran the bases for McKinley), Roosevelt and Taft, the prospect of securing a man who was not running after the office with his tongue out was such a diversion that the movement for Hughes gained in direct proportion to his unwillingness. Folks said, "If this man Hughes would refuse a chance at the presidency to keep the Supreme Court out of politics, he might be just the kind of man we want for president!"

The Republican party had first turned to Hughes in 1912 to ward off the impending war between Taft and Roosevelt. He had declined the nomination on the grounds that he would not oppose Taft, who had appointed him to the Supreme Bench only two years before. For a solid year before the 1916 convention he firmly declared that he was not a candidate; he had written countless letters to this effect, had insisted upon it to newspapermen seeking his views; he repudiated all friendly party workers who attempted to form Hughes organizations. When the Republicans convened in

Chicago he informed the assemblage that he was not a candidate, that no one had the right to speak or work on his behalf.

Following the lead set so admirably by Alton B. Parker, he had never expressed a political opinion, refused to commit himself on the problems of the day. No one knew what he thought about the invasion of Belgium or the sinking of the S.S. *Lusitania;* no one knew what he thought should be done about the civil war in Mexico which was overflowing the American border; no one had heard how he would prepare the nation against invasion. If he had a program for America, there was no way to persuade him to announce it.

But when the convention opened, the party whips were strangely silent; the boomers of favorite sons had few words to speak; there were no deals, bargains, intrigues or cabals. The public had said in unmistakable terms, "A good man is a good man, and he will believe in the right things. We will take Justice Hughes on faith."

He received a quarter of all the votes on the first ballot, and on the third ballot had every vote except eighteen diehard Roosevelt ballots. For once the people had spoken, instead of being spoken to.

The Republicans now had a powerful candidate, one respected throughout the country for his integrity and good works, the only one who had a chance to defeat President Wilson. Would he accept the nomination? Had he been stalling, or would he refuse to step out of the ermine robes of the Supreme Court and once again enter partisan politics?

2

"I always taught Charles," said his father, "that a straight line was the shortest distance between two points."

For a future politician, this was heresy.

David Charles Hughes was a Baptist preacher who had been ordained at Wesleyan University. Before entering the ministry he had taught Latin, Greek and English at West River Collegiate Institute in Maryland. He had been born in Wales and was related to Joseph Hughes, the well-known London preacher who had founded the English Bible Society. He was a man of strong, independent and individualistic faith; his son took after him in everything: his politics, his religion, his feeling for individualism.

"Like most boys," reminisced the father, "Charlie had difficulty in keeping still—standing on one foot, then on another. I called his attention to this and impressed upon him the need for self-control. He took a seam on the carpet as a

119

dead line, placed his feet down firmly and toed it. From that day he had himself under complete control."

It was to remain one of the most classic examples of control ever to appear on the American scene.

The effect of the father's teachings upon the character of the son is exemplified by the portrait done of him by the *Nation* at the time of his nomination for the presidency. "He is a man of plain thought and manners, cheerful temper, and businesslike ways, with a trait of positiveness which you would scarcely suspect from his urbanity. He knows what he knows, and what he thinks he thinks. No one could bully or wheedle him into a conclusion towards which he had not been headed by his own mental processes."

The Reverend Hughes's income while pastor for the churches at Glens Falls, Sandy Hills and Oswego in New York had varied from four hundred to a thousand dollars a year. In this sense the Hughes family were always the poor mice of the church; but they were rich in mental and spiritual resources. It was a self-imposed poverty which did not embitter the household; young Charles's home was well stocked in those qualities for which money can be but a down payment. His mother, the daughter of a New York physician, had been educated at the Claverack Institute, where she had won honors in mathematics and languages. Charles Hughes's cultural life was as bountiful as his economic life was lean.

He was born on April 11, 1862, at Glens Falls, New York. He was precocious, his mind active and eager. Entered when he was six in the one-room schoolhouse, he evolved what he called the Charles E. Hughes Plan of Study, a schedule for breaking the day into specialized periods. By the time he was eight he had persuaded his parents that he could make better progress at home, studying under his own discipline. Every few days he would place his books before his mother or father and recite his lessons; they in turn instructed him in the subjects they knew best. Delighted with his progress, the family decided that he too should be a clergyman, and set him to writing sermons. By the time he was fifteen he had written a good many, but having also read the novels of the worldly Mr. Smollett, he had determined that he would be a lawyer instead of a preacher.

The youth changed his school as his father changed his pastorates: Oswego, Newark, New York City. When he was fourteen he entered Colgate, which he attended for two years, and then entered Brown University, where he graduated in 1881, at the age of nineteen. Despite the fact that he did not study very much he took top honors in the classics, the prize in English, and one of the two prizes awarded the students "showing the greatest promise as based on scholarship and character." He went in for college amusements, joined a fraternity, and was well liked for his humor and affability.

Like Alton B. Parker and other young men of the period who had to help their families and at the same time lay aside funds for their further education, Charles Hughes went looking for a teacher's job. At nineteen he was tall, gangling, meticulous, with a disarming smile. He hied himself to the Delaware Academy at Delhi, New York, which was in the market for an instructor of Greek, English and mathematics. Bravely he flashed his diploma from Brown.

"Why, my dear boy," said the head of the academy, "while I may not doubt your ability to teach those subjects, I frankly doubt your ability to handle two hundred and fifty youngsters. You have no more hair on your face than an egg."

"If you will give me the employment, sir," replied Hughes, "I'll start a beard growing and handle my classes."

He got the job. He also got the beard.

After a year of teaching, during which he read his first law in the office of a local judge, he returned to New York City. Here he studied law at Columbia University while clerking in an office. He graduated at the top of his class in 1884, winning the prize fellowship which was to earn him five hundred dollars a year for tutoring. He was admitted to the bar, taught a night law class at Columbia, and transferred his clerking to the law firm of Chamberlain, Carter and Hornblower. In 1888 he was made a member of the firm, and in December of that year he married Antoinette Carter, daughter of his employer, a graduate of Wellesley. As with Alton Parker, who also had married his boss's daughter, he was to enjoy a happy and gratifying home life. Mr. Carter broke all father-in-law precedent by saying to his daughter, "Nettie, I don't know whether I love Charles Hughes more for his attributes of the heart or for his attributes of the mind. But I love him. Someday Charles Hughes will be the acknowledged leader of the New York Bar."

Charlie Hughes became known as a lawyer's lawyer. An indefatigable worker, scientifically precise in his study of a subject, with a wide-ranging and penetrating mind, he established his ability to handle intricate legal matters. "His cases were won before they came into court. His presentation of facts was lucid and convincing, and his clear statement of applicable rules soon won him the confidence of the bench." He was no emotional jury pleader; he was a specialist in commercial law and litigation.

After three years of intensely hard work he accepted a position as professor of law at Cornell. He was so tired he was a little ill, but mostly he took the job because he preferred the theory of the law to its actual practice in the market place. After two years of teaching he found it necessary to return to his office in New York, where he practiced private law for the next sixteen years, keeping alive his studies in theory by lecturing at the New York Law School.

By 1905 Charles Evans Hughes was a successful and prosperous New York attorney. He took good care of his parents in their older years, had a comfortable home on West End Avenue, with pictures of Lincoln, Webster, Huxley, Hobhouse, Bright and Tennyson on the walls. In the bookshelves was evidenced his catholic taste in reading: the novels of Dumas and Balzac, the histories of Carlyle, the heavy tomes of the philosophers and the light volumes of the detective-story writers. He taught a Sunday-school class in the Baptist church, liked to fish and golf and take vacations in the Adirondacks or go hunting in the Maine woods. Each summer the family went to Switzerland to vacation in the Alps, where he engaged in his favorite sport of mountain climbing. A home-loving man, he spent his leisure with his family rather than in clubs. A friend says of him:

"Like most men of intense purpose and an insatiable appetite for work, he paid the penalty in a certain fixed sternness of expression, and the reputation of being an iceberg." The *World's Work* added, "No one, not even his closest intimates, would ever dream of slapping him on the back. I think likewise that most men would hesitate before telling a risqué story in his presence."

Thus he stood at forty-three, over six feet tall, slender, immaculately garbed, with quiet gray eyes under huge brows, a Jovelike head and handsome austere face, with flaring reddish-brown whiskers parted in the center and brushed precisely and exquisitely to each side. It was at this moment that fate picked him up and carried him toward one of the most useful careers in American public life.

He was selected out of the clear sky to serve as counsel for the state legislative committee investigating the monopoly which controlled the gas supply in New York City. His law partners and his wife, who was known as his "invariable court of first and last resort," were skeptical about his taking the appointment.

"This committee," they said, "despite its promises, will let you go so far and then draw the reins. If you refuse to acquiesce, you will be scuttled."

"In that event," replied Hughes, "I will appeal to the newspapers. If they will not be fair I will go over their heads straight to the people. New York is not without its public meeting places. Cooper Union still lives."

When it was announced that he was to be counsel for the Stevens Committee the people of New York asked, "Who is Charles Evans Hughes?" while those who knew groaned aloud. He was a Republican; he was a conservative; he was a corporation attorney; he belonged to the same church as Rockefeller. Once again they had been sold down the river!

Hughes had only four days in which to prepare his material. Reporters clamoring for interviews found him inaccessible. This increased their suspicions: instead of assuming that the man was up to his ears in work they asked if he were consulting with the gas and electric company officials. They created around him an Ice Myth, making of him a cold, unapproachable machine. When he finally was able to see the press the reporters dubbed him a curious specimen.

"We missed the humor in his voice," said one of them, "the desire for fellowship. His voice sounded harsh, cold, raspy; the gray eyes seemed incapable of fun. We suspected this man, and our resentment mounted as very gravely and not without a tremor in his voice, he said:

" 'I have accepted their employment because I am free to do so. There are no social or business connections that will prevent my carrying out the intentions of the investigating committee, an investigation that is to be absolutely uninterfered with, either politically or socially.' "

On the way out one reporter asked another, "Does that man think he is putting it over on us?"

But from the instant the investigation opened, this son of a man who had taught mathematics and a woman who had won honors in mathematics conducted what became known as the Hughes Class in Advanced Mathematics. The cartoonists who had been amusing the public by drawing caricatures of Hughes with ribbons and curlers tied on his whiskers promptly took them off; the whiskers became a broom, sweeping out error and inaccuracy, concealment and manipulation. With his intense powers of concentration and penetration he had pierced the accounts of the gas company and revealed them as charging monopolistic prices which bore no relation to the cost of production. He demonstrated the validity of his father's theory about the shortest distance between two points: through his talent for figures he was able to show the public exactly what it cost to manufacture and distribute gas and electricity, then pointed out the waste, political corruption and public extortion which underlay the existing rates. He wrote a report based on his findings which was to change the conduct of the industry, place it under state control and bring reasonable gas rates to the people of New York City.

The press and public were elated. Overnight Charles Evans Hughes became a hero. The reporter from the *World* who had distrusted him now said, "We had been watching, not a machine, not an iceman, but a master draftsman, an artist, an architect of law and order and justice."

The managers of the gas monopoly, who were not liking the relentless and incontrovertible exposure, set out to alienate public sympathy from Hughes by continuing the theme of his having ice water in his veins, accusing him of not being human. The newsmen, now his most ardent supporters, asked him to fight this kind of propaganda because it lessened his effectiveness. They said, "Mr. Hughes, you must help us combat the Ice Myth. You must give us personal stories to get before the public, so people will know you and love you."

"Ice Myth?" asked Hughes, his eyebrows raised. "What might that be?"

They showed him an article in which he was described as "one who communed in the Alps with Kant, solid geometry and Lycurgus."

Hughes laughed. "I'll plead guilty to knowing Kant," he chuckled, "but not guilty as to the solid-geometry charge. As to Lycurgus, I don't know what that may be. Do you think it is anything intoxicating?"

A moment later he added quietly, "You fellows know I'm not stuffed with sawdust, and as long as you know it, this sort of thing doesn't matter."

In this gas investigation he had done a good job, but it was only a prologue. It was his next call to public service which was to make him revered throughout the nation, cause President Taft to call him the Republican party's greatest asset.

His hard-earned vacation in the Tyrol was interrupted by a cablegram from a legislative committee asking if he would serve as counsel for the investigation of the life-insurance companies. He wired back, "Yes, on the condition that I shall be absolutely unhampered by any influence, direct or indirect."

When the Armstrong Life Insurance Commission started out it sought to probe only into the mismanagement and manipulation of insurance funds. In the middle of the investigation the nature of the inquiry changed from one of local business to one of national politics and the future of the democratic form of government.

As the *Independent* put it, "There was a widespread impression that the great wealth and vast power of the large life-insurance companies had been used to influence legisla-

124

tion, control elections and effect political action, both state and national."

No one ever had been able to document this charge; now Hughes, with his painstaking research, had come upon the proof.

That morning he told the committee of the evidence he had found. When they appeared frightened and unwilling to continue he announced in the quietest of his icy tones, "I mean to have your permission to follow that trail, or I mean to resign and give to the people my reason for quitting."

There then took place one of the most dramatic investigations witnessed in the United States up to that time. The major clash occurred between Charles Evans Hughes and John A. McCall, president of the New York Life Insurance Company. "Mr. McCall, bold, arrogant, courageous, apparently ready to meet all contingencies, occupied the witness chair. Mr. Hughes, calm, even kindly, stood before him with a New York Life Insurance Company check for one hundred thousand dollars in his hand.

" 'Mr. McCall, would you kindly tell us for what purpose this check was used?'

" 'Yes, Mr. Hughes, it was one of the several checks issued to pay for a block of property in the rear of the New York Life Building.'

" 'Mr. McCall, you will see on the back wall a real-estate map showing this block of property, with each parcel marked off in red lines. Let us now identify each parcel with the check that was issued to pay for it.' "

As McCall described each purchase and it was indicated on the map, Hughes produced the check with which it allegedly had been bought. But when every parcel had been identified, the hundred-thousand-dollar check in question remained unclaimed. Trapped, under oath, the president of the New York Life Insurance Company confessed that the real-estate setup had been a blind, that the hundred thousand dollars had been part of a two-million-dollar fund with which the New York Life had bought legislation. Republican Hughes put on the stand the Republican boss of New York State, who admitted that for fifteen years he had been taking large sums of money from the insurance companies, repaying them with favorable legislation.

Throughout the investigation Hughes had found himself baffled by an item known as the "Hanover Bank office account." His requests for information were avoided. Finally a friend tipped him off: this account contained a contribution of forty-eight thousand dollars to the Republican campaign fund. "As a good Republican," said the friend, "you can understand why we have been avoiding your questions. So just investigate around it!"

Hughes was a good investigator first, a good Republican second. He put an insurance official on the stand and gently led him to the admission that the Hanover Bank account was a secret political weapon. "I am glad you brought that out," said the official, suddenly gone noble, "because it is a matter of far-reaching importance and should be brought out."

Counsel for the committee displayed his only elation of the ten weeks' investigation when he murmured, "Yes, I intended that it should be brought out!"

If he was winning the applause of the honest businessmen, administrators and the public, he was putting panic into the hearts of the Republican leaders. They went to him crying, "You're ripping the party wide open. We'll not stand a chance at the polls in the next twenty years!"

Hughes replied, "A trust has been betrayed. Funds belonging to widows and orphans have been misappropriated. I'm going to lay the truth on the records for the public to read." The *World's Work* commented, "As an investigator Mr. Hughes has no enemies and no friends; one felt that even though his revelations were to affect his closest relatives, he still would not hesitate. He uncovered facts that reverberated the world over, almost without displaying a sense of personal triumph; he never browbeat witnesses, never threatened, hardly ever lifted his voice above the conversational tone."

Yet Charles Evans Hughes had a boiling point. He reached it when, exposing the use of policyholders' money for extravagant agency promotions, an insurance official tried to wiggle out by comparing these expenditures to Hughes's fees as a lawyer. His right arm shot out like a piston rod, and his long index finger shook under the official's nose.

"My fees, sir," he cried, "are not trust funds!"

Not knowing where he would strike next, the Republican bosses kicked him upstairs: without his knowledge or consent they nominated him for mayor of New York City, an honor for a man who had been unknown only a few months before. Hughes politely handed back the nomination on the grounds that he was "already engaged in work of a public character which must be kept absolutely free from political bias, and that he was bound by every obligation of duty to see the thing through, as the public had asked and expected him to do."

As a result of his exposures some rascals were driven from political office, government supervision of the insurance companies was instigated, the abuses corrected, confidence in insurance restored. A less able man might have done his job so well he would have destroyed the insurance companies and the institution of insurance as well. Charles Evans Hughes, after exposing the existing evils, then worked equally hard to demonstrate that the companies still were sound, their type of business important to the life of the nation.

There was no such thing as Saturdays or Sundays off, or nights for relaxation or sleep. He worked twenty hours a day, every day, spending his days in court and his nights poring over ledgers, account books, records, tracking down the elusive truth through a jungle of figures. Having worked most of the night, he showed up in court the following morning fresh as a daisy, groomed as though he had just stepped out of a bandbox, ready to fight down some of the cleverest business brains of the nation. It was a brilliant performance, one which won him the admiration of his country, and the nickname of Long Legged Bulldog.

3

His nomination for the governorship was almost automatic. Tom Platt didn't want him, nor the other Republican leaders, any more than they would want him for the presidency in 1916. But in meetings, letters to the press, club and society resolutions, in widespread conversation in their homes, business offices and on the streets, the people of New York State demanded his nomination.

It was a strange campaign. Folks went to hear him speak, applauded lightly when he came on the stage, listened in silence to his quiet, factual talk, showed no signs of enthusiasm, pleasure or emotion, engaged in no cheering, backslapping or excitement. It was impossible to tell what they thought of Charles Evans Hughes. But vote for him they did, in sufficient numbers to make him the only Republican to be elected in a Democratic landslide. He had been instrumental in discrediting and defeating his own party, but that was only part of the reason why the people knew him to be bigger than the job for which he was running.

His first act as governor was to move the desk out of his private office into the large waiting room, where anyone who had business with the governor could step right up and state it. He made no swaps or bargains, but appointed the best man he could find for each position, regardless of party. He was a militant crusader against the abuses of trusts and monopolies; he secured the passage of the Public Service Law enabling the public to control the activities of those corporations which functioned under charters granted by the people: the utilities and railroads. His efforts were always directed

127

against the abuses, never against the businesses themselves. Nor was he a blind reformer: when the legislature passed a law fixing railroad rates at two cents a mile he vetoed the measure until a Public Service Commission could make sure that the two-cent rate was fair to the roads. When the New York Stock Exchange came under fire he appointed a commission of recognized bankers and lawyers to investigate and make recommendations.

He believed in scientific government. He worked to achieve a government based on a full knowledge of facts.

The Hughes family in the Executive Mansion in Albany gave a cheering example of democracy: two or three times a week children from the St. Joseph's Catholic Home at the back of the Mansion were invited over for games, ice cream and cake; the Hughes children found their playmates among the orphans. Mrs. Hughes was up at seven each morning to get the girls and boys off to school, worked through the day as the mistress of her home, and assembled her family at eight every evening around the dinner table. Governor Hughes had been presented with a white bull terrier by a neighboring fire company; he loved the dog so much he frequently asked that a chair be set for him at the table so that they could have a visit.

"Hughes has no genius," said one observer, "except the genius for thinking and doing the direct and obvious thing."

In 1908 he was opposed for re-election by the party bosses and legislators with whom he had refused to traffic, by the monopoly interests whose activities and profits he had curtailed, by the Hearst papers. But the people of the state knew a good governor when they had one. He was re-elected. Despite the wrangling and sharpshooting of his opponents, he continued his work for the direct primaries and control of public utilities. Like his fellow jurist Alton Parker, he had confidence in the judgment of the people, fighting to keep political control in the hands of the voters and their elected legislatures. He gave his state four years of honest and efficient government, a contribution of incalculable value to the American way of life.

Toward the end of his second term he was offered a justiceship on the United States Supreme Court by President Taft, and transported his family to Washington. Despite the fact that his four years as governor had exhausted his savings, he turned down a hundred-thousand-dollar bequest left him by Joseph Pulitzer of the *World*.

He became a solid middle-of-the-road judge, devoted to the principles of justice and a root adherence to the Constitution. During his six years on the Supreme Bench he wrote one hundred and fifty decisions which were handed down as the opinion of the Court. In only nine cases did other judges dissent from his opinions; when he dissented from the majority it was because he had taken a more progressive view than his associates.

"With chest well out, head held erect, full beard breasting the wind, arms loosely swinging, the face of one who is at peace with the world, here comes Charles Evans Hughes walking down Capitol Hill at the close of a day's work."

And here he was when the Republican convention nominated him for the presidency in June of 1916. The convention could not be blamed for nominating him, nor the people for wanting him. His record had been superb; of such material should presidents be made.

But he had sworn he would not run.

He was greatly attached to the Republican party, as had been his father before him. He wanted to see its wounds healed after the disruption of 1912. He wanted to see the Republicans again in power. The convention proved that he was the only candidate who could persuade the scattered forces of his party to unite. He believed in the two-party system, felt its continuance to be imperative to the democratic form of government; and he believed it necessary that both parties should operate always at the height of their strength. If he rejected the nomination, if the convention went into a dog-fight to secure someone else, their forces again would be split. He read in such papers as the Milwaukee *Free Press* that "service on the Supreme Bench is of the highest importance to the country, but at this critical time, when the most vital interests of the nation are being largely disposed of in the White House, the presidential office assumes an importance with which no other government function can compare."

He had before him the example of Alton B. Parker, to whom the newspapers were likening him, and whose descendant he was just as surely as Bryan was Clay's. He would have to give up his good life and his good work. If defeated, he doubtless would be forced back into private practice.

Yet he felt he had no choice. He had to accept.

Only Alton B. Parker could know what his decision cost him. Only Parker could tell him how tragically his life and his work might be blasted.

4

In the split second of his entrance into the campaign he made an error which was symptomatic of a series of incomprehensible errors; for nowhere as a presidential candidate was Charles Evans Hughes the man he had been as gas and insurance investigator, governor of the state of New York, or Supreme Court justice—or any part of the man he doubtless would have been as president.

Deciding to accept the nomination, Hughes dispatched a telegram to President Wilson which read, "I hereby resign the office of Associate Justice of the Supreme Court of the United States." This curt telegram was an insult, not to Wilson, who happened to be president at the moment, but to the office of the chief executive. For the moment Hughes believed that he had been appointed by Taft, a Republican, and hence was under no obligation of courtesy to his president and opponent, who was a Democrat. In his excitement and perturbation he struck a blow at the dignity of the highest office in the land by failing to remember that no man or party makes an appointment to the Supreme Court, but only the indestructible office of the presidency.

In his telegram of resignation Hughes could have put himself on solid ground at once, endeared himself to whole sections of the nation by stating simply and honestly his reasons for resigning from the Supreme Court after he and his chief justice had sworn he would not. His discourteous telegram made him appear a routine opponent who would fight a partisan fight.

Thus at the very instant that he accepted the nomination, Charles E. Hughes defeated himself.

Despite the fact that he had few enemies, that his record was known and admired throughout the land, he entered the presidential campaign handicapped. By repudiating his pledge not to become a candidate he not only set a dangerous precedent for the Supreme Bench, but destroyed a part of his public's faith in his promise. As Walter Lippmann observed, his conscience hurt him. For four years he had served alongside of President Wilson, seen the staggering problems under which the president labored, and been on excellent terms with him. As a humanitarian and a progressive he must have approved many of the socially modernizing acts sponsored by Wilson: the Federal Reserve Act, the Child Labor Laws, the Agricultural Credits Act.

He inherited the Republican case against the Democrats from Theodore Roosevelt, who had launched the first attacks as a matter of routine party politics in 1914 and followed them with a campaign of ridicule when Wilson announced that "a nation can be too proud to fight." Hughes was in the position of a general who must take over in midbattle and is obliged to carry through, though he may not agree with the prescribed strategy. He was also a little upset, precisely as

Parker had been, at the thought of what might happen to him if he lost; that uncertainty deteriorated both his poise and his skill.

For six years he had not participated in the immediately pressing problems of the nation; for six years he had done the work of a highly technical specialist protected by the seclusion of an ivory tower, cut off from people and their everyday needs and thoughts. He had done no mixing, no public speaking; he could know but little of the ordinary life of his compatriots.

Could he warm up to folks? Could he make them warm up to him? Could he convince that wedge of a million independent voters which decided the outcome of elections that he was really a liberal, that he understood the world that was being brought about by the war? He said:

"I would not be here if I did not think of the Republican party as a liberal party."

He came into his candidacy in a world in upheaval, in a year when the important issues would be of foreign policy rather than national policy. What would he do about Germany, whose submarine had sunk the *Lusitania* and whose government was threatening the United States? What would he do about Mexico, torn by warring factions, attacking American troops and property along the border? What would he do about an army and navy which would be able to defeat all comers? These were among the questions he had to answer satisfactorily if he hoped to be elected.

Not since the Parker-Roosevelt campaign of 1904, and only a few times in the history of the republic, had the people enjoyed the opportunity of choosing between two such excellent men. To make the choice more difficult the similarities between Hughes and Wilson, as between Parker and Roosevelt, were startling: both were sons of clergymen; both had shown mental power at an early age; both had been university professors; both had been progressive governors of their states; both had fought for the people against the trusts; both had cast off the rule of party bosses; both had brought the divergent factions within their parties to work in harmony.

The *Outlook* suggested that "Wilson is keener, cleverer, more adroit and subtle, has more mental delicacy and skill in managing men. Hughes has a more powerful intellect, a greater toughness and piercing quality. Wilson is flexible, practical, ready to sacrifice details in pursuit of the large object. Hughes is determined, settled, inclined to hew unflinchingly to a definitely marked course."

Republican Hughes found himself confronted by the identical problem that had stymied Democrat Parker: if, admittedly, Wilson was a good man, as Roosevelt had been a good man, and the two candidates were so alike in background and qualifications, what must Charles Evans Hughes do to convince the public that, in this hour of international crisis, with half the civilized world ablaze, they should vote Wilson and his Democrats out, to be replaced by Hughes and his Republicans?

He attempted to answer the impending questions and solve his problems by one bold and, for him, courageous stroke. Against the advice of his friends and advisers, who were afraid that he might alienate the mass by his aloofness and bring a return of the Ice Myth, he took to the road. In Detroit he jumped onto the roof of the players' bench to shake hands with both ball teams and chat with Ty Cobb; in Butte he got into miner's clothes and went down into a copper mine; in Reno he attended a barbecue and rodeo and mingled with the cowboys. He was warm, hearty, cordial: people liked him. He liked them too, for this was no act on his part: he was having a great time. When he emerged from a railway station or an automobile crowds would cry, "That's him, the tall chap with the whiskers!" and give him a good hand. The newsmen in his entourage reported to their papers that he was genuinely human and responsive.

The New York *Post* wrote that "he is making one of the most remarkable records of successful campaigning of any presidential candidate in recent years." For a man of Hughes's temperament and background it was an astonishing tour.

He spoke strongly for women's suffrage, the merit system, efficiency in government, the budget system, elimination of politics from diplomatic appointments, a firmer stand with warring nations over American rights. On many fronts he established a valid case against the Wilson administration: many of Wilson's appointments had been poor; civil service and diplomatic posts were given to men whom Bryan had called "deserving Democrats"; there had been logrolling; there had been inefficiency and lack of sound business sense; there had been vacillation in the United States' attitude toward Germany and Mexico; there had been a laxness up to the very last minute in preparing America to defend herself. In these attacks Hughes presented the trained lawyer's brief against the opposition, with documentation of the errors, stupidities and failures.

But his cogent case against his opponents disclosed not even to the Republicans a constructive program of his own or a *modus operandi* by means of which he would correct the faults of a harassed but intelligent administration. When the tour was over, and the public was able to judge what he had said in its entirety, it boiled down to, "Throw the incompetents out!" Norman Hapgood asked in the *Independent,* "Has Mr. Hughes any issue, any program, or has he nothing but a lawyer's criticism of detail?" His campaign, which would have been a good campaign in 1908, 1912 or 1920, was not quite good enough for the embroiled world of 1916. One magazine said, "We are living in exceptional times, which demand a clear, bold voice. Mr. Hughes's first stumping tour still leaves his position undefined."

The New York *World* stated the case for the Democratic press when it maintained that it could not find the Hughes of 1908 in the Hughes of 1916, ". . . none of the frankness, none of the courage, none of the devotion to high principle. He is merely a Republican office seeker, dodging and twisting and evading and angleworming his way toward the White House." The New York *Herald* considered it an open secret that Republicans were disappointed in him, while the *Nation,* which for years had beaten the drums before Hughes's tent, commented sadly, "In no aspect of the campaign has Hughes seemed to realize the need of making the impression of breadth and power, of creative energy. There has been hardly a trace of largeness of treatment, of magnanimity of tone. Republicans will vote for him, but they have not been stirred or thrilled." The independent San Francisco *Star* predicted that California would go Democratic in November.

Walter Lippmann observed caustically, "The human interest of this campaign is to find out why a man of rare courage and frankness should be wandering around the country trailing nothing but cold and damp platitudes. If we had to judge Mr. Hughes by what he has been saying since he was nominated we would have to grant that he is a Republican of the nineties, superstitious about the tariff, frock-coated about labor, and with a regular Union League attitude. Why has this hero of the insurance investigation, the merciless and accurate enemy of corruption, been willing to stultify himself as a candidate?"

The *World's Work* lamented, "We had not expected that he was leaving the Supreme Bench to enter an ordinary political campaign." He himself had convinced the public that a Supreme Court justice should not step down unless there were a great and meaningful battle to be waged.

Two of his stands in particular antagonized large blocs of voters. His insistence upon a high-tariff wall to protect American industry indicated the kind of Republicanism practiced by the father rather than the son. His attitude toward the hyphen vote, the German- and Irish-Americans who were publishing a seditious press, abusing Wilson because of his antagonism toward Germany, displayed the only evidence of cravenheartedness of his career. For these ingrates he could have had nothing but contempt, yet, knowing that the election would be hairsbreadth close, he did not want to antagonize them. This bloc of votes was part of the mathematical equation he had worked out in his acceptance speech, and he did not dare upset the equation.

His acceptance speech contained the epitome of his campaign and the seeds of his defeat: he had handled it as a scientific task to be performed in a laboratory. With almost geometric precision he wooed the camp followers of Taft, placated Roosevelt and his recalcitrants, shined up to the liberal independents, made sheep's eyes at the diverse and quarreling anti-Wilson forces. The speech had achieved a formula of adhesion; as a piece of political mathematics it was a stroke of genius. But like most mathematical formulas, it lacked a soul. The public thought of Hughes as one of its few great men; it now asked confusedly, "What did he actually say? What would he have done if he had been in Wilson's place? What would he do if he were in office now?"

Hughes was playing it safe. He was relying on the normal majority of Republican votes to carry him into office without committing himself. The man who never had wanted to be a politician, who had refused to indulge in politics, who had twice been elected to the governorship of New York for the very reason that he was a poor politician, now with the ultimate honor and office within his grasp, became overly solicitous of success, behaved like a smart vote getter.

He had come into the election like a two-ton bomb. Was he going to fizzle out like a Fourth of July firecracker? If he had despised ordinary political maneuvers, repudiated the traitorous hyphen vote; if he had honestly granted the virtues of the Wilson administration but set forth bold and blueprinted specifications of what he would do about the war in Europe and the conflict in Mexico; if he had behaved like the gubernatorial candidate of 1906 and 1908, he could have become an American idol.

The campaign was a tragedy for Charles Evans Hughes because it destroyed the legend. In exposing himself to public examination he revealed that although he had a magnificent *mechanism* of thinking, he had no magnificent *content* of thought. His ability to handle a job honestly and scientifically was not to be denied. But in his social ideology, in his concept of a great people's state, he was uncreative, a benevolent patrician.

The election was a clean one: the newspapers were polite and restrained. Though the atmosphere was tense there was no mudslinging, no personal invective, rancor or class warfare. If anything, large sections of the press seemed pained to have to say anything against Charles Evans Hughes at all! Except for a few key speeches such as Franklin D. Roosevelt would make in 1940 when Wendell Willkie's breath was getting a trifle too hot on his neck, Wilson did little campaigning.

The battle was astonishingly close. Because of his high-tariff stand and the fact that he did not seem really to understand the modern labor union or its problems, Hughes had the Independent vote pretty solidly against him. His anticipated normal Republican majority was offset by the happy Democratic campaign phrase: "Wilson kept us out of war." Wilson made no promises that he could continue to keep the United States out of war; by 1916 it already was beginning to appear that neither candidate could accomplish that miracle, yet large portions of the public voted for Wilson on the grounds that he would continue to do so.

The Republicans appeared to have won the election. Hughes carried New York, Illinois, Indiana, Iowa, Massachusetts, Michigan, Wisconsin, Minnesota, Pennsylvania, and Wilson's home state of New Jersey, an overwhelming bloc of votes. Hughes fell asleep that night thinking that he had been elected president of the United States, just as he had fallen asleep on election night in 1906 believing himself to be defeated for the governorship.

He awoke in the morning to find that to everyone's astonishment, except that of the San Francisco *Star*, Wilson had carried California by a majority of some four thousand votes, that the state's thirteen electoral votes had given Wilson the decision. Hughes was alleged to have snubbed Senator Hiram Johnson, leader of the California Republicans, when they both had been in the Palace Hotel in San Francisco. Hughes denied having known he was there. His feelings hurt, Senator Johnson was accused of having swung enough votes to spoil Hughes's breakfast on the day after the election.

Wilson received 9,129,606 votes; Hughes 8,538,221.

It is not a matter of record whether Charlie Hughes said to his wife over the breakfast table that morning, "My dear, I congratulate you. You have just escaped four years of genteel poverty in the White House."

5

If he had been elected president in 1916, Charles Evans

Hughes would have carried out the will of the people, as expressed by the legislature; he would have been scrupulously ethical; he would have secured the best man for each job, attempted to put the business of government on a scientific basis. As an executive who implemented the program and the wishes of the legislature he would have been one of the most efficient in the country's history. But as a leader, as a man who strode ahead of his people, formulating their inarticulate will, as a visionary and a prophet fighting for a better world and a more equitable economic democracy, Hughes could not have held a candle to Wilson. As President Harding's secretary of state from 1921 to 1925, and once again as chief justice of the Supreme Court from 1930 to 1941, Hughes proved that he could be as big as his job, that he could perform the duties of his office in a high-minded, efficient and forward-looking manner. There was only one position in the United States in the turbulent and despairing days of 1916 which he could not have handled better than Woodrow Wilson: the office of the presidency.

It was not only that Hughes did not have the temperament for revolutionary leadership, that he was no idealist or social philosopher, but also that, as Alton Parker before him had stated, he did not believe this to be the function of the president. He believed it to be the job of the executive to put into effect whatever the legislature demanded, as efficiently and as inexpensively as possible. His was the legal approach to the office: it would be his duty to make the machine run as it then existed, not to experiment, replace, or even improve on the machinery, except in the mathematics of execution.

At that particular moment the people needed an idealist, a vision of a better and more equitable world rather than a more efficient government under the status quo. Hughes would have been a superb president in times of "normalcy"; in 1916 his opponent was better suited to lead a people in a world that was in dire need of leadership.

Or at least so thought the half million or so voters who threw in their lot with Wilson instead of Hughes, changing one of the closest elections in history. Perhaps that was symbolic; perhaps the need to change and the need to stay as we are always will be that close—with one side or the other going to sleep at night confident that it has won, only to waken in the morning to find the other seated in the place of power.

The tragedy for the United States was not that Charles Evans Hughes ran for office in 1916 and was defeated, but that he was nominated one campaign too soon. Good a man as he was, he was not needed in 1916. He was badly needed in the rebound election of 1920, in place of Warren Harding as the Republican nominee; his talents were the precise ones needed by the United States in its postwar period.

The story of Hughes exemplifies the gambler's chance behind democratic elections: so many good men are lost to the presidency because they run one election too soon or too late, are defeated because the season is not quite ripe; while other and poorer men are elected because the times and the elements combine to remove the superior opponent.

The Republican defeat did more than put Charles Evans Hughes out of the running; it also served to eliminate the Supreme Court as a source of presidential candidates. For six consecutive elections no high-court judge has been obliged to abandon his robes for the political arena, though in 1940 the Republicans sounded out Justice Harlan F. Stone. How many years must pass before a major party, hard pressed for a worthy candidate, again will attempt to raid the Bench? Or has the defeat of Parker and Hughes established a jinx on justices, as that of Greeley and Cox did on newspapermen?

Because he scored a near win, Charles Evans Hughes was able to function with the full respect and confidence of the American people as Harding's secretary of state, and again as chief justice of the Supreme Court when reappointed in 1930 by President Hoover; while Parker, who had taken a severe drubbing, had been obliged to return to private life and remain there. The margin by which they have been defeated often has been the determinant of the Also Rans' status among scoreboard Americans. That was part of the reason why Clay and Bryan could run three times, why they did not lose face by their defeats; while candidates like Cox and Parker, who have been given short shrift, are not even considered as potential candidates for the following election.

Americans will string along with a loser—providing he has lost by a nose!

BOOK FOUR

Generals Die in the Army

I: WINFIELD SCOTT
II: JOHN CHARLES FREMONT
III: GEORGE B. McCLELLAN
IV: WINFIELD SCOTT HANCOCK

The people idolize their military heroes—yet they kept these four generals out of the White House. Will World War II put another general in the White House?

CHAPTER ONE

Winfield Scott

HE WAS THE DADDY OF THEM ALL, the founder of America's professional army.

From 1807, when he borrowed the first of his countless uniforms from a friend and captured a boatload of British sailors, down through the War of 1812, incessant border clashes, the Indian Wars, the Mexican War and Civil War, until he was unhorsed by the ambition-driven General George McClellan, he was the courage, the brains, the driving power and the monumental loyalty behind the American Army. He was the first since George Washington to become a lieutenant general. Soldiers fighting on Bataan Peninsula in 1942 carried the proud name of Winfield Scott Smith or Winfield Scott Jones.

As a military leader he had only one weakness, attacking superior numbers; by dint of this idiosyncrasy he kept the ambitious armies of Europe at a respectful distance while the United States was still weak from growing pains.

He spent a good part of his lifetime proving that the pen is not only mightier than the sword, but that it can get a fellow into a lot more trouble. He had a gift for turning a phrase; his opponents usually managed to turn that phrase around and stick its point back into him. For years at a time his reputation would be impaled upon the point of a sharp exclamation of his own making: he would have to win another war to get himself off.

In a field of good-looking men he was by far the most gorgeous to be defeated for the presidency. He stood six feet five, with perhaps the most overpowering physique produced in America in the nineteenth century. He literally soared above his contemporaries. The greatest tribute to his appearance was paid by the defeated Mexicans when he entered the square of Mexico City on his tremendous charger, his plume waving in the air. They had been watching the American troops in sullen silence, but General Scott was so awe-inspiring they cheered him. It is perhaps the only time in history that a conqueror drew applause from the bleachers because he was such a beautiful sight to behold!

If Winfield Scott could have given five inches off his six feet five to his brother general, George B. McClellan, he might have saved General McClellan from his inferiority complex and himself from much of the vanity which kept him from becoming a great man; the shifting of that focal five inches, critical to both men, might have turned two half geniuses into two whole geniuses. If McClellan's dementia praecox had not forced him to drive Scott out of power and out of Washington in order that he might glory in the sole command, the team of Scott and McClellan might have ended the Civil War two years earlier.

In appearance Scott was Nietzsche's Superman, the Man on Horseback if there ever was one. Yet he had no desire to become a dictator. He never wanted to use force, except against an enemy; he wanted no power except the power necessary to accomplish his job of building a proficient army and winning battles; he wanted no honors or titles except those granted by the people for work well done. Offered the role of military dictator of Mexico by a group of wealthy Mexicans, and promised that later he could bring Mexico into the United States, he instead gave up the command of his intensely loyal troops and returned to Washington to face an investigation of his professional conduct. When this happened a Mexican observer paid the highest possible compliment to the genius of the American democracy:

139

"General Scott returned to the United States, deprived of his military command, leaving reflecting men to admire the moral force of the American government which, by a slip of paper, written at a distance of two thousand leagues, could humble a proud and victorious soldier and make him descend from his exalted position."

Winfield Scott would have been astonished at the Mexican historian's astonishment. Of course he obeyed his people's government; for whom else was he fighting these battles? Had not his father fought in the Revolutionary Army for the right of the American people to set up and control their own government?

It is a curious bit of Americana that the more handsome the man, the greater his capacity for swearing. The only soldier who almost could equal General Winfield Scott for looks was also the only one who had an equally diverse vocabulary of cuss words: General Winfield Scott Hancock, his namesake and protégé. By an amusing coincidence it was the lone vice indulged in by either man; in the flush of his youth Scott once made a pass at a farmer's buxom wife, but that good lady broomed him out of the house with such ferocity that he never again was guilty of philandering—though his wife sometimes would remain in Europe for five years at a time.

Winfield Scott was a man of gargantuan appetites: for food, for dress, for battle, for accomplishment, for honors; yet great as were his appetites he never was content to satisfy them with second-rate ingredients: the food had to be the very best, prepared by culinary artists; the wines had to be of the finest vintage; his uniforms had to be the most colorful and resplendent to be found in military annals; his work had to be of the utmost importance, not alone to him but to his profession and his people; his victories had to have meaning for his country and its place in the world; his hard-earned honors had to set him off as a conquering warrior and be bestowed by a loving citizenry.

He alone among those who Also Ran looked upon the presidency as the ultimate honor to be pinned upon his breast in gratitude for past valors.

Yet his life story reveals that he would have made a good president: he was a man of fierce and unquenchable love for his country and its institutions, of complete honesty and integrity, of an inexhaustible courage that was the despair of his military opponents. A successful diplomat at settling embroilments, of a gentle nature, with a love for the common soldier and the common citizen; intelligent, cultivated, well

140

read, well traveled, he was respected at home and admired abroad.

Somewhere in the middle of his long career he was dubbed "Old Fuss and Feathers" because of his weakness for elaborate and colorful uniforms. Though he unquestionably loved his sashes, plumes and tight britches, he wore them not only to pay tribute to his magnificent body but also to do honor to the United States Army. Many who saw him at public functions, dressed in his gold braid, medals and sword, thought him to be conceited and ostentatious. In reality Scott was standing as a symbol for an army which neither Congress nor the people would give him to train: an ever-present one-man lobby for preparedness.

"In my person," General Scott seemed to be saying to a public suspicious of the purposes to which a large standing army might be put, "you see how big and strong and beautiful is your army. Keep it that way! Make it more so!"

As a consequence of the disregard of Scott's advice, every time there was trouble the country was caught with its muskets down.

As for his medals, had they not been won with the taste of blood in his mouth? Had not that very sword saved the nation time and again from humiliation, loss of territory and loss of faith? Had he not been a good servant of democracy for half a century?

He thought he had. Nothing made him prouder.

Scott never looked better than when in the midst of a fiercely contested battle, with bullets thickening the air about him. He looked particularly good in the presidential battle of 1852, when one of his contemporaries remarked of him:

"Scott does seem to me to be happy. Like the consumption, this ambition for the presidency may be called a flattering disease."

2

Three generations of Scotts had fought England; instead of the fighting blood running thin by the third generation it had developed into a perfect tornado in Winfield. His grandfather, a Scotchman, fought the Duke of Cumberland, was defeated and fled to Virginia, where he studied law; Winfield's father, a prosperous farmer, fought in the Revolution as the captain of a Virginia regiment; Winfield himself spent half a century keeping England off America's neck.

His mother was known in the county as a "woman of superior mind and great force of character." She died when the boy was only seventeen, but he writes of her in his *Memoirs:*

"If in my protracted career I have achieved anything worthy of being written, it is from the lessons of that admirable parent that I derived the inspiration."

Winfield Scott was born on the family plantation of Laurel Branch on June 13, 1786, entered high school in Richmond in 1804 and William and Mary College the following year. He cared little for organized classes, preferring to choose his own books. His taste in literature was the best: Goldsmith, John Locke, Adam Smith, Addison, Milton, Johnson, Shakespeare. From these authors he picked up a colorful though somewhat bombastic vocabulary, as well as a knack for the felicitous phrase; if he had read them a little less attentively he would not have become so effective a letter writer, and might have saved himself a great deal of trouble. *Plutarch's Lives* was his favorite book because he felt that he could be as good a man as any he was reading about, yes, even as good as Julius Caesar and Scipio Africanus. He said to himself:

"When some future Plutarch writes the *Lives* of the great of the nineteenth century, the students of William and Mary College will be reading about me."

It was fatheaded conceit; it was illusion of grandeur; it was the simple truth.

Brought up in Thomas Jefferson's Virginia, Scott was an avid democrat fighting the aristocratic Federalists at college; coming of age in a state where Bishop Madison refused to call Heaven a Kingdom because that sounded too Federalist, referring to it instead as "that great Republic where there is no distinction of rank, and where all men are free and equal," Scott was to his dying day "a violent democrat."

Deciding to follow in his grandfather's steps and become a lawyer, he left college after one year to go into the office of a successful practitioner in Richmond. "Already he towered above his fellows and attracted admiring glances by his superb good looks and herculean proportions. Never an actor on the Thespian boards craved applause in greater degree than Winfield Scott, or was more resolutely certain of his ability to merit the plaudits of the world. Proud, passionate, and scrupulously honest, burning with ambition, intensely patriotic, absolutely fearless, he faced the future with impetuousness, earnestness and perfect self-confidence."

He was admitted to the Virginia bar when he was twenty, began riding circuit, and doubtless would have remained a fair-to-middling lawyer if the British had given him half a chance; for although he had a tremendous admiration for Caesar and Africanus, believing that he could become an equally great general, he was living in a country which did not believe in war, did not think it could be attacked, and wanted no part of an army. Then the British, who had been seizing American vessels on the high seas, refused to obey President Jefferson's order to remain out of American waters; by so doing they jettisoned a lawyer, replacing him with a soldier.

Winfield Scott rushed to answer the call for coastguardmen, was made a corporal, and nearly precipitated a war by capturing a rowboat full of English sailors. He loved the feel of his father's Revolutionary War saber in his hand, this first touch of combat and fleeting fame: for President Jefferson, who was not anxious for a war with England, had to caution the overzealous young man not to do it again! It is unlikely that anything Scott achieved in the law courts in the following years of peace brought him a tithe of the excitement or pleasure.

By 1808, when it became apparent that another war with England was inevitable, President Jefferson asked the Congress for a larger army and new officers. This was the great moment for which Winfield Scott had been waiting: he was one of the first to apply. While his commission was coming through he made his first charge upon the rampart: between court cases this youth who had been a mediocre student at college dug into the history and science of military operations with the eager-eyed avidity of a Greeley throwing himself into journalism or a John C. Fremont into exploring, to make himself one of the best-trained military minds of his century.

Great and joyous was the day for Winfield Scott when his commission arrived from Washington, for on this day he was really born. He was now Captain Scott of the Regulars—only he had no troops! He had to scour the countryside to enlist a company over which he might be captain.

Out of his own pocket he had circulars printed asking for Virginia volunteers, but before he went on recruiting duty he visited the best tailor in Richmond to have his uniform made. He understood the effect of a resplendent uniform on a prospective enlistee; for fifty years he was to utilize the psychology of the uniform to bring prestige to his despised and eternally inadequate army. His first regalia, worn at the age of twenty-two, was one to make the mouth of a European marshal water: "Tar-bucket or high glazed hat crowned with a lofty white pompon tipped with red, a blue coatee with a high choker collar and tails, adorned with three rows of gold buttons and gold epaulets on the shoulders, white breeches tied around the middle with a red sash, and black knee boots."

This was a slight case of gilding the lily, but Scott had a sense of humor about his physical vanity: thirty years later

143

he was to tell about how he strutted up and down in front of the mirror admiring himself.

Now fittingly attired, he bought himself a horse and galloped through the countryside persuading young men by a combination of legal eloquence and military fervor how critical it was for them to join his company. Often he had to buy their uniforms out of his own funds; upon one occasion an irate mother appealed to Washington to get her boy back, claiming he had been mesmerized by Captain Scott.

His company at length completed, he took them to New Orleans, where the men wasted and died from the fever and from the incompetence of the malevolent General Wilkinson. Disgusted with this inefficiency, with the bungling and waste and callous manner in which the officers permitted their men to suffer, Scott rashly uttered a public criticism of Wilkinson. He was wounded in the scalp in a duel and cashiered from the army for a year as reward. It was an inglorious start, but he improved his year by an intensive study of supply and organization, of the Napoleonic campaigns—and an observation of the sloth and inability of the army officers in power. He resolved that when he came into command of the army he would create a highly trained and efficient corps, with good men and a high morale, a promise he was to fulfill to the letter.

With the War of 1812 about to break, young Scott rushed to Washington where he begged to be allowed to see action at once. He was appointed a lieutenant colonel of the artillery. Eight days later he was in his first battle.

Scott was always out in front where the bullets were the thickest, and where his enormous figure made a superb target. During his first campaign he crossed the river into Canada in an attempt to capture Queenston. Only three hundred troops crossed with him, the militia standing on its rights and refusing to leave American territory to fight. Receiving word from his commander to retreat in the face of superior numbers, Scott assembled his officers, "told them that their condition was desperate, but that the stain of Hull's surrender must be wiped out.

"Let us die arms in hand," he cried. "Our country demands the sacrifice. The example will not be lost. The blood of the slain will make heroes of the living. Those who follow will avenge our fall, and our country's wrongs. Who dare to stand?"

His brother officers did not know that they were listening to the purple language of Plutarch. They cried that they would stand. Hopelessly outnumbered, they were driven slowly back to the river—where the boats that were supposed to transport them to safety had somehow failed to appear. Scott was forced to surrender to save his troops from annihilation. Two soldiers carrying white flags of truce were shot down by Indians fighting for the British. Scott grabbed up a stick and a white cloth and crossed to the enemy lines, with the Indians shooting wildly and rushing at him with tomahawks. Only the intervention of the British saved the future lieutenant general of the United States Army. The Indian chief ran his hand over his prisoner's enormous bulk murmuring:

"I fire ten times! I hit you not once?"

"Hands off me, you filthy scoundrel," shouted Scott. "Hit me? Why, you fired like a squaw!"

So anxious was he to be in the heart of the fighting at all times that he pursued battles, on one occasion riding his horse for thirty hours through a sleet storm to reach a battlefield where he might see action!

If all this was the courage of heroics, of an actor playing a grandiose part, Scott portrayed another kind of courage which he could not have learned from the promptbooks. In 1832, while transporting a force of officers and troops to Detroit to fight in the Black Hawk War, an epidemic of cholera broke out on the *Henry Clay*. Scores of soldiers in perfect health at nine in the morning suddenly would collapse and be dead by three in the afternoon. Cholera being considered contagious, the ship's surgeon deserted to his bunk. Winfield Scott took over. With his own hands he nursed the stricken men, fed them medicine, worked night and day to establish cleanliness, to lighten the suffering, presenting such a calm and courageous front that the men were inspired to fight the disease, not to give over to panic and death.

There were no medals or promotions to be gained from this kind of heroism: only an ugly and instantaneous death and an end to his cherished career. Yet he fought the battle of the cholera with all the dash and courage and skill with which he fought the battles of Chippewa and Lundy's Lane. This he learned from an educated heart, and not from Plutarch.

He did not depend for success upon his height, his strength or his dash; he was the lone military scientist among the personnel of the American army. When he was dispatched to Fort Niagara in 1812 he hauled with him a complete library on military organization and tactics, including the very latest French book on the Napoleonic organization of a general staff. By means of his studies Scott, now an adjutant general, revolutionized the structure of his corps, set up an efficient general staff, started a steady flow of supplies coming in, put

145

new recruits under vigorous drill. His brother officers laughed at him for dragging along a "five-foot shelf of books," but upon these books was founded the modern American army.

His wisdom in military affairs went deeper than detailed organization; he knew that it was not enough to win battles, that his troops had to pursue and destroy the opposing forces. He was alone in thinking this: each time he and his fellow officers won a decisive battle and could have annihilated the enemy by vigorous pursuit, the right orders were not forthcoming.

"Scott fought nine tenths of the battle!" wrote a fellow officer. He also fought it with a broken collarbone; if his superiors had permitted him to fight the final tenth, a major portion of the war would have been won.

He had been cashiered once for criticism of his superior officers, and he did not wish to be sent down again; yet if he had been in command of the American forces in 1813 the war might have ended that year with a decisive American victory; a considerable portion of Canada would have come into the possession of the United States.

When Scott was exchanged by the British in 1812 and returned to Washington he found that he was a hero: the defeat had been laid to General Van Rensselaer's bad planning. Stories of Scott's heroism under fire had preceded him to the Capitol. On the night he reached Washington, President Madison and his Dolley were giving a reception; not uncharacteristically, Scott had stopped en route to have a new uniform made. When his six feet five of sartorial elegance entered the White House he instantly became the lion of the party, surrounded, congratulated and flattered by the president, his cabinet and congressmen. Scott held his audience spellbound with his tales of the war: for the boy who had ridden circuit in Virginia was no mean storyteller; his court could hear the bursting shrapnel, smell the acrid smoke of battle.

It was at this moment, garbed in a magnificent costume, his dark wavy hair brushed to either side of his great brow, his eyes big and clear and friendly and pleased, that Winfield Scott, only twenty-six, took his place on the stage of national importance.

At Christmas of 1813 President Madison summoned him for advice on the state of the war and how further to wage it. Appointed a brigadier general though not yet twenty-eight, he was sent to upper New York to take charge of the ragged and hitherto useless militia. Scott proceeded to whip it into a powerful and efficient army, more effective in combat than the regulars. He trained his officers and men so thoroughly in the craft of soldiering that his commanding officer was able to say about the important battle of Chippewa:

"Brigadier-General Scott is entitled to the highest praise our country can bestow—to him more than any other man I am indebted for the victory of the fifth of July."

He was a fierce adversary, but a courtly one as well. When his soldiers had captured a town and broken into the personal effects of the British officers, Scott purchased from one of his men a lovely miniature and some letters which he returned to the enemy officer with his compliments. He was a gentleman as well as a fighter, a gentle soul, sensitive and sympathetic, as well as a holy terror on a battlefield. He spoke quite openly about his own virtues and abilities, but he was equally eager to speak of the outstanding qualities of others.

Neither the United States nor England won the War of 1812, but Scott emerged as a victor. Though he took second money to Andrew Jackson, the winner of the battle of New Orleans, he found himself an authentic national hero. On the point of death from an ugly wound which he received in one of the greatest series of charges in military history, the battle of Lundy's Lane, he was brevetted a major general, voted a gold medal by Congress, swords from grateful state legislatures, honorary degrees from colleges.

Twenty-six years later he and Henry Clay, both candidates for the 1840 presidential nomination of the Whig party, were playing whist with other members of the Executive Committee in the Astor House while the convention was balloting. It is probable that both men were having a hard time concentrating, for whichever Whig received the nomination was certain to be elected, and they were the favorites. When word was flashed that they had been cast aside for William H. Harrison, Clay flew into a rage, striking Scott a hard blow on the left shoulder. Scott said grimly: "Senator Clay, I beg you not to lay your hand so heavily on that shoulder. It is the shoulder wounded at Lundy's Lane."

While the honors were pouring in, his main concern was for the recognition of the work done by the officers under him, for the public declaration that every man in his brigade had been a hero! Always ambitious, sometimes vain, when offered the position of secretary of war he refused on the grounds that it would put him in command of officers much older than he, and might lead to dissension.

He was a big man, cut to a big pattern. Before he was thirty he was one of the outstanding figures of his day. He had everything: looks, figure, brains, courage, culture, dash, confidence, leadership, loyalty, one of the best all-around equipages to be found in young America. If he charged into

147

the political arena with the same superb courage, science, self-confidence and heroic determination to win, what force could keep him out of the White House?

3

The years between wars were not easy ones for restless, volatile Scott. He enjoyed his task of overhauling the drill and tactics regulations of the army; he enjoyed the honors heaped upon him during his vacation in Europe; but "the decade from 1819 to 1829 was to bring bitter disappointments and humiliations, resulting from his too rapid rise and his inability to hold his ambitions in leash."

The most lengthy, frantic and useless battle of his long life was to be waged over the supreme command of the United States Army. When the ranking major general died the command had to pass to either Scott or Edmund P. Gaines; Gaines was older, had been in the army longer; Scott had been brevetted earlier. Scott believed with all his heart and soul that his prior promotion, his accomplishments and manifest abilities entitled him to the command; to attain this end he threw the entire country into a turmoil, disrupted Congresses, harassed presidents, created a national scandal with his thousands of argumentative, pleading, quarrelsome letters, pamphlets, reports of two hundred pages in length to prove that he had a priority and greater qualifications. He kept the government and the army in a state of siege in the single worst brawl for promotion and command in the military history of the country: for Gaines was just as determined to secure the command for himself, and had equally powerful political backing.

As a result of the strength of both sides neither presidents, cabinets nor Congresses dared name either man. For years the army remained under the joint command of Scott in the east and Gaines in the west, both of whom loathed each other. At length President Adams, sick of the embroilments, passed them by, appointing to the supreme command an officer who had been inferior in rank to both of them.

This decade of fighting put lines in Scott's face. At twenty-nine, when he began the struggle, he had been young and beautiful and unconquerable; at thirty-nine he had injured himself more painfully than any adversary was to injure him in fifty years of fighting.

Meanwhile he had been rendering invaluable service to his country. He fought the Indian wars when fighting was unavoidable, but more often he made peace with the Indians and succeeded in getting them to sign friendly treaties. Sent to South Carolina by President Jackson to man the Union defenses when that state was threatening secession over the tariff in 1832, he was so diplomatic with the enraged Carolinians that he played a crucial part in averting them from war. Ordered to the scene of his old triumphs on the Canadian border in 1837–38 to keep hotheaded American patriots from starting still another war with England, he won international renown for the manner in which he quieted the hostilities, "giving not an inch to the British and yet satisfying bands of Americans already armed and fighting."

By 1840 Winfield Scott once again had so endeared himself to the public that his conflict with Gaines was forgotten. As an enthusiastic Whig he had been mentioned as a possible presidential nominee long before the convention had opened. The Whig *Journal* spoke of his "honorable services, his repeated triumphs of mediation, his patriotism, his intellectual attainments, his disinterested character . . . If merit, and neither favor nor party is to win the honors and higher trusts of the Republic, where shall we find more merit than in Scott?"

Up to 1840 Scott steadfastly had refused to take sides, declaring, even as Parker and Hughes had as judges, that an army officer must not become involved in politics because the opposition might take it out on the army. Leadership was in a sense forced upon him, and always he accepted such attentions as honors for work well done. His discerning mind was intensely interested in the issues of the day and so he entered the political arena as had so many generals before him, little suspecting that this move nearly would keep him out of the Mexican War.

When the Whig convention of 1840 opened it appeared that Scott had an excellent chance, particularly since his campaign managers, the fandanglers Seward and Weed, were in power. But political-innocent Scott could not suspect that Seward and Weed were merely using him as a decoy to kill off Henry Clay, then to sneak in their candidate, General Harrison, by the back door.

When Harrison was nominated Scott was disappointed, but he took his defeat in good season. Clay cried, "My friends are not worth the powder to blow them to hell!" Scott said, "I preferred the success of either Harrison or Clay providing the convention believed their chances of election better than mine." Later he was able to write with a fair measure of truthfulness, "I was absolutely indifferent whether I ever reached the office of the president."

By an odd twist of fate Scott was defeated for the presidency in 1840, and not in 1852 when he was a candidate. As had been the case with Alton B. Parker and Charles Evans Hughes, his defeat was entirely a matter of timing: if he had been nominated in 1840 when the Whig party was in its full strength he would have won by an overwhelming majority; by the time he received the nomination, twelve years later, the Whig party had reached the end of its road. Scott may have thought, as he learned that General Harrison had won the nomination, that that was just the beginning of his political career; actually it was the end.

He spent the years between the 1840 nomination and the beginning of the Mexican War in 1846 modernizing the army, in such projects as the founding of the first summer camp at Plattsburg for the training of officers. So minute was his love of detail and his interest in his men that he wrote the recipes for the army's food, insisting that the bread be thoroughly baked so that it would be health giving, the meats boiled or baked, never fried. He kept up his omnivorous reading of books and journals, not only on military science but in literature, history, philosophy. Now that he was an important Whig he also considered it his duty to read all the Whig newspapers and inform himself on the political issues. There was a movement to have him nominated at the convention of 1844, but Henry Clay won the prize.

His hour had not yet struck. He would have to win still another war before he could gain the nomination.

President Polk sent for Winfield Scott when the Mexican War broke out, asking him to take charge of the new army to be raised for the war. From the very first instant there was conflict, for although Polk wanted to win the Mexican War of 1846 he also wanted to win the election of 1848; he knew that if Scott defeated the Mexicans he would also defeat Polk. Polk was a patriot, he wanted the war to end successfully, but he did not want it to create a rival candidate; he preferred it to be won by generals who belonged to his own party. That was what the youthfully astute Scott had had in mind when he had refused to engage in politics from 1808 to 1840.

With his tremendous energy and background Scott set out to build a powerful war machine, only to find that his efforts were being hamstrung. Outraged at being thwarted at his work when his country was at war, Scott wrote a letter complaining that he had "a fire upon my rear, from Washington, and the fire, in front, from the Mexicans."

The note became famous as the "fire upon my rear" letter, and so incensed President Polk that he relieved Scott of his command. No bullet through the heart could have wounded Scott more critically. Receiving his notice of demotion while sitting in a restaurant, he again rushed to pen and paper, writing to Polk in an effort to apologize, explain, to get back his command. "Your letter, received as I sat down to take a hasty plate of soup, demands a prompt reply." This "hasty plate of soup" letter, published together with the "fire upon my rear" letter by President Polk in his explanation of why he was refusing to reinstate Scott, hurt Scott considerably with the American people.

Having committed what appeared to be an irreparable folly, he now engaged in a consummate piece of wisdom. Instead of acting hurt or abused, he glued himself to his desk in Washington during the long hot summer, working to keep General Zachary Taylor's army in Mexico supplied with an unending stream of troops, munitions, foodstuffs, ordnance, for he was as good at paper work as he was at leading a charge upon an enemy battery.

The war was not going very well; when the strategists in Washington decided that the best way to win was to capture Vera Cruz and proceed overland to the conquest of Mexico City, General Scott applied for the command of the army to be shipped to Vera Cruz. President Polk, still insisting that a Democrat win the war, refused. So complete was Scott's plan of attack that Secretary of War Marcy became convinced that only he could accomplish the task, and persuaded Polk that if he wanted to win the war he had better send General Winfield Scott to take charge.

The major general's capture of Vera Cruz, his victories at Contreras, Churubusco and finally Mexico City were won by campaigns scientifically mapped before they began, by the complete equipping of his forces, by his method of utilizing the best counsel of his general staff, and by his flaming self-confidence which inspired his men. Though the Mexican fire upon his front was never very scientific, the fire from Washington continued to keep him always on the hot seat. Polk loaded him with newly created Democratic generals as well as a political coadjuster who was to hold him within bounds of the administration's desires. The Democratic generals and coadjuster gave Winfield Scott rather more trouble than the Mexicans.

Scott arranged a friendly peace with the Mexicans, setting up such an excellent civil government that the conquered people came to regard him with affection. This was too much for Polk; seeing the election close at hand he began a campaign to discredit Scott at home. After having won the war to everyone's satisfaction, Scott was called to Washington to face a board of military examination. Since he would not permit his name to go before the 1848 convention while under inquiry, General Taylor was elected president for having won the first battle of Buena Vista. The Board of Inquiry certified that Scott had waged a brilliant campaign in Mexico —but the vindication came too late to secure him the nomination and election.

Having superseded Zachary Taylor in Mexico, he had made an enemy of the general; he knew that as long as Taylor was president he would remain in eclipse.

Growing old, his body shattered by the wounds and diseases of war, his hair turning white, his giant head sinking slowly onto his chest, his magnificent face settling into crevices from nose to mouth and from lips to the jawbone, every sign on the horizon indicated that the major general was washed up. Then the death of President Taylor put into the White House his old friend Millard Fillmore, who said:

"Now, General, your persecutions are at an end!"

Throughout the Fillmore administration Scott lived and worked in Washington surrounded by friends and admirers, his organizational plans carried out. A married daughter came to live with him, the Scott home becoming one of the high lights of official society where one found the best foods, wines and conversation in the capital. As proof of Fillmore's assertion, Congress at long last named him a lieutenant general, the first since Washington.

Though his name was now the most prominently mentioned to succeed Fillmore to the presidency, there were many who felt that the lieutenant general should remain at his soldiering. The New York *Herald* said, "A deep movement is on foot for General Scott, but if he is wise he will have nothing to do with it. He has glory enough and honor enough to satisfy the higher ambition."

Having elected two Whig generals, Harrison and Taylor, Seward and Weed, the Whig whips who had double-crossed Scott in 1840, decided that their best chance of a third victory lay with a third general. Scott was the country's outstanding general; the worst that could be said against him was that he had a tendency to monopolize the dinner-table conversation. Though he had worked for the passage of the Missouri Compromise because he felt it would prevent a civil war, he was the only big-Whig who had committed himself so little on the question of slavery that he would be acceptable alike to the north and south.

The campaign managers who could have elected him in 1840 or 1848 put their money on the general's nose after they already had come into bad odor and lost a considerable portion of their prestige. In the flush of their power they had cuckolded him; now their jaded embrace was to prove the kiss of death.

A flood of letters reached the general asking for his opinions on important questions. He had been too often burned by writing letters and, at the age of sixty-six, finally refused to rush into print, replying courteously without committing himself. Advised by the outstanding Whigs that he should remain absolutely silent, he agreed that he would say nothing and do nothing which would embarrass their efforts to get him nominated.

It is the only instance of docility in his tempestuous career. The south, afraid that he would be dominated by anti-slavery Seward, stormed against this silence, insisting that he make a positive statement in favor of the Fugitive Slave Law, that he declare the Missouri Compromise to be the last word on slavery. However, if the south was skittish, the north liked the idea of Winfield Scott as president, instructing their delegates for him. Horace Greeley approved the general as a candidate, believing him to be the most pre-eminently available.

The last great Whig convention—for its scattered forces were to be drawn into the new Republican party—opened on June 16, 1852, in Baltimore. Every step of the way was ardently contested by the advocates of President Fillmore, Winfield Scott and Daniel Webster. On the first ballot Fillmore had 133 votes, with Scott only two votes behind. Fifty-three ballotings were required, spread over four fever-ridden days, before the nomination came to the general. But the convention already had adopted one plank in its platform which would defeat any candidate it named.

The Scott forces had battled to have the candidate named first so that he might have some control over the platform for which he was going to be responsible; the combined Fillmore and Webster camps had defeated this move. The plank which nominee General Scott was now made to walk read "The acts of the Thirty-Second Congress, the Fugitive Slave Law included, are received and acquiesced in by the Whig party as a settlement in principle and substance of the dangerous and exciting questions which they embrace; we will maintain them and insist upon their strict enforcement."

More than a million northern Whigs who were for Scott, and whose votes were imperative for his success, loathed this plank as a piece of abominable treason. Should he repudiate his platform and lose the south? Or approve it and lose the north? There could be only one answer: maintain an absolute silence, let the election be decided on his past record.

Scott was not politically subtle enough to understand that a candidate can ignore the platform with which he has been

153

strapped. He was a loyal Whig; the Whig convention had set up this platform; therefore it was his duty to endorse it. Caught off guard when the telegram informing him of his nomination arrived, he dispatched an immediate reply to the convention, "Having the honor of being the nominee for President by the Whig National Convention, I shall accept the same, with the platform of principles which the convention has laid down."

When that telegram went out the front door the general once again was unhorsed by the truth of his own immortal phrase, "Fire upon my rear." He was caught by the hopeless dilemma of slavery: if he turned to the south, the north would fire upon his rear; if he turned to the north, the south would fire upon his rear. The northern Whigs said, "We accept the candidate, but we spit upon the platform!" The southern Whigs said, "We accept the platform, but we spit upon Seward, the campaign manager!" In the election of 1852 Scott's sizable rear was caught in the murderous cross fire of the slavery and anti-slavery forces.

In such fashion were the Whigs torn to shreds while the Democrats were united under an obscure party hack by the name of Franklin Pierce whom even the delegates hardly knew. No one outside of New Hampshire had ever heard of Pierce; Lieutenant-General Winfield Scott was known to every last man, woman and child in the country. Certainly the unknown could not defeat the national hero?

4

There was only one way for Scott to win the election: by being as great a statesman as he had been a soldier, by riding for thirty hours through a sleet storm to catch up with the enemy; by getting in front of his troops and leading them through shot and shell; by superb self-confidence that his cause was right and that he would triumph. He must plan his campaign as a scientist, blueprinting to minute perfection every detail before going into battle, make the same intuitively accurate split-second judgments that he had made in the clash of arms. He must attack superior numbers, be undaunted, a great eagle soaring above the petty fears, hesitancies, mistakes of the milling crowds below. All these virtues had made him one of the world's great generals. Could he apply the same character, the same technique, the same genius to the world of politics?

As a general he had understood what was meant by the command, *"L'audace, toujours l'audace!"*; as a presidential nominee and the leader of a political party he showed no audacity whatever. He took a defensive stand, letting the enemy attack. He fought no lost causes, he revolutionized no antiquated techniques, he whipped no bodies of raw recruits into scientifically trained militia. He did not understand the tactics of an election. He took orders instead of giving them, did not jump upon his horse and lead the charge; the flaming courage and inspiration of Chippewa and Lundy's Lane he somehow could not transfer to an election battle.

The Democrats cried triumphantly, and much to Scott's discomfort:

"We Poked you in 1844, we shall Pierce you in 1852!"

"Slander, vilification and ridicule of both Scott and Pierce were the order of the day. The most outrageous libels on their characters, habits and personal histories were shamelessly bruited about. In this warfare of calumny, abuse and general disparagement the Democrats were more plentifully supplied than the Whigs."

No one knew much about Mr. Pierce. Scott had been a public figure since 1812; every move he had made had been highly publicized. He was lampooned because of his love of uniforms, was called a drunkard; his seven-year feud with General Gaines over promotion was aired for all its unpleasant implications; his wounds were declared to have been incurred in duels rather than battles; he was charged with having acquired a small fortune from the government in pay; he was labeled an aristocrat who had no love for the people; to the Protestants he was called a Catholic sympathizer because one daughter had become a nun, to the Catholics he was declared a murderous enemy because he had hung certain Irish Catholics who had deserted to the Mexican army. There was little that the poisoned mind of political man could invent that could not be found in the Democratic press of 1852; in its ultimate implications the institutions of free press and free speech took a more mortal beating than General Scott: Scott would die in a few years, but the freedoms of speech and press had somehow to be sustained through the centuries.

The press whipped itself into its usual ill-bred frenzy, but the public was disinterested. The New York *Herald* commented that "there never had been such a ludicrous, ridiculous and uninteresting presidential campaign." In the sweltering heat of summer the campaigns of both parties died aborning.

Scott finally broke precedent and went touring, ostensibly to inspect soldiers' homes, but actually to renew old friendships. He made a number of speeches in key cities, more amiable than political, receiving ovations wherever he went. The throngs that turned out to hear him speak afforded the general great pleasure; from these rousing receptions he became convinced that he was winning the election. Dining with Weed in Albany, he told his comanager that he anticipated an easy victory in November. When November rolled around he appeared to be the only Whig in the country who did not know that his cause was lost, the Whig party dead.

By midnight of election day General Winfield Scott was stunned and grief-stricken, for he felt his defeat to be a slur on his past. He carried only four states, but in his popular vote he did not run so far behind: 1,386,580 for Scott against 1,601,474 for Pierce. Horace Greeley wrote:

"His proud form was never more erect, nor his eagle eye brighter than it is today. He stands alone amid the wreck, grand and unconcerned, like a lighthouse after a dreadful storm."

He was a soldier first, a politician second. He allowed no one to know how keenly he felt his defeat.

5

What kind of president would Scott have made?

Is it better to have an experienced politician like Franklin Pierce, who had served in a state legislature, who had been re-elected four times to the House and the Senate, who knew the inside workings of administrative government; or a man like Scott whose sole training was that of the military organizer and leader? Do ability and pre-eminence in another field fit a man to move into the complicated world of politics, of which he knows little and perhaps suspects less? Or is it better, in a democracy, for a shoemaker to stick to his last?

Even genius in another field does not fit a man to carry out the highly specialized job of president. Yet in the case of Winfield Scott it was the inexperienced man who would have made by far the better chief executive!

In comparison to the great statesmen of American history Scott would have made a fractional president; but he does not have to be compared to statesmen, he needs only to be compared to Senator Pierce of New Hampshire, about whom R. H. Dana exclaimed in horror and awe, "A third-rate county politician President of the United States!"

Historians aver that Scott would not have made a good president because he was not clever in the same sense that the men around him were clever: Daniel Webster, Henry Clay, Seward and Weed. Scott was open and forthright, not clever enough to connive and double-deal, to compromise or play factions, betray his ideals or double-cross his associates or his country.

He had many small vanities and posturings of the ego: he

talked too much about himself, he had a love of gaudy uniforms, a quick temper which led him into "hasty plate of soup" letter writing which so frequently kept him in the soup, an unquenchable desire to rise to the supreme command of the army, an ability to settle disputes between states and nations with more tact than he had the ability to settle his own disputes. But these were tolerable peccadillos in a tower of strength, resolution and integrity. He was one of the best-educated and most scientifically trained men of his day, numbering among his lifelong friends the great writers, thinkers and doers of his age. He was a passionate follower of Jefferson, with a burning zeal for freedom and democracy, an understanding of the problems of a federated government, a love of every disparate section of his vast country.

As a civil governor he had done an efficient and intelligent job in Mexico; as a diplomat he had enjoyed outstanding success with the Indians, the South Carolinians, the British; as an organizer and executive he had modernized the American army, brought it up to the level of the best in Europe; as a fighter he had shown inexhaustible courage, as a tactician, inexhaustible skill; as a leader he had taken loving care of the least of his men; as a servant of a democracy he had proved a thousand times over his respect for representative government and his willingness to obey its commands; as a citizen of the world he had achieved a fine cultural standing, won respect for his country wherever he went.

The major charge against him was that since he was politically inexperienced he would have taken orders from Seward during his presidency, as he had during the campaign. Scott knew little about campaigning, but he knew as much as the best of them about the issues of the day, which he had been studying for years. He had a fast, clear, powerful, daring and scientifically trained mind; there is reason to believe that he would have turned these talents to the presidency as he had to every other task he had undertaken. General Scott had organized a highly efficient general staff, seeking the best men available, and then had afforded himself the benefit of their best advice; but no man under him had ruled or controlled the general. As president he would have organized a general staff of governmental advisers, and he would have utilized their skill and knowledge the better to make up his own mind.

Franklin Pierce was as mediocre and feeble a president as the United States had yet suffered. His one talent was for party organization, for keeping his state party intact in New Hampshire, for cracking the whip which would make all Democrats vote the straight Democratic ticket. According to his biographer Pierce rarely understood what the issues, policies or principles were about; he understood only that he had to herd the party vote. He was weak of character, fled from harsh realities into mental comas, drink and a mystical religion. He understood nothing of the structure of society, was incapable of grasping the nature and needs of constitutional government.

That he was congenitally incapable of handling the job of president is less than half of Pierce's shortcomings. He spent his entire four years in office playing man against man, faction against faction in an attempt to insure his re-election; almost his sole activity was appointing Democrats to jobs of which they most often understood nothing. Because he played the game of giving out patronage and offices not as rewards, but as potential vote getters for the next election, he turned his own administration into a cage of snarling tigers who tore to pieces not only the government but the Democratic party as well.

Winfield Scott would not have spent his days playing power politics; he would have considered that to be treason! He loved his country so deeply that he would have given his lifeblood, as he had at Lundy's Lane, to provide an honest, courageous, conciliatory and loving government.

Against Franklin Pierce's crumbling limestone of a character Winfield Scott stands out like a granite mountain peak. Virginia born, he remained loyal to the Union in 1861, did valuable work as Lincoln's chief of staff and, at seventy-five, so ill he could not leave his bed, mapped the strategy of the battle of Bull Run, which has been called "the best-planned and worst-fought battle of the war." If General Scott could have been carried onto the battlefield, the battle might have been won and the offensive retained by the Union forces.

As a youth Scott had saved his Quaker schoolmaster from a thrashing at the hands of a bully. Later, when he returned triumphant from the War of 1812, his schoolmaster said, "Friend Winfield, I always told thee not to fight, but since thou wouldst fight, I am glad that thou wast not beaten!"

Alas, he spoke too soon!

CHAPTER TWO

John Charles Fremont

JOHN FREMONT was only a few months old when shots rang out in the hotel in which his parents had taken lodgings in Nashville, and a bullet entered the room in which the infant was sleeping. Thus was young Fremont rudely introduced to his future father-in-law, Thomas Benton, who was feuding with Andrew Jackson. There was no connection between the shot and the marriage, but there was a considerable relation between the marriage and Fremont's rise to fame. Without the one he might have enjoyed little of the other.

By another strange coincidence the first two presidential candidates of the Republican party, John Charles Fremont and Abraham Lincoln, went through life under the burden of family illegitimacy. Though Fremont never mentioned his illegal birth, it remained as a barb and a spur in his consciousness. Much of his dramatic and superbly heroic conduct is understandable in the light of his flight from childhood.

By the time he was forty-three this flight had carried him a long way: he had been offered the nomination for the presidency by the powerful Democratic party and, having rejected their offer, had been nominated by the dynamic new Republican party.

The matrons of Washington declared him to be the most exciting young lieutenant ever to ride down the mud-crusted streets of the capital when he arrived there in 1838, yet his eyes were sad, almost melancholy. He had little humor, was rarely known to laugh, was sincere and serious, quiet and well mannered. Even in his early twenties his full-face beard gave him an appearance of settled maturity. He had a driving ambition which he miraculously managed to keep within the bounds of good taste.

The country revered him for his undaunted spirit and his contribution to the exploration and literature of the wilderness, yet he had none of the attributes of the demagogue: he was shy, soft-voiced, unassuming. In moments of gravest peril he gave his orders with a gentle tact, yet no man failed to obey. He could be impetuous, volcanic, rash; he was capable of passionate tempers; but with the exception of two errors of judgment during four long expeditions, he acted consistently

159

as a scientific explorer of boldness, imagination and integrity.

Fearless frontiersmen, indomitable characters, hunters, trappers, explorers, all had the utmost respect for John Fremont, considered it a privilege to serve under him even in the face of death. Kit Carson, who acted as his guide on two dangerous expeditions, treated him as an equal as a frontiersman and as a beloved friend. A group of Delaware Indians followed him as their master for many years; none but a brave and instinctively wise man could have maintained such devotion.

Most of the friends he made remained loyal to him all of his days: generous, of deep and earnest sympathies, a poet both by nature and expression, himself capable of lifelong friendships, he could inspire and maintain love in others. Yet like so many of those who Also Ran, he was another of America's *génie manqué:* something was lacking in his character or his brain, that last mysterious element which would have enabled him to rise to full stature and achieve greatness.

He was an indefatigable worker; he could endure the most devastating hardships without even disliking them: starvation, burning heat and freezing cold, agonizing thirst, the tortures of unceasing pain, the immediacy of violent death, none of these frightened or distressed him. He marched himself and his men into dangers against which the hardiest frontiersmen had warned him; he found passes through the glacial Sierras when Indians who had spent their lives in the mountains swore there were no passes; with one tragic exception he conquered the insuperable difficulties by sheer force of will.

Combined with the hard steel of his mind and slight body was the sentimentalism of the Gallic romantic and poet. He was a careerist, an opportunist, yet he never tried to serve his own career unless he were serving the interests of his country and his people first. Sometimes he was cruel, as with the Indians who attacked settlers, but more often he was generous with his opponents. He was never vulgar, petty or base; he never would accept slaves as gifts, and refused to use them in his gold mine when their cheap labor could have netted him additional millions.

Many times he had his hands wrapped securely around success, only to have that fragile dish fall and shatter to a thousand pieces: by his third expedition he had established himself as the outstanding trail blazer of his day, only to embark on an unwarranted fourth which ended in disaster and cost him part of his reputation; he played an important role in the conquest of California, was its first American governor, only to be dismissed from his post, taken back to Washington a prisoner and court-martialed; he discovered gold on

160

his apparently worthless land in California, becoming a millionaire, only to go broke through frenzied finance; he was appointed one of the first major generals by President Lincoln at the outbreak of the Civil War, saved Missouri from capture by the Confederacy and achieved fame as the first issuer of an emancipation proclamation, only to be cashiered and retired in disgrace; he became the shining star of a new and great movement arising from the plains of America, only to be defeated and turned aside, while the party surged forward to triumph. In his every success there was contained the germ of his next defeat; in every defeat, the seed of his next victory. Like Winfield Scott his career rode a Ferris wheel: every time he was on top something happened to swing him to the bottom; on the bottom something propelled him to the top.

When John Charles Fremont was nominated for president by the newly formed Republican party in 1856, Emerson, Whittier, Walt Whitman, Washington Irving and other outstanding literary lights, artists and intellectuals sang his praises and wrote poems about him. University presidents and professors campaigned for him under the charge that "it was the duty of the American scholar" to elect him. Henry Ward Beecher and other religious leaders fought for him as leading a mighty crusade. Greeley of the *Tribune,* Dana of the *Sun,* Bryant of the *Evening Post,* and most of the other outstanding editors gave him their papers and their eulogies.

The spontaneity and rapidity with which Fremont Clubs sprang up all over the country was not to be equaled until the advent of the Willkie Clubs in 1940. Giant crowds gathered to hear speeches about Fremont: thirty thousand in Kalamazoo, thirty-five thousand in Alton; the rally in Indianapolis took five hours to pass the reviewing stands, fifty bands played along the line of march, almost five thousand men parading in one unit alone, and at night "a torchlight procession which turned the streets into streams of fire."

Something tremendous was on the march in the fall of 1856, sweeping the nation into a fervor and ecstasy. New forces were at play, new social and political ideologies aborning, a new political party surging forward with an irresistible force.

And a new national hero was in the making: ex-Captain John Charles Fremont, with his hair parted neatly in the center, his eyes strong and sad and quiet, his face covered with a young, pointed beard, his wiry body small, taut, indestructible.

What had made John Charles Fremont the most colorful and dramatic character on the American stage? Why had both parties tendered him the nomination, with the reasonable certainty that he would be elected no matter which offer he accepted?

2

His mother, Anne Whiting, came of one of the best Virginia families, her father having been an important figure in the Virginia House of Burgesses. Colonel Whiting died when Anne was young, and the family fortune was dissipated by a stepfather; at seventeen the girl was married off to sixty-year-old John Pryor of Richmond. After twelve years of fractional marriage Anne fell in love with a young and romantic French refugee who had fled his country during the revolution and was now working as a teacher of French in a fashionable academy in Richmond. The young couple were happy in their intimacy for about a year; then Pryor learned of the relationship and threatened to kill his wife. The following morning Anne and Frémon were gone. Anne seemed to have some small resources, which Frémon supplemented in their wanderings by teaching French, working as a fresco painter and upholsterer.

On January 21, 1813, a year and a half after the couple fled Richmond, John Charles Fremont was born in Savannah. There may have been a marriage performed, but since the Virginia legislature had refused to grant Pryor a divorce by the time of the arrival of Anne's first son, the ceremony could not be considered legal.

Frémon died when Anne was thirty-four, at which time she moved to Charleston with her three children. Though her money was gone and Charleston knew of her irregular elopement, she was accepted everywhere because of her family, which was reputed to be connected with the Washingtons, and because the important French colony in Charleston was pleased about the French blood in the children.

John Fremont favored his father in appearance: slender, wiry, quick of movement, restless, with unbounded physical energy and the beautiful dark eyes of the Gallic race, a "very handsome lad, with dark hair, olive skin and snapping eyes." His warm charm and pleasant personality made the boy popular in Charleston. At sixteen he entered college to study botany, chemistry, astronomy and mathematics, in which he stood at the top of his class. John had inherited much of the mental strength of his grandfather, Colonel Whiting, for his mind was quick as a cat: he learned fast, retained well, correlated what he knew and used it to advantage.

He had the makings of a first-rate nature, yet he lacked

one essential quality, a lack which was to dominate his entire life, bring him fame and fortune and, ultimately, failure: emotional stability.

After a year and a half of college, during which he had made a brilliant record, he stopped going to classes because he had fallen in love with a beautiful Creole girl, Cecelia, and was too much in ecstasy wandering the hills and sailing the bay to bother with discipline or books. Threatened with expulsion, failure to graduate, John smiled his warm though reserved smile and continued to pass the hours with Cecelia. The school put him out.

He worked for a time as a teacher, and then in a library, reading books on travel and exploration which excited his alert and adventuresome mind. When he was only nineteen he began a series of friendships which were to make him the best-trained man in his field, honored for his contributions by the scientific societies of Europe. His charm brought him friends, his brain enabled him to keep them.

The first of his friends was Joel Poinsett, congressman, minister to Mexico, world traveler and cultivated gentleman. Poinsett enjoyed Fremont's flashing spirit and mercurial mind, first secured him a position as instructor of mathematics on the navy ship *Natchez*, and later as a surveyor for a proposed railroad between Charleston and Cincinnati. Pleased with Fremont's work, his superior officer, a West Point graduate, chose the boy as an assistant to survey the country into which the Cherokee Indians were being moved. He received invaluable training from the army officer; this journey of exploration, surveying and map making brought him endless delight, for he loved the nomadic out-of-doors life, was uncomfortable and cramped in the civilization of cities.

John Charles Fremont decided to make exploration his lifework. No young man ever made a decision which fitted more perfectly his nature, his talents, and the opportunities of the times.

When Joel Poinsett was appointed secretary of war by President Van Buren he secured for Fremont a commission as second lieutenant in the Topographical Corps of the army, and immediately attached him to the Nicollet party just leaving Washington to make the first official maps of the unexplored country between the Mississippi and Missouri rivers. Once again Fremont enjoyed a piece of good fortune, for Nicollet was one of the world's outstanding scientists of exploration.

Himself of French blood, Nicollet took a great liking to Fremont, made of him almost a son, training him thoroughly in the crafts of surveying, sketching, map making, astronomy,

163

topography, geology, botany. John Fremont made good on the Nicollet expedition, for he was a "natural" when it came to frontier life, as Winfield Scott had been at soldiering. Exposed for months to the finest guides, hunters, trappers, trail blazers, scouts and Indian traders, he sopped up their knowledge and skill with the thirst of the ardent young man who was even more passionate about his work than he had been about Cecelia.

He spent the better part of three years in the wilds of the northwest, sketching the country, surveying, setting down descriptions of everything he saw. When the expedition was completed he returned to Washington with Nicollet to draw up a full report of their findings. Fremont and Nicollet went to live in the house of a distinguished scientist by the name of Hassler, the greatest map maker of his day. Hassler too became attached to Fremont and continued his training.

Only twenty-seven, appealing in his army uniform, genteel, polished, skilled, well read, confident, with a tremendous warmth of manner, liked and respected by his associates, already a little known from having been associated with the Nicollet expedition and the Hassler maps, the son of the French refugee was on his way to success. He was now to make his most important union, with the beautiful and brainy Jessie Benton, daughter of the resolute senator from Missouri, which was to open the heavy doors of the future and make him the best-known frontiersman of his age, the popularizer of exploration and of the lands of the west.

Jessie Benton was only sixteen when she fell in love with Fremont, but already she was a mature woman, of iron resolutions and magnificent loyalties, well educated by her father, who had made her his companion and confidante, admired in Washington circles as a lovely and promising girl. She could have had her pick of Washington or southern society, so it is perhaps not to be wondered at that her father was outraged when she chose, at so early an age, to fall in love with a penniless army lieutenant of questionable birth and resources.

In an effort to halt the headlong courtship Senator Benton, one of the most fiery expansionists in Congress, secured Fremont a commission to head an expedition which was to survey and map the Des Moines River in the Iowa Territory. Though the separation was painful to Fremont, he proved in the six months' journey that he could assemble and command an expedition successfully; the material he brought back enabled Nicollet and Hassler to complete the map making of the entire region.

When, after many tempestuous scenes, Senator Benton had at last to face the fact of his daughter's marriage to Fremont, he took the young couple into his spacious home, proved himself a model father-in-law by working to have a Far West expedition authorized with Lieutenant Fremont in command. It was 1840; the times sorely needed trail blazers. Fremont had the best scientific training of any young American at precisely the time when the people were clamoring to have Oregon, California and Texas become part of the United States, at the time when the great migration westward was about to begin.

Fremont took part in the discussions going on constantly in Benton's home concerning the need for new and less dangerous trails to Oregon and California which, once filled with Americans, must inevitably cease to be British and Mexican. "The discussions gave shape and solidity to my own crude ideas," said Fremont. "I felt that I was being drawn into the current of important political events. The object of this expedition was not merely a survey; beyond that was its bearing on the holding of our territory on the Pacific."

Thus even before he had been put in charge of his first major expedition, John Fremont had coupled his two desires: to map and chart scientifically the wilderness between the Mississippi and the Pacific; to use these expeditions as mechanisms with which to secure further expansion of the United States.

Congress appropriated thirty thousand dollars for the army expedition. Nicollet was old and ill, he wanted Fremont to command; it was agreed in official circles that the twenty-nine-year-old lieutenant was Nicollet's successor and heir. He was to command three brilliant journeys in all, by means of which he won fame for himself, aided immeasurably the westward migration, and played an important role in securing California from Mexico. On these three expeditions he achieved the height of his adventure, of his value and his contribution.

3

He left for St. Louis to assemble his party: topographers, hunters, trappers and, by a lucky meeting, Kit Carson as his guide. It was a well-organized expedition, carefully guarded against the dangers of the wilderness, and carrying such scientific equipment as a sextant, telescope, barometer.

Fremont's outstanding qualities emerged at once: he was calm in all emergencies, had no sense of physical fear; he was indefatigable, this man of slight stature, outworking the strongest of his crew. After a long day's march, when the rest of the camp was asleep, he would sit by the campfire to write his observations, draw sketches and rough maps, file away the botanical and geological specimens he had collected since sunup, and finally take his bearings by the stars.

He wound up the Kansas River Valley, crossed to the Platte, climbed into the Rockies, explored the Wind River Mountains of highest Wyoming, then carried out his appointed task of traversing and mapping South Pass. He was gone until October first, traveled through hundreds of miles of uncharted country with only a single mishap: he impetuously decided to use his new collapsible rubber boat to descend the cataracts of the Platte. The boat overturned, most of the heavy scientific equipment, foodstuffs and guns were lost, the party left at the mercy of the countryside and the Indians.

Fremont knew that his next step must be to have Congress authorize an expedition to Oregon for the following spring, a plan in which the expansionists joined wholeheartedly. He sat down at his desk to write his report, not as a dry factual journal, but as a literary effort, one which would serve as an impetus to western migration.

For three days Lieutenant Fremont sat; for three days his head pounded; for three days not a word emerged. When on the fourth day Jessie went into her husband's study and found him in the midst of a nosebleed from having been concentrating too long and too hard indoors, she took his face in her hands and said:

"My dearest, for weeks you have been telling me the story of your journey, making me see and smell and feel the country. Why not let me write it down just as you tell it?"

Fremont was elated at the idea, as indeed he had reason to be, for Jessie's was the sharper intellectual mind, better trained in the matter of books and writing. Each day they worked together, Fremont reliving his adventures, Jessie by her adroit questions helping him to expand to his subject.

Fremont was both a naturalist and a poet; his notes on the fields of wild flowers, on the icy lakes of the Rockies, the beauties of the forest at night would have done credit to Thoreau. Jessie had a creative flair, with lean values and impeccable taste; by their collaboration they produced a report that was one of the finest pieces of exploration literature the world had known. He was praised in Congress, which ordered a thousand copies to be printed for distribution; the newspapers reprinted it for their readers; accolades were bestowed by the scholars and scientific societies of Europe.

The report assured him another expedition, this time to more distant fields. It was to be his task to demonstrate that the Oregon Trail was both accessible and safe. This time he equipped what was called the best-fitted expedition, private or governmental, that ever had been assembled in the United States. His party consisted of thirty-nine men, well armed, a covered wagon for his scientific apparatus, and a cannon.

Somehow the War Department in Washington heard about the cannon. Since Fremont was going on a peaceful expedition, what need had he for the cannon? Relations with England and Mexico were in a delicate state, which Fremont's artillery might blow up. A letter was dispatched from the Topographical Department summoning him back to Washington to explain his conduct. If he returned someone else would have to be put in command, or the expedition be disbanded, for it would be too late to leave.

Jessie Benton Fremont received the letter while Fremont was with his party at Kaw Landing, four hundred miles from St. Louis, jumping-off-place for the Oregon Trail. Seeing the expansionist dream of empire crash, along with her husband's career, she dispatched a horseback rider to Fremont with the message: "Do not lose a day. Start at once, upon the receipt of my letter."

In a few days a messenger returned with a reply from Fremont. It read:

"I trust, and go."

Starting out on the Sante Fe Trail he found it an almost continuous train of covered wagons moving westward. Failing to discover a new pass to Oregon which would be easier and safer, he pushed on to Salt Lake, which he explored and mapped, then led his men through a falling winter to the Columbia River and Walla Walla. Up to this point he merely had made a scientific survey of a much-traveled trail; having no further orders he could have returned by the same route. But Lieutenant Fremont was not content to be a trail marker; he wished also to be an explorer and empire builder. No white man ever had traversed the vast region southward between Walla Walla and what is now Reno; he had no authority to do so; he was not adequately equipped; most of it was foreign territory. Yet he and his men made their way painfully through the snow and ice and wilderness, through bitter hunger and exhaustion, without complaint, finally emerging, utterly spent, on the Truckee River.

Here he could have rested and recouped on the ample game and fish of the region, returning to Washington with important new material. However, he had set his heart on reaching California. Without waiting to rest his men or animals he plunged blindly into the vast, frozen, uncharted Sierras, originating the slogan which was to move so much traffic

167

along the Lincoln Highway a century later: California or bust!

The Indians he met assured him that the Sierras were impenetrable at that point, urged him to turn back lest he perish. Fremont exhorted his men, in sub-zero weather, snowblind, skeletons living on dog meat, facing endless chains of icy crags, to push forward, to think of the opulent Sacramento Valley only seventy miles away—according to his calculations. He was headstrong, reckless of his men and himself; he was whipped, his men knew he was whipped, but he would not stop. He had destiny in his blood, and he was going to fulfill that destiny.

When it was obvious that the party could proceed no farther Fremont took a picked group, including Kit Carson, and explored for a pass that would take them down into the Sacramento Valley. Suffering such torture as only the tragic Donner Party could have known, unflinching, his slight figure cutting through the snow and ice and gales, John Charles Fremont found his pass, led his entire expedition down into the safety of the Sacramento Valley. He had forced the crossing without losing a man. It was a great feat, not only of human strength and courage, but of navigation as well, for Fremont had found his pass at precisely the point where his sextant told him the valley must lie.

He was never happier nor more alive than when in the wilderness or on the icy ranges: hardship was nothing to him, he could conquer where stronger men trembled and died; for in conquering hardship he was conquering the one element he never could change nor obliterate, his illegal birth, the sense of being a social outcast. In the wilderness, at the head of his men, the last had become first.

While his party was being outfitted at Sutter's Fort, Fremont investigated central California, gathered material on the Mexican California situation. Then he led his men back to St. Louis, never taking established routes, always seeking out the unexplored, hoping to further chart the wastelands.

In collaboration with Jessie he wrote his second report, which proved to be more valuable and exhilarating than the first, a warm, human, colorful, authentic, endlessly dramatic and poetic account of his adventures and the new lands he had seen. Congress ordered ten thousand copies to be printed; it was published in book form, sold widely. Fremont found himself the hero of the hour, was promoted by General Winfield Scott to be a captain, praised by Secretary of State Buchanan, against whom he was to run for the presidency twelve years later.

War was brewing with Mexico while he prepared his third

expedition. It was agreed in unofficial congressional conversation that if the war had started by the time he reached California, Captain Fremont was to see to it that the state did not fall into the hands of the British, that it became a part of the United States. The captain took sixty well-armed sharpshooters with him; California was sparsely settled, and Fremont's sixty men became the nucleus of a conquering army.

He made the passage of the Sierras easily, before snow fell, again descending into the Sacramento Valley. There was no reason for him to remain there, but he was convinced that war would begin, and John Fremont had every intention of using his expedition for military purposes. He settled with his men near San Jose where they rested, hunted and botanized, killing time. At last Captain Fremont received orders from General Castro, commanding the Mexican forces, to leave California under pain of arrest. Fremont replied that his country had been insulted, that he would resist. He established a fort on top of a hill, raised the American flag and prepared to give battle.

For all this he had not one line of written authority.

On advice of the American consul at Monterey he retired after a few defiant days, slowly winding his way out of Mexican territory into Oregon. Here he dallied until two army officers reached him with official dispatches which had been written in Washington months before, telling him to be prepared for an outbreak of hostilities. By a dramatic coincidence war with Mexico had begun that very day. Fremont had no way of knowing this, except that his intuition—his most dependable weapon—told him so. He marched his men back into California, swore in volunteers, and bloodlessly captured the Mexican fort at Sonoma. He encouraged the American settlers to rise in the Bear Flag revolt and establish California as a republic; this having been accomplished he took command of the force, organized the California Battalion and captured central and northern California for the United States with a loss of ten lives.

Captain Fremont now combined with Commodore Stockton, and with all his men was sworn into the navy and transported on American warships to San Diego, where he cut off the Mexican supply line, marched on General Castro in Los Angeles, again joined with Commodore Stockton's men and made an almost bloodless conquest of southern California. Under appointment of Commodore Stockton as the first civilian governor of California, he granted the Mexicans a friendly and generous peace. He was doing a good job as an executive with progressive rather than militarist ideas when complications began.

General Kearny, coming overland with a force of soldiers, was defeated by a group of still hostile Californios and had to be rescued by Fremont and Stockton. Both Kearny and Stockton had been instructed to institute civil government in California when that territory had been conquered. Fremont was an army officer, yet his work in southern California had been done as a naval officer under Stockton. Stockton was his friend; the two men worked extremely well together; he knew that General Kearny was a martinet, hard to work with. Caught between Commodore Stockton and General Kearny on the question of command, he elected to recognize Commodore Stockton as the highest authority in California. This was a mistake in judgment, for he was an officer of the United States Army and had been one for eight years. His permanent allegiance was to the army; he should have recognized General Kearny, who subsequently received orders from Washington to take sole command of the state. Captain Fremont was placed under arrest, hauled back to Washington a virtual prisoner, vindictively refused permission to take with him his scientific equipment, maps, charts, botanical and geological specimens, all of which he needed to write and document his third report.

President Polk wanted the quarrel to blow over, but Fremont and Senator Benton insisted upon a public court-martial as the only means of securing a complete investigation. John Fremont, with his dark eyes and distinguished manner, became a *cause célèbre*. He was charged with conduct prejudicial to discipline, disobedience of lawful command, and mutiny. The case received tremendous space in the papers; his exploits in helping to win California became known nationally and were largely responsible for his nomination to the presidency ten years later.

A jury of West Point officers found him guilty on all three charges. The press almost universally resented the verdict. President Polk pardoned Fremont, ordering him to "resume his sword and report for duty." Emotionally volcanic, Fremont refused the pardon on the grounds that it implied his guilt; he resigned from the army and put an end to his useful career. He wrote no report on the third expedition; on his fourth expedition, privately financed for the purpose of finding a railroad route through the Rockies, he failed to force a crossing, lost his equipment and eleven of his men in one of the west's major pioneering catastrophes, barely reaching California alive.

Before leaving for Washington he had handed the American consul the sum of three thousand dollars, almost his total resources, to buy him a fertile stretch of ranch land to which

170

he intended to bring Jessie and the children and settle down permanently. Instead of buying the piece that Fremont had chosen, Larkin spent the money, or some part of it, for an isolated piece of land, overrun by Indians, called the Mariposa Ranch. When Jessie and the children joined Fremont in San Francisco they were practically destitute, without plans or future.

Then, in one of those flashes of fortune which spun the Fremont wheel of life, gold was discovered on the Mariposa Ranch! John Charles Fremont rapidly became one of the few millionaires of the day. As "the colonel" he was the single best-known man in California, was elected to represent the new state in the United States Senate. Repatriated, there followed a long visit to Europe with Jessie and the children, where honors were heaped upon him, and his popularity continued to grow. Once again he seemed destined to play an important role in American life.

The nomination for the presidency afforded him that opportunity. Would he who had been court-martialed and broken out of the army in disgrace now return to Washington as president of the United States?

4

The Democrats were the first to approach him, offering the nomination on condition that he endorse the enforcement of the Fugitive Slave Law, that he sanction the introduction of slaves into Kansas and the new territories. Fremont had refused to use slave labor in his mines in California; Jessie consistently had refused to accept slaves from her family and friends as gifts, though sometimes she had to do heavy housework herself. After careful thought Fremont informed the Democratic leaders that he was against the extension of slavery, and the offer was withdrawn.

The Republican party had been organized a few months before by a group of Wisconsin citizens, and the idea had spread like a prairie fire. A young man was wanted for the young party; a vigorous man to represent its vigorous beliefs; a dashing, daring, courageous man to represent its revolutionary attitudes; a man who had been out of the Kansas and slavery warfares, who would not bring old hatreds and enmities to the new party; a man who was known throughout the nation, about whom a legend could be spun.

John Charles Fremont fitted this description almost miraculously. His name was mentioned with the very birth of the party; the movement in his direction gained strength with the passing of the weeks. The New York *Tribune* said, "A sort of intrusive feeling pervades the people that Fremont will be nominated and elected. He seems to combine more elements of strength than any man who has yet been named." Fremont himself was pleased but did nothing to further his candidacy.

The first Republican convention met in Philadelphia in June of 1856 and, with the hot-eyed fervor of a revival meeting, nominated Fremont on the second ballot. Instantly a huge pennant: JOHN CHARLES FREMONT FOR PRESIDENT! was strung across the hall, and the thousand delegates went mad with joy, shouting, cheering, singing, crying. One of the most telling campaign slogans in American politics was originated:

FREE SPEECH, FREE PRESS, FREE SOIL,
FREE MEN, FREMONT AND VICTORY!

A wave of enthusiasm not to be duplicated until the Bryan campaign of 1896 swept the country. Newspapers of the north, midwest, northwest and west published his praises in endless eulogistic articles; poetry was written, songs composed, his portrait hung in shopwindow and home, campaign biographies were read widely, torchlight parades and mass meetings were held in all non-slave cities. Women, for the first time, campaigned, sang songs about "Jessie Bent-on Being Free"; the clergy, the educators, the intellectuals, the artists and writers gave their time and talents. Voluntary campaigners by the thousands took to the stump; thousands of halls shook with Republican oratory. Bear Clubs sprang up in California; young men's clubs called "The Wide Awakes" spread across the land; roads were clogged with every manner of vehicle carrying enthusiasts to town to work for Free Soil, Free Men, Fremont, and Victory. "The Northern heart was fired as it never had been before."

The Pathfinder was going to find a path through the impenetrable wilderness of slavery.

Fremont's record and character lent themselves to enthusiasm, but the fever of the drive was for the eradication of slavery, the taking of national power from the south-dominated Democrats. He became the center not of a campaign but of a religious, moral and ethical crusade, the most intense since 1800 when Thomas Jefferson created the Democratic party. In 1800 Jefferson and the Democrats had been bitterly assailed as radical, exactly as Fremont and the Republicans now were assailed as radical in 1856.

The Democrats were badly frightened, for had not they too tried to cash in on the popularity of Fremont? Through the early summer months it appeared that nothing could stem the tidal wave from overwhelming "Old Obliquity" Buchanan, Democratic wheel horse, mollifier, political corkscrew. Thereupon was organized the dirtiest campaign in the American political record. The Catholics were voting solidly against Fremont because they thought him sympathetic to the Know-Nothing or anti-Catholic forces, yet the Democrats started a whisper going that Fremont was a Catholic, practicing his Catholicism in secret, believing in Catholic control of the United States, thereby alienating the Know-Nothing vote and an astonishingly large bloc of the Protestant vote. Just as in 1928 Alfred E. Smith would in part be defeated by the vicious whispering campaign that the White House would be ruled by the Pope, John Fremont was in part defeated in 1856 by a religious issue, false in fact and false in implication. An Episcopalian, he refused to make a public denial of the charge that he was a Catholic on the grounds that he would not appeal for votes through religious fanaticism.

Having rejected the Democratic nomination because he would not sanction slavery, he now was publicly accused of being a slaveowner and slave trader; a man of impeccable honesty and integrity, he was charged with being a swindler, a manipulator of money, an appropriator of public funds. An abstemious man, he was accused of being a drunkard; because his father had been born in France he was labeled a foreigner, a French actor, a bastard of low birth; because of the court-martial he was branded a mutineer, a usurper of authority. A gentle man of indestructible loyalties, he was alleged to have mistreated the unfortunate Californios, to have deserted his men and caused their death on the ill-fated fourth expedition: "a shallow, vain-glorious, mule-eating, free love, nigger-embracing, Black Republican, a financial spendthrift and political mountebank."

Much of the muck was effective, costing Fremont great blocs of votes. At this point, in 1856, the democracy still had not solved the fundamental problem of how it could maintain a free press while controlling criminally irresponsible slander during elections. By 1940 political manners would improve a trifle, but the problem of controlling poison pens and poison tongues still would not be solved. People were saying that it was a dilemma which never could be resolved, that if election campaigns were restricted to a telling of the pure truth, if impersonal issues alone were permitted, such action would constitute a deathblow to the basic freedoms of speech and press. Other observers, witnessing the passions unleashed by ungrounded personal slander, believed that if this type of manufactured invective were not outlawed it one day might be the reef upon which democracy could be shattered.

The most important strategy waged by the Democrats was the fiery threat that if Fremont were elected the southern states would secede from the Union. A politician by the name of Toombs typified the thousands of incendiary speeches being made in the south when he cried to a frenzied assemblage, "The election of Fremont would be an end to the Union, and ought to be. The object of Fremont's friends is the conquest of the south. I am content that they should own us when they have conquered us, and not before."

The south declared Fremont a traitor to his country, while the north looked upon him as an emancipator. But with the south girding itself for war, a considerable portion of the north did not want an emancipator at the cost of a rebellion. Chief among these was Senator Thomas Benton, who came out against his son-in-law and the Republicans as a sectional and geographic party which would rend the nation. Many honest northerners, such as Rufus Choate, the sons of Clay and Webster, opposed Fremont on the grounds that his election would bring disunion.

Fremont was dazed by the fratricidal passions that had been unloosed, suffering keenly under the hysteria and dementia which four years later were to drive the south into a war which would lay them waste for half a century. Through the bitterest of the turmoil he kept as calm and dignified as he had in the dire peril of his explorations. He remained quietly at his home on Ninth Street in New York City, refusing to answer the canards or sanction similar attacks, welcoming people at his home, speaking to them simply and informally, conducting himself with the utmost of breeding, taste and public spirit.

"The campaign was full of personalities," writes Fremont's daughter; "my father was used to life in the open and wanted a square fight." However the Democrats were fighting a catch-as-catch-can brawl and didn't give a hoot for the Marquis of Queensberry rules.

In spite of the tremendous Republican spirit there was little money available with which to finance a campaign—as so often happens in a popular movement. The Democrats on the other hand had a great deal of money, about ten dollars for every one in the Republican coffers. Money was needed desperately to wage the campaign in Pennsylvania and two other doubtful states; if these could be won, the election would be won. But the new party simply could not match the contributions given to the Democrats by those interested in the southern trade: fifty thousand dollars by August Belmont, a hundred thousand by Wall Street financiers. The Republicans lamented that they were being defeated by the monied interests, a charge that would be brought against them by the Democrats only a few years later.

Slander, the threat of secession, and a lack of campaign funds defeated John Charles Fremont for the presidency. He carried eleven states to Buchanan's seventeen, received 1,341,264 votes against 1,838,169 for Buchanan.

Although the Republicans ostensibly were defeated, actually they had scored an astonishing success: completely unknown and unorganized only five months before, they had come within a half million votes of unseating the oldest party in the country. The results boded so well for 1860 that there were immediate plans to renominate Fremont: it was evident that his reputation and demeanor had helped popularize the Republican cause.

Fremont took his defeat quietly and with good grace. He knew that although the election had been a victory for his party, it was a defeat for him. Too much dust had been kicked up, too many names called, too many charges levied. He would not be nominated again; he would never be president of the United States.

5

What kind of president would John Charles Fremont have made?

Would he have been better than James Buchanan?

Might he have saved the nation from the civil war which followed four years later?

He would have found the president's desk at the White House very different from the unexplored South Pass of the Rockies; he would have found his task far more difficult and dangerous than his hardiest exploit in the wilderness. He had had little political training; would he become snow-blind in the wastelands of professional politics?

He would have been a strong president. If in a democracy the weakest and least government is the most and best government, perhaps the kind of strength that Fremont possessed is not the highest desideratum in a president: the greater his strength the greater may be his will to usurp the alternative powers of government, take away the power from the people's representatives.

John Fremont liked to be the sole commander; he disliked restraint over him; he acted without authority when he thought it necessary. He had in him the germ of the dictator: when one member of his expedition expressed conscientious scruples against joining Fremont's California Battalion for the purpose of waging war on Mexico, he had him jailed

175

overnight in Sutter's Fort to change his mind. He began a war with General Castro without specific orders, captured the fort at Sonoma, organized an American army and captured northern California, all without authorization. The peace terms he granted to the Mexicans, though wise and generous, were not in his power to grant, for he was second in command under Commodore Stockton. When he became major general of the Department of the West in 1861 he issued an emancipation proclamation for the slaves of rebels in his district without authority from President Lincoln, threw the north into an uproar and forced the president to rescind the order as untimely and precipitate.

How would John Charles Fremont have behaved as chief executive of the land? Would he have been irked at the system of checks and balances imposed upon all three branches of the government? Would he have tried to browbeat and imprison overnight the Congress and the Supreme Court until they came around to his way of thinking, insisted upon being the King who could do no wrong?

Fremont had a deep sense of love and loyalty for the American tradition; he was a man of culture, refinement and grace; he understood and liked the common people; he was intimately acquainted with every farflung section of the vast continent. He was a man of action rather than thought, more comfortable on the trail than at a desk, yet he had spent years over desks with Nicollet and Hassler, done the close, confining work of map making and done it so well that he was considered one of the best in the world. His scientific training would have been of value to him in the presidency, for it would have given him a method with which to attack problems; the respect felt for his accomplishments in Europe would have added cachet to the American government.

Fremont had been brought up to respect the congressional tradition, he had been a tactful and gentle leader on his expeditions, he had behaved superbly during the election; there is reason to believe that he would have been a good leader. For the most part he would have accepted the will of the people as expressed by the Congress with the same confidence that he had accepted the guidance of Kit Carson on the wilderness trails. If on certain critical matters he had tried to expand the powers of the president, he would have done so for the good of the people as he saw that good, not for personal aggrandizement; in so doing he would have carried on the tradition, begun by Jefferson and implemented by Jackson, of strengthening the executive's powers.

One of Fremont's biographers angrily accuses him of having played too little part in the bringing of peace and order

176

to California, avers that he had no sense of statesmanship, had neither experience, liking nor cleverness for the making of civil government. Fremont's two experiences with civil government refute this charge: even Buchanan agreed that he had done an excellent job as governor of California, while during his brief term as senator from California "he introduced eighteen useful bills to satisfy the political and economic needs of his state," voted with other free-soilers to abolish the slave trade in the District of Columbia, showed a good grasp of the political economy of the day.

Sent into St. Louis as a major general and commander of the west in the early days of the Civil War to take over Missouri and the neighboring states, obliged to work without supplies, money or men, Fremont did a superb job of organization; he trained recruits and instilled a high morale into his forces, set up a unified transportation system, made St. Louis safe for the Union and relieved the Federal forces at Cairo, worked twenty hours a day at his overwhelming task of bringing order out of chaos. He also equipped gunboats, his own idea, as was the buying of arms in Europe without governmental approval when he was caught there at the outbreak of the war. In his frenzy of work he made mistakes: he surrounded himself by a general staff of European officers, made himself unavailable to private citizens, gave contracts to some of the wrong people, was frequently cheated. His accomplishments outweighed his faults, but the pressure of his opponents caused President Lincoln to remove him after a hundred days of command.

He was rash, impetuous, headstrong, self-willed. These charges are substantiated by his utilizing of the newfangled rubber boat on the Platte; by his insistence that his men push through the icy wall of the Sierras; by his insistence upon taking new routes and covering unfamiliar ground when there were safe trails available; by his early emancipation of the slaves in his district. Yet these are the charges brought against pioneers in all fields: the arts, the sciences, the professions, the humanities. Fremont simply used initiative, imagination, and daring; without such men this world would have remained undeveloped. For years he was on the trail and in the wilderness, making thousands of decisions, and with very little exception his judgment had proved sound and effective.

For his expeditions Fremont had selected unerringly the best men in the country, but later when it came to business and finance his trusting nature made him gullible. When his Mariposa mines fell into debt he turned over the business of incorporation and exploitation to a set of sharks who defrauded him of most of his holdings. In 1870, when he had lost the remnants of his fortune trying to build a railroad from Norfolk to San Diego, he permitted more than five million dollars' worth of bonds to be sold in France by agents who misrepresented to the French people. He knew nothing of the misrepresentation, but he had selected the men who proved to be dishonest. A great deal of his usefulness as president would have depended upon whether he chose his Washington associates with the penetration of his pioneering days or the naïveté of his business ventures.

Historians guess that if civil war had broken out in 1856 Buchanan would have made a better president than Fremont because he was an old hand at politics, a compromiser, because he knew how to twist, placate and wangle. The exact opposite might also be true: if civil war had broken out, John Charles Fremont, as a military man, would have been a great asset in the presidency. He would have taken immediate, bold, direct action which might have cut the ground out from under the revolt. He would have occupied with loyal troops all Federal property in the south: forts, armories, arsenals, camps, harbors, military fields. He ruthlessly would have confiscated the arms of the south, blockaded her harbors, arrested those southern politicians who were crying for revolt. He would have emancipated and armed the slaves, which would have complicated the south's effort to wage a war. He would have refused permission to army officers to resign and go over to the Confederacy; those who refused to fight for the Union would have been imprisoned; much of the fighting brains of the south would have been made unavailable.

He would have used force to prevent a secession by force; in so doing he would have been guilty of abridging civil liberties; in terms of the amount of blood shed and misery actually endured this may have been a lesser crime than Buchanan's abetting of the Civil War. Fremont would have struck like a hurricane to break the secession. Loving the south and its people, once the revolt was put down he not only would have granted them a friendly and generous peace, but would have used all available Federal funds to repair the damage, make the south well and strong again.

As a prewar president he would have been superior to Buchanan because he would have used every weapon at hand to prevent the south from arming for the struggle, as it did so effectively during Buchanan's administration. He would have prevented the nation's store of munitions from being raided by southern congressmen and cabinet officers, would have bought heavily of arms in Europe, built northern arsenals, ships, forts, set the factories humming with the manufacture of army supplies. He would have built up a strong Union army from the northwest and the west, an army of men who joyously would have followed the Pathfinder. He would have fought bitterly the seditious and mutinous talk of southern politicians and the southern press, policed the southern cities with a peacetime army whose presence would have outraged the south but which would have prevented it from preparing for war until every available solution to the problem of slavery had been worked out.

For four years weak and irresolute Buchanan shut his eyes to the arming of the south, granted concession after concession, maintained as his secretary of war Jefferson Davis, the most rabid of the southern Fire Eaters, justifying each surrender with "Peace for our Times," bringing the United States toward flames and destruction: he was the worst possible man for the presidency at that particular moment in American history. Described as "obtuse and small statured," he spent the major portion of the four years playing politics, more interested in his personal feuds and power than in the unity of the nation—even as Pierce had been before him.

Four years before, the people had had to choose between Pierce, an experienced politician, and Scott, who was without training in office. They had made a tragic blunder in Pierce. Once again they had had to choose between Buchanan, who had been a state legislator, member of Congress, secretary of state, and Fremont, whose knowledge of the inside workings of politics was derived from the expansionist discussions in his father-in-law's house. And once again the nation was saddled with the wrong kind of experience. What was wanted in a president was courage, vision, love of his people over his party. Pierce and Buchanan had none of these; they had only the disadvantages of experience: cutting the corners, picking up the marbles. In eight of the nation's most critical years the White House was occupied by small-minded politicians who had absorbed all the bad tricks of their profession without assimilating much of the good. Had either Winfield Scott or John Charles Fremont been elected there is a possibility that the Civil War might have been little more than a short-lived insurrection.

There are countless ways in which John Charles Fremont was superior to Buchanan: in brain power, in scientific training, in sensitivity, integrity, boldness, leadership, in culture, courage, character, loyalty and love of the entire nation. He had his weaknesses, his phobias, his limitations and his faults. Withal he was a good and brave man, built on heroic proportions. It would have been impossible for him to have done a worse job as president than Buchanan, or to have done more harm to his country.

179

If as a southerner Fremont could have placated the south or prevented them from arming for war, or swiftly crushed their uprising—and all three of these were possible—then the legend of Abraham Lincoln could have been the legend of John Charles Fremont.

By rejecting Fremont for the presidency, history missed one of its most potent "might-have-beens."

CHAPTER THREE

George B. McClellan

FROM THE MOMENT in August of 1861 that he was put at the head of the Army of the Potomac, the talk of making George Brinton McClellan the next Democratic presidential nominee began. This was not because he was considered a statesman or even an experienced politician—he had voted for the first time in 1860—but because the Democrats, weakened by the loss of the southern vote, were seeking for a man with sufficient popularity to give them a chance against Abraham Lincoln in 1864. The Democrats grabbed hold of his regimentals in precisely the fashion that the Republicans in 1942 would fasten onto General Douglas MacArthur for his thrilling defense of Bataan.

Only three years before, in 1858, McClellan had been vice-president of the Illinois Central Railroad. His company had engaged the services of Abraham Lincoln to defend them in a court case. At the last moment counsel for the defense had to request a postponement.

"Why is the company not ready to go to trial?" asked the judge.

"We are embarrassed by the absence, or rather want of information from Mr. McClellan," replied Lincoln.

It was an answer he was to make many times, some of them in anguish, during the months that General McClellan commanded the Union forces.

One evening President Lincoln, accompanied by Secretary Seward and Hay, called at McClellan's home to confer with him over the unsatisfactory progress of the war. They were informed by a domestic that the general was at an army wedding but would be back soon. For an hour the president and his aides waited in the drawing room until McClellan returned. Though informed that the president was waiting he went directly upstairs. After another half-hour Lincoln sent the servant after him. The man returned, murmuring apologetically:

"General McClellan has gone to bed."

"The president is nothing more than a well-meaning baboon," said McClellan of his commander-in-chief. "He is the original gorilla. What a specimen to be at the head of our affairs now!"

Summoned to a meeting of the president, the cabinet and the general staff, McClellan replied loftily to Lincoln's request that he divulge his plan for the coming campaign:

"If the president has confidence in me, then it is not right or necessary for him to trust my designs to the judgment of others. But if your confidence is so slight as to require the commanding general's opinions to be fortified by those of other persons, then you ought to replace me by someone who fully possesses your confidence."

It was a staggering brush-off. The general got both his wishes: he was permitted to leave without divulging his plans; later he was replaced.

"I understand there is a good deal of talk about making a dictator," remarked General McClellan to an officer of his staff.

"Mr. Lincoln, I suppose."

"Oh no," he replied, "it's me they're talking of."

Riding before his cheering troops, he commented, "How those brave fellows love me, and what a power that love places in my hands. What is there to prevent me from taking the government in my own hands?"

The officer to whom he was speaking replied, "General, don't mistake those men. As long as you lead them against the enemy they will adore you and die for you. But attempt to turn them against their government and you will be the first to suffer."

McClellan dug his spurs into his horse and dashed off in high dudgeon.

He was obsessed with the idea of becoming a dictator. In a series of astonishingly indiscreet letters to his wife he keeps referring to the subject: "I find myself in a new and strange position here," he writes from Washington. "President, Cabinet, General Scott all deferring to me. By some strange operation of magic I seem to have become THE power of the land. I almost think that were I to win some small success now I could become dictator or anything else that might please me."

George Brinton McClellan had been a manic depressive since childhood. He alternated between periods of arrogant confidence and wretched self-abasement. In his efforts to offset a gnawing sense of inferiority he was never able to think, "I want to become good at my job; I want to do it just as well as it can be done." He thought, "I've got to be better than everyone else in the world." He looked at everything through the lenses of how well he could lead or conquer it;

all problems revolved about him rather than their own characteristics. Though he tried to attribute his idea of dictatorship to the Democrats who hated Lincoln, most of the planning originated in his own mind. His attitude toward his superiors revealed the kind of insolence indulged in by men who are congenitally incapable of acknowledging that they have superiors because that would make them feel inferior.

"I have this moment received a dispatch from the president, who is terribly scared about Washington, and talks about the necessity of my returning in order to save it. Have just finished my reply to His Excellency! It is perfectly sickening to deal with such people."

His normal state was one of exaltation and supreme faith. "Everything here needs the hand of the master, and is getting it fast. 'Our George' the soldiers have taken it into their heads to call me. You can have no idea how the men brighten up when I go among them. I can see every eye glisten. I believe they love me from the bottom of their hearts. Wherever I go it seems to inspire the fullest confidence."

When he was halfway up or down the ladder he was capable of combining his arrogant confidence with his groveling fears in one sentence: "Any day may bring an order relieving me from command; if such a thing should happen, our cause is lost!" In the trough of depression his persecution mania blossomed. "I feel that the fate of a nation depends upon me, and that I have not one single friend at the seat of government. I am tired of public life; when I am doing the best I can for my country in the field, I know that my enemies are pursuing me more remorselessly than ever."

As an instructor at West Point he had prepared a paper on Napoleon's campaigns of 1812. This was an unfortunate accident; himself a short and stocky man, it is not long before he began to envisage himself in Napoleon's boots. When after his first successes his admirers changed his nickname from Little Mac to Little Napoleon, the die was cast. In his own mind he became the Man on Horseback.

"Crowds of the country people who have heard of me and read my proclamations come in from all directions to thank me, shake me by the hand and look at their 'liberator.' It is a proud and glorious thing to see a whole people looking up at me as their deliverer from tyranny."

Of all the leading generals, both Union and Confederate, who have come down through history, McClellan is the most forgotten. Yet President Lincoln one day "sitting in the October sunlight on a hillside with McClellan, had said, 'General, you have saved the country. You must remain in command and carry us through to the end.'" Few aside from scholars know that he ran against Lincoln for the presidency in 1864.

He saved Washington twice; he took over the disorganized and defeated remnants of the Union armies after Bull Run and built them into a powerful organization. He was a military engineer of insight and prowess; he won several of the important battles of the early campaigns; it was partly with his plans that General Grant put an end to the war. He was a strict disciplinarian but a superb morale builder: he took fastidious care of his men, went to great pains to see that they were well fed, clothed and armed; he never wasted human life. The men under General McClellan genuinely loved him, were always in high fighting spirits. He could command and lead; he could not follow or obey.

The New York *Times* stated: "We cannot fully account for his lack of success by pronouncing him the victim of circumstances, since he was rather the victim of temperament."

The story behind the temperament of George B. McClellan is a weird and most confounding one. His biography inevitably becomes a psychograph.

2

George Brinton McClellan came from one of the best Philadelphia families; his father had been a respected surgeon and professor of medicine, his grandfather fought as a lieutenant in the French and Indian Wars of 1763 and took part in the battle of Bunker Hill. George was born on December 3, 1826, the youngest of four children. From the outset he was conscious of the distinctions between classes, wanting to associate only with the "best people." He attended the University of Pennsylvania for two years and though he was not yet sixteen was admitted to West Point, an exception being made because of his precocity.

The cause of his inferiority complex has never been determined, but his character pattern immediately became evident. He was plunged into the deepest gloom: a neglect mania, the forerunner of a persecution phobia, bursting into full flower. "I am as much alone as if in a boat in the middle of the Atlantic," he wrote to his sister; "not a soul here cares or thinks of me—not one here would lift a finger to help me . . ."

His wailing was interrupted by the call to drill. By the time he returned he had made a complete swing of the cycle. "I feel so much encouraged by *my successful endeavors to do better than all the rest* that I feel like an entirely different person."

From the viewpoint of outward appearance there was little need for young George to be depressed or unhappy, for he was a fine-looking chap, with warm blue eyes, a light complexion, strong, symmetrical features and a rich stand of sand-colored hair. Though he was husky and strong, his figure sturdy and graceful from fencing and horseback riding, he never grew taller than five feet eight. His outward manner was gracious and lovable, the kind that inspires friendships. His lack of height, the fact that he was the youngest of four children, the youngest of his class at West Point, that his father, who perhaps spent too much time founding the Jefferson Medical College, went into debt and George was strapped for funds, these are the only clues to be found for his pathology. Somewhere in his nervous or glandular system lies concealed the cause of his instability, a flywheel missing on his overly fluid emotion.

At West Point he took to the southerners because he thought they had better manners, more social grace. He bragged to his family that he was at the head of his class, a distinction which none of his classmates at the earlier schools could have achieved "to save their lives." At graduation he delivered the valedictory address, then entered the Engineering Corps. In 1846 he was sent to Mexico to take part in the war; before leaving he penned another of his frequent letters revealing his strangely brooding ego-distortion:

"I am the only one of my class of engineers who is to go to Mexico, and I must confess that I have malice enough to want to show them that if I did not graduate at the head of my engineering class, I can nevertheless do something."

Both as an engineer in the siege of Vera Cruz and as commander of a section of artillery Lieutenant McClellan turned in a good job. He took care of his men, was ever considerate of their welfare. For this, for his warmth, his charm, his brightness, the men loved him. At the same time he despised his fellow officers, abusing them as incompetents: "He was one of the worst subordinates and best superiors that ever lived. As a subordinate he was restless, critical, often ill at ease and seemingly unwilling to co-operate. He knew what was best, and others were, in his estimation, ignorant or insincere."

While fighting in Mexico two horses were shot from under him, he was hit by grapeshot, and his life was saved when the hilt of his sword stopped a bullet. He did not like this proximity to death. During his brief span as commander of the Union forces in the Civil War no one ever saw him with his troops when a battle was in progress. "At Williamsburg he was twelve miles at the rear; at Seven Pines he was across the river; at Malvern Hill he sat smoking on the gunboat *Galena* with the thunders of the battle rolling about him, and Heintzelman sending messages that his absence depressed the men and that disastrous results might ensue."

It was at Antietam that he created a world's record. At ten o'clock in the evening, having instructed his officers how to fight their battle the next morning, he went to sleep in the comfortable Pry House and slept peacefully until the following eight o'clock, straight through the roar of Hooker's battle, which had been waging since dawn! So far behind the lines did General McClellan remain that one of his political opponents later would remark, "In the retreat General McClellan for the first time in his life was found in the front."

By the time he was twenty-one he had been cited for "gallant and meritorious conduct in battle," been brevetted a captain, had an early start on a brilliant career. Returning to West Point he soon undid himself by his quarrelsome nature, his fear that he was being slighted or not being given sufficient credit. He began a three-year series of brawls with his superiors by going over the head of the superintendent of West Point, refusing to relinquish command of his company until ordered to do so by Washington. He refused to attend compulsory chapel, informing Washington that he would attend only if it could be voluntary. His greatest row he caused over his quarters, which did not end until he had worn everyone out and been rebuked by the secretary of war for the offensive tone of his letters.

"I do not think I am of a quarrelsome disposition," he wrote plaintively to his sister, "but I do have the luck of getting into more trouble than any dozen other officers."

It wasn't luck; it was genius.

The next years George McClellan spent as an army engineer in the construction of forts, on an exploration of the Red River in Arkansas, in surveys of rivers and harbors in San Domingo and Texas. He did his work well, sometimes with an original flair, though on one expedition he failed to find either of the two available passes which would have made possible the wagon road he had been sent to locate. He was only twenty-eight when he was chosen as one of a commission of three army officers to go to Europe to study the Crimean War. In England he was received by the most important government officials and engineers; in France he was presented to Napoleon III and the Empress Eugénie; in Russia he was wined and dined but refused permission to visit the battle front. With his two associates he made a dash to Sebastopol where he studied the war at firsthand; after many months of a magnificent tour he returned to the United States and wrote up his valuable observations in a report published under the title of *The Armies of Europe*.

186

Mrs. Jefferson Davis says of him at this period, "Captain McClellan was quite young and looked younger than he really was; his modesty, his gentle manner and the appositeness of the few remarks he made gave us a most favorable impression of him." Nathaniel Hawthorne wrote, "His forehead is not remarkably large, but comes forward at the eyebrows; it is not the brow nor countenance of an intellectual man, a natural student or abstract thinker, but one whose office it is to bring about tangitive results."

He selected this moment, when his prospects for promotion and for becoming an international military authority were the brightest, to resign from the army. He long had been dissatisfied with the smallness of the pay, had decided that he needed more money to win Nellie Marcy, daughter of his commanding officer on the Red River expedition. He had been wooing the lovely Nellie for five years.

On January 1, 1857, he went to work for the Illinois Central Railroad as chief engineer. He was now thirty, making three thousand dollars a year; by the following year he had been promoted to a vice-presidency and was making five thousand. So great were his organizational and executive skills that two years after joining the company he had wiped out its more than three hundred thousand dollars of debts. The Ohio and Mississippi Railroad offered him the presidency of their company at a salary of ten thousand dollars a year, and he was on his way toward becoming one of the leading railroad men of the country.

Having accomplished his first ambition, business success, George McClellan now realized the greatest dream of his life. Nellie Marcy finally married him in May of 1860. He enjoyed a beautiful married life, for Nellie was an intelligent and loyal wife, but he knew that she had been in love with another army officer, failing to marry his rival only because of the opposition of her parents; that she had married him after an eight-year courtship in part because her parents favored him so strongly. To his gnawing inferiority was added the dread that his wife did not love him; perhaps that accounts for his letters to her in which he tried to prove that he was the greatest general, the greatest leader, the wisest statesman, the most widely loved, the most generous liberator in the world.

Nellie did love him. Her only mistake was that she made her husband's letters available to the public after his death.

He was as good an engineer for the railroads as he was a business executive, yet his inability to win the Civil War could be sighted even then: in his failure to provide his attorney with the material with which to conduct an important case, in the fact that "he built the strongest bridges on the road, yet hesitated to give the order to send over the first train."

Only two years later he was to build the Army of the Potomac, the greatest the country ever had known. Completely formed and equipped and raring to fight, it was impossible to get him to put it into action. Once his work was completed, be it a bridge or an army, he did not like to see it soiled, disrupted; the Army of the Potomac was both the symbol and arm of his power: once used it might not hold; it must lose some of its men, its perfection, its strength.

His rise to national glory was spectacular: upon the outbreak of war the governor of New York telegraphed for his services; he was offered the command of the Pennsylvania Reserves; the Pennsylvania Militia asked him to become their chief engineer. McClellan preferred to accept the urgent invitation of the people of Cincinnati to build an Ohio regiment. With little available money or equipment he did a fast and efficient job of organizing both troops and surrounding country, working out a campaign for his district which he dispatched to General Winfield Scott, head of the army. Within three weeks he had been appointed a major general in the Federal army, in charge of Ohio, Indiana and Illinois; his command had grown from a hundred men to ten thousand. Confidence in his abilities ran high. Ulysses S. Grant, sitting in McClellan's waiting room for three successive days in the vain hope of seeing the major general, said, "He had a way of inspiring you with the idea of immense capacity. I saw in him the man who would pilot us through, and I wanted to be on his staff." Sherman said, "The Mississippi River is the hardest task of the war, and I know of no one competent unless it be McClellan."

Missouri was added to his department, as well as parts of Pennsylvania and Virginia. Washington began to talk of him excitedly. When he won the first important skirmish of the war, at Hart's Farm, he found himself in the headlines. President Lincoln and General Scott praised him unstintingly. The New York *Herald* called him "the Napoleon of the present war."

McClellan promptly issued a series of bombastic proclamations: "Soldiers of the Army of the West, I am more than satisfied with you. You have annihilated two armies commanded by experienced soldiers entrenched in mountain fastnesses . . ." Cut constantly between the giant blades of timidity and arrogance, his schizophrenia is graphically described by an associate. "McClellan's personal intercourse with those about him was so kindly, his bearing so modest

188

that his dispatches, proclamations and correspondence are a psychological study, something to be spoken in character by a quite different person from the sensible and genial man we knew in daily life."

In the mind of a public desperate for any evidence of Union success he had risen to the position of conquering hero. His minor victories in West Virginia, added to his reputation as a military expert earned by his book *The Armies of Europe*, made it inevitable that he should be called to the command of the Army of the Potomac after the disastrous Union defeat at Bull Run.

George McClellan was only thirty-five years old. His light complexion had become ruddy from years in the open. He parted his hair in an angular cleft at the right side, brushing the shorter thatch over the top half of the right ear. He wore a heavy, untrimmed mustache and chin beard which completely concealed his mouth, giving his face an untailored appearance though the rest of his face was clean shaven. He had the strong head and ample shoulders of the big little man. He liked that phrase, Big Little Man. He smiled pleasantly when he read it in the press. But better yet he liked to be called Little Napoleon, for then, as with Fremont at the height of his dangers in the wilderness, the last had become first, the little man had become the biggest of them all.

3

It was in his building of the Army of the Potomac that George Brinton McClellan achieved a permanent position in military history. When he took command the recruits were disorganized and disheartened, their equipment pitiful, their discipline non-existent, their morale low.

"To this congenial task of reorganization McClellan brought the love of order and system, a thorough knowledge of detail, and an insistent habit of mind which nothing could deflect from its purpose." He knew as much about the armies of the world as any man living; he was a competent engineer; he was a hard worker, devoted to the Union. On the basis of these gifts he built the strongest army to be known in the United States up to the American Expeditionary Force of 1917. Discipline became rigid, but the soldiers were brought to such a high state of morale that they approved the discipline; supply was improved to the point where the men enjoyed good food, clothing, shelter; new troops were brought to Washington, drilled within an inch of their lives, welded into a cohesive unit; defense fortifications were erected, modern equipment made available to the forces.

While accomplishing this tremendous task George kept himself in hot water by his ingrained habit of quarreling and going over the heads of his superiors: he quarreled bitterly with General Scott, went over his head to the secretary of war; he quarreled with the secretary of war, went over his head to President Lincoln; he quarreled with President Lincoln and went over his head in sporadic bursts of dictatorship.

There also emerged the basic weakness of his character: having built the most powerful army of its times, he could not be persuaded to use it. He held parades in Washington, rode up and down on horseback before his troops to the sweet music of their tumultuous shoutings, conceived superb plans of defense—but he could not be made to fight. The north did not want a defensive war: they had been attacked, the Union had been shattered, the people were clamoring for a vigorous campaign. But McClellan was interested in protecting Washington, in keeping General McClellan's Army of the Potomac intact and shiny!

He permitted the Confederates to build strong batteries on the Potomac without challenging them, refusing to make any decisive movement until he had built up the perfect army, the complete army, the army which would conquer all. Slowly it became evident to the administration, and then to the nation at large, that his ideal of preparedness was a chimera in McClellan's mind, an idea of perfection which receded no matter how far forward he moved. His temperament engendered other weaknesses: his fear of the enemy and consequent exaggeration of their strength. He could have won smashing victories with the troops, plans and equipment on hand, but he forever was afraid that his army was still outnumbered, too weak to win. His indecision provoked President Lincoln to exclaim:

"If by magic I could reinforce McClellan with a hundred thousand men, he would go into ecstasy over it, thank me, and tell me he would go to Richmond tomorrow, but when tomorrow came he would telegraph that he had certain information that the enemy had four hundred thousand men, and that he could not advance without reinforcements." To this Secretary of War Stanton added, "If McClellan had a million men he would swear that the enemy had two million, and then would sit down in the mud and holler for another million."

Unlike his fellow general, Winfield Scott, who organized the forces on hand, supplied them as best he could and rushed them into battle, or John Fremont, to whom the conquest was all-important, McClellan was only half a general; another half was needed to wage the fight.

Any hope there may have been for a fall offensive in 1861 was lost when a Union force was defeated at Ball's Bluff and its commander killed. The Comte de Paris, who was with McClellan at the time, says that the news of the defeat was a great shock to McClellan, from that day "a fatal hesitation" unnerved all his activities. McClellan did not like defeat; he could not take defeat; in his mind he resolved never to fight because then he never could be defeated.

In November of 1861 he finally succeeded in having eighty-year-old General Winfield Scott retired and himself put in command of all the Union forces. For five months he continued to build his army, quarrel with the administration, turn a deaf ear to the clamor of the press and the public that he fight. He set up supply bases, established lines of communication, mapped out the engineering works, placed armies in the field—but never fired a shot! Opposition to him mounted steadily. In March of 1862 he was removed by President Lincoln when it became evident that he was impotent to give the command which would send his men into action.

A large segment of the administration believed that McClellan refrained from fighting and was ineffective in rushing the rebels because he had no desire to crush them or defeat them in battle, that he hoped to outmaneuver the enemy, exhaust them until they laid down their arms and limped back into the Union. He was detested by the Liberal Republicans who wanted the slaves emancipated, who believed that the war was not being fought merely to hold the Union together, who were convinced that if slavery were not abolished once and for all these civil wars would recur. With this point of view McClellan differed sharply. He liked the southern people better than the northern, the southern way of life better than the northern; he felt it to be more aristocratic. One reason he loathed Lincoln so bitterly was because Lincoln was plain and without social grace. McClellan was not opposed to slavery; he did not believe the slaves should be freed, or any other form of southern property confiscated or destroyed.

Having been demoted from the position of commander, he was on his way out of the army, his egress being hastened by his genius for tactlessness, this man who worshiped manners and social grace in others! To the administration he kept sending such telegrams as the one to Secretary of War Stanton: "If I save this army now, I tell you plainly that I owe no thanks to you or to any other person in Washington. You have done your best to sacrifice this army." He was momentarily saved by a crushing Union defeat, even as smashing

Union victories later would defeat him for the presidency: the Army of the Potomac, which had been turned over to General Pope, was soundly beaten at the second battle of Bull Run.

The Army of the Potomac had loved McClellan and was intensely loyal to him; so outraged were the men at his removal that officer and soldier alike fought listlessly, without the will to victory. McClellan was accused of having sabotaged General Pope, of having encouraged the army not to fight under him. It was also claimed that "wild was the rage of Stanton and those in his clique when the news came in of the defeat of Pope, for it meant also the defeat of their plot to get rid of McClellan." Whatever the cause, the Army of the Potomac was once again in rout, and Washington in danger.

Against the wishes of the Liberal Republicans President Lincoln again called upon George McClellan. "I am conscious of the infirmities of McClellan," he said, "who has the slows, was never ready for battle and probably never will be." But this was an emergency; Washington was threatened; and for defensive preparation McClellan had no superior. Put into command of the Army of the Potomac he again converted it into the powerful weapon it had been when he was relieved.

In the one major battle he commanded, at Antietam on September 17, 1862, he was charged with fighting in "driblets," yet the magnificent work of his officers and men stopped Lee's invasion of the north, enabling President Lincoln to feel strong enough to issue his Emancipation Proclamation. It was the last military battle McClellan ever fought. It was felt that he could have destroyed the Confederacy had he moved against them on the day after the great battle, but he had been too shaken by the twenty-three thousand men lying dead and wounded, too dispirited to pursue General Lee. When after a number of days he asked for remounts for his cavalry, Lincoln telegraphed in reply:

"I have just received your dispatch about sore-tongued and fatigued horses. Will you pardon me for asking what the horses of your army have done since the battle of Antietam that fatigues anything?"

A few days later McClellan was relieved of his command and sent to Trenton, New Jersey, to await further orders. When his army heard the news it was outraged; there was talk of marching on Washington, with one officer crying, "Lead us to Washington, General, we will follow you there!" General Winfield Scott Hancock put a stop to the mutinous talk when he exclaimed, "I do not sympathize with the movement going on to resist the order. I tell the gentlemen around me they are serving no one man. We are serving our country."

Though the Civil War was only half over, though he was the best organization man turned up by either side, Major General George Brinton McClellan never again was called to the service of the north. His military career was ended. But another career was in the offing, one in which he had an excellent chance of achieving even greater fame and importance.

In August of 1864 President Lincoln would observe, "I do not see how we can defeat McClellan in the election."

4

McClellan was pleased and flattered by the idea of becoming the next president. He had not encouraged the talk greatly, he had merely listened with sympathetic interest, writing in his own story, "My ambition was fully gratified by the possession of the command of the army, and so long as I held that, nothing would have induced me to give it up for the presidency." However the prospect doubtless influenced his thinking; his astonishing letter to Lincoln at Harpers Ferry, telling the president how to conduct the war, the government and the affairs of the nation, can be explained only by McClellan's having in his own mind already superseded Lincoln.

On September 24, 1862, just a week after the battle of Antietam, McClellan gave a dinner at headquarters for his general staff, proclaiming to his officers that he was being urged to denounce the Emancipation Proclamation, that the soldiers were so devoted to him they would back his decision with their arms. Shocked at this invitation to mutiny, he was informed that "not a corporal's guard would stand by him in insubordination." McClellan next announced to his soldiers that "the remedy for political errors, if any are committed, is to be found only in the action of the people at the polls," an open encouragement to his men to defeat Lincoln at the next election.

The northern Democrats, who were opposed to the emancipation of the slaves as an unconstitutional and revolutionary act which endangered all private property, immediately embraced McClellan. His nomination from that time on was inevitable: they believed too that he agreed with their desire to end the war by making concessions to the south to get them back into the Union.

Horace Greeley says of McClellan's war years, "His house was thronged with partisans of the extreme peace wing of the

Democratic party, who must have held out to him the golden lure of the presidency as the reward for a forbearing, temporizing, procrastinating policy which would exhaust the resources and chill the ardor of the North."

The Democratic convention meeting in Chicago on August 29, 1864, nominated George B. McClellan on the first ballot, almost unanimously, amid cheering and enthusiasm. At this point it appeared that he surely would be the next president: many war-weary Republicans were ready to desert to the Democrats; Lincoln was growing increasingly unpopular due to his inability to end the conflict; his renomination had been made as a matter of necessity, without enthusiasm either in the convention or the press.

Though it was McClellan's war victories that had originally attracted the Democrats, they now put him into the stocks by writing into their platform a repudiation of the war and a demand for an immediate peace through an armistice. This doctrine that the war never should have been fought, that the sacrifices had been in vain and now should be abandoned, was a blow to the thousands of northern families whose menfolk had been killed.

For General McClellan, who had suffered over the death of his brave men on the field of battle, this philosophy ought to have made an acceptance of the nomination unthinkable. But George McClellan wanted the nomination: to revenge himself upon Lincoln, to repatriate himself in the eyes of the nation, to vindicate himself in his disturbed inner depths for his enforced retirement. Though he later was to write, "When I allowed my name to be used as a candidate for the presidency I was well aware that I was sacrificing my future so far as public life was concerned," at the time he accepted the nomination he was certain that he would be elected.

A tremendous and heartfelt wail went up as the country realized what the "repudiation of the war" plank meant. The New York *Herald* announced, "If McClellan will set aside the Chicago platform and stand boldly upon his record, he will save the country and be triumphantly elected president."

In his letter of acceptance McClellan repudiated the platform and with it the Democratic party:

"The Union must be preserved at all hazards. I could not look into the face of my gallant comrades and tell them that we had abandoned that Union for which we have so often periled our lives."

In many ways the election was a Civil War in miniature: with so many men dead and dying the canvass could not but be deathly bitter and malignant. McClellan was assailed as a traitor to his country and his soldiers; he was accused of being a coward under fire, his record torn to shreds, his abortive mutinies exposed; he was charged with a plot to murder Lincoln, with being sponsored by some of the worst Copperheads, saboteurs and traitors at large in the country.

The campaign waged against Lincoln was even worse. He was accused of destroying the Constitution, of causing a revolution which would wreck the country; he was called vacillating, incompetent, stupid, vulgar, ugly, a disgrace to the White House. He was catechized by a parody of the Lord's Prayer:

"Father Abraham, who art in Washington, thy Kingdom come and overthrow the Republic; thy will be done, and the laws perish."

McClellan himself, now only thirty-eight years old, behaved in an exemplary manner. He remained in retirement, made few speeches, and those brief and in good taste. He made no overt efforts to get himself elected. At the time of his retirement McClellan had accused Lincoln of jealousy, of having removed him to destroy his growing popularity and power; during the campaign the two candidates partly compensated for the dirty work of their cohorts by remaining respectful toward each other.

The campaign against Lincoln convinced a large portion of the electorate that any change would be a blessing, since things could not possibly be worse. So strong was the swing to McClellan after his repudiation of the Democratic platform that Thurlow Weed, astute politician, said he could not find anybody in New York who held out any hope of success for Lincoln, while the chairman of the Republican National Executive Committee wrote Lincoln that "I hear but one report, the tide is setting strongly against us."

On August twenty-third Lincoln was convinced of his impending defeat; he asked each member of his cabinet to sign a sealed paper which, opened after the election, was found to read, "This morning, as for some days past, it seems exceedingly probable that this administration will not be re-elected. Then it will be my duty to so co-operate with the President-elect as to save the Union between the election and the inauguration, as he will have secured his election on such ground that he cannot possibly save it afterwards."

The election was suddenly jerked out of the hands of the campaign managers when the war took a sharp turn. Grant, Sherman and Sheridan turned in major victories; it became obvious that the rebellion soon would be over. As a poetic young officer of a Michigan regiment put it, "Every shell from Sheridan's guns knocks a plank from the Chicago platform. Go to gallant Farragut, who, lashed to the mast amidst

195

a storm of lead and hail, went on to victory, and ask him if the war is a failure. Go to Grant, who is cutting every artery of the Rebellion, and ask him if the war is a failure . . ."

Thus was McClellan defeated by his brother generals whose victories heartened the flagging Republicans and knocked the props from under the "peace at any price" Democrats.

He carried only three states and received but twenty-one electoral votes against Lincoln's two hundred and twelve, yet his popular vote was amazingly high: 1,835,985 against Lincoln's 2,330,552, a count which never ceases to astonish those who believe that Abraham Lincoln was as popular during his lifetime as the legends have made him after his death, and who have never heard of Little Mac. The vote would have been closer if as many Democratic soldiers had been furloughed home to vote as had Republicans. McClellan took his defeat quietly, perhaps deriving some consolation from the fact that he captured Lincoln's home county by a majority of almost four hundred votes.

If the Democratic party had not established a war-repudiation platform, if the victories of Grant, Sherman and Sheridan had not come until a few months later, the inferiority complex of George Brinton McClellan might at last have been fully appeased.

5

In comparison to Abraham Lincoln, what kind of president would George Brinton McClellan have made? He was a skilled organizer, combining the vision of the over-all executive with a talent for detail, but as in his army days he would have refused to consult his governmental generals or to build a staff which could have replaced him; he would have sought no counsel, taken no advice. As a capable engineer he would have planned an extensive building campaign for the nation; as a shrewd businessman he would have worked to wipe out the vast war debts and put the government on a paying basis; yet his uncontrollable temper, his will to rule alone, his pathological need to be king in order to make himself feel as important as other men would have kept him in the midst of destructive clashes with his cabinet, the Congress, the Supreme Court, with every function of government which attempted to limit his control.

McClellan was a sympathetic leader, one who inspired love and confidence in those under him, and doubtless he would have tried to take as good care of his people as he had of the soldiers in his command, been a sometimes benevolent despot

—but those of independent mind who don't like despotism even when it is benevolent would have been ruthlessly suppressed. He would have created a veritable jungle of quarrels in Washington: all difference of opinion would have been considered personal persecution, the government effort turned into a yapping, growling, biting melee of fighting dogs, enmeshed in the intrigues which he would create against those who he believed were against him. Only his yes-men could have survived.

His inability to go into action would have rendered the central government impotent. George B. McClellan would have built bridges, but he would not have been able to summon the courage to cross them. The country would have lain prostrate under his inability to take a bold stand. While major battles of the day were being fought he would have been twelve miles to the rear or across the river, conjuring up mutinies, making plans to lead his people in a march on Washington against the Constitution, the Supreme Court, the Congress. He had no sense of interdependent government, of co-operation, of the balance and limitation of powers; his pathology could not let him respond to those things which make a democracy.

His sympathy for the south would have urged him to deal gently with them. Lincoln and Andrew Johnson also wanted to deal gently with the south, both of them far stronger and more able than McClellan; both were wrecked by the south-hating Republicans.

George Brinton McClellan might have made a good king for a court of Europe; he would have made a maladroit president for a democracy. He joins the ranks of Henry Clay and William Jennings Bryan as Also Rans whom the United States were profoundly blessed in missing.

CHAPTER FOUR

Winfield Scott Hancock

"HANCOCK WAS SUPERB!" telegraphed General McClellan after the Battle of Williamsburg.

From that time on he was known as "Superb Hancock." He never had occasion to be embarrassed by his nickname; so valuable was he to the Union cause that President Lincoln said, "When I go down in the morning to open my mail, I declare that I do it in fear and trembling, lest I may hear that Hancock has been killed or wounded."

"At seven o'clock on the night of the election," writes Hancock's wife, "he yielded to extreme weariness and went to bed."

"Don't you want to know whether you've been elected President?" she asked, astonished.

"I can't know until morning," replied the general, "so I may as well sleep until then."

This was not indifference, it was superb command of nerves. Battles were not new to him; he had been in hundreds of them, had had his horses shot from under him, seen four of his five staff officers fall, been severely wounded himself, and had never flinched. When there was a battle to be fought, he fought it, calmly but fiercely, on the field or the election ground. When the good fight was over, it was time to rest.

At dawn he awoke and asked his wife, "What's the news?"

"It has been a complete Waterloo for you," replied Mrs. Hancock.

"That is all right," he murmured. "I can stand it."

He turned over on his pillow and in another moment was fast asleep.

Mrs. Hancock had not remembered her military history aright: her husband had suffered no Waterloo, but the very closest of defeats, being bested by less than ten thousand votes in a total of nine million votes cast! The general was used to close shaves: at the battle of Fredericksburg a bullet "went through my overcoat, just missing my abdomen"; a quarter of an inch closer and he would have been killed; a quarter of an inch closer and he would have been elected president. To both of these incidents Hancock would have said smilingly, "Almost doesn't count."

He was a soldier's soldier and an officer's officer, as much a natural at the military life as the men after whom he had been named, as Greeley at journalism or Fremont at pathfinding; he did so well that Lieutenant General Winfield Scott loved and admired his namesake. Hancock was enough like Scott to be, not his blood brother, but his son. He was broad as an oak and six solid feet tall, one of the most imposing figures on the landscape, with classical features, clear, bold eyes and a magnificently sculptured head. "He was a perfect blond, powerfully formed yet easy and graceful in his movements, strong without a trace of ferocity or even of habitual severity."

He combined the best qualities of Fremont and McClellan without the shortcomings of either. Like McClellan he was an expert at ordnance and supply, believed in equipping an army fully and scientifically before it struck, but the moment his force was ready he struck hard and fast. He too awakened the greatest love in his men, but he was no haystack general. At Gettysburg, "the shells now fell thicker and faster every moment. General Hancock rode at once to the right of his line of battle, and from thence passed along it for a mile or more, under a furious fire, to its extreme left, in order to inspire confidence among his troops."

He consulted with his officers, asked their counsel, took their advice. He had no phobia about ruling alone, no fear that if he gave the men under him a chance they might prove to be better than he, replace him. He was as rigid a disciplinarian as McClellan, took equally good care of his men, but he also went out of his way to pay honor to the volunteers, who were being looked down upon by the regulars and their officers. He could give orders; unlike either Fremont or McClellan, he could also take them. While neither Fremont nor McClellan was interested in politics up to the moment of their nomination, Scott and Hancock inherited their passion for the politics of freedom and democracy from the seed of their fathers.

When he was only eleven years old his uncle had founded a paper to help wage a political campaign; young Winfield spent all his free time at the plant, setting type, working the hand press on the political articles. At the age of thirty-eight, reporting at Washington to begin his work in the Civil War, he said, "My politics are of a practical kind: the integrity of the country, the supremacy of the Federal government, an honorable peace or none at all."

This political philosophy made him a great and honored

general during the war; after the war, as military governor of Louisiana and Texas, the identical policy brought upon him his only defeat to compare with a lone Civil War defeat at Ream's Station. From this defeat he was not able to extricate himself, and was carried off the field unhonored and unsung. Yet he had displayed greater courage in trying to save the south from a harsh military dictatorship than he had shown in riding into the hail of bullets at Gettysburg.

Among the Also Rans he is closest to Alton B. Parker for temperament and functional balance of nerves, brain and body. In the best sense of the term he was a normal man. Such a decent life did he lead that during the presidential campaign the worst the Republicans could do was to ridicule him a little for not fully understanding the intricacies of the tariff. He was almost too good to be true; as a saving disgrace, he possessed one of the most extensive and graphic cuss vocabularies of his day. "Only one habit marred Hancock's otherwise invariable dignity and impressiveness under all circumstances: this was an extravagant indulgence in harsh and profane speech."

He wanted to rise the good way, and was willing to rise the hard way; that was the way he made it.

One reads of his life with a kind of wonder and joy: lo, here is a good man, a sweet man, a kindly man, a brave and honest and courageous and able man with a social as well as a personal conscience. He was no meddler or reformer, no softy or sissy; he pushed and shoved no one, let no one push him; he was no idle dreamer or impractical martyr; he was a man of action who drove everyone hard, most of all himself, to achieve a desired result. He was no genius, but a man of modest talents developed to their highest degree. Watching Winfield Scott Hancock's story unfold, a spectator is inclined to think, with reverential awe:

"If only the world were full of men like Hancock, what a sweet world this would be!"

2

His grandfather was taken prisoner by the English while sailing a merchant vessel during the War of 1812; when the boy was born in Pennsylvania on February 14, 1824, the family paid tribute to General Winfield Scott, who had revenged the unjust imprisonment, by naming one of their twin sons after him. Winfield's grandfather was English, his grandmother Scotch; his father had been born in Philadelphia and named after Benjamin Franklin. Benjamin Franklin Hancock had taught school while reading law in Bucks County, Pennsylvania, and, when admitted to the bar, went to Norristown to begin a successful practice. He was a deacon of the Baptist church and superintendent of its Sunday school for three decades: it was not from his blood father that Winfield acquired his profanity, but from his spiritual father and idol, Winfield Scott.

In all other respects the son was a dead ringer for his father. Benjamin Hancock was six feet tall, broadly built, blond, with a strong and attractive face, "an industrious lawyer, patient and careful in his investigations, of calm, equable temper, his character marked by great decision." Change this to read soldier instead of lawyer and it is a fine likeness of his offspring.

On his mother's side young Winfield came from a long line of American soldiers who had been officers in the French and Indian Wars, the War of Independence and the War of 1812. The military was strongly ingrained in the lad's nature, an aptitude which was heightened by his having been named after Winfield Scott. While still in elementary school he formed a military company which he drilled and led in parades on holidays.

Hancock, like Scott, was one of the few among those who Also Ran who did not come of poor parents or have to work for their own education. He spent a pleasant childhood in Norristown, had the best schooling available, was particularly interested in mineralogy, geology and the other sciences, and at the age of sixteen was admitted to West Point. It is about this phase of his life that Hancock utters his lone complaint: it had been too early to enter him upon such a rigorous life. At sixteen he was a sprouting weed, with all his strength going into growing; he did not take his studies too seriously, though he was among the twenty-five who graduated from a beginning class of one hundred.

"My father intended me to become a lawyer," says Hancock.

To this end he had young Winfield read Chitty's *Blackstone* six times through while he was at West Point. Upon graduation from West Point in June of 1844 he was sent as a second lieutenant to the Indian country near the Texas border, where he spent two delightful years in the open, hunting, fishing, riding the plains and filling out his tremendous frame. He was not successful in getting himself dispatched to Mexico until the fighting was nearly over, but he still had time to engage in several battles and to be brevetted first lieutenant "for gallant and meritorious conduct." Once Winfield got a whiff of powder during the Mexican War he deserted his father's side of the family for his mother's, and the six readings

201

of *Blackstone* apparently were so much waste material. But only apparently.

In Mexico he received his first experience as regimental quartermaster and commissary, a job which was to join his talents for fighting with paper work, a combination at which his father had been so successful in another profession. The next few years Lieutenant Hancock spent in widely separated parts of the country, learning his trade under difficult and often harrowing conditions. It was while working as adjutant of his regiment in St. Louis that he married Almira Russell, daughter of a local merchant. Mrs. Hancock proved to be a woman of outstanding intelligence and integrity who helped him at every turn of his career. In almost every instance the wives of the men who Also Ran had much to do with their husbands' success and good works.

Success came slowly for the young married couple, particularly slowly for Hancock who wanted to rise in the world but would not cajole or play politics to win promotion. He was kept a lieutenant for twelve years and even then, when offered a captaincy, it was not in the service he wanted. In 1861, when the Civil War broke out, Hancock still was an obscure captain, living with his wife and children on a modest wage, wondering how many hundred years it was going to take him to become a major and then a colonel. He had a right to wonder, for his rate of advancement was in inverse ratio to the quality of the service he had been giving his country.

Sent to Fort Myers during the Seminole War, he had to maintain an army that was working in broken country, without roads or lines of communication. There was nothing in the history books to tell Hancock how to provision the troops; he worked out an ingenious method of his own, assembling a fleet of a hundred and fifty boats, all the way from canoes to steamers, by means of which he kept the men in the field supplied with food and ammunition. So well did he do his job that his commanding officer asked that he be sent with him when Federal troops were being rushed to Kansas to prevent the border clashes over slavery from bringing on a civil war. From Kansas he was dispatched to the Utah country during the Mormon disturbances, and from there to Fort Bridger where he accomplished one of the outstanding supply jobs in the history of the United States Army.

Arriving at Fort Bridger, he became regimental quartermaster just in time to be given the responsibility of outfitting an expedition to California. It was a desperately difficult place from which to provision, for the supplies were limited, there were no fresh animals to be had, the repair facilities were non-existent. The regimental wagons were in bad state, the animals half starved; the gear and equipment needed to be overhauled before the voyage could begin. Hancock did his job with such resourcefulness and minute attention to detail that "the troops and trains were brought into Benicia, California, in even better condition than when they started."

Though he was under no obligation to submit a report on the country through which the expedition passed, he wrote one of the finest to reach Washington since the Fremont reports. Hancock undoubtedly had read and admired Fremont's accounts, and his was based on those of the Pathfinder: there were maps of the route, distances accurately observed between geographical points, the nature of the wood, water, grass and food to be found on each day's march, and well-drawn observations on the botany and geology of the country.

The Hancock family spent three years in the sun-baked village of Los Angeles, where Fremont had been the first governor; Captain Hancock had the much less important job of quartermaster, providing the troops of southern California and Arizona. He was well liked in Los Angeles, where he averted a good deal of trouble by his friendliness. "Though he was one of the most soldierly men that ever lived, authority was exercised by him with tact and with a great deal of diplomacy. No man ever had a livelier sense of the virtue of courtesy, conciliation and considerateness in the use of power." There was unrest in California, as well as agitation for the southern cause. In 1861 Captain Hancock quieted the community with a flowery but adroit Fourth of July speech, in which he gently reminded his audience of the Federal government's ability to deal with its enemies.

Essentially a man of action, Hancock became one of the best authorities on regulations in the service: "He became educated in that very important branch of military labor—the skillful, accurate, concise, scholarly preparation of reports on military operations."

When it was time for action he plunged into battle with tremendous verve and éclat; when it was time for office and desk work he attacked his papers with a thoroughness that made him one of the outstanding supply men in the United States Army. He was a good man; he knew he was a good man; he wanted the chance to do a bigger job. But from the looks of things he would remain stuck away in this sleepy hacienda, Los Angeles; he would never become a major or a colonel. In this prophecy he was right: General McClellan, knowing how greatly he would need supply experts to help him organize the Army of the Potomac, asked President Lincoln to appoint Captain Winfield Scott Hancock a brigadier general.

Ulysses S. Grant was to write, "Hancock stands the most conspicuous figure of all the general officers who did not exercise a separate command. He commanded a corps longer than anyone, and his name was never mentioned as having committed in battle a blunder for which he was responsible."

In spite of his magnificent record he was at no time in command of the Union forces or of a complete army. He wrote to his wife, "I have been approached again in connection with the command of the Army of the Potomac. Give yourself no uneasiness—under no conditions would I accept the command. I do not belong to that class of generals whom the Republicans care to bolster up. I should be sacrificed." He had no wish to share the fate of Generals Fremont and McClellan. He wanted to fight, not to wrestle with a cabinet or be made a scapegoat; of fighting no man ever got more of a bellyful. He knew many officers who had gone through agonizing inner struggles before they cast their lot with the Confederacy, and he would tolerate no wild talk about traitors or "hanging them to a sour apple tree." But, unlike McClellan, his commanding officer, his understanding did not lead him to pull his punches. "He knew too much of the southern temper to make light of the task before the nation, or to predict a holiday parade for the Union armies."

One small incident illustrates Hancock's character better than all the tales of his commanding and fighting. When he captured the Confederate General George Stuart, whose wedding he had attended, he sought to comfort General Stuart by giving him news of his wife, whom he had seen in Washington a short time before. When Stuart refused to take his outstretched hand Hancock said quietly, "General, such an affront should not be put upon me before my officers and soldiers."

As a commanding officer Hancock asked no special privileges, gave none to his friends, investigated all complaints impartially, redressed grievances for a private on the same basis that he did for an officer, established a heartening spirit of comradery among the volunteer troops. Most important, he carried out orders given to him by his superiors with the same alacrity and dispatch with which he demanded that his own be carried out. He understood war.

His first victory came at Williamsburg during his first encounter with the enemy, a victory sorely needed by the Union forces. It was here he showed the "tactical skill, calm courage and majestic bearing" which stamped upon him

McClellan's epithet "Superb." This action took only twenty-three minutes, but the military records describe it as sharp and decisive. Though greatly outnumbered he caused the enemy to evacuate their fortifications and to retreat. "He displayed a perfect command over his men—energy applied in exactly the right way and at exactly the right moment."

Summoned in the midst of the battle of Antietam to succeed General Richardson, who had been mortally wounded, he became commander of the Second Corps. "On the trampled battlefield strewn with bloody stretchers and wrecks of caissons and ambulances, the dead and dying thick around, the wounded still limping and crawling to the rear, with shells shrieking through the air, Hancock first met and greeted the good regiments he was to lead in a score of battles."

It was at Gettysburg that he rendered his greatest service to the Union cause. Sent forward to take command, he found upon his arrival that the Federal troops had been defeated, their equipment smashed, the soldiers in a disordered state of retreat. He not only had to stop the rout but had to save them from being captured by a pursuing enemy. There had been no time to bring his now famous Second Corps with him; he had only himself to save a disheartened and scattered army from another Bull Run.

"As the confused throng was pouring through Gettysburg, and General Hancock arrived on the ground, it was clear that if the flight was not stayed, a great disaster might follow. If there is in the commander that mysterious but potent magnetism that calms, subdues and inspires, there results one of those moral transformations that are among the marvels of the phenomena of battle. This quality Hancock possessed in high degree, and his appearance soon restored order out of seemingly hopeless confusion."

Like Scott at Lundy's Lane, he re-formed the shattered regiments, rallied the men to their lost colors, established a new line of battle, brought up ammunition, presented such a formidable front that General Lee, believing he was facing fresh troops and solid reinforcements, failed to pursue his advantage and attack. Hancock sent word back that Gettysburg appeared the most favorable spot in which to engage the enemy; the subsequent action proved his judgment to be sound, while his holding off of General Lee's forces until the Second Corps arrived turned Gettysburg from a shattering defeat to a decisive victory.

It was the next morning, when gunfire opened the battle of Gettysburg, that Hancock mounted his horse and, with his staff behind him and the colors flying, "rode slowly along the front of his line so that every man might see that his general was with him in the storm . . . Streams of screaming projectiles poured through the hot air. Men and horses were torn limb from limb. No spot within our lines was free from this frightful iron rain. At this moment Hancock rode slowly along the terrible crest while shot and shell roared and crashed around him." Soldiers trying to crawl into the earth to escape the deadly hail of shrapnel must have looked up at Hancock, riding with his chest out, affording a magnificent target to the enemy, and murmured to each other, "If he can stand it, we can." They had unwavering confidence in their commander's tactical skill and unerring judgment; they knew that no blunders would be made, no lives wasted.

No one knew until the Confederate attack had been repulsed that President Lincoln's fears at last had been realized: Hancock had suffered an ugly wound in the side. He telegraphed to his wife, "I am severely wounded, not mortally. Join me at once in Philadelphia." In reporting to his commanding officer he indulged in the one piece of melodrama of his career:

"I did not leave the field so long as there was a rebel upright!"

He was almost too stricken to be moved. His journey to his father's home in Norristown, which he had left twenty-four years before to enter West Point, was a procession that had a parallel only in the carrying of the wounded Scott in 1814 a hundred miles on the shoulders of relays of men: at Philadelphia the fire brigade turned out to transport him painlessly to the station; at Norristown he was met by a detachment of invalid guards who carried him in a stretcher to his home, through streets lined solid with quiet and reverent people watching an authentic hero go by.

His wound yielded but slowly to treatment. Hancock was back in command, now a major general, before he was entirely healed. He was transported onto the battlefield of the Wilderness in an ambulance, but once the battle began he had himself lifted onto his horse and led his men into the thickest weather. He suffered only one defeat during the war, at Ream's Station on August 25, 1864. The Second Corps of the Army of the Potomac had been one of the greatest fighting units in the history of the army, but it was decimated and shattered from almost three years of bloody warfare. Defeated and pushed back, Major General Hancock tried to rally his corps for a last supreme effort. The men had nothing more to give. Covered with the dust, powder and grime of the daylong battle, Hancock rode up to one of his officers, put a hand on his shoulder and said:

"Colonel, I don't care to die, but I pray to God I may never leave this field."

At the close of the Civil War the Union League Club in New York City hung his portrait in their main salon. With the advent of peace he embarked upon a service to his country which required greater moral stamina than he had displayed at Antietam or Gettysburg.

3

Appointed military commander of Louisiana and Texas, Hancock had it in his power to control the minutest act of every person in his domain. But Winfield Scott Hancock was not thirsting for power; he was a passionate believer in civil liberties and the rights of a people to govern themselves. The Liberal Republicans in Washington wanted the south treated as a conquered people, to be held in a state of virtual imprisonment; to this effect the Congress had passed the despotic Reconstruction Acts. For Hancock this appeared a form of fratricide, if not downright treason: he had fought against the south with every ounce of his strength, but now that the conflict was over, the southern states back in the Union, their people once again citizens of the United States, he wanted to see their health, prosperity and self-government restored as quickly as possible, the citizens enjoying the same privileges as those of Pennsylvania or Connecticut.

This attitude was no sudden departure on his part: his father had been a strict constructionist of the Constitution, had raised his son in the belief that the rights guaranteed to the people of the United States under the Constitution were inviolable. Dispatched from Washington to be a military tyrant, Hancock performed while en route to New Orleans with his wife and children what was probably the first disobedient act of his career: with pen and ink while the steamboat slipped quietly down the waters of the Mississippi he wrote his General Order No. 40, which remains one of the truly humane and broad-visioned documents to come out of the greed, brutality and corruption of the Reconstruction era.

"The General Commanding is gratified to learn that peace and quiet reign in this department. As a means to preserving peace he requires the maintenance of the civil authorities and the faithful execution of the laws. When insurrectionary force has been overthrown, the military power should cease to lead, and the civil administration resume its rightful domain. The General announces that the great principles of American liberty are still the inheritance of this people. The right of trial by jury, the habeas corpus, the liberty of the press, the freedom of speech, the natural rights of person and property must be preserved."

To the southerners this proclamation appeared too good to be true; to the carpetbaggers and politically ambitious Negroes, too bad to be true. Hancock set out to prove that he meant precisely what he said: local officials who had been removed to make way for carpetbaggers were restored to their jobs; military orders which had made it impossible for southerners to be tried by a jury of their peers were revoked; disputes which the carpetbaggers wanted settled in Washington were referred by Hancock to the local courts and judges; urged by northern settlers to set aside elections on the grounds that they were irregular, and to remove officials who were charged with malfeasance, Hancock replied:

"Only the people can set aside an election or remove their officers."

"We are unwilling to permit the civil authority and laws to be embarrassed by military interference," he announced in an official decree, and to this end he forbade the appearance of soldiers at the polls during a Texas election. Harassed by a railroad to grant it rights which included eminent domain and the obstruction of navigable rivers, he informed his petitioners that such rights belonged to the state of Louisiana and could be granted only by the people; asked to interfere with lawsuits, he replied, "The rights of litigants do not depend upon the views of the General; they are to be judged and settled according to the laws." Urged by the governor of Texas to set up a military commission to try prisoners accused of murder, he insisted that the civil authorities assume jurisdiction, castigating the governor by saying:

"It is an evil example, full of danger to the cause of freedom and good government."

His six readings of Chitty's *Blackstone* bore fruit, for his reasoning shows an understanding of the nature of the law and the character of a free government. He refused to break the law—even upon order of the Congress!

His executive skill and understanding won him warm friends in the south, but not quite so fast as they won him hot enemies in the Congress. He was not guilty of mutiny; he was simply giving the Reconstruction Acts their most liberal interpretation. A movement was begun to get Hancock out of the south: Liberal Republican General Garfield, chairman of the Committee on Military Affairs, introduced a bill reducing the number of major generals in the United States Army, an act aimed solely at Winfield Scott Hancock. Hancock was too popular with the people to be destroyed by such obvious means. A more subtle scheme was set on foot to overrule his decisions, to siphon off his powers, to humiliate his program, to make him impotent. Federal agents in Louisiana fought him; military commanders of adjoining states sabotaged him; incited Negroes swarmed about his home, threatened the life of his family. Realizing that his usefulness to the southern people was at an end, Hancock asked to be relieved of his command.

Thus ended one of the brightest pictures in the Reconstruction period. Hancock was defeated by Garfield in 1868 even as he was to be defeated by him in the presidential arena in 1880. The Union League, which had charged Horace Greeley with treason for the same liberality to the south took Hancock's picture off its wall and stored it in the cellar.

4

Hancock had been a soldier before the Civil War began and, unlike Fremont and McClellan, continued to be a soldier after its close. Nevertheless from the nomination of 1868 down through the election of 1880 he remained one of the outstanding figures of the Democratic party. He did not seek the office, he engaged in no political activity, yet on the eighteenth ballot the convention of 1868 gave him two thirds of the number of votes needed for the nomination. Because of his liberal stand in Louisiana and Texas and because he was an enormously popular figure Hancock retained both his popular favor and the respect of his party.

Two weeks after President Grant's inauguration General Hancock was sent to St. Paul, where he commanded the military department of Dakota for three years. In 1872 he became commander of the Atlantic Division, with headquarters in New York. His only major conflict was a political one: the disputed election of 1876 between Democrat Samuel Tilden and Republican Rutherford B. Hayes. Hancock's wife writes:

"The exciting Presidential campaign of 1876 was one of engrossing interest, and the only one that I can recall that my husband followed with intense interest and anxiety, not even excepting that in which he was himself the nominee of the Democratic party."

Hancock became the center of wild and incendiary rumors: that he was preparing to lead a Democratic army against the Republican usurpationists, that he was going to use force of arms to place Tilden in the White House, begin the Civil War all over again. Upon the heel of these rumors, which now found their way into the press, it next was alleged that President Grant had ordered General Hancock to the Pacific coast to prevent him from seizing power for the Democrats. In a rapidly rising crescendo Hancock was charged with incipient mutiny, with refusing to obey President Grant's order banishing him to the Pacific coast!

General Hancock got on his horse and, with the shrapnel bursting around him, rode quietly before the ranks of the American people, his chest exposed to the cannonading. "I have not refused to obey such an order," he wrote to the papers, "for the simple reason that I have received no such order. Nor would it be conceivable for me to think of renewing warfare and bloodshed."

The Democratic convention of 1880, meeting in Cincinnati on June twenty-second, nominated Winfield Scott Hancock on the second ballot. For fourteen years, since his military governorship in the south, the forces for his selection had been gathering strength. In 1868 he had received two thirds of the votes needed for the nomination. The Democrats withheld his nomination during three successive conventions, at last concentrating on the general as the single best and strongest force at the fourth convention. As a piece of political time reasoning this delayed-action bombing of the Republicans with Hancock almost hit a bull's-eye, missing by only ten thousand votes.

The Pennsylvanian who nominated him said, "I present to the Convention one who on the battlefield was styled 'the superb,' yet whose first act when in command of Louisiana and Texas was to salute the Constitution by proclaiming that, 'the military rule shall ever be subservient to the civil power.' I nominate one whose name will suppress all faction and thrill the republic."

Against Hancock the Republicans put up James A. Garfield, who had led the movement to have Hancock retired from the army because of his sympathetic attitude toward the south while in command in New Orleans, a member of the Liberal Republican clique which had advocated the confiscation of rebel property and had brought the reign of misery and terror upon the south; the same Garfield who had been connected with the Crédit Mobilier graft scandals in 1873. Garfield always had been one of the boys in the back room, a mediocre legislator who knew how to wangle, compromise, roll the barrel. He was the exponent of co-operative government who ascribed Tilden's Democratic victory of four years previous to the "combined power of rebellion, Catholicism and whisky." He was the Warren Harding of his day. In his long legislative career the historians are able to find only one instance in which he showed courage and the willingness to fight for his beliefs: in the greenback legislation.

Garfield was an experienced politician who knew all the

tricks of the trade. Hancock was a student of government who knew none of the tricks of the trade. As when Scott ran against Pierce, the country had to ask itself, "Which type of man can serve us best?"

"I never aspired to the presidency on account of myself," wrote Hancock. "I never sought its doubtful honors and certain labors and responsibilities merely for the position. My only wish was to promote, if I could, the good of the country, and to rebuke the spirit of revolution which had invaded every precinct of liberty. Principles and not men is the motto for the rugged crisis in which we are now struggling."

Hancock had to wage a fight against a Republican machine built up from five successive elections: twenty years of Republican rule from Lincoln in 1860 through Hayes to 1880. "It was the first of our national campaigns in which money talked out loud. The bankers took alarm because the Democrats had won in Maine, and they aroused the business interests to take a hand in the campaign. The officeholders also were warned of their peril of being turned out, and the assessments on them helped to swell the biggest campaign fund in history up to that time." It would set a pattern for Mark Hanna's management of McKinley in 1896.

To this campaign Garfield, the amoral politician, made his contribution. In a letter to "My Dear Hubbell," written by Garfield to the chairman of the Republican congressional campaign, he approved the taking of part of all governmental salaries to help win his election, kept tabs on how much money was being collected in this manner. "As this was one of the worst abuses of the spoils system, it discredited Garfield's open protestations of friendship for reform."

Chester A. Arthur, the vice-presidential nominee who succeeded to the White House when Garfield was shot by a disappointed office seeker, declared, "We won this election with plenty of . . . !"

Winfield Scott Hancock set out to win the campaign with plenty of principles, by a vigorous attempt to lay before the American people the inefficiency and corruption at the base of the Republican power machine. He sensed that the electorate was becoming frightened and disgusted at the manipulations of the inner ring, at the constant exposures of graft and dishonesty, that the time was coming ripe for a rigid change of party and principles. His perceptions deceived him by only the slimmest time margin: he missed his destiny by only one election!

"Our home was invaded from the beginning to the end," writes Mrs. Hancock. "All was turmoil, excitement and dis-

211

comfort of every known kind. The ordeal to the General was severe, requiring herculean strength."

The general treated the canvass as though it were another military campaign, figuratively snatching moments of sleep on a cot at field headquarters, keeping out in front of his troops when the gunfire was the heaviest. He spent the months mapping strategy, writing, speaking, giving interviews, trying through every available means to put before the country his conception of a government that would be as fair and decent and open and generous as his own nature and concept of the State.

"No form of government, however carefully devised," reiterated Hancock, "no principles, no matter how sound, will protect the rights of the people unless its administration is faithful and efficient. It is a vital principle in our system that neither fraud nor force must be allowed to subvert the rights of the people. It is only by a full vote, free ballot, and fair count that the people can rule in fact."

In large measure he succeeded, if not quite enough to get himself elected, then sufficient to start in motion a tidal wave of indignation which only two years later, in 1882, began washing Republicans, both good and bad, out of the government.

Hancock was the recipient of little personal abuse during the campaign: his record allowed for none. In only one other campaign in American history, that of Alfred M. Landon in 1936, was a candidate left so free of calumny and slander. His own conduct throughout the campaign was so much of a piece with his past record that even those who did not vote for him admired and respected him, a rarity in the barbarous clangor of American elections. "Although I did not vote for General Hancock," wrote Republican General Walker in 1893, thirteen years later, "I am strongly disposed to believe that one of the best things the nation has lost in recent years has been the example and influence of that chivalric and splendid gentleman. Perhaps much which both parties now recognize as having been unfortunate and mischievous during the past thirteen years would have been avoided had General Hancock been elected."

Garfield on the other hand was savagely attacked; not satisfied with the charges which they could sustain, the Democrats invented fictitious ones, circulated on the Pacific coast a forged letter which purported to show Garfield's approval of the introduction of cheap Chinese labor.

The speed with which Hancock's stock went up after the election was exceeded only by the rate at which Garfield's went down. During his inauguration he had made a strong plea for civil-service reform, the outstanding governmental need of 1880, but when his letter to "My Dear Hubbell" was made public his speech was seen to have been so much wind-breaking. At the same time there came the exposure of the Republican mail frauds, with the guilty defendants being supported by the Republican power ring, of which Garfield was now the head.

By the time he was shot, only four months after taking office, the reaction to Garfield was so intense that he had forfeited any potential leadership. The shooting, the long illness and his death saved him on the eve of national repudiation, in exactly the manner in which Warren Harding would be saved by his sudden death in 1923.

"My God," exclaimed Garfield bitterly, after two months in the White House, "what is there in this place that a man should ever want to get into it?"

Winfield Scott Hancock would have been incapable of that kind of thinking. He would have done his job calmly and up to the hilt of his abilities. Thousands of people in widely scattered parts of the country had spontaneously urged his nomination; in nearly every instance where the people have demanded a candidate he has been of high caliber. Garfield had been nominated by the machine clique, which nearly always selects its most obscure and acquiescent stooge: Garfield, Pierce, Harding. Until Democracy evolves a method of taking nominations out of the hands of the political machine, putting them permanently into the hands of the people, the weakest man in the party too often will be selected for the highest position in the land.

Many factors contributed to the defeat of Hancock by the slight edge of ten thousand votes out of nine million: the Republican extortion of campaign funds and profligate use of industry's money; Hancock's endorsement of the Democratic plank of a tariff for revenue only, enabling the Republicans to frighten businessmen with the dread cry of Free Trade; the fact that many northerners still were afraid of a man sympathetic to the south; that labor was indifferent to him because he had been in charge of Federal troops used to police the first railroad strikes of 1877; because the Greenback party, with a liberal program, rolled up three hundred thousand votes, practically all of which would have gone to the Democratic party as its closest economic kin; and lastly because the wave of revolt against the Republican machine had not quite reached its peak.

Winfield Scott Hancock's name must be written in red on the debit side of American electoral judgment, a political asset which the voters allowed to remain frozen.

Unlike General McClellan, General Winfield Scott Hancock would have made a poor dictator for Europe, but he would have made a good president for a democracy.

He might even have been Superb.

Interlude at the Halfway Mark

———— ⊷ ◆ ⊷ ————

WINFIELD SCOTT HANCOCK *joins Horace Greeley, James M. Cox, Winfield Scott and John Fremont, superior men who got lost in the democratic shuffle. Alton B. Parker and Charles Evans Hughes, two excellent public servants who Also Ran, could not quite convince the country that there was any shattering need to make a change, to evict the incumbent. Three Also Rans, Henry Clay, George B. McClellan and William Jennings Bryan, were better defeated.*

At the halfway mark democracy has thus run two dead heats, been dumb in five elections and smart in three. Twenty per cent of the time the voters have passed up first-rate men for other first-rate men; thirty per cent of the time they have avoided dangerous and inferior men; fifty per cent *of the time they have rejected good and superior men and bought gold bricks.*

Part of the reason for this astonishingly poor box score— so bad that one wonders how democracy has managed to survive—has been the blind, unreasoning support given to both parties by vast blocs of voters who will vote the straight party ticket at any cost, who don't give a continental how injurious their party's record has been, nor how feeble, corrupt and incompetent the candidate may be. Almost ninety per cent of the orthodox party vote is cast for its own side regardless of issue, and on the basis that their worst candidate is preferable to their opponent's best candidate; some vote as sheer automatons, others because they are convinced that their party's conception of government is what keeps the country going. Die-hard Republicans voted against James G. Blaine in 1882 because of the exposed corruptness of his personal character; lifelong Democrats voted against Bryan in 1908 because he had proved himself to be a false prophet. Aside from these two exceptions it has taken a national catastrophe, such as the depression of 1932–36, to make voting servitors break their party lines. The only incentive for a party to nominate its best and strongest man has been that independent bloc of voters which, as it has gained in strength, holds the balance of power between the two parties and decides the outcome of elections.

What will the other half of this story tell? Will the electorate improve in judgment as this narrative goes along, or will it grow increasingly worse? Will the people continue to select a Franklin Pierce over a Winfield Scott, a James A. Garfield over a Winfield Scott Hancock, and prove James Bryce to be right when he wrote in 1886 in the American Commonwealth:

"Europeans often ask how it happens that this great office is not more frequently filled by great and striking men. It might be expected that the highest place would always be won by a man of brilliant gifts. The safe candidate may not draw in quite so many votes from the moderate men of the other side as the brilliant one, but he will not lose nearly so many votes from his own ranks. Even those who admit his mediocrity will vote straight when the moment for voting comes. The ordinary American voter does not object to mediocrity."

The ordinary voter is right if the mediocre man is a safe one and the brilliant man a dangerous one; for the people do not wish to delegate too much power or to be pushed around by too strong a force. That was why they founded a democracy: so that they could not be led, even to salvation, by a nose ring. Unfortunately the score shows that too often the voters got their signals mixed: mediocre weaklings such as Pierce, Buchanan, Garfield and Harding were the dangerous ones, while Greeley, Scott, Fremont, Hancock and Cox, the brilliant men, were safe.

BOOK FIVE

Heroes Stand Alone

Martyrdom was thrust upon him. Perhaps that was why he carried it so well.

———— ◆◆◆◆◆ ◆◆ ————

CHAPTER ONE

Samuel J. Tilden

HE WON THE RACE BY A HEAD, but it was before the day of the photo finish, and the judges ruled him out. No American ever had a greater right to cry, "I was robbed!"

He wasn't built to be a hero: slight of figure, racked by illnesses—real and imaginary—cold by nature, battle-worn at sixty-two, without luster or fire. Yet he proved to be the outstanding hero among the Also Rans.

Samuel J. Tilden had it in his power to renew the Civil War, to plunge his country once again into bloodshed and disunion. Victim of a guerrilla uprising against the democratic form of government, no man would have said he was wrong to put down the revolt with force. No man, that is, except himself. All around him he saw people who loved their country with blind passion; he loved democracy with an icy and penetrating intellect. That intellect would not permit him to shatter the peace which was slowly emerging from a war already twelve years ended.

Rutherford Hayes is the man who Also Ran in 1876. But his is not half so interesting a story.

The Ice Myth with which Charles Evans Hughes was erroneously charged was true about Tilden: most of his life was spent inside his brain-pan; aside from his parents he loved no

217

one, and no one loved him. He had a big and powerful brain lodged on top of a weak and ineffectual body; his body was something he dragged grudgingly behind him all his days: his mind pulled him ahead of the field like a champion.

Tilden's life was compounded of ironies: though he became a millionaire through his work for the railroads, mines and manufacturers, he was interested in working people; though he loved the Democratic party above all things, he smashed it wide open in New York City when he prosecuted the Tweed Ring; though he had a cold, unapproachable personality, thousands revered him in every section of the land as the unconquerable warrior for reform; though he was a hypochondriac who was forever dosing himself with medicines and cures, he could work any group of healthy men into exhaustion; though he was a laboratory technician in the science of politics, he refused to utilize his skill to seat himself in the White House even after the people had given him a quarter of a million popular majority. He is the only man elected to the presidency who never got his foot inside the White House.

He was a rational man first and a human being second; that was why he never served as president.

The Tilden fiasco of 1876 provides the only major case in American history where the tradition that the majority must rule broke down. Frequently the elections have been corrupted by an unconscionable use of money; sometimes they have been befogged and muddled until everyone except the officeholders seemed to lose; sometimes the elections were lost to the nation in the convention halls, where the weakest men were selected; sometimes they were lost at the polls, where an efficient machine rolled up a majority for a useless man. But the election of Tilden was the first and only time that the majority, choosing the superior candidate, had their ballots flung back in their faces.

Tilden knew the nation could not endure many such breakdowns. They had to be avoided at all costs; and if one of the first costs was that of the presidency, Samuel J. Tilden was willing to pay it. Though he started with more handicaps than most of the Also Rans, he emerges through his self-abnegation as perhaps the greatest of the lot. Only Parker and Hughes would have endured the decapitation with the same legalistic phlegm.

He accepted the decision, but it came as close to killing him as the defeat did Greeley. He went into the campaign resolute, strong of will and purpose; when Hayes was finally inaugurated, to the hisses and groans of more than half the nation, Tilden was an old man, worn out.

Young Samuel had learned his politics at his father's knee; he took to it the way Greeley took to journalism, Scott to soldiering and Hughes to law; he became trained in the mechanics of carpentering or animal husbandry. In the home of his father, who was the leading political mind of the countryside, he listened to penetrating discussions of the issues of the day, of the manner in which elections best could be waged and won. In his father's home he met the political leaders not only of New York State, but of the nation. These men liked young Sammy for his eagerness and interest in politics; they discussed the complicated affairs of the nation with him seriously. What Sammy heard he absorbed.

Just as Greeley preferred to sit in a corner of the family cabin and read literature rather than go out of doors and play ball, young Tilden preferred to discuss the rechartering of the Bank of the United States to playing games with the neighboring children. While he was still a boy his father took him with him to visit William Cullen Bryant in the office of the New York *Evening Post;* all through the discussion the father solemnly would ask the son for an opinion on each of the national issues, and just as solemnly Samuel would reply. By the time he was eighteen he had published a paper in the Albany *Argus* outlining why the National Republicans and Antimasons should not combine against the Democrats, which the Albany *Journal* attributed to the hand of Martin Van Buren! This tract was symptomatic of Tilden's approach: written in cool, emotionless prose, the arguments were presented with such clarity and authenticity of research that there could be no answer.

When he was nineteen he wrote a paper on the tariff, defending President Jackson's stand. At twenty he wrote "Is the Treasury an Executive Department?" in which he defended Jackson's right to refuse Nicholas Biddle a recharter for his bank. By the time he was twenty-three he was publishing letters in the New York *Times* defending President Van Buren from attacks within the party.

In the meantime he was failing at everything else! He attended for scattered months at neighboring schools, mostly being unhappy and learning little. Sent to New York to further his development he wandered the city, read fitfully, was interested only in a course in elocution. He went to Yale for one semester, did barely average work, then dropped out. He attended New York University for a semester now and then, when he could find time to sandwich it in between elections and the writing of polemics. At twenty-four he apparently exhausted his course, finishing his work at the university without graduating.

He was a completely disorganized young man. He was still being supported by his father, who could ill afford the money; his health was precarious, his energy low, his determination and direction non-existent. He had no interest in girls, no physical pleasures; he is the lone bachelor among the Also Rans. He was a brilliant and erratic young man with no discernible future except the vague feeling that he might like to be a lawyer since he enjoyed writing and debating. There was little reason to believe that he would make a better lawyer than he had a student or that he would have the health or determination to do anything but eke out a meager living. The bookies would have given heavy odds against him, with a few tempted to play him as a long shot.

From this unpromising beginning he developed into one of the keenest legal minds of the country, became a bulwark of the Democratic party, carrying it to its first presidential majority in twenty years, since the election of Buchanan in 1856. Anyone who had put two dollars on his nose would have collected the equivalent of the daily double: for he became, momentarily, the great man of his day.

How could Samuel J. Tilden, legally elected to the presidency, allow an opponent to foul him on the home stretch and spill him ingloriously into the dust?

2

Samuel Jones Tilden was born at New Lebanon, New York, on February 9, 1814. As was almost universal with the Also Rans, both of his grandfathers as well as most of his granduncles fought in the Revolutionary War. Sam was a fighting man too, even though most of his battles were waged for such abstract causes as civil reform and efficient government.

Samuel's father, Elam, was a successful farmer as a young man, but being a social creature, interested in the problems of the day, he found the solitary life on a farm too lonely. He opened a general store at the crossroads of New Lebanon, where he became a sort of town-meeting moderator: with every keg of nails he sold to one of the hundred householders of the vicinity went a discussion of hard money versus soft, and with each pound of cheese an analysis of whether the state or Federal government should pay for internal improvements. Elam loved nothing better than political discussion, but he was no idle talker: he soon became the political sage of the community and for many years helped formulate the platforms and policies of the Democratic party.

Young Samuel grew up in an aura of respect and homage

220

paid to the political sagacity of his father, a conditioning which gave the boy confidence in his own powers of analysis and deduction. From the time he was fourteen and Martin Van Buren came into control in New York State, the leaders of the Regency were in and out of the Tilden home. Consequently Sam followed the trade of politicking as surely as the blacksmith's boy grew up in the trade of the smithy.

In spite of his political activity and the debt of his party to him, Elam Tilden never wanted nor would accept any office other than that of local postmaster. His son followed him in this trait: though he was elected governor of New York and president of the United States, he did not want either office, preferring to earn his living at his profession. From his father Sam inherited his hypochondria, love of politics, power of analysis, interest in books: by the time he was fifteen he had bought out of his own spending money a copy of Adam Smith's *Wealth of Nations* and had read Thomas Jefferson's published letters many times over.

His mother was the adopted daughter of a physician, well educated for her day, a woman of unending love and loyalty for her family. Sam loved his mother; he looked a good deal like her, and from her he inherited his tendency to aloofness. The boy was as unsocial as his father was social; he had no young friends, played no games, never had a home or a wife or a woman he loved or a group of intimates whom he trusted. He would discuss political economy at the drop of a hat but cared little for other forms of social intercourse. Serious and literal-minded, with an occasional flash of dry humor but no laughter, he had been too delicate as a boy to learn the rough-and-tumble of comradery. Homely, sickly in body, awkward in manner, unable to speak freely or with pleasure except to his elders about politics, he became shy and then inhibited. He held himself apart from his contemporaries, and they in turn, though they easily might have liked him if he would have permitted it, kept away from him. Young Samuel steeled himself to do without people, closeting himself in a world of ideas. His shyness and discomfort in the presence of others was something he had to fight all his life; he preferred to stay out of public affairs, to be obliged to meet only those with whom he had business, whose relationship would be confined to law and industrial management.

It is one of the more diverting humors among the stories of the Also Rans that the man who least understood the human nature of people, and least wanted to associate with them, should have the greatest understanding of their political motivations and be forced into the most pitiless political spotlight in all American history. He was a lone wolf who, by the inexorable demand of the times, found himself at the head of a great pack.

In 1837 he became a law clerk in a New York office, entering at the same time the newly opened law school of New York University. During his three years' study of law and early American history he kept plowing as an artisan in the vineyards of the Democratic party. During the presidential campaign of 1840 he spent six full months working for the re-election of his friend Martin Van Buren, writing pamphlets and newspaper articles on political economy, resolutions for meetings of workingmen, addressing audiences on such subjects as "Prices, Currency and Wages," speaking at open meetings for Democratic causes. He anticipated by a full century the revolution which was to take place in American law when he announced that "institutions are founded not on property but upon humanity."

In addition to his other activities he was also preoccupied in his spare hours with such assorted ailments as rheumatism, chills and fever, neuralgia, swellings and lameness, to which afflictions he was applying poultices, mustard plasters, ice packs, being bled, taking mild narcotics and otherwise enjoying the adventure of bad health.

Tilden hated to make up his mind to anything which would project him into action; he was a congenital delayer, but once he reached a decision the movement that followed was irresistible. He was admitted to practice in 1841, was earning from fifteen to twenty dollars a week by the end of the first year, became a consultant for the leaders of the Democratic party as well as one of their most astute writers on controversial subjects, and soon enjoyed a flourishing law business which followed in the wake of his political activity. As his work and income increased, as he began to feel confident that he had found his place in the world, many of the illnesses began to fade.

The only office he ever ardently desired was that of corporation counsel of New York City, which was appointive. He held this post for a year before he was removed by a rival political faction; from it he received the experience he had wanted in matters of city business and procedure. In 1845, though he had no appetite for the job, he campaigned for the state legislature on the insistent demand of his friend Governor Wright, who was in sore need of him to command the Democratic forces. His outstanding achievement as a state legislator was indicative of both his character and his future career: he investigated the long-standing land-tenure troubles in New York State, bringing in a report which gave justice to the tenants and yet won the approval of the landowners;

when he had drafted the laws and helped push them through the legislature he found himself lauded throughout the state as a master of economic compromise, as a moderate and scientific reformer.

Due to the falling off of his practice, his activities as a legislator had cost him money, but he now was better acquainted with the inner workings of a state government, had overcome some of his shyness and inability to mix with people and had won the respect of the industrialists. When he returned to his office in New York City he found that railroads, banks, foundries, mills were knocking at his door, asking that he take over their reorganization, put their finances on a sound basis, handle their incorporations and mergers. He proved to have an almost uncanny ability to salvage, rearrange, combine and otherwise rescue sinking industries. From his reorganization of failing railroads he made large sums of money; this he began to invest in coal mines and new ironworks; and above all he had a nose for stocks.

By the time he was thirty-two the weak, sickly, irresolute boy who had been without any discernible prospect of success or fulfillment was a legal power in the inner sanctums of industry, an outstanding political power in his party, a polished man of the world who had become a patron of the opera and was assembling a magnificent library. He would give any amount of time and counsel to the needs of his party, but he was resolute in his determination to remain out of public office.

He appeared to be just another corporation counsel, a smart and capable lawyer who would become wealthy through his work, associate largely with the rich, dabble in politics, occasionally speak his piece for honest government and reform, and slowly disappear from public view. This was what he wanted. But just as was to happen to his lineal descendant, Charles Evans Hughes, in the same city and for the same causes thirty years later, the irresistible rush of events picked up his frail body and swept him to fame. Never again would he be able to retire to the simple pleasures of earning millions.

He had never been physically attractive; the older he grew the less handsome he became: he had sallow skin, a biggish nose, small, standoffish eyes, the thin, almost cynical mouth of the ascetic, a jutting, upturned chin which somehow gave his face an expression of contemptuousness. His thin graying hair he combed broadside to cover his growing baldness; his voice was hoarse and unpleasant from some obscure throat ailment. His figure had lost some of its awkwardness but it was still unsightly, the shoulders thin and stooping; he looked as though the first strong gust of wind would surely blow him off the legal and political scene. He had none of the external appurtenances of a giant; the last thing in the world he wanted to become was a giant.

Shakespeare said, "Some are born great, some achieve greatness, and some have greatness thrust upon 'em." Greatness was never thrust upon more reluctant shoulders than the frail shoulders of Samuel J. Tilden.

3

For every political poison there is an antidote: the Tweed Ring was the poison, Tilden the antidote. Yet Tilden wanted to be a reformer as little as Tweed wanted to be reformed.

The Tweed Ring of New York City was not only the most corrupt of local governments in the history of American commonwealths, but it came to stand as a symbol for depravity and bold burglary in machine-dominated cities. Tweed had worked himself into control of the Democrats' Tammany Hall, but after a time he realized that he could not seize really empire loot unless he controlled not merely the machinery of the city but of the state. To this end he started to buy election officials, councilmen, legislators and judges. When he needed votes to win an election one of his judges solemnly would citizenize thirty-five thousand immigrants! His election officials would report the results in their districts without counting the votes; upon one occasion he put in his governor with more votes than there were voters.

Tilden was a Democrat; he had helped build New York City's Tammany Hall; as a practical politician he knew that the Democratic party needed the Tammany vote in order to help win state and national elections. If Tweed had confined his stealings to the modest scale of a few millions he would not have died in prison through Tilden's efforts, nor yet made a presidential candidate of Tilden.

By 1870 the Tweed Ring so completely controlled every facet of government within the state, including the force of public opinion, which they molded by the purchase of newspaper editors, that they grew careless and contemptuous of their victims. Safes whose value was three thousand dollars were charged against the city for half a million; a contractor of fire alarms who submitted a bid of sixty thousand dollars for a job was asked by Tweed if he would give the Ring half of the loot if he were paid four hundred and fifty thousand for the work. This overreaching ultimately outraged public opinion; all that was needed was a leader who would make their righteous wrath effective.

Tilden did not want to be the spokesman of the drive: he knew that the revelations would be injurious to his party; he knew the strength of the opposition that would be unleashed against him. But he was repelled by the use of the machine for brigandry. He became convinced that in order to preserve the strength of the Democratic party it must be the Democrats themselves who threw out the rascals, rather than the Republicans who would use the revelation as a club with which to beat the National Democratic party over the head. The Democrats turned to him to undertake the job not only because he was one of their most able and reputable men, but because they had confidence that he would destroy Tweed as an individual malefactor without seriously hurting their party.

Tilden tackled the problem, not by shooting off vocal firecrackers, hurling charges or demanding indictments, but by working patiently within the framework of political procedure. Instead of starting criminal prosecutions which he knew would be thrown out because the Ring controlled the courts, he started a drive to nominate honest judges to the Court of Appeals in the election just coming up, then campaigned arduously to put over the reform slate. When the state convention met he framed a platform of repudiation of the Tweed Ring and Tammany Hall, saw to it that anti-Tammany Democrats were selected to run for state officers and for the legislature, contributing a hundred thousand dollars out of his own pocket to have the polls policed. Some of his campaign speeches, in which he presented a scientific analysis of the evidence against the Tweed Ring, are among the best of his long career.

New York City and New York State rose in its electoral might, giving Tilden's reform candidates tremendous majorities. Tweed judges were swept off the Bench, his legislators out of Albany, his henchmen out of the city jobs. Tilden then began his impeachments of the remaining corrupt judges and his prosecutions of the Tweed Ring, spending a large portion of his time sending to prison all those who had not fled the country. He waged the four-year battle not only without compensation or hope of reward but at tremendous expense to his health and resources: for whenever there were no public funds to cover the costs of the investigations and prosecutions he would pay the money himself. At the beginning of his attack upon the Ring he was known in corporation circles as an able lawyer, in Democratic circles as an astute campaigner, to a small group of New Yorkers as a penetrating writer on political subjects; but to the nation at large he was unknown. At the termination of the prosecutions he had become a national hero, not only for the blows he had struck for honest government, but for the quiet skill and sagacity he had displayed as a commanding general of the citizen army.

For many years his name had been put forward by committees, clubs, newspapers and party groups as a proper man to hold office. He had rejected the suggestions. He had gone into the Tweed investigations as a private citizen and had had every intention of returning to private life when the job was done. But the deeper he got into the problem the deeper he saw he would have to go in order to be successful. Though the idea of holding office was still repugnant to him, he ran for the state legislature in order to complete the task he had undertaken, to secure the passage of laws to protect New York's cities from future gang raids.

In 1874, at the height of his Tweed purges, a movement as spontaneous as that to run Hughes for governor after his gas and insurance purges took form to elect Tilden the next governor of the state. He was so obviously the most capable man at the moment that outstanding Republicans and their journals joined in the boom. His unwillingness to hold public office was no longer tenable. He had been importuning the best men among the Democrats to train themselves and run for office. By what right could he now refuse to serve, when he was the best man available for that particular job at that particular moment and the people needed him?

Having decided, in his slow-moving, cautious, secretive way, that he must become the next governor, he threw all of his energies and experience into winning the battle. He waged a laboratory campaign, directing every slight move himself: collecting the funds, supervising every dollar spent, issuing a continual stream of articles and pamphlets from his own and the pens of the best writers he could find in the state, setting up an educative barrage the like of which had not been known before, speaking to thousands of voters in every section, speeches ringing with incontrovertible truth and zest for decent government. He knew more about the actual blueprint and mechanism of elections than anyone since his master, Martin Van Buren: he maintained an active list of fifty thousand Democrats, two in each school district, who supervised his campaign, while he estimated by a mathematical formula just how the vote was veering. He knew at every moment of his campaign exactly what his chances were. His winning majority of fifty thousand votes was precisely what he had estimated it would be.

He turned in an excellent record during his two years as governor, finishing off the Tweed Ring, smashing the upstate Canal Ring by a statistical investigation which revealed their plunderings beyond contradiction. From the moment he had been elected people talked jubilantly of moving him from Albany to Washington in 1876, and during his administration his candidacy grew apace. Nor was Governor Tilden any longer dilatory or reluctant: the die was cast, he was going to have to serve as a public officer; since the Grant Ring in the capital was the national counterpart of the Tweed Ring, it was merely a continuance of his job to be elected president, go to Washington, throw out the rascals and set up reforms which would protect the nation from further depredation.

How does a man secure the nomination for the presidency?

Bryan got his by setting the convention on fire with oratory; Parker got his because the conservative Democrats of the east saw in him an antidote to the silvery vocal Bryan. Greeley got his because his opponents accused him of wanting it, thus putting the idea in the nation's head. Clay got his by manipulating men, by keeping the party in line with magnetism and tongue-lashings. Cox got his by being an Ohio governor and editor chosen to oppose an Ohio editor and senator. Fremont got his because he had established a name as an explorer and pathfinder just when the infant Republican party needed a name and a man to blaze new political paths; McClellan got his because he publicly opposed Lincoln's Emancipation Proclamation, setting himself at the head of the northerners who wanted southern property protected, including the slaves; Hancock got his because, as a military governor in the south after the war, he manifested a desire for unity and brotherhood of the states, and no one could wave the bloody shirt in his face. Scott got his because he was the greatest general since Washington, because the only two of his fellow Whigs ever elected had both been generals. Hughes got his because the voting Republicans thought him the party's greatest asset, an idealist whose record equaled Wilson's.

The professional manipulators of the New York Democratic machine did not want Tilden any more than the Republican machine would want Hughes forty years later: he had made powerful enemies by his reform movements; he was what they called a "cold fish," not the kind of good egg with whom the boys could drink and play poker and hold smut sessions.

Some nominations are accidental, others are a result of wangle and wampum. Tilden's came out of a test tube. He waged a more detailed and meticulous campaign to win a unified nomination from his party than most candidates waged to win the election.

First he established a Newspaper Popularity Bureau which sent out paid advertisements to some twelve hundred rural

227

newspapers and furnished the city papers with interesting and well-written articles about himself. A Literary Bureau, an extension of the idea he had used so successfully in his gubernatorial campaign, employed the best authors available to write articles, pamphlets, human-interest stories which were mailed out by the hundreds of thousands. Such an inventive manager was he that he selected the most attractive combinations of reds, blues and greens to be used in printing the circulars, an innovation in campaign literature. Nothing that modern thought had made available was neglected in his design to win the Democratic nomination. The material with which he blanketed the country was extremely high in caliber, for he believed wholeheartedly in a campaign of education. The articles and pamphlets included analyses of governmental expenditures, taxes, civil service, the eradication of patronage and graft, the structure of a businesslike administration.

He set up the equivalent of the modern Gallup and Fortune polls: reports poured into his office every day from the remotest sections of the land, surveying and estimating the sentiment of the people. His researchers took a census of college commencement exercises, found that a majority of them were about reform and Governor Tilden; the Fourth of July speeches also were tabulated, showing that the majority had made Tilden and Reform the heroes of the year. By such methods Tilden knew that reform was on the march, that it could sweep the country in an election; but even here he did not stop. He also kept an unsleeping eye on his enemies and opponents in order to gauge the direction and strength of their opposition.

Democrats in every state in the Union made it known through their newspapers, committees and rallies that they wanted Tilden nominated. Tilden, the technician, had left nothing to accident; when the doors of the convention hall swung open no one could be found to wager a dollar bill that he would not be nominated. Elam Tilden and Martin Van Buren would have been pleased with their protégé.

Five thousand people jammed the auditorium in St. Louis, for the sweet smell of victory was in the air, the first in twenty years for the Democrats. The platform, with its sharp cry for immediate and sweeping reforms, sent the delegates into an ecstasy of political fervor. The historical conjunction of Tilden, the country's greatest reformer, with the crying need for reform brought Tilden more than four hundred votes on the first ballot and the nomination by a landslide on the second.

It is claimed that his nomination was received by the voting Democrats with more enthusiasm than any leader since

Jackson. However, the Democrats were a minority party. With the Republicans able to extract a fifteen-million-dollar campaign fund for their three hundred thousand officeholders alone, could Tilden gather a sufficiently large fund to cover the country with a hailstorm of educative literature? Could he entice enough Republicans into his camp, lure enough of the independent vote to secure a majority?

Could Samuel Tilden, a man without warmth or charm or attractiveness or personality, fire a nation for a great cause?

He was not a vote cadger, he was a vote manufacturer. He published a seven-hundred-page campaign bible exposing the Grant administration's frauds and mismanagement; his own principles of sound government were contrasted to the evil record. The Democratic campaign was rich in courage, energy and faith; it was poor in only one ingredient, cash, the national fund not being over half a million dollars, of which Tilden himself had contributed a hundred thousand.

Sam Tilden always had been a man of ideas: he waged the campaign of the Idea. It was successful. Then the Idea was blown to bits by surviving Civil War artillery.

4

The Republican nominee, Rutherford Hayes, had been three times governor of Ohio, had had an honorable if unspectacular career in Congress. He had pulled himself up by his bootstraps from a poor boyhood to considerable means, culture and comprehension of national affairs, including civil-service reform. However the majority of the public did not give him credit for wanting reform; they gave that credit to the man who already had proved that he could make reform effective.

The campaign started on a high plane, as directed by the two candidates, both of whom were high-minded men; then it sank lower and lower in both tone and manner as the fighting fell into lower and lower political hands. When it finally reached the hands of the ward politician, the county bigot, the frightened Repulican officeholder, the job-smelling Democrat, the canvass conformed to pattern, the country suffering one of its recurrent ravages of filth, vituperation, chicanery, libel and slander. Tilden was accused of having been a Copperhead, of approving of slavery and secession; the Boys in Blue were fired to wage the war all over again, to vote as they had shot.

He was called the harlot of the railroad kings—all of whom had deserted when he cleaned out the Tweed and Canal rings; he was accused of being a millionaire aristocrat, an enemy of the working people and the common man; he was accused of wrecking industries in order to cheat the public out of their funds and pocket the profits, of evading his income tax; he was charged with being a crony of Tweed, of perpetrating election frauds; he was called a wirepuller and consummator of deals. Among the other accusations levied against him in print, in whispering campaigns, in speeches, was that he was "a drunkard, a liar, a cheat, a counterfeiter, a perjurer and a swindler," a defrauder, a sham reformer, a grafter. No tiny shred of his record or reputation was left untouched.

This same machine, spewing the same filth, had helped to kill Horace Greeley only four years before. Was it any wonder that Tilden had wanted to stay out of public life? That many men would not voluntarily endure this calumny?

Tilden was made of sterner stuff than Greeley; besides, he knew more about the inner workings of politics. The campaign of vilification neither caught him by surprise nor distressed him. In the great mass and crush of work he refused to become worried or excited. He spoke quietly, made momentous decisions with a barely discernible nod of the head. While working twenty hours a day and supervising every detail he kept himself detached and objective in relation to rising problems. The people around him thought him indifferent; he was merely the engineer refusing to land himself in the soup through emotion or hysteria.

Tilden answered the worst of the canards himself in letters and articles to the press. No one could tell whether the calumnies were traveling faster than the denials; one of the most encouraging signs was that a number of outstanding Liberal Republicans, men of the best families, artists and scholars such as James Russell Lowell, Lyman Trumbull, Charles Francis Adams, Professor William Sumner of Yale, Henry Cabot Lodge, came out for Tilden as the superior man.

The fever rose as election day came closer: there were huge bonfires, parades during the day with bands and marching men; at night crowds surged through the streets, singing campaign songs, wearing oilcloth over their hats and shoulders to catch the warm tallow that melted from the candle lamps. There were speeches and hecklings and fights and gnashed teeth and broken bones. But when election day dawned the patient had passed his crisis, the fever subsided, the nation cast its ballots quietly and in good order.

As post time drew near, Tilden was a five-to-two favorite. The bookies, with seven hundred thousand dollars to put on his ample nose, could find few takers. On the eve of election Tilden and his lieutenants pored over the mathematical formulas which Tilden had set up, and what they saw on the sheets convinced them that they had a clear victory on hand. The staff and workers of the Democratic committee were wild with joy, but Tilden sat by quietly, his left lid falling low over his eye, his thinning white hair combed neatly, parallel to his brow, his high stiff collar and black bow tie immaculate, his face a mask.

When it was learned on election day that New Jersey and Connecticut, both doubtful states, had gone for Tilden, there was every indication of a landslide. By nightfall Tilden also had captured New York State, and everyone knew that the election had been decided.

Rutherford Hayes went to bed that night saying that he had been defeated; Tilden, like Hughes, went to sleep believing himself to be president.

The following day the press in all parts of the country informed the people that Samuel J. Tilden was their nineteenth president. The New York *Herald* and the New York *Times*, though conceding that Tilden had a lead, refused to acknowledge his victory. Editor Reid of the *Times* had undergone great privations while held in a southern prison during the Civil War; his implacable hatred for everything connected with the south included the Democratic party and its candidate. His vituperation and ridicule of Tilden had been frenzied; it was Reid who now started the movement which put Rutherford Hayes in the White House.

The plot began at three forty-five in the morning of the second day after the election, while Reid and two of his assistants were sitting in the editorial rooms of the *Times*. At that moment they received a message from the chairman of the State Democratic Committee asking, "Please give your estimate of the electoral votes secured by Tilden. Answer at once." Reid exclaimed, "If they want to know the electoral vote, that means they are not certain they have won. If they are still in doubt, then we can go on from here and win the election!"

On November tenth the popular vote was 4,285,992 for Tilden against 4,033,768 for Hayes. The electoral vote stood: Tilden 184, Hayes 166, with the nineteen votes of South Carolina, Louisiana and Florida still doubtful. If the Republicans could establish a majority in all three states, Hayes would be elected by an electoral majority of one vote!

Going to the Republican National Headquarters at the Fifth Avenue Hotel, Reid awakened the Republican chairman and set before him his plan to capture the election. Securing the chairman's approval, Reid telegraphed south, "Hayes is elected if we have carried South Carolina, Florida

231

and Louisiana. Can you hold your state? Answer immediately."

But how could the Republicans split up the south, solidly Democratic since Jefferson?

5

In South Carolina, Louisiana and Florida there were two separate factions, each with its own electoral board, still fighting the Civil War: the Republican carpetbaggers with their shepherded Negro vote, and the local white residents, all of whom were Democrats. Reid's telegram was asking whether the Republican Certifying Boards could set up a carpetbag-plus-Negro vote which would be larger than the resident white vote.

Rutherford Hayes wanted no part of these monkeyshines; he told a Cincinnati newspaper two days after the election, "I think we are defeated in spite of recent good news. I am of the opinion that the Democrats have carried the country and elected Tilden." Tilden, aware of the power of his adversaries, said, "The fiery zealots of the Republican party may attempt to count me out, but I don't think the better class of Republicans will permit it."

This was one of the few political errors of his long and sagacious career: for President Grant already was pouring Federal troops into the south to enforce the carpetbag count at the end of a bayonet. General Sherman, in charge of the Federal troops, later wrote, "The probabilities were that Tilden was elected." However that did not stop him from playing an important part in swinging the election.

There did not appear to be much doubt in anyone's mind that Tilden had won; the only issue was whether the Republican machine could force a majority in the three southern states.

In South Carolina the seven-man Certifying Board which was to determine whether Hayes or Tilden got the electoral votes was solidly Republican; in Louisiana the board of four also was solidly Republican; in Florida the board again was solidly Republican. Combined with the presence of Federal troops under Republican commanders, this potent fact, plus the promise of Federal patronage, plus the passage of certain large sums of money, plus the promise of southern amnesty and independence if its Democrats would throw in with the Republicans, made a formidable task force.

Letters, messages, telegrams poured in upon Tilden urging him to act, to take a stand, to make a strong statement, to choose his cabinet, to plan his inauguration, to denounce the plot and, with his usual mathematical genius, to expose what was already being termed a Mexican election, decided by bullets instead of ballots.

Samuel Tilden, pale-faced, sick at heart, his left lid drooping ever lower over his eye, could not be booted into action. He kept his finger on the minutest detail, pursuing a course of watchful waiting. If he had issued the kind of icily devastating blast of which he was capable, he might have chilled the plot and put an end to it. But he did not consider that this would be dignified conduct. He was first of all a lawyer, with an overpowering respect for the law and the Constitution; he would make no claims to the presidency even though his infallible charts proved that he had been elected. The people would have to decide this election within the framework of the existing legal machinery; he would do nothing to help.

He had conquered through ideas, but ideas were having a rough time surviving in the world of force.

The Democrats of the country wanted no part of Tilden's reserve: they staged victory parades, fired victory salutes, sang of their quarter-million majority. The more hotheaded ones among them began talking of fighting with their bullets if their ballots were powerless to win; this feeling was accentuated when in Louisiana, where Tilden had a seven-thousand majority, the board threw out thirteen thousand of his votes; it burst into flame when in Florida, in spite of Tilden's conclusive majority, the board certified the Hayes electors.

When all of the electoral votes had been dispatched to the Senate it was found that Tilden still had one hundred and eighty-four votes. Hayes had one hundred and sixty-six. In dispute were nineteen votes of the three southern states where both parties claimed a majority. The Republicans, who had a majority in the Senate, claimed that that body not only had the right to count the electoral votes but to decide which ones were valid. The Democrats, who had a majority in the House, claimed that only the House could decide upon contested votes. The Constitution was vague on the subject.

Tilden was completely convinced that the House should decide between conflicting electoral returns; to prove his point he wrote and published a brilliant study under the title of *The Presidential Counts*. At times he seemed more interested in the case as a lawyer than as a prospective president, preparing long and detailed briefs because he believed that the election laws needed clarification so that this kind of impasse could not occur again. By distributing his material to the newspapers, by seeing that *The Presidential Counts* reached a large part of the influential public, he prevented the Senate from accepting the Republican votes of the southern states. Thus he put himself in the lead at the first turn, but it was to be a long race: for the Republicans were threatening war if the House tried to seat him.

The cooler Tilden remained in his legal fight, the closer the rest of the country approached the boiling point. The battle cry of "Tilden or Blood!" arose; Democrats began re-forming their old companies; officers demanded that he allow them to fight their way into Washington; thousands of men offered their services and their lives.

Another Civil War was in the making. It required only one word from Tilden, one barely perceptible nod.

He refused to say the word. He would countenance no force. He insisted on being installed in the White House through the existing legal machinery, by the decision of the House.

Since the Senate never would accept a decision of the House, nor the House a decision by the Senate, it became increasingly obvious that the affair could be settled only by arbitration. Numerous schemes sprang up in Congress, some of them involving the drawing of lots. Tilden killed these proposals by saying, "I do not care a snap of my fingers for the presidency, and will not consent to raffle for it."

He maintained that he would accept the arbitration of no extralegal body: according to his reading of the law the Constitution provided a means of settling electoral disputes and definitely did not provide for the setting up of arbitration commissions. However, inauguration day was drawing close, it was known that Grant wanted a third term, that he was hoping that Tilden and Hayes would stymie each other. Believing that justice would emerge out of the right on their side, the Democratic congressmen used all their persuasion to make Tilden accept an Arbitration Commission; he disapproved of the plan, but finally acceded to the wishes of his confreres.

Congress therewith passed a bill setting up a commission to be composed of five members of the Senate, five of the House and five from the Bench. Having declared the bill unconstitutional, Tilden and Hayes agreed to accept its decision. Of the fifteen men on the commission, seven were Democrats, seven were Republicans, and one, Judge Bradley, was to be neutral and objective. Some time before midnight of the last day one of Tilden's campaign managers read an opinion written by Judge Bradley in favor of Tilden's electors. He reported back to headquarters that Tilden would be selected. However he had left the judge's house a bit too early: a Republican senator and Republican cabinet officer spent the rest of the night with the judge.

The following day the commission declared Rutherford Hayes to be the legally elected president. Fourteen of the fifteen members of the commission were lawyers, yet they made their decision on straight party lines; the evidence played no part in their judgment.

When told of the result Sam Tilden smiled quietly and murmured, "It is what I expected."

But the nation was rent by cries of "Fraud! Dishonesty! Corruption!" Once again Grant sent Federal troops marching, while Tilden's supporters begged him to, "Lead us! We will put you in the White House, where you belong!"

Samuel J. Tilden relinquished all leadership. Bitterly disillusioned, exhausted, he reasoned that it was better to let Hayes and the Republicans have the election than to plunge the country once again into bloodshed and destruction. He permitted Hayes to be inaugurated under the heaviest burden ever carried by an American executive, to spend a miserable and execrated four years in the White House.

"I can retire to private life," said Tilden, "with the consciousness that I shall receive from posterity the credit of having been elected to the highest position in the gift of the people, without any of the cares and responsibilities of the office."

Though he lived for another ten years he was never in robust health; he remained as a counselor of his party, but refused the nomination in 1880.

It had been a photo finish, with history serving as the infallible camera. By the time the film could be developed the wrong people had collected their money and gone home, the stands were deserted, the track dark. Yet there remains the picture for all time, with Tilden out in front by a nose.

6

What kind of president would Tilden have made? Four million three hundred thousand American voters had rallied to his banners with the zeal of warriors. He had inflamed the nation as no man since Fremont or Lincoln. Such public enthusiasm is not always an indication of a man's ability to deliver, but in the case of Tilden, who had no personal charm or warmth to awaken interest, this zeal had to be based upon a record of past performances.

With Tilden as president there would have been no family life in the White House; an undemonstrative man with few friends, the White House might have been a chill place. He was methodical, secretive, cautious, wanting complete and perfect proof before making a decisive move. In certain upswing periods of American history these characteristics might have been a drag upon the country, but in 1877, when the greatest need of the day was to bring honesty, economy and prudence into the government, administrative conduct based upon fact and science rather than grab and revenge, they might have made Samuel J. Tilden one of America's most able presidents.

It is not necessary to minimize Hayes's solid competence to indicate that Tilden had the broader and deeper mind, the greater courage, the profounder conception of the structure of the nation. While he had been campaigning brilliantly on cogent issues, not even the most experienced newspaperman in the nation could get a syllable out of Hayes. "Seldom has a candidate more wholly ascended his party than did Tilden; seldom has a candidate been more completely submerged by his party than was Hayes."

As the legally constituted chief executive Tilden would have searched the country high and wide for the most able men to run the various services; he would have set on foot a movement to impeach corrupt officers, would have kept up a continuous education of the public on the work being done in reform. His activities as a legislator and governor had been precisely the kind needed in a president in 1876: he had helped put the state finances on a sound basis, abolished much graft, rescued New York-owned enterprises from the hands of mulctors, helped draw up a new and modern constitution for the state. He would have striven to make his administration run as efficiently and cheaply as possible, setting up the Federal government as a model for lesser governments.

In relation to the south he would have made a complete and scientific study of conditions, then set up a progressive program to bring peace and prosperity to the ravaged states. Certainly he would have taken the corrupt carpetbagger off the neck of the south, helped it to function under its own government; this alone would have made him a great administrator.

Though Hayes's biographer admits that Tilden won the election, and "was one of the ablest men of the country, if not the ablest," he still believes that it was better for Hayes to have occupied the presidency because the Republican hatred of Tilden would have prevented him from accomplishing anything, either for the south or in the way of reform. This judgment leaves out of account two crucial factors: Tilden's adamant character, and the fact that he had a quarter-of-a-million majority of the votes. As an astute and scientific politician he would have known how to handle his die-hard opponents. He had handled them in New York with great success for the state. He would have made his reforms stick: in spite of his poor health and delicate condition he was a bulldog of tenacity whenever he was convinced that something had to be done.

Considering the handicaps under which Hayes took office he turned in a good record: he helped break up the unscrupulous Senate Ring of Roscoe Conkling and his followers, fought the corruption in the port collector's office, made attempts to reform the civil service—though he paid off for the electoral votes swung to him in the election. He made efforts to help the south, yet he remained at heart an insular governor of Ohio who knew little of the outside world.

Tilden's attitude would have kindled respect and enthusiasm for the democratic form of government, whereas Hayes, labeled with "Fraud!" across his forehead in several of the nation's papers on inauguration day, through no fault of his own created contempt for the system of popular elections.

Tilden was a better man than Hayes to start with; his defeat in an honest election would have been a blow to the nation. But to have him elected by a sizable majority, and then despoiled of his office by a corrupt machine, multiplied the tragedy of his loss by a mathematical formula which could have been worked out only by Sam Tilden himself.

BOOK SIX

Main Chance Politicos

I: STEPHEN A. DOUGLAS
II: JAMES G. BLAINE

*They tried too hard. In politics, as in love, a soupçon
of reluctance aids in the conquest.*

◆━◆━━◆━◆

CHAPTER ONE

Stephen A. Douglas

WHEN Stephen Douglas was only a few weeks old his father, who was holding the baby in his arms before the fire, suffered a heart attack. The infant fell to the floor, but "a neighbor, happening in the door at that moment, saved the child from the flames." There was no rescuer handy when Douglas dropped the nation into the flames.

Of all the Also Rans it can be said of him with the greatest truth that "he did not sneeze without reference to the presidency."

He was the man who brought Abraham Lincoln into national politics: it was his defense of the right of slavery to be extended to the territories, his exclamation that "I don't care whether slavery is voted up or down!" which caused Lincoln to mint the line which resolved slavery to its ultimate issue: "A nation cannot exist half slave and half free!" If there had been no Abe Lincoln, Douglas might have been forgotten; if there had been no Lincoln, Douglas also might have been president.

Douglas was called "a steam engine in britches." He won his name because of his unflagging energy; it doubly was

238

earned by his proclivity for letting off steam: the more steam he let off, the faster his puffy, stubby locomotive scooted down the tracks toward the White House.

His yearning was apparent to everyone. When he was only twenty-seven, Joseph Smith, leader of the Mormons, said to him, "Judge, you will aspire to the presidency. If you ever turn your hand against me or the Latter Day Saints you will feel the hand of the Almighty upon you."

Stephen Douglas began aspiring to the presidency when he was twenty-one; he ended by holding Lincoln's hat at the inaugural services of 1861, there being no room on the little table for Lincoln's tall beaver. Symbolically this was the hand of the Almighty resting on Douglas' brow: he who had determined to be the First Man of his times comes down through history holding the hat of the inelegant rustic whom he had defeated for the senatorship of Illinois only two years before.

He appears to have been called the Little Giant more because he was little than because he was a giant. He was a beautiful youth: his dark brown hair he wore as long and bushy as a woman's, parted on the left side and combed with a mass of rich waves rolling halfway down both sides of his head; his skin was dark but animated by a glow of vigorous youth; his eyes were dark blue, big, sentimental in repose, flashing in action; he had a strong, projecting nose and a mouth which slanted downward on the left side. He was short of neck, his chin riding only a couple of inches above his chest, but he was able to divert attention from this deficiency by centering it on his luxuriant hair. He had a huge head, impressive as a cannon ball; square, small, pudgy hands and abbreviated legs. One night while campaigning through the countryside he put up at a one-room cabin. After he had peeled off his outer garments Serena, the seventeen-year-old daughter of the family, observed sagely, "Mr. Douglas, you have got a mighty small chance of legs there."

When he left his home in New York at nineteen and his mother asked, "When will we see you again?" he replied, "I will stop by and see you on my way to Congress within the next ten years." Actually it took him eleven years to become a congressman.

He had a magnificent speaking voice, its sexual vibrations enchanting men as well as women; he was a clever and resourceful debater; he was an adroit maneuverer for compromises; he was a party whip; he had the courage of his ambitions; but above all he had charm and personal warmth. His tremendous personality excited people: once they had met him or heard him talk they remained excited about Stephen A. Douglas the rest of their lives. Because he rose to national

239

fame so young, in a field dominated by oldsters, projected so much youthful vigor and enthusiasm, the young people of the country came to think of him as their champion. In all elections he had a powerful youthful backing.

He was a perennial Fourth of July sparkler, an effervescent soda pop that never lost its bubbles. He served his own career with magnificent faithfulness during his twenty-seven years in public life; like Henry Clay he also served the nation's interest whenever their tracks happened to run parallel.

Among the Also Rans he was the most subtle artist at protective coloring and self-deception: any move which he thought would bring him a step closer to the presidency became in his mind the best possible move for the country. When almost singlehanded he secured the repeal of the Missouri Compromise, which had kept the slave and free states at peace for thirty years, and replaced it with the Kansas-Nebraska Act which led directly to the Civil War, a tactic for which he was bitterly criticized, he cried to a young friend:

"Stick to the law, my boy. Never go into politics! If you do, no matter how sincere and earnest you may be, no matter how ardently you devote yourself to the welfare of your country, you will be misinterpreted, vilified, traduced, and finally sacrificed to unreasoning passion!"

In mental equipment, character and driving ambition Stephen A. Douglas was the descendant of Henry Clay, the progenitor of James G. Blaine. He had "a wonderful faculty for extracting from his associates, from experts and others, by conversation, all they knew of a subject he was to discuss, and then making it so thoroughly his that all seemed to have originated with him."

In 1852, the first presidential race in which he was a factor, he said to the editor of a Boston paper, "I do not consider myself a candidate in the field. I am young and can afford to wait." In a private letter he wrote, "Things look well and the prospect is brightening every day. All that is necessary now to insure success is that the northwest should unite and speak out." He did not consider himself a candidate, yet he lashed himself and his followers so hard that "Douglas' case has been overworked, and thus was spoiled. With one fourth the effort on the part of his friends, and no more, he would have been the nominee."

Douglas called Henry Clay his master. From him he learned the miracle of the hummingbird: reversal in mid-air without first stopping the forward movement, the great whirring of wings without moving an inch in any direction.

Douglas' life is synonymous with slavery—but only because he willed it so. He could not leave the issue alone. He

240

saw no moral question involved. It was a millstone around his neck which he imagined he was crafty enough to convert, by a skillful rounding of its edges, to a wheel for his presidential chariot.

2

Stephen Arnold Douglas was born at Brandon, Vermont, on April 23, 1813, the son of a physician. His paternal grandfather was with Washington at Valley Forge; his mother was declared to be a woman of "courage and character." When Dr. Douglas died of the heart attack which almost consigned infant Stephen to the flames, his mother moved with her two children to the farm of her bachelor brother. Stephen was a normally bright lad; he attended school in the winter and worked on his uncle's farm in the summer. When he was seventeen his mother married into a prosperous family of Clifton Springs, New York; he enjoyed two years at Canandaigua Academy, where he read in the classics; this appears to have been his first and last venture into literature.

Stories of the pioneer west excited the young man: he reasoned that he could grow up with the new country. He read law for a short time in St. Louis and Cleveland, taught school in Winchester, Illinois, to earn a living, and within a year applied for his license as a lawyer. The examining judge granted the permit grudgingly, saying:

"You must apply yourself closer to the study of the law."

Stephen never took the advice. He moved to Jacksonville, the county seat, and, finding that there was no law work to be had, jumped into local politics feet first. He made quite a splash. Like Clay before him, and Blaine to come, he was a natural actor: he donned a pair of Kentucky jeans, adopted a frontier vocabulary, threw himself into a vigorous defense of Andrew Jackson's policies. He wrote to his mother, "I have become a western man, with western feelings, principles and interests." If this would seem to be a too-quick conversion, it is the adaptability of the born actor who can play any role convincingly after a short rehearsal.

A gamecock of a man, quick on the vocal trigger, a straight and logical thinker when in the heat of argument, courageous against any odds, he became a valuable campaigner for the Democrats by the time he was twenty-one. He secured his first public office by a party cabal, legislating the incumbent Whig out of the office of state's attorney, then slipping neatly into the niche himself, a bit of wangling for which he was to do considerable explaining. The examining judge who had advised him to apply himself closer to the law exclaimed irately when he heard the news, "What right has such a stripling with such an office? He is no lawyer and has no lawbooks."

Douglas didn't want to be a lawyer; he wanted to be a politician: "He started at once for the presidency." He rode circuit as state's attorney, was witty, resourceful, dramatic, charming, energetic, hearty, assets which served as a working substitute for a knowledge of the law in pioneer Illinois. Winning a difficult case by a daring bit of bravado, he evolved a lifetime motto:

"Admit nothing, and require my adversary to prove everything."

To him the law was a contest of wits; on the national scene he was to treat political issues as a series of games in which he strove for personal victory.

Within a year after securing his first public office he took to the stump in his own behalf and had himself elected to the state legislature. His next job was register of the Federal Land Office in Springfield, after which he lost a race for Congress by a bare fistful of votes. This defeat did not cramp his style: in 1840 he became chairman of the Democratic State Committee and showed such a tremendous talent for political organization that he carried Illinois for the Democrats and Van Buren though the Whigs won the national election.

As a reward he was appointed secretary of state for Illinois, then justice of the Supreme Court. If he didn't know too much law he at least knew how to clear the docket, for he cut through years of held-over cases with a combination of honesty and common sense which made him known affectionately throughout the state as "the Baby Judge."

By the time he was thirty he had organized his congressional district within an inch of its life, stumping the region in dramatic fashion. "I live with my constituents, eat with my constituents, drink with them, lodge with them, pray with them, laugh, hunt, dance and work with them; I eat their corn dodgers and fried bacon and sleep two in bed with them."

It would be difficult to tell whether it was the eating, sleeping or praying, but in 1843 the district elected him to the House of Representatives. In his ten years in Illinois he had developed into a first-rate party organizer, an expert dissector of issues, a smart campaigner; his skill in handling people and making himself liked, his driving force and warm charm earned him a battalion of loyal friends. He believed his party always to be right; he fought to the last ditch when, deep in his crafty unconscious, he knew both his party and himself to be wrong. The odds were a thousand to one against his ever turning on his own organization.

Named chairman of the Committee on Territories by the House of Representatives he worked, like all westerners, for expansion in the southwest and the Pacific coast. He became known as a fiery orator and brilliant debater. The House was but another stop on his journey to the presidency: after two years the Illinois Democratic machine of which he was now the undisputed boss named him to the United States Senate.

When he was thirty-three years old Stephen Douglas married Martha Martin, beautiful daughter of a North Carolina plantation owner. He had never been farther south than St. Louis, knew little of the actual workings of slavery; up to the time of his marriage he had never held any brief for slavery. When his father-in-law offered him a plantation with a hundred and fifty slaves as a wedding gift, he refused on the polite grounds that as a northern man he knew nothing of slaves and could not manage them. Through the Martin family Douglas was introduced to southern life in its most agreeable form, becoming definitely sympathetic.

Basically he disapproved of slavery but in his public utterances he remained amoral: "I have no sympathy for Abolitionism on the one side, or the extreme course on the other which is akin to Abolitionism." To the southerners he said, "We stand up for all your constitutional rights, in which we will protect you to the last, but we protest against being made instruments, puppets, in this slavery excitement. We have molded our institutions at the north as we have thought proper; and now we say to you of the south, 'If slavery be a blessing, it is your blessing; if it be a curse, it is your curse.'" The Douglas marriage was an entirely happy one, he was devoted to his wife and two sons; nevertheless it was to make him increasingly obtuse to the moral issue, so that Abraham Lincoln would be able to say about him, "Douglas' Popular Sovereignty simply is, 'If one man would enslave another, neither that other nor any third man has a right to object.'"

When Stephen Douglas entered Congress in 1843 the country was enjoying the comparative peace engendered by the Missouri Compromise of 1820, under which the north agreed to admit Missouri as a slave state and the south agreed that slavery should be excluded from all American soil north of 36:30, temporarily establishing the right of Congress to exclude slavery from the new territories. Neither side had been overly happy about the compromise: the northern abolitionists talked about setting up "a new Union of thirteen or fourteen states unpolluted with slavery," the more extravagant southerners spoke of the establishment of a Slave Confederacy; for

243

twenty-three years the two sections, about equal in strength and representation, had kept each other from doing anything rash or dangerous. Cooler political heads felt that although the Union might have been a weak and tottering thing in 1820, when the Missouri Compromise was passed, its strength was growing, and if the compromise could continue for a few more years the feeling for the indivisibility of the nation would become so strong that not even slavery could split it.

Douglas felt this way when he stepped up to the Senate in 1847. So crucial to the unity of the nation did he believe the Missouri Compromise to be that he said, "It is canonized in the hearts of the American people as a sacred thing, which no ruthless hand would ever be reckless enough to destroy." Had the twenty-nine United States remained permanently set as a nation when Douglas reached the Senate, there would have been little likelihood of civil war. But new lands were being pioneered; war was waging with Mexico over Texas, California and what later became the states of New Mexico, Nevada, Arizona and Utah; the government was struggling with England over the possession of the Pacific northwest. America was on the march! Was it on the march to become a free or slave country? The north said the new lands must be free; the south said at least half of them must be slave. Between these two factions Douglas set about to effect a compromise: it was while groping his way through this No Man's Land that he was blown up by his own hand grenade.

Stephen A. Douglas reasoned that no man could become an outstanding national figure who remained outside the arena of the slavery embroilment. Because of his single-tracked ambition he felt impelled to whip the conflict into a unifying compromise, believing that the man who settled the problem of slavery would roll into the White House on a giant wave of acclaim. Had he remained quiet in the manner that Pierce and Buchanan had remained quiet he would in all likelihood have followed his two Democratic predecessors into the White House in 1860. His use of slavery as a whipping post was the tactical error of his career.

When the war with Mexico was over and there arose the problem of slavery in the newly acquired territories, Douglas, as chairman of the Senate Committee on Territories, suggested that the line of the Missouri Compromise be extended to the Pacific, making Texas, New Mexico, Arizona and southern California slave states, all the territory above this line to be free. This seemed to him to be a fair and workable solution.

The south was pleased; the north was outraged. In order to preserve the balance of power the south was determined to secure one new slave state for every free state admitted to the Union; the north was determined that there should never be another acre of slave territory, insisting that the Missouri Compromise gave Congress the right to exclude slavery from all new territories. Douglas was politically embarrassed by the uproar his suggestion had caused, but it was not until the Illinois legislature passed a resolution publicly rebuking its own senator for his attempt to extend slavery that he realized that he was in serious trouble. A more rigorously ethical figure might have resigned in the face of this repudiation by his own people; Douglas only stuck his battering-ram of a head into the wind and went seeking still another compromise, one which would placate the voters of Illinois.

"Douglas' interest in Popular Sovereignty seems to have developed largely out of a purely local situation."

He did not want slavery to spread to new territories; he believed it doomed by geography and climate to remain precisely where it was. After winning the favor of the south by voicing the right of slavery to be extended, he now suggested that slavery would not be extended to any of the territories because cotton could not be raised in them profitably. Having lost his friends in the north for appearing to want the spread of slavery, he also lost his admirers in the south for implying that his plan was a hoax.

It was to extricate himself from this painful dilemma that he worked with his friend and political master, Henry Clay, to bring the Compromise of 1850 into the Senate. Douglas' bills, combined with Clay's, achieved the admission of California as a free state, admitted New Mexico and Utah as territories without any prohibition against slavery and put into effect a stronger Fugitive Slave Law. When the senator went home to Chicago he was asked to explain why he had been in New York when the Fugitive Slave Law was passed; he heard the epithet that was to ring in his ears until the day of his death; "Traitor!"

Because of his work for the Compromise of 1850, Douglas conceived of himself as the logical candidate for the 1852 Democratic nomination. He believed he had pleased the south by agreeing to a Fugitive Slave Law, by opening the new southern territories to slavery without offending too greatly over the admission of California as a free state. He believed that he had pleased the north by securing the admission of California, which the south had been holding up, by assuring the north in a series of asides that it could do no harm to allow slavery to be introduced into New Mexico and Utah because cotton could not be grown there, by assuring a

245

northern terminus to the country's first transcontinental railroad.

"Prospects look well and are improving every day," he wrote to a friend. "If two or three western states will speak out in my favor the battle is over."

But for all his efforts he had not appeased the south sufficiently, receiving only two votes from that region on the first ballot. His strength rose from twenty votes to ninety-one on the twenty-ninth ballot, when he was trailing the leading Buchanan by only two votes. If he could have had the support of the south at this point, a support he felt he had earned, the nomination would have been his. He and Buchanan continued to stymie each other; a dark horse by the name of Franklin Pierce was brought in and nominated.

His defeat convinced Douglas that he had to have southern support if he hoped to become president. His newly hatched Kansas-Nebraska Bill was his answer to the problem: by throwing all of the nation open to slavery he surely would win the undying love of the south; when the new territories voted for freedom instead of slavery, as he was convinced they would, he would prove to the north that he was the wisest compromiser of his age, the inevitable nominee of his party in 1856, the right man for the White House.

It was on January 4, 1854, that Douglas fired what may have been the first shot of the Civil War: he brought in the Kansas-Nebraska Bill, which repealed the Missouri Compromise, denied the right of the Federal government to legislate slavery out of the territories, opened the territories of Kansas, Nebraska, Montana, the Dakotas and parts of Colorado and Wyoming to slavery—if its settlers wanted slavery. This was Douglas' theory of Popular Sovereignty. He made powerful speeches, filled with brilliant sophistries, declared the Missouri Compromise to be unconstitutional because it was a restriction on the peoples of the north, forbidding them to hold slaves! "If the people want slavery, they have a right to it, and if they do not, it should not be forced upon them. The determination as to whether a new state shall be slave or free depends not upon the north or south, but upon the people themselves. The principle of self-government is that each community shall settle this question for itself; I hold that the people of a new state have a right either to prohibit or establish slavery, and we have no right to complain either in the north or the south, whichever they do!"

Harriet Beecher Stowe, who listened to Douglas fighting for his bill in the Senate, wrote, "His speeches, instead of being like an arrow sent at the mark resemble rather a bomb which hits nothing in particular, but bursts and sends red-hot nails in every direction." Douglas' opponents were so busy dodging the hot nails that they had no opportunity to counterattack.

Only a few years before Stephen Douglas had said, "The Missouri Compromise is canonized in the hearts of the American people as a sacred thing, which no ruthless hand would ever be reckless enough to destroy." After his Compromise of 1850 he had declared that slavery was now a dead issue, vowing never to discuss it again. The Union was in no danger when he introduced his Kansas-Nebraska Bill. "There was not even any demand for the legislation until Douglas created it." Instead of calming the strife it brought such a storm on the country as it had never known before, and was never to know again except when engaged in civil war.

By this bill which Douglas rammed through both Houses by sheer magnetism, manipulation and drive, he awakened the anger and fear of the north as it had never been awakened before. Abolitionism took a tremendous spurt. He was burned in effigy, condemned by vast organizations of clergymen, educators, editors; called a Judas, handed thirty pieces of silver, howled down for four solid hours when he tried to justify himself to the home folks in Chicago. An examination of history reveals not the tiniest shred of an excuse for his having introduced the bill . . . except that it looked to Stephen A. Douglas like the Main Chance to achieve the presidency.

The south was delighted with his work; he could count on their votes in the 1856 convention. The independent Democrats of the north cried:

"Will the people permit their dearest interests to be thus made the mere hazards of a presidential game?"

All he needed now was for Kansas to declare for freedom, for Kansas and Nebraska to become free states and prove to the north that he had done the cause of freedom no harm; that Popular Sovereignty was, after all, the best solution to slavery in a democracy; and he would have demonstrated himself to be the cleverest manipulator in the history of the country, the man who, singlehanded, had solved the unsolvable problem of slavery. The nomination and election of 1856 were in the bag.

Then the first guns were fired in Kansas, the first men died in the prologue to the Civil War. Stephen A. Douglas was among the casualties.

3

Under Douglas' Kansas-Nebraska Bill the residents of

Kansas could vote whether they wanted to be free or slave—only there were no residents. Freedom and slavery men rushed to Kansas in order to be there when the voting took place. Up to this moment the conflict over slavery had been waged largely in terms of excited argumentation; now the two opposing sides met in Kansas with guns in their hands. When it came time to elect the legislature which would exercise Douglas' theory of Popular Sovereignty by deciding whether Kansas was to be slave or free, three quarters of the votes were cast by heavily armed invaders from neighboring Missouri, who crossed the line solely to vote and secure the state for slavery. Anti-slavery men were driven from the polls by mobs; every fraud was exercised in electing a complete slave legislature.

Douglas' theory of self-government had broken its front axle the first time it went out on the road.

The pro-slavery legislature drew up a slave constitution. The Free Staters held their own convention in which they drew up a constitution prohibiting slavery. Armed forces clashed; there were shootings, killings and a siege of the town of Lawrence. Douglas had assured the north that Kansas never could be anything but a free state; the south had assured itself that Kansas never would be anything but a slave state. The Missouri rifles now came in conflict with Horace Greeley's "Beecher Bibles."

The three candidates for the 1856 Democratic nomination were President Pierce, Douglas and Buchanan. Pierce started twelve votes behind Buchanan, but by the tenth ballot he had disappeared. Douglas started with thirty-three votes, absorbing Pierce's support as the president faded. By the sixteenth ballot Douglas had gathered a hundred and twenty-one votes, but Buchanan lacked only eighteen ballots of the necessary two thirds. Once again it became evident that Stephen A. Douglas had run in the second money when there was nothing to be awarded but a first prize. Yielding to the blandishments of Buchanan's lieutenants that they would repay his loyalty in 1860, Douglas admitted defeat, threw his votes to Buchanan, then went on the stump to campaign for a victory over John C. Fremont.

He was still only forty-three years old. He had plenty of time.

But political misfortunes began to fall like hailstones on the Little Giant's head. Buchanan, instead of being grateful for Douglas' support, stripped him of all patronage and power, ostracizing him from administration circles. The violence, guerrilla warfare and destruction of self-government in Kansas were making him out to be a fool, a knave or a conniver. Chief Justice Roger Brooke Taney handed down the Dred Scott decision, which said that an owner's property rights over his slaves extended into all states and territories of the Union, consequently neither the Federal nor the state governments had any right to prohibit slavery. The people of a territory or state had no right to prohibit slavery, even though the Free Staters might be in a majority!

Douglas put up a show to prove that the decision confirmed his Popular Sovereignty; the southerners laughed in his face, the northerners grew frightened and rebellious.

Stephen Douglas' chickens came home to roost in Kansas, where the Lecompton Convention, made up of pro-slavery men representing about a quarter of the state's voters, drew up a new constitution containing alternate planks on slavery: the Free Staters could reject the constitution which endorsed slavery, but if they did they had to vote to protect the slaves already in Kansas, and their increase as well; whichever way the Free Staters voted they got slavery. President Buchanan fired the governor of Kansas for denouncing the Lecompton Constitution as a fraud, gave it administration backing, made it a test of party loyalty and jammed it through both Houses. Douglas knew that Buchanan was attempting further to discredit him, to hold the allegiance of the south and to insure his own renomination in 1860.

Stephen Douglas broke with the party he had loved and served since he had been twenty-one. With a fiery speech in the Senate he announced to the world that another war had been added to the war in Kansas: the war between Douglas and Buchanan. He was outraged at the fraud and violence being practiced in Kansas, he was outraged at the Free State majority in Kansas having a slave constitution stuffed down its throat, he was outraged at the administration for making it a test of party loyalty to vote for the Lecompton fraud. Yet there was more to his revolt than virtuous indignation. The Kansas fiasco, in exposing the underlying weakness of Popular Sovereignty, had exposed him as a statesman. It was clear that the administration could force the Lecompton Bill through both Houses and, when that happened, Stephen A. Douglas would be out in the cold. The war in Kansas, Chief Justice Taney, President Buchanan and the solidarity of the Democratic party were in process of making him a dead duck.

There was only one way to come back into power: smash Buchanan, discredit his administration, denounce the Lecompton Constitution in the Senate, demand that Kansas be admitted as a free state, put himself in solid with his Illinois voters and provide a barrage for the northern drive against

Buchanan. For this tactic he was read out of his party, only five Democrats voting with him against the admission of Kansas under the Lecompton Constitution.

His first wife having died in childbed, Douglas had married the young and gracious Adèle Cutts, a charming southern woman who captivated Washington society by her brilliant dinners and soirees, and made Senator Douglas' home the social center of Washington. It is interesting to contemplate whether Douglas, if he had married a northern woman originally, if he had not become a "Doughface," a northern man with southern principles, would have fought for the repeal of the Missouri Compromise, battled for the right of the people in a new territory to decide for themselves whether or not they wanted slavery. If he had not forced through the Kansas-Nebraska Bill there would have been no John Brown's raid on Harpers Ferry, no *Uncle Tom's Cabin,* no opportunity for Jefferson Davis and his Fire Eaters to rouse the south to a frenzy over secession. He might have had Lincoln's side of the argument in 1858, and the Republicans would have had to go scratching for an issue. With a unified Democratic party behind him he could have defeated Lincoln and become president.

Instead, in 1858, he found himself disavowed by his party, in danger of losing his seat in the Senate to an upstart Republican. He would stage a whirlwind campaign, discuss national rather than state issues, prove himself to be the one leader of the true Democratic party! Certainly there was nothing that Buchanan could do that would stop him?

His plans were well laid; they would have carried—except for one factor. He had reckoned without Abraham Lincoln.

The Douglas-Lincoln debates are the most famous of modern times. They ranged the width and breadth of Illinois, with the nation following them avidly in the press. No two men could have been in greater contrast: Douglas was short, chunky, handsome, urbane, rich, polished, world-famous, fashionably dressed, superbly poised; Lincoln was grotesquely tall, awkward, homely, crude, ill at ease, dressed in ill-fitting clothes. However Douglas did not underestimate his opponent: "Lincoln is as honest as he is shrewd, and if I beat him my victory will be hardly won."

Douglas was carried to Chicago to open his campaign in a special train, convoyed to his hotel in a carriage drawn by six horses, with a military escort, a crowd of many thousands jamming the neighborhood of the Tremont Hotel. Lincoln arrived on foot, alone. When stumping the state Douglas traveled in a private car with a swank entourage, red carpets, the best of food, drink and entertainment and endless changes of fresh linen; the days when he ate, prayed and slept two in a bed with his constituents were gone. Lincoln rode the dusty day coach in his battered high hat, long coat of which the sleeves were too short, trousers of which the legs were too short.

The Illinois senatorial election of 1858 was a dress rehearsal of the presidential election of 1860, with the Democrat Douglas pleading for Popular Sovereignty, the Republican Lincoln arguing that "this government cannot endure permanently half slave and half free. I do not expect the Union to be dissolved—I do not expect the House to fall—but I do expect it will cease to be divided."

Douglas struck out on a vigorous speaking tour, renewing friendships and stirring the large crowds to enthusiasm. Lincoln trailed him from town to town, speaking from the same platform the following day. When Douglas was challenged by Lincoln to a series of debates he knew that he had everything to lose and nothing to gain: he was the incumbent; he was the better known; he was drawing larger crowds than Lincoln; there was every reason to believe that he was winning the contest. If he submitted to the debates they could only have the effect of raising Lincoln to his own stature, giving him a better opportunity to be heard and increasing his chance of winning.

Stephen Douglas was never a coward. He accepted Lincoln's challenge, and the seven debates began, debates in which Douglas was to win the election but lose the argument.

The Douglas-Lincoln debates were a review of the history of slavery legislation as well as a prognosis of its future status in the United States. Douglas stuck to his guns for Popular Sovereignty: "Whenever you put a limitation upon the right of a people to decide what laws they want, you have destroyed the fundamental principles of self-government. Mr. Lincoln asserts that there must be uniformity in the local laws and domestic institutions, and he therefore invites the non-slaveholding states to band together and make war upon slavery in all the slaveholding states until it shall be exterminated."

Douglas held a clear advantage in the early debates, for he put Lincoln on the defensive, kept him explaining that he neither favored the extermination of slavery nor advocated civil war. He threw away this advantage by charging Lincoln with statements which the press quickly proved he had never made. The two men finally came to grips over the conflict between Popular Sovereignty and the Dred Scott decision: Lincoln asked Douglas, "Can the people of a Territory in any

251

lawful way exclude slavery from its limits prior to the formation of a State Constitution?"

Douglas was trapped: if he said no, he negated his own theory, the right of a majority to reject slavery. If he said yes he not only would infuriate the south but would be flying in the face of the Supreme Court, which had said that a slave continued to be private property no matter where he was taken. Douglas elected to stand by Popular Sovereignty: "I answer emphatically that in my opinion the people of a Territory can, by lawful means, exclude slavery. No matter what the decision of the Supreme Court may be on that abstract question, still the right of the people is perfect and complete under the Nebraska bill."

Lincoln then showed that only two years before Douglas had said in the Senate that "whether the people should exclude slavery prior to the formation of a Constitution or not is a matter for the Supreme Court." Douglas was hoisted by his own petard; the debates began going seriously against him.

The Lincoln delegates received 190,000 votes to 174,000 for Douglas. Because of the arrangement of voting districts, the Douglas electors were in a majority and the Illinois legislature returned him to the Senate.

He had assured his own nomination for the presidency in 1860. By his sporting acceptance of Lincoln's challenge he also had assured the nomination of Abraham Lincoln to run against him.

4

Douglas entered the 1860 Democratic convention as the strong man of his party, having made Buchanan's renomination impossible. He was now forty-seven years old. In every section of the country, north, west, south, he had bands of followers, particularly among the young people. There seemed little chance this time that a dark horse would outrun him in the homestretch, some other favorite flash across the turf, kicking dust in his eyes.

Unfortunately for Douglas and the Democrats, the convention was held in Charleston, South Carolina, the very heart of the Fire-Eater Secessionist south. Had the convention been held in New York or Chicago there might have been less pyrotechnical display for the home folks, and Douglas might have held his party together. Just as Henry Clay had wrecked the Whigs in his attempt to wreck President Tyler in 1840, so Douglas had split the Democrats in the wake of the wrecked Buchanan. Douglas controlled at all times a clear majority of the electors, but the southern Ultra-Slavery men made it impossible for him to secure the necessary two-thirds vote. Finally, in exhaustion, the convention adjourned for a month, to meet again in Baltimore. In spite of Douglas' heroic efforts to mollify the southern Ultras they bolted the party at the Baltimore convention. The main body of the Democrats nominated Douglas on a Popular Sovereignty platform; the bolters named John C. Breckinridge as their candidate; a fourth party was formed, the Constitutional Union party, which nominated John Bell of Tennessee. Douglas now had three opponents instead of one.

He fought the campaign with the red glare of war shining in his face, a glare he accelerated by telling the nation they had better not elect Lincoln or the south would secede. Emphatically denying the constitutional right of the south to secede, he spread the virus of disunion by using it as a campaign bugaboo. He attempted to achieve a final compromise to avert secession and war, stumped the country with demoniacal energy trying to persuade both sides to stop their inflammatory talk, to work within the Constitution, to mind their own business within their own states, to let Popular Sovereignty determine the fate of slavery within the new territories. But everywhere the specter of "bleeding Kansas" rose up to haunt him.

To his neighbors in Chicago he poured out his heart in one of his bilingual speeches. "I believe that this country is in more danger now than at any other moment since I have known anything of public life. It is not personal ambition that has induced me to take the stump this year. The presidency has no charms for me. But I do love this Union. There is no sacrifice on earth that I would not make to preserve it."

Stephen Douglas traveled thousands of miles in an effort to sell the country the idea of himself as a Union candidate. He made two and three major speeches a day, invaded the hostile south, where stories sprang up of his having been fired upon, of attempts to wreck his train. Lincoln remained quietly in Springfield, answering correspondence but refusing to make any statements on slavery beyond his 1858 debates. The west was confused, the south sullen and incendiary, the north feverish with joy at the prospect of a Republican victory and the beginning of the end of slavery. The Republican "Wide Awakes," covered by shining oilcloth capes, carrying burning torches, tramped all night. There were constant parades, with lines of decorated wagons, and a half million young men marching in military formation. A craze for rails and rail splitters swept the country, with a delegation of six-foot-two rail splitters marching in the streets of Boston.

The Republican party was vigorous, unified, unafraid, on the march; the Democrats were torn, frightened, nervous, hedging, voting to avoid trouble. Buchanan backed Breckinridge, throwing him the administration support. Pierce also backed Breckinridge, splitting the Democratic party even wider. Milton in his *Eve of Conflict* offers abundant proof that the Civil War was needless, blaming it largely on the Fire-Eater politicians of the south who wanted secession and a war to consolidate their waning power. He portrays 1860 as "a mad election; madness reigned." Surely there was more emotion and less reasoning exerted than in any single election in United States history.

Douglas moved hard and fast so that his magnetic presence would have its effect on people and gather in votes; he was hampered by the reluctance of wealthy eastern Democrats to contribute to his campaign fund because they were "afraid to lose their southern customers." Douglas spent his own money, worked himself into exhaustion. The harder he worked, the more ground he lost.

He opened his campaign in the slave states, on the levee in St. Louis where he had first stopped on his trek west after leaving his home at the age of nineteen. "I am not here tonight to ask you for your votes for the presidency. I am not one of those who believe that I have any more personal interest in the presidency than any other good citizen in America. I am here to make an appeal to you on behalf of the Union and the peace of the country."

He was sincere in his appeal for the Union; what he omitted to mention was that he had been one of the main instruments in cracking it open, that everything he had done since introducing his Kansas-Nebraska Bill in 1854 had cast the Union deeper into the fire.

By October, with Pennsylvania and Indiana carried by the Republicans, Douglas said, "Mr. Lincoln is elected President. We must try to save the Union. I will go south."

After months of trying to frighten the electorate out of voting for Lincoln by telling them that if the Republican were elected the south would secede, it was a courageous act for him to plead with the Fire Eaters to accept the verdict of the people. It took courage for him to say, "In my opinion there is a mature plan through the southern states to break up the Union. I believe the election of a Black Republican is to be the signal for that attempt, and that the leaders of the scheme desire the election of Lincoln so as to have an excuse for disunion." But he would have shown greater courage had he fought the election without fostering rebellion.

He was sitting in the office of the Mobile *Register* on election night when he heard that Abraham Lincoln was to be the next president. He had received 1,376,975 votes against 1,866,452 votes for Lincoln. However, Lincoln had received almost a million less votes than a majority! Breckinridge's 849,781 Democratic votes would have made Douglas president. Had the 588,879 votes garnered by Bell, who was running on a Union ticket similar to Douglas', gone to Douglas, he would have defeated Lincoln without Breckinridge's vote.

Like so many of his confreres among the Also Rans, like James G. Blaine to follow, Stephen A. Douglas had been nominated one election too late.

He lived only a few months after the election, dying in June 1861 at the age of forty-eight. During these months he worked to preserve the Union, to support President Lincoln, to prevent the war. Disappointment, heartbreak, bitterness caused his death, and perhaps a gnawing realization of the part he had played in bringing about the holocaust.

5

Stephen A. Douglas would have made a better president than he made an aspiring candidate. Once he had achieved the only possible cure for the ravages of presidentitis the fever would have fallen off and he would have been free to do good work. Aside from the maneuvering he might have had to do to insure his re-election in 1864, he would have striven for the national welfare, for the development of the west, for the cooling of both the Abolitionists and the Fire Eaters, for a plan of peace.

There would have been no Civil War in 1861 if Douglas had been elected: the south knew that he was friendly to their interests, would make no attempt to injure slavery where it already existed. During these four years a more moderate set of politicians might have come into power in the south, men who were not trying to establish a new nation; Popular Sovereignty might have proved to the south that slavery was unprofitable in the new territories, that their salvation lay in the continuation of slavery only within the states in which it then existed. Certainly Douglas would have worked with every ounce of his considerable strength and resourcefulness to make secession and war impossible. He might have succeeded.

Douglas had the juxtaposition of virtues and vices usually to be found in the professional politician: he was interested in the material progress of his country, and particularly of his section; he believed in granting public lands to homesteaders, in making grants to prospective railroads and canals. He believed in the free institutions of the American system, encouraged education by donating the land on which the University of Chicago was built, by helping to build the Smithsonian Institution; he urged Congress to admit all works of art free of tariff so that American artists could study from the old masters at home. He had an excellent memory, the ability to correlate facts into a cogent argument, was honest in governmental money matters. He was of a forgiving nature, was a good husband and father, had a host of loyal friends.

He was also a professional handshaker and charmer who used his personality to gather votes, was frequently invective in his speeches, could use illogic, bombast and quarter-truths to gain his point; he used the spoils of office to reward his followers and made political deals, used his power as a senator to develop regions where he owned great blocks of land; he was an opportunist and careerist who served himself first, his region second, his nation third.

The story of Stephen A. Douglas demonstrates that although a democracy needs specialists in government, the young men who clasp politics to their bosoms as a career often become too clever, too experienced in the tricks of the trade to be valuable to the nation as a whole. Thus democracy is sorely beset by a dilemma: experience is needed in the men who are to run the government, yet experience in this particular field has turned out more self-seeking party servitors than public servants. There can be no good government without experience, yet in politics, above all other callings, experience corrupts!

It is not difficult to compare Stephen A. Douglas and Abraham Lincoln as men, as thinkers, as humanists, yet we know Lincoln only as a war president; had Douglas been elected he almost certainly would have been known as a peacetime president. Lincoln's election cost us the war but earned us the Emancipation; Douglas' election might have saved us the war at the cost of a prolonged slavery in the south.

CHAPTER TWO

James G. Blaine

JAMES G. BLAINE came of a wealthy and important family that had run itself into the ground by the time he appeared on the scene. If the Blaine family had never been affluent, or if it still had been prosperous when James was growing up, he might have escaped the twists of character which made him money-mad. Resolved to return the Blaines to their former substance, he made large fortunes by devious means, owned palatial homes in Augusta, Maine, Washington, D.C., and Bar Harbor, employed six servants to wait on his family, traveled the world in state.

"Where does Blaine get his money?" folks asked.

The answer to that question deprived him of the presidency: he had made too much of it too easily. When he was told that he was hurting himself politically by fraternizing exclusively with millionaires, Blaine cried from the bottom of his heart:

"But I like rich people!"

James G. Blaine became important in American politics at the very moment that Stephen A. Douglas died; if there be anything to transmigration he inherited Douglas' political soul, complete and intact. They were two of the fiercest party men of their times; like the chorus girl who wouldn't go anywhere without her mother, Blaine and Douglas rarely would go anywhere without their parties—but their parties would go anywhere.

He was a container rather than a content: he could empty himself on the shortest notice and refill with any new material which he deemed expedient. As a supreme opportunist he was furnished with all modern political conveniences, including hot and cold running ideas.

He was the leader of the railroad lobby in Congress during the years of their colossal depredations of public funds. "Blaine has valuable suggestions on the Pacific Railroads and legislation," wrote Henry Cooke to his promoter brother, Jay. "He says that if we manage our case with discretion we can get a handsome money subsidy from Congress." While Speaker of the House of Representatives he was working as a railroad promoter, selling blocks of stock on the implication of the land and cash grants he could manipulate through Congress. Attempting to sell Jay Cooke a quarter of a million dollars' worth of Little Rock and Fort Smith Railroad stock for $91,500, he wrote to Cooke, "My position will enable me to render you services of vital importance and value. Are you not willing to aid me when you can do so with profit to yourself?"

The most able parliamentarian in Washington, he worked so brilliantly and vigorously against bills introduced into the House to control the railroads that he became known as Jay Gould's errand boy. His fellow congressmen did not know that Jay Gould held a thirty-thousand-dollar mortgage on Blaine's imposing Washington home. He was as blind to the moral issue involved in a congressman's acceptance of blocs of railroad stock from promoters as Douglas had been to the moral issue involved in slavery; it was on this moral obtuseness that both men foundered.

Blaine would not have accepted cash in payment for his vote on a bill favorable to a group or business; he simply felt it fair that business should let congressmen in on the legitimate profits of such enterprises as railroads, which were helping to develop the country. Never during the years that he was under attack, through the exposure, scandal and disgrace, did he give any indication that he understood the dangers involved in the earning of large sums of money by public officials through individuals and interests needing protection or favors in the national capital. Business and money were his gods; he honestly considered them incapable of doing wrong: they alone were responsible for the development and prosperity of the United States; any slight excess of which they might be guilty, such as the ladling out of money or land from the public funds, were a thousand times compensated for by the magnificent good they were doing the entire nation. When he was told that by such practices the people lost control over their government, that democracy was superseded by a financial oligarchy, he was sincerely astonished and hurt.

James G. Blaine and Stephen A. Douglas were the long and short of the same proposition: Blaine was as tall as Douglas was truncated; yet there are no two figures to be found in American annals, unless it be their political relatives, Henry Clay and William Jennings Bryan, who are so astonishingly like father and son. Both were naturals in politics, became successful very young, had no other craft than politicking; both were consummate actors who never for an instant forgot they were playing roles on the national stage;

both were brilliant debaters, swift and clear on their feet, with a devastating gift of sarcasm; both were in all publicized issues up to their mouths. They both were experts at parliamentary maneuvering, with photographic memories; both attracted fanatically loyal followers through their animal magnetism. Both were party whips in Washington who held their state organizations in a dictatorial vise, and both broke their parties' decades of power by leading them to defeat. The blow with which Douglas felled the Democratic party made it possible for Blaine to rise to power as a Republican. Thus Douglas unwittingly helped prepare the way for his successor. They both were shrewd businessmen who made fortunes from their extracurricular activities, hummingbird politicians who lined their nests with plush.

Blaine liked people and people liked him; he had tremendous personal charm, and therein lay his grip on fame. "Providence," murmured Blaine, "has been pleased to bless me with a retentive memory." While traveling through the west, where he went not oftener than every fourth—presidential—year, he was able to stage such amazing scenes at every small-town stop of his train as:

"Why, my dear friend, Mr. Watkins! How do you do? And how is your father? Well, I hope. Why, Mr. Hodgkins! Delighted to see you again! And have you brought Mrs. Hodgkins and that bright, talented son of yours? And Willie? He must be nearly ready for graduation by this time. Ah, Mr. Tompkins! Have you still that gray horse you told me about that was so speedy? Your nephew? Glad to make your acquaintance, young man. I suppose, Mr. Adkins, you have finished that house you were building? What! Living in it? I wish I could see it."

Blaine was acting, reading from an ever-lengthening play script which he memorized through the years; it was superb acting because he loved both his role and his audience. One of the spectators recounts that it was done "not perfunctorily, not effusively, not condescendingly, not unctuously, but with a masterly finish, with sincerity, with warmth, with delicate and perceptive skill, with calm and gentle dignity, with a suggestion of greatness."

When maneuvering in Congress for his first presidential nomination it was said of him, "He is not a coy candidate. It is an honest aspiration and he indulges it like a man."

Blaine's political aspirations were out in the open; his financial aspirations he kept hidden in the dark labyrinth of his acquisitive soul. He had a genius for concealment; except for the exposures of the Congressional Investigating Committee, no one ever learned where James G. Blaine got his money, or how much, or why. He not only knew on which side his bread was buttered, but he also had a taste for jam; he used the gifts of his mind and personality to promote his career and garner his considerable share of the world's goods.

Blaine would take a bold stand in the midst of his cohorts, but no one ever found him standing alone. Should his party show signs of abandoning him on an issue, he promptly abandoned the cause.

He had the courage of his investments, not his convictions.

2

James G. Blaine was the fifth generation of Scotch-Irish stock, his great-great-grandfather having arrived in Pennsylvania from Londonderry in 1745. His great-grandfather fought in the French and Indian Wars, became Commissioner of Purchases and Provisions for the Revolutionary Army; his grandfather migrated west and made a sizable fortune by trading and acquiring large blocks of land. His father was admitted to the bar as a lawyer, but never practiced; he married Maria Gillespie, also of Scotch-Irish stock, and the young couple carried on the family tradition of moving ever westward, settling near Pittsburgh. No Blaine ever continued to live in the place of his childhood; it was not until the fifth American generation that one of them doubled back on the family tracks.

When the Blaines had been married for ten years they returned to the wife's home in West Brownsville, Pennsylvania, where James Gillespie Blaine was born on January 31, 1830. His father had failed as a settler, trader, land manipulator; he was now reduced to supporting his brood through political activity. A fervent Henry Clay Whig, he was elected to the office of county clerk, moving his family to the little town of Washington, the county seat, where they enjoyed the closest thing to a secure livelihood they had known.

Young James was brought up with Henry Clay as the household god: by the time he was ten he was a die-hard Whig, remaining one until 1856, at which time he was absorbed with tens of thousands of other Whigs into the new Republican party. To the young boy Henry Clay was the greatest man in the United States; he studied his speeches, conned his writings, determined to model himself in his master's image. He succeeded: just as Stephen Douglas before him had been the Henry Clay of 1850 to 1860, so Blaine became the Henry Clay of the period from 1865 to 1895. Like his predecessors, he had the gift for the felicitous phrase which upon examination proved to be the gift for the felicitous fraud.

At thirteen James entered Washington and Jefferson College in his home town; he was tall for his age, gawky, with a large nose which earned him the nickname of Nosey Blaine. He suffered from an impediment of speech that made him so sensitive he kept out of all debates and public discussions even though he was burning to argue politics. His mother had given him his education up to this time; he was the youngest in his class but he graduated in the top three. He did not drink, smoke, gamble or swear; his only vice was politics: he took to politics the way other boys took to baseball, was so much a natural in the field that it was later said of him that he was born under the rotunda of the Capitol in Washington. He had the identical mental gifts which carried Douglas so far, the same amorality in their utilization: a spongiose memory which recorded every line of his wide reading in history, literature, politics; the ability to knife through to the core of an issue, to bring every fact he had read to bear on a subject, swiftly and logically, when it was logic that would best serve his purpose. Twenty-two years before he was to hold the position he assured his boyhood chums that he would one day be Speaker of the House of Representatives.

He graduated at seventeen, a tall spindly youth with warm gray-brown eyes and a heartiness of manner which drew his young comrades to him. He had realized very young that he would have to compensate for his ugly impediment of speech, and this he accomplished with an overflow of kindliness, interest and magnetic projection. He wanted people to like him; in the eagerness of his desire he developed a physical emanation, a seed that entered people whether he was talking to them alone or in large crowds, which impregnated them with a devotion to James G. Blaine.

Seventeen-year-old Blaine wanted to attend Yale Law School but the family funds were low. Following the family tradition he set out for the west, locating a teaching job at the Western Military Institute near Lexington, Kentucky, and the home of his idol, Clay. Here he taught for three years; his ability to make people like him served him well, for although some of the pupils were his own age he was a popular and respected teacher. For diversion he went to hear Henry Clay speak at every opportunity, began to write concise political analyses of the issues of the day. His colleagues were astonished to find him an oracle on elections: he could always tell who was going to win and by how wide a margin, even when it was his beloved Henry Clay's defeat that he had to predict.

Douglas had become a full-blown westerner in one month; Blaine too was a man of quick and easy attachments: when he was in Pennsylvania he assured his intimates that nothing could ever take the place of Pennsylvania in his heart; when he was in Kentucky it became the greatest spot in the world; when later he moved to Maine he adopted that state as his parent home with the deepest of devotion. He was adaptable, he was social-minded, he would like any place, he would get along anywhere.

Stephen A. Douglas had had his outlook and political career shifted by marriage to a southern woman; James G. Blaine found in Kentucky a New England girl teaching at a female seminary twenty miles from his school, married her and moved to her home in Augusta, Maine. Douglas, through his marriage, became known as a Doughface; Blaine as "Blaine of Maine." Again his charm was his most valuable asset: he was taken in and called a son by the rock-ribbed people of Maine.

He was teaching and reading law on the side when he was suddenly offered a half interest and the editorship of the Kennebec *Journal*. He had never worked on a newspaper; he had never written anything for public consumption. He was "genial in character, persuasive in argument, versed in politics and ardent in his devotion to the Whig principles"; these were his qualifications. Now twenty-four, he borrowed money from his brother-in-law to invest in the newspaper, threw away his lawbooks and excitedly took the first steps of a career which would make him absolute master of Maine politics for twenty years, the acknowledged head of the Republican party and the idol of almost five million voters. He came into his editorship in November of 1854, just as the Whig party was fading and the Republican party was about to be born. From the moment of its inception Blaine was with all his heart a Republican.

He wrote the leading editorials for the *Journal:* vigorous, crystal clear, well informed, piercing, saying the things about local and national politics that the home folks were thinking. He was the flawless gold-backed mirror: in Kentucky he had been a secessionist, in Maine he was sympathetic to the abolitionists; in Kentucky he had believed in a low tariff, in Maine he was calling for high protective tariffs; in Kentucky he had been a greenback advocate, in Maine he was a hard-money man: ever a container, never a content.

His editorials were reprinted in other Maine papers, the *Journal* increased its circulation, the Republicans secured him the state printing contract, and before long Blaine was able to announce with justifiable pride that he had earned four thousand dollars in one year. He lectured at the Augusta Lyceum, slowly and painfully overcoming his impediment, became acquainted with the leading political figures of the state while reporting the proceedings of the Maine Senate, was sent to the first Republican convention in Philadelphia in 1856 to represent his district, and helped the Republicans carry Maine with a twenty-five-thousand majority by his brilliant work for Fremont.

Fremont was defeated by Buchanan, but the Republican party was launched in politics—and so was James G. Blaine. He was elected to the Maine legislature, served three consecutive terms and was named Speaker in 1861, a rehearsal for his coming performance in Washington. To further implement his training as a Republican he fell in love with the one political figure of the era whom he openly acknowledged to be his superior: Abraham Lincoln. He had heard the Lincoln-Douglas debates when in Illinois in 1858 preparing a report on prison reform for Maine. It is one of the more delicious ironies of politics that the man who was to pick up the mantle of the Little Giant when it fell from his defeated shoulders should completely repudiate Douglas, declare Lincoln to be the outstanding man of the country, work assiduously for his nomination in 1860 and, as chairman of the Maine State Committee, wage a fierce campaign against the Democrats.

In 1864 Blaine was elected to Congress for the first of seven consecutive terms, a period of twelve years which were to prove the happiest and most valuable of his life. He was now thirty-three, with a tall, broad figure which he carried with magnificent poise, excellent presence no matter how large or small the stage, brown eyes that were soft and luminous, friendly and intelligent. His impediment was almost completely whipped; because of a full-face beard his nose no longer seemed so prominent. He had a large head with an amplitude of black and gray hair, a gentle and winning personality. Having overcome his handicaps he did not throw away the tools that had won him friends and position; instead he sharpened and refined them for use on the national scene. In his first victorious brush in the House his opponent facetiously referred to his magnetic manner; he was dubbed Magnetic Blaine.

He entered Congress just as the Civil War was ending; the problems of his first two terms were concerned with the south. In the beginning he was for moderate treatment of the south, but he would not stand alone; he voted for the Reconstruction Acts and President Grant's Force Bills, going down the line with his party that it might show its greatest possible strength. He opposed the impeachment of President Johnson, demonstrating to the House that it had no case, but when the roll was called he voted for impeachment, elected to serve his party rather than justice and good government.

The one consistency of his congressional career was his insistence upon sound money, a virtue ingrained in his acquired vice of worshipping wealth and the men who controlled it. He waged crusades for the maintenance of national credit and the redemption of government bonds in gold instead of depreciated currency, crying, "No repudiation of obligations! It will doubtless cost us a vast sum to pay our indebtedness, but it would cost us incalculably more not to pay it." His economic reasoning was valid, yet Blaine needed a stronger motivation than being in the right: his intimates, who held large blocs of government bonds, stood to lose a portion of their investment if the bonds were redeemed in currency.

By 1870 he had made himself the leader of the Republican majority in the House; he accomplished this by reason of his power to make friends, his outstanding mental gifts, his clever adroitness in parliamentary maneuver. As a reward for his leadership he was elected Speaker of the House, achieving the first of his life ambitions. Thirty-nine-year-old Blaine had been preparing himself for the job of Speaker since he had been seventeen: he had read widely in parliamentary history and mastered the technique of procedure. It was commonly admitted that he knew more about this complicated and difficult science than any man of his times; added to this careful preparation was his equally careful preparation, dating back to his childhood, of making people want to agree with him, ride along with him, crusade for him. Coming into command when the House was known as the Bear Garden, perhaps the most disorderly period in its history, Blaine brought about order and as much good feeling as was possible in the postwar passions.

He had vowed not only to become Speaker of the House, but one of the best the House had known; he had tremendous love for the office, and from his love arose a high quality of service. He worked hard, was faithful to his duties, was fair to the opposition, handed down his rulings not on a partisan basis but from the established necessities of parliamentary procedure. He remained untouched by the scandals that rocked the Grant administration, refusing to accept a bonus that Congress voted itself; even his opponents respected him for his efforts.

At forty-three he was at the height of his power and fame. He had bought a home in the fashionable district of Washington where he was surrounded by the most important men in the government. His wife, who was a brilliant woman with

264

greater spiritual strength than her husband, gave the best parties and dinners in Washington, with Blaine always the center of attraction: he had become the wittiest and most delightful talker in the capital. He had the assured and powerful yet courteous manner of the leader, the indomitable one. After six years as Speaker he had risen from leader of the House to undisputed leader of the Republican party. When he handed over his gavel to the Democratic majority in 1876 he received an ovation from colleague and opposition the like of which had not been heard in the House since Henry Clay had stepped down. The newspapers, which had been singing his praises, announced that his high-minded conduct in office for six years made him one of the most valuable public servants in the country, one who should aspire to higher office not only because he was deserving of the honor but because he would be able to fulfill its duties.

Blaine's ambition to become president was not nearly so well planned or implemented as his ambition to become Speaker. It was not until this moment that he decided to use his position as a steppingstone to higher things, rather than a glorious end in itself. That single decision led to the tragic scrambling of his hitherto successful career.

For then the storm broke.

3

The most serious scandals of the eighteen seventies were centered around the railroads: groups of promoters would go to Congress with requests for subsidies to build new railroads; a compliant Congress would grant them millions of acres of land bordering the proposed lines, then approve building contracts so fraudulent that the stock and bond buyers would pay four times over for the building of the roadbeds. When the roads were completed the syndicates not only owned the railroad, which had not cost them a dollar of their own money to build, and millions of acres of valuable land, but in addition had pocketed a profit off the building of the road!

How could congressmen be persuaded to make such munificent grants of land to financiers and then approve contracts so liberal that the railroad spikes could have been hammered out of gold? As Congressman Oakes Ames said, "By placing shares of stock where they could do the most good." Or as Collis P. Huntington said, "Jay Gould went to Washington, since which time money has been used very freely. Gould has large amounts of cash and he pays it without stint to carry his points."

Blaine not only approved the action of businessmen in thus

persuading legislators to make them princely grants out of the public domain; he approved as well the acceptance of the honorariums. He was congenitally unable to understand why anyone should object to this procedure: he used the office of Speaker to bring James Garfield back into favor after he had been charged with accepting cash from the Crédit Mobilier railroad organization; he also used his Chair to prevent the expulsion of Oakes Ames, who had been responsible for the frauds.

The reform movement of 1874, which had given the Democrats a majority in the House and reduced Blaine's status from Speaker to minority leader on the floor, was gaining impetus with each fresh revelation of malpractice within the Grant administration. To win the presidential election of 1876 the Republicans realized that they were going to need, if not an outstanding reformer to defeat the reform champion, Samuel J. Tilden, at least a man whose honesty and incorruptibility could be proved to the country by his untarnished record. Despite his championship of Garfield and Ames, Blaine had come through the pyramiding scandals with his personal reputation intact. By common consent he seemed their man. All he needed was to make one strategic move to unite the Republican masses behind him.

Blaine was not long in developing a strategy. On January 6, 1876, he threw his hat into the presidential ring by contesting a bill granting amnesty to those southerners who still were excluded from citizenship by the Reconstruction Acts. By a clever ruse he centered his objections to repatriation on Jefferson Davis, resurrecting the charges that he "was the author, knowingly, deliberately, guiltily and willfully, of the gigantic murders and crimes against northern prisoners at Andersonville," reviving the horrible details for the consumption of the public. The south, outraged, countered with charges of atrocities against southern prisoners. Blaine had known that a Democrat would be elected president in 1876 unless the bloody shirt of the Civil War once again could be waved successfully; as he had anticipated, the Civil War was refought in the Congress, the press, the passionate public. When peaceful men of both north and south accused him of willfully rejuvenating sectional hatred and strife in a bid for the presidential nomination, Blaine smiled quietly, for he had killed two birds with one stone: he had assured his nomination, and he had assured a Republican success. That he was protracting the bitterness between brothers meant as little to him as it had to Stephen A. Douglas when he sponsored the Kansas-Nebraska Act. Two main-chance politicos, Douglas had plunged his country into war in his avidity for the presidency, Blaine was perpetuating the wounds of that war.

Congressman Cox of New York rose to his feet in the House to make one of those strangely prophetic speeches which illuminate a dark landscape:

"Whether Blaine is led like Macbeth by the dangerous vision of the crown, or hopes to divert the public from the maladministration, it is a bad, malicious purpose which will never elect him to the presidency if he lives a thousand years."

Large portions of the Republican voters approved his attack on the south; he was deluged with letters of approval and congratulations; his name was praised in newspaper editorials and pulpit sermons. "Hitherto he had friends, supporters, admirers; now he had devotees. The masses hailed his denunciation of the 'rebel chieftain' and his defense of the 'boys in blue' with shouts of enthusiasm. State after state in the north declared him their choice for the coming nomination for the presidency. It was freely predicted that he would win on the first ballot. The 'Blaine legion' increased to millions. Their hero was already taking on the legendary proportions of an American idol."

If he had been willing to remain a congressman, if he had not used the Civil War to win a presidential nomination, the fates might have ignored him. But dire means often bring dire results: of all the multitude of blows that might have fallen upon his broad and graceful shoulders and easily been shrugged off, there came the one blow which felled him like an ox.

In February of 1876, two months before the Republican convention, a government director of the Union Pacific claimed that the railroad had loaned James G. Blaine sixty-four thousand dollars on some worthless Little Rock and Fort Smith Railroad bonds. Blaine ignored the charge until the newspapers circulated the story, then in a pyrotechnical speech to a jammed House he denied categorically that he had received any money from the Union Pacific or had ever deposited Little Rock bonds with the Union Pacific. He read letters from officials of the Union Pacific which stated that he never got one dollar from them.

Blaine's rabid followers declared their hero exonerated, labeled the charges a "democratic smear." But their exultation was short-lived: to the Congressional Committee set up to investigate Blaine's railroad activities came a James Mulligan from Boston, with a packet of business letters written by Blaine over a period of years. It was James Mulligan who defeated James Blaine for the presidency.

267

Mulligan had been a bookkeeper for Warren Fisher, through whom Congressman Blaine had sold Little Rock and Fort Smith bonds. Mulligan testified that Blaine had sold a hundred and thirty thousand dollars' worth of bonds to individuals in Maine, for which he had received the astronomical commission of a hundred and thirty thousand dollars' worth of land-grant bonds and thirty-two thousand dollars' worth of Little Rock and Fort Smith first-mortgage bonds. Thus Blaine was faced by his first public deception, for in his defense against the original charges he had declared in the House that his sole connection with the Little Rock Railroad was that of a bond buyer, like any other member of the public; he had not let the public know that he had used his office to sell railroad bonds.

Mulligan further testified that Blaine had turned over his thirty-two thousand dollars' worth of first-mortgage bonds, which had been made worthless by the failure of the road, to the Union Pacific, and on this worthless collateral the Union Pacific had paid Blaine sixty-four thousand dollars in cash. When Mulligan mentioned that he had in his possession a packet of letters written by Blaine to Warren Fisher, Blaine grew perturbed, asked a Republican member of the committee to request an adjournment.

That night he went to Mulligan's hotel, asked to see the letters, then refused to return them. While protesting loudly that they contained nothing that possibly could embarrass him, he also refused to show them to the Investigating Committee. The Democratic members of the committee moved to have him expelled from the House for tampering with a witness and for seizing important evidence under consideration. With every move he made James Blaine was falling deeper into the dark pattern of his private past.

Before the House could act on his expulsion Blaine rose for the second time to defend himself; once again the galleries were packed, for he had let word get around beforehand that he was going to speak. Like an actor in an overdirected melodrama he flung the packet of letters down on his desk with a renunciatory gesture, crying:

"I am not afraid to show the letters, thank God Almighty! With a mortification which I do not pretend to conceal, with a sense of outrage which any man in my position would feel, I invite the confidence of forty-four millions of my countrymen from this desk!"

It was a grandstand play; the bleachers cheered; but Blaine had rearranged the letters, edited them. He carried on a rapid-fire monologue of self-defense as he read, leaving out parts he did not care to divulge. He still refused to turn the letters over to the Investigating Committee, accusing the members of having received and suppressed a cablegram from Josiah Caldwell of the Union Pacific which exonerated him of the charges. He was resolved to win this contest by maneuver and stratagem, as he had won all other contests in the House. Forced to admit by Blaine's clever jockeying that they indeed had received a cablegram from Caldwell, the meeting broke up in pandemonium; his friends surrounded Blaine like a conquering hero, showered him with their congratulations.

The facts, however, were growing increasingly ugly: the committee had not released the Caldwell cablegram because it had been sent from London without an address. They still were trying to determine whether it had been sent by Caldwell or someone signing his name, though the denial still proved no more than that the Union Pacific was defending its own reputation as well as Blaine's. Actually Blaine's intimates had sent a cablegram to Caldwell telling him word for word what he must cable back to the House Investigating Committee in order to clear Blaine of the charges against him. That was how Blaine had known that the committee had received the cablegram; the likelihood of his having written the message himself was demonstrated by a letter he wrote to Warren Fisher which was not made public until the election of 1884. In it he wrote a long and detailed defense of his conduct, which he begged Fisher to copy and mail back to him immediately:

"I want you to send me a letter such as the enclosed draft. It will be a favor I shall never forget if you will write me the letter and mail the same evening. Kind regards to Mrs. Fisher. Burn this letter." Blaine did not mail the letter to Fisher's Boston address; he sent it instead to the Parker House, instructing Fisher by telegram to pick up the letter at the hotel.

While the Investigating Committee was rebuking Blaine for having edited the letters while reading them, for having refused them to the members and for having been guilty of unethical conduct in the Caldwell cablegram matter, the public was coming to understand why it was that Speaker Blaine had been able to make the grandiloquent gesture of refusing a five-thousand-dollar bonus voted by the House. Bit by bit Blaine's method of making large sums of money was emerging:

In 1861, when he was military agent for the state of Maine, Warren Fisher had summoned him to Boston to tell him of a new rifle which he had been unable to bring to the attention of the secretary of war. Could Mr. Blaine bring it to the secretary's attention? He could, and did. The government gave the company an opening order for twenty thousand rifles; Blaine received ten thousand dollars' worth of stock in the company. He had not mentioned to the secretary of war that he was acting as agent for the manufacturers.

He got a cut on nearly every railroad that was organized during his twelve years in the House. He saw to it that the roads received the largest possible appropriations and land grants; when they fell into trouble he used his influence to secure them a profitable reorganization. When Senator Thurman of Ohio introduced a bill to compel the railroads to build sinking funds from which to redeem their bonds, Blaine worked and lobbied and fought against the bill with all his art and all his strength. Senator Thurman's denunciation of Blaine left the congressman completely unruffled: the railroad magnates were his friends, and he would defend them to the last ditch because they were doing more to expand the country than any other group.

"It is false that the railroads have exercised undue pressure on Congressmen," said Blaine; "the railroads can be trusted to be honest, to pay their debts and redeem their bonds when they fall due; they should not be punched and knocked and worried and harrowed by Congress interfering with their business and charters."

Yet he went to labyrinthic ends to conceal his private activities, the size of his take. An editor of the New York *Tribune,* which supported Blaine for years, said privately, "When the Hocking Valley railroad scandal was under inquiry Mr. Blaine publicly declared that he had never owned a dollar's worth of stock in the railroad, nor been interested in it in any way. And yet some months before the scandal broke I had a note from him asking me to do all that I could to help Hocking Valley because he was heavily interested in that road."

The Republican convention which assembled in Cincinnati two months later rejected James G. Blaine for Rutherford Hayes, an honest man.

4

He was still Blaine of Maine, and his state sent him to the United States Senate for a six-year term. Here his political career scraped bottom, for he served mainly as a lobbyist for railroad interests, blocking everything constructive President Hayes tried to accomplish: he opposed Hayes's liberal treatment of the south and its return to self-government on the grounds that the president was abandoning the Republican party in the south; he opposed Hayes's civil-service reform on the grounds that it was weakening the power of the Republican party, that the civil-service reformers were "upstarts, conceited, foolish, vain; noisy but not numerous; ambitious but not wise; pretentious but not powerful."

Blaine worked hard for the nomination in 1880, but his forces were locked against those of Ulysses S. Grant, who still was striving to secure a third term, and the convention compromised on James A. Garfield, whom Blaine had repatriated in the House after his involvement in a railroad scandal. Blaine and Garfield were close friends; Blaine threw his votes to Garfield, insuring the nomination. In return Garfield named James G. Blaine his secretary of state. For Blaine this was a new lease on life: he would be honest and courageous and farsighted, he would give his country the very best that was in him, and after eight years of outstanding performance the old scandals would be forgotten, he would be elected to the presidency. Everyone had suspected that he would be the power behind the throne; soon he made his position evident by his dictatorial treatment of Garfield.

For ten months he was a vigorous secretary of state; he created friendship in Central and South America, worked for hemispheric solidarity and an increased exchange of goods; he took a tough and often undiplomatic attitude toward Great Britain, whom he disliked, which greatly strengthened the hand of the United States in European negotiations. He was building a good record when President Garfield was assassinated, and Blaine found himself with no job at all. For the following three years he remained in Washington, entertained widely, made new friends, held the scattering reins of the Republican party. He wrote a book called *Twenty Years of Congress,* which proved to be popular.

President Arthur found no favor, no other strong man arose, and at last in 1884, in Chicago, James G. Blaine won his coveted nomination at the convention which the *Nation* described as "a mass meeting of maniacs." So strong had been his hold on the voters during the years that when his name was mentioned "pandemonium broke loose, whole delegations mounted their chairs and led the cheering; hats, coats, umbrellas were thrown in the air, banners torn from the walls to be wrapped around the paraders."

To run against the magnetic Blaine the Democrats selected Grover Cleveland, governor of the state of New York; he was not as smart an operator as Blaine, in fact he was not clever at all. He was not nearly so brilliant a talker nor glib a writer; he was not so resourceful at maneuvering, and he had no outstanding magnetism. Blaine found himself up against a simple, solid and honest man in somewhat the same fashion that the charming, cultured and clever Stephen Douglas had found himself up against a simple, crude and honest Abraham Lincoln. Douglas and Blaine were political icing, Lincoln and Cleveland were bread and butter.

A group of Republicans had threatened to bolt if Blaine received the nomination; these Independents, or Mugwumps, as they came to be called, held a first meeting in Boston, attended by such men as Josiah Quincy and Charles Francis Adams, in which they repudiated Blaine. A week later a second meeting was presided over by President Eliot of Harvard, at which five hundred of the so-called best brains of Boston "united to rebuke corrupt men and corrupt methods in politics." The movement spread, similar meetings were held in New York, the New York *Times* printed three columns of letters from Republican bolters. Carl Schurz stated the case for the Mugwumps when he wrote to ex-President Hayes, "I oppose Blaine because I believe that the election of the man who wrote the Mulligan letters and who stands before the country as the representative of the practices which they disclose would be a precedent fraught with incalculable evil. It would be a terrible thing to teach our young people that such a record does not disqualify a man for the highest honors and trusts of the Republic."

The Independents had urged the Democrats to give them a candidate they could indorse; Cleveland, like Alton B. Parker, was so much like the best of the Republicans that the Mugwumps took him to their seething bosoms with great joy. Most of the influential newspapers deserted Blaine for Cleveland: the *Times, Herald* and *Telegram* in New York; in Philadelphia the *Times* and *Record;* in Boston the *Advertiser, Transcript* and *Record.* It was the fastest and most effective bolt under which any party had suffered since the Fire-Eater southerners bolted Stephen A. Douglas in 1860.

Blaine still had many of the good men of the country supporting him, educators, editors, clergymen who did not believe him guilty of malfeasance; the mass of uncritical Republican voters was behind him; because of his hard-boiled attitude toward England he was particularly strong with the Irish voters. The race would be close, but there could be felt the rising tide for Cleveland; Democrats were exulting that the victory which had been snatched from Tilden in 1876, that had been denied to General Winfield Scott Hancock in 1880 by only nine thousand votes out of nine million cast, was at last coming home.

Then a bomb struck the Democratic campaign: an obscure Buffalo newspaper charged that twelve years before Grover Cleveland had had a liaison with a young widow and that a child had been born of their union. Here was a charge of moral turpitude against Cleveland to offset the charge of political turpitude against Blaine. Cleveland's supporters were plunged into the deepest gloom; his chance of election appeared to be blasted. When his managers cried in despair, "What shall we do?" Cleveland made a characteristically blunt answer:

"Tell the truth!"

Maria Halpin had come to Buffalo as a young and attractive widow. Here she met Grover Cleveland. She had had relations not only with him but with three or four other men at the same time. Cleveland had no way of knowing whether the child were his; since the others were married men, and he did not care to face a court trial to determine the parenthood, he had accepted the responsibility and contributed to the child's support; he saw nothing more of the mother.

Had the story been made public before the Democratic convention, it is not likely that Cleveland could have secured the nomination; had it broken a week before the voting, he would not have won the election. Coming as it did in the middle of the campaign, the gossip died down; Governor Cleveland's manly conduct in facing the accusation won him back a large portion of the public which charged it off as a youthful indiscretion. Besides, a new batch of Mulligan letters was discovered in Boston!

An investigating committee of Democrats released the letters to the press without comment. Blaine admitted their authenticity but denied that there was anything incriminating in them. In their midst however was the confidential letter sent to Warren Fisher at the Parker House begging Fisher to send him a rewrite of his own statement of vindication, and ending with, "Kind regards to Mrs. Fisher. Burn this letter."

After the exposure of Cleveland's illegitimate child, Blaine cohorts had paraded the streets singing: "Ma, Ma, where's my Pa?"

The Democrats retorted: "Gone to the White House, Ha, Ha, Ha!"

When the Cleveland parade moved up Fifth Avenue the marchers carried huge writing-paper banners while lighting matches and chanting:

> *"Burn this letter, burn this letter,*
> *Kind regards to Mrs. Fisher."*

The line "Kind regards to Mrs. Fisher" was a masterpiece of American satirical humor, making Blaine look like such an outright fraud that it actually cost him more votes than the charges implied in the line "Burn this letter."

The Democrats piled up a tremendous case against him, some of it accurate, some fictional canard. He was called "a friend of the railroads, musket in hand, firing from behind the breastwork of Jay Gould's lobby," which was true, and a "persecutor of the foreign-born and Roman Catholics," which was viciously false. He was labeled "a corrupt jobber who first tried to conceal and then to pervert the evidence which convicted him of prostituting his high office for personal gain," which was roughly true, and of being "a Jingo who pursued an atrocious foreign policy in the State Department," which was a grave injustice to his excellent performance as secretary of state. He also was called the usual group names of liar, crook, cheat, hypocrite, to offset the names being called Cleveland: "hangman, lecherous beast, obese nimcompoop, drunken sot."

The campaign reached its dregs when the Democrats, still trying to offset the morals charge against Cleveland, started a whispering scandal against the Blaine marriage: the Blaines had been married secretly in Kentucky in 1850, followed by a public marriage of few months later; the Democrats now charged that there had been no secret marriage in Kentucky, that the first Blaine child, who had died in infancy, had been conceived out of wedlock. Charges of a similar nature spread about Andrew Jackson's beloved Rachel had killed that good woman.

Arrogant and overconfident after twenty years in power, the Republicans were making a number of tactical mistakes: so crudely had they insulted the Temperance League that Temperance members nominated their own man, set up headquarters in New York to campaign against Blaine. The Republicans also put up an independent adventurer who they had thought would siphon off Democratic votes; to their horror they found he was drawing Republican support instead. Frightened, Blaine's campaign managers called on him at his home in Augusta, Maine, where he had been spending the summer months, and pleaded with him to take to the stump, to utilize his personal magnetism in the doubtful states.

Blaine agreed to make a tour of New York, Massachusetts, Pennsylvania, Ohio, Michigan, Indiana, Illinois and West Virginia. His conduct was dignified, he indulged in no personal abuse against Cleveland, telling his vast and enthusiastic audiences that the sole issue of the campaign was the tariff. An examination of his speeches, however, reveals several hummingbird reversals in mid-air: the man who had fought every attempt to bring civil-service reform into the government under President Hayes now assured his audiences that he always had been a champion of reform; the man who had waved the bloody shirt in Congress in an effort to secure the nomination of 1876 now assured his listeners in West Virginia that the friendship between the north and south never again could be broken.

When despite his blandishments the voters of West Virginia gave Cleveland a majority and its electoral votes, Blaine cried out to an assemblage in Indiana, "The Democrats dream that they will seize the government of the nation. I do not believe that the men who added luster and renown to your state through four years of bloody war can be used to call to the administration of the government the men who organized the great Rebellion!"

No ward heeler, no narrow-minded county-vote warden could have fallen lower than to make such a statement a full twenty years after the close of hostilities. There were no depths to which Blaine would not sink to win the presidency, but his chances appeared to fall with his political ethics, for Indiana ignored his fulmination and went Democratic. Further alarmed, his managers urged him to close his campaign in New York City instead of going straight home to Augusta.

In the lobby of the Fifth Avenue Hotel, where Blaine put up, several hundred New York clergymen gathered to pass a resolution on the "purity of Blaine's personal character," then collected at the foot of the staircase to wait for their hero to descend. The ministers' chairman congratulated Blaine as he walked down the steps, then said, "We expect to vote for you next Tuesday. We are Republicans and don't propose to leave our party and identify ourselves with the party whose antecedents have been rum, Romanism and rebellion."

Blaine either was not listening or was too tired to grasp the significance of the phrase, but an astute reporter dashed it to Democratic headquarters. The next Sunday morning handbills were distributed at the doors of every Catholic church in America, and the Catholics rose in rage against the slur on their religion. Thus, through the efforts of what the New York *Sun* called "an early Paleozoic bigot," Blaine lost the Irish-Catholic vote that had been sewed so neatly in his pocket.

If the religious intolerance had been no fault of Blaine's, except in that he had not instantly repudiated the clergyman's sentiments, his next catastrophe arose directly from his character: he accepted an invitation to a dinner at Delmonico's tendered him by some two hundred of the wealthiest men of the nation, including all of New York's millionaires. It was a feast befitting the men who controlled American finance and industry, but unfortunately the nation was suffering from a severe depression, thousands of men were out of work, their

275

families starving. Stuffed with the rarest of foods and the choicest of wines, Blaine made a speech in which he extolled the great gifts which these men had made to the nation, praised the record of the Republican party which had "elevated the standard of America and increased its wealth in a ratio never before dreamed of."

The next day the press excoriated Blaine and his millionaires, many of whom had been involved with him in the railroad scandals, for the "Belshazzar's Feast" and "Boodle Banquet." The *World* published a cartoon showing an unemployed, skeletonlike man, holding his sunken-faced wife and puny child by the hand, begging crumbs from the millionaires filling themselves at the feast. Blaine's counselors had advised him against going to the banquet, but he had thought them crazy: why shouldn't he have dinner with his friends? The attack the following day stunned him, as he had always been stunned by these attacks against the men who were, in his opinion, building the nation. He could not realize the cruelty of such a banquet in the face of nationwide hunger because he never knew there was any hunger; he associated only with the rich, he knew nothing about the working masses and cared less—except when it was time to gather in their votes. The Boodle Banquet cost Blaine a good part of the labor vote.

On the last night in October of 1884 Blaine reviewed a great Republican torchlight parade in New York City. The following day Grover Cleveland, who had remained working at his governor's desk in Albany during the entire campaign, stood in the stands at Madison Square and watched forty thousand excited supporters march up Broadway and Fifth Avenue reciting:

> "Blaine, Blaine, James G. Blaine,
> Continental liar from the state of Maine."

The following day Blaine lost New York State by eleven hundred votes, and with it the election. His total vote was 4,851,981 to Cleveland's 4,874,986. He proved to be a bad loser, stirring up geographical hatred and attempting to discredit Cleveland's victory. Two days after his defeat he told a group of friends serenading before his house that the transfer of the political power to the south was deplorable:

"Toward Cleveland personally I have no slightest cause of ill will; with entire cordiality I express the wish that his administration may overcome the embarrassment which the peculiar source of its power imposed on it from the hour of its birth."

Blaine continued to be important in national politics until 1892; except for his ten months as secretary of state under Garfield and for another three years under Harrison, his record is a shabby one for a man who gave such brilliant promise. The insinuations against Mrs. Blaine during the campaign so turned her against public elections that she persuaded her husband not to accept the nomination in 1888. One of Blaine's biographers says, "What bitter discomfiture was caused him by the lure of the market place; it consumed some of his fondest hopes in its tormenting grasp." The other writes, "Blaine was a phenomenon to move the thoughtful patriot to pondering and maybe to fear. For this man had two paths that he walked, one in the daylight that was straight, one in the dark that was as twisted as a ram's horn."

His shuttle record on such crucial issues as rehabilitation of the south and civil-service reform proves him a meandering opportunist even in the honest light of day. His virtues can be recorded in one sentence: he was an able parliamentarian, a forceful exponent of solidarity with South America, a charming, well-informed talker and a loving family man. There is no balance sheet long enough to compute what he cost his country in squandered resources, in blasted faith in the democratic form of government, in the ability of men to govern themselves honestly and for the common good. As president he would have gyrated with the main chance until he had the electorate dizzy, and in the resultant confusion would have run the country in the exclusive interests of the gentlemen who had entertained him at Delmonico's.

In comparison to the solid-wall honesty and conscientious executive abilities of Grover Cleveland, Blaine shows up like a wavering shadow, a butterfly to a grizzly bear. James G. Blaine started out with many gifts but few principles; if he had begun with many principles but few gifts, he could have ended by making a contribution to the good of his country.

With his stablemate Douglas he joins Clay and Bryan as main-chance politicos whom the sometime genius of democracy—by one half of one per cent!—kept out of the White House.

BOOK SEVEN

"Governors, Pardon!"

The Governor's Mansion is the halfway mark on the road to the White House.

CHAPTER ONE

Lewis Cass

TWICE IN HIS LONG LIFE, once at the beginning of his career, again at the end, he broke a sword across his knee. He was a powerful fellow: he had no trouble smashing the swords.

The first American to spring onto Canadian soil in the War of 1812, he was ordered by his commanding officer to surrender to the British without a fight. Positive that he could defeat the redcoats and drive them out of Canada, Colonel Cass broke his sword in two rather than hand it over to the British intact.

"Basely to surrender without firing a gun!" he groaned. "Tamely to submit without raising a bayonet!"

Both the sentiment and the rhetoric were revealing.

Half a century later, in 1861, he begged President Buchanan, for whom he was secretary of state, to send reinforcements to Charleston, to man the garrisons, to prevent the south from appropriating Union guns and supplies. President

Buchanan replied, "The interests of the country do not demand a reinforcement of the forces at Charleston."

Cass resigned: it was the only way a seventy-nine-year-old diplomat had left of breaking a lance.

He had been six years old when his mother had held him up to the window of their home to watch the bonfires blazing in the streets of Exeter, for New Hampshire, the ninth and last state necessary, had ratified the Constitution. When he resigned as secretary of state in 1861 he said:

"I saw the Constitution born, and I fear I may see it die."

South Carolina seceded and he cried, "The people in the south are mad; the people in the north are asleep; the president is pale with fear, for his official household is full of traitors, and conspirators control the government. God only knows what is to be the fate of my poor country!"

In temperament and quality of service Cass is closest to Parker and Hancock among the Also Rans: he came from a loving and well-adjusted home; his married life was always a delight; he enjoyed the finest synthesis of nerve, gland and muscle structure. He was handsome, had a big, overpowering frame, was always in robust health. A blistering fighter for self-government, he worked with a heroic phlegm and courage for public causes, hating no one, speaking no evil word, making few enemies, liked wherever he went: honest, persevering, social-minded, brave to the point of foolishness, as plain and easy to get along with as an old shoe; another of those rare miracles, a perfectly adjusted human being, a delight to the eye and an inspiration to the mind, the apotheosis of that overworked figure, the invaluable public servant.

Next to Alton B. Parker he is the most neglected and forgotten of the Also Rans. He was an authentic giant; he contributed magnificently to the building of the United States; he missed becoming president only by the sabotage of a fifth columnist at the heart of his party. Yet none but the student of northwest pioneer history ever encounters the name of Lewis Cass.

He was the first white man to cover the Indian trail from Detroit to Chicago, spent eighteen years teaching the Indians of the northwest to feel friendship for the "Great Father at Washington." But Washington was too remote; the Indians came to love the "Great Father at Detroit" instead. They frequently visited him at his home; Mrs. Cass never knew how many redskins would push in the front door of her tepee and sit down with the family to supper.

When he went on his long canoe trips of exploration or treaty making Cass would take with him a sack of heavy tomes, journals and newspapers, reading in the prow of the

279

boat as it swept down unexplored rivers where at any moment an Indian arrow might cross his vision to serve as a bookmark. In this manner, though he lived for two decades in the wilderness, he kept himself well educated and abreast of world affairs.

He received his first official appointment from President Jefferson in 1807, as a United States marshal; he served as a colonel and brigadier general under President Madison, as governor of the Michigan Territory under Presidents Monroe and Adams, as secretary of war and ambassador to France under President Jackson, as a senator under Presidents Polk and Taylor, and as secretary of state under President Buchanan. He also bears the dubious distinction of being the only presidential candidate to be twice defeated within his own convention by a dark horse, the first in American history.

2

Lewis Cass was the son of a blacksmith who laid down his hammer for a musket to fight at Bunker Hill, Princeton, Trenton and Monmouth, emerging from the Revolutionary War as a captain. He was a powerful man from his years over the forge, big and erect, with black eyes and attractive features; his outstanding characteristics were a love of order and authority, no matter whether he was on the giving or the taking end. In looks, in figure and in character Lewis Cass was a ringer for his father.

His mother was a Gilman from Norfolk, England, whose people landed in Boston in 1635. The boy was born in a comfortable house in Exeter on October 9, 1782, entered the Academy when he was ten, and had several years of rigorous training which gave him a lifelong love of scholarship. Daniel Webster, who attended the Academy with Cass, described him as: "A clever fellow, good-natured, kindhearted, amiable and obliging."

After a few years in civilian life Cass's father went back into the army as a major to continue the battle against the British, a heritage he was to pass on to his son as Scott's father passed his on to young Winfield. While his father was stationed at Wilmington, Delaware, seventeen-year-old Cass taught at a local school; when his father resigned his commission Lewis accompanied him into the wilderness of Ohio. The family settled near Marietta in 1799.

Young Cass studied law in the office of a practitioner in Marietta, dividing his time between reading and helping his father clear the family land, build a log cabin and set out a crop. Lewis proved to be a natural frontiersman. He loved its every aspect: the giant forests, the felling of great trees, the hunting and fishing for one's food, the life on the Indian trails while exploring the countryside. He liked the frontiersmen, too, and they found him to be their kind: hard hitting, hard working, without pretension or complaint: a man's man.

He never outgrew his love of the frontier nor his belief that it was the cradle of democracy. Though as American minister to France he lived in a style called "sumptuous—the table is splendid, servants in small-clothes constantly supply you with some new luxury," Cass wrote in his book, *France, Its King, Court and Government,* "God be praised, we have no Paris with its powerful influence and its inflammable materials. He who occupies the lowliest cabin upon the very verge of civilization has just as important a part to play in the fate of our country as the denizen of the proudest city in the land."

He was admitted to the bar when he was twenty, the first lawyer to be licensed under the new Ohio constitution of 1802. He settled in the three-year-old town of Zanesville and proceeded to grow up with the country. For a robust young stalwart filled with love of the frontier this could not help but be the most delightful time of his life. He rode circuit in pursuit of a practice, covering a hundred miles between county seats, sometimes following an Indian trail, sometimes blazing his own way through the forest, fording swift-flowing streams, occasionally being thrown off his horse, baggage and all, into the water; spending weeks in the wilderness, sleeping in the forest when there was no settler's cabin available.

"These were the troubles of the day," said Cass, "but they were compensated by the comforts of the evening, when the hospitable cabin and the warm fire greeted the traveler, when a glorious supper was spread before him: turkey, venison, bear's meat, hot corn bread, sweet potatoes and pumpkin butter—and then the animated conversation, succeeded by a floor and a blanket and a refreshing sleep."

Judges and lawyers rode into the county seat together, the judge looking for a bench, the lawyer for a client. All the countryside was collected to see the show, and each litigant circulated among the lawyers like a farmer among prize stock. Young Cass was soon getting his share of the cases, for he was bronzed, smiling, clear-thinking, with a good mind for detail, a powerful adversary who combined quiet dignity with vigor. By the time he was twenty-one he was making a comfortable living from his law work; by the time he was twenty-two he was elected prosecuting attorney for his county, and by twenty-four he was elected to the Ohio legislature.

His outstanding case in his short career as a lawyer was his defense of two Ohio judges who were up for impeachment for having declared an act of the state legislature unconstitutional. Cass's defense received national attention, helped to establish the right of the judiciary to pass upon the acts of the legislature, thus strengthening the system of checks and balances in American government. His judges were acquitted, their ruling held valid, and Lewis Cass, not yet thirty, became one of the most important figures in his rapidly growing state.

He made money, married the daughter of a Revolutionary War general, built a log cabin on his father's land in which to sire sons. He played an influential part in the legislature, was a zealous Democrat who succeeded in having Ohio's lawmakers pass a resolution of strong approval of Jefferson's policies, an act of loyalty for which President Jefferson bestowed upon him the token job of marshal.

If he had remained in Ohio he doubtless would have become governor, then senator, and perhaps wended the same long trail toward the presidency. However, the War of 1812 broke; Lewis Cass laid down his lawbook in favor of a sword, recruited a regiment of Ohio volunteers, trained them, then led them to the war in Canada.

This act was to change his life. Never again would he live in Ohio. Fate would cast him down in a vaster wilderness.

Cass marched his regiment of Ohio militiamen to Detroit, training them en route. They were good fighters and eager for action—but General Hull was old, weak and vacillating. Not even a threatened mutiny on the part of his officers could induce him to fight. Cass and his fellow officers secured proof that they outnumbered the British, that the British positions were untenable, that the first vigorous action would drive them out of that portion of Canada. Still Hull would not fight, but he permitted Colonel Cass to make a sortie with a small band of men, as a result of which Cass won the first victory of the campaign at Tarontee. He wanted to pursue the advantage, use the full American force which was spoiling for contact with the enemy. Hull refused to approve any further attacks, withdrawing the troops across the river to Detroit, where he handed over the fort, the settlement and the army at the first shots fired by the British. Cass, returning to the fort with a crack body of men, found that he and his regiment had been surrendered.

It was then he had broken the first sword of his public career.

When paroled, Cass went to Washington where he tesified against Hull, then returned to Ohio to raise another regiment. He rose to the position of brigadier general in the regular army, fought through 1813 until the British and their Indian allies were defeated. General Harrison, whose aide-de-camp he had been, named him as governor of Detroit and west Canada; shortly thereafter President Madison appointed him governor of all the Michigan Territory.

No man could have been given a tougher assignment. The Indians still were hostile, marauding and murdering the scattered settlers; huddled in the fort for protection and sustenance were the whites of the region whose homes, stock and crops had been destroyed in the course of the war. With little food available Cass had to provide for the community of Detroit, the French settlers, the peaceful Indians who previously had been provisioned by the British. Through the long, arduous winter he saw to it that every man, woman and child in his territory was fed, but he understood that the feeding of a people was a temporary rod: he had to get the settlers back onto their land, persuade them to build new cabins, plant crops, begin raising livestock again. How was he going to resettle the country when Indians still were massacring the families who braved their isolated farms?

He organized a group of volunteers in Detroit and went on a hunt for the Indians who were using British guns and bullets. On his first expedition a member of his staff urged him to fall back into the center of his group so that he should not be hit by a sudden burst of fire.

"Oh, Major, I am pretty well off here," replied Cass; "let us push on."

After a few bloody encounters the attacks fell off. In one of the more dramatic exploits of his career he went into a conference of heavily armed, hostile Indians to ask for land treaties. Becoming angered at General Cass's firm tone, the chiefs withdrew to their camp on an adjoining hill and broke out an English flag. Alone, unarmed, Cass strode into their midst, tore down the British flag, gave the Indians a blistering harangue about the supremacy of the American flag on American soil, turned his back on the outraged warriors and walked down the hill with the captive flag under his arm.

No one shot at him. The Indians accepted the treaty. After a time it became known that Governor Cass not only kept his word but that he fought in Washington for full justice to the Indians, never taking advantage of their weaknesses.

"I never broke my word to an Indian," said Cass, "and I never expected to find that the red man had broken his." Peace came to reign upon the Michigan Territory.

Having achieved his first objective, Cass set out to sell the Michigan Territory to the rest of the country: he needed more families, settlers by the thousands to conquer the wilderness and break it to the plow. He worked tirelessly, a one-man Chamber of Commerce, to have Congress offer the lands as bounty settlements to soldiers, to spread word in the east of the new and rich and available, that a wave of migration might begin. The first government surveyors who ventured into the wilderness on Cass's promise that Indians would not murder them brought back a report that Michigan Territory was wasteland, unfit for cultivation or settlement. Cass saw his work go for nothing: few easterners could be tempted to move to Michigan in the face of the adverse report. It was not until 1818 that he was able to secure a land office for Detroit where the acreage of the territory was offered for sale.

During these years Lewis Cass's most important labor was bringing the American principles of self-government to the territory where the settlers were mostly backwoods Frenchmen, uninterested in democratic processes. He was in sole and complete command of the territory, appointing its officials; he could have been a virtual dictator. But he had been raised in New England, had matured in pioneer Ohio: he had the virus of townhall self-government in his blood. For years he made every effort to strip himself of his powers and hand them over to the people. As settlers began filtering in and forming little communities he insisted that they elect their own men to office, carrying on a tireless campaign for self-government in the face of blank indifference and even hostility from the French: in 1818 he asked the people to vote on the question of representative government, waging a superb campaign of education for the cause. He was defeated: not enough of the French settlers would bother to vote.

It took Cass another five full years of work to imbue the territory with American ideals. He codified the rough nail-of-thumb laws into what became known as the "Cass Code," set up a judicial system to administer the laws; he built schools and churches, maintaining, "Of all purposes to which a revenue derived from the people can be applied, there is none more interesting and important than education. Wherever education is diffused among the people generally, they will appreciate the value of free institutions."

The governor's campaign to "popularize the schoolbook and the ballot" took as much skill and courage as had any of his campaigns as a soldier. He had his people elect their own council, then secured them the right to have a representative in Congress.

"In proportion as all governments recede from the people," he said, "they become liable to abuse."

He had started in 1814 with a wrecked, war-torn, poverty-stricken wilderness. Within fifteen years he had attracted thirty thousand settlers; he had quieted the Indians, made them friendly, kept the ever-hostile British off the neck of the young community; he had built roads, was exporting flour to the east, had prepared an American commonwealth to become a full-blown state. It was an accomplishment of herculean proportions, brought about with infinite patience, boldness, tact, industry and skill. Lewis Cass had become known as one of the world's great empire builders—and he had accomplished it all before he was forty.

Only half of his life had been spent.

3

In 1832 Lewis Cass was appointed secretary of war by President Jackson. He combined successfully his qualities of vigor and tact in handling the threatened secession of South Carolina and the Black Hawk uprising. At the end of a year, because of the Peggy O'Neill controversy, he was the only original officer left in Jackson's cabinet. He did not fare well in the internecine political warfare of Washington, this man who was used to fighting big battles in wide, open spaces; he became, pale, ill, dissatisfied with both his post and his work. When he asked to be relieved President Jackson sent him to France as the American minister. This job proved to be no sinecure: relations were strained between the United States and France due to the refusal of France to pay for the Napoleonic raids on American commerce.

In spite of the fact that he had spent so many years in rough, out-of-door living he was considered as successful a minister as Benjamin Franklin and Gouverneur Morris had been before him. He became friendly with King Louis Philippe and the court, wrote an interesting book about the country, restored good feeling between the two governments.

As good-will minister to France, Cass was in an excellent position to continue his observation of England's bad will. For thirty years he had been fighting the British who had carried on their subtle warfare against the northwest, invaded American territory with armed troops to recover deserters from their own ships, "seizing and searching" American ships bound for Detroit, keeping the Indians stirred up, in every way attempting to weaken the hold of the American government on the territory. His unrelenting front had been one reason the British were ineffective in keeping Michigan from becoming a loyal American state.

While in France Cass reported to his government the preparations of the British fleet for a possible attack on the American coast, and on February 1, 1842, published a pamphlet dissecting the evil slave-control treaty, outlining the entire career of Britain's aggression, offenses and untrustworthiness. The pamphlet was reproduced in the American press and won him a tremendous following in the United States. He who had been a strong arm and a strong front on land against Britain from 1812 to 1842 now became famous as the defender of American rights on the seas.

The publication of his pamphlet proved to be the first round fired in Cass's presidential war. His resignation as minister in protest of the disadvantageous Ashburton Treaty with England, when it was signed in Washington, was the second cannonade. By the time his ship reached the United States he had become a popular legend, the fighting minister. Congress gave him an official reception at Washington; the legislatures of Ohio and Pennsylvania declared a holiday, the governors and other important officials riding out on the roads to escort him into the capital with bands blaring and banners flying. There were crowds and parades and receptions and cheers and cannons fired in his honor.

A new hero had been born.

His admirers at the Harrisburg convention passed a resolution in favor of Lewis Cass as the next Democratic candidate for the presidency. The New York *Herald* featured the story, adding its emphatic approval by calling Cass a new Jackson who would lead his party to triumph. "He could be carried into the presidency," claimed the *Herald*, "with a universal shout of acclamation!"

The Democratic party had been run out of office by the Whigs under General Harrison in 1840. They were casting about frantically for a new name, a new face, a new personality, a new record which they could nail to their guard and behind it march back into power. Lewis Cass had been a supporter of Jefferson and Jackson, both of whom had given him their blessing, hence he was a true child of the Democratic party; he had a good record as a general in the War of 1812, a superb record as governor of the Michigan Territory, a distinguished record as minister to France; he had numerous friends and almost no enemies; he had been abroad for six years and so had been cut off from local politics, incurring no obligations or enmities.

The Democratic party needed a new candidate. Lewis Cass needed a new job. He returned to his country at precisely the right time. The needs of the Democratic party at that particular moment joined with Cass's popular stand against England at that particular moment made a happy marriage, thrusting Cass upward toward the presidency.

Cass is an indication that the need creates the presidential candidates rather than the candidate creating the need. The leaders of the Democratic party got together and asked, "Who can win a victory for us?" They answered themselves, "Lewis Cass just came home from abroad; he is well known and well liked; he has made no commitments which will embarrass him in the campaign. His anti-British stand is popular with the people. He is the most available man in the country today. Boys, Lewis Cass bears looking into!"

4

He had been home only a short time when he perceived that the annexation of Texas was the issue of the day: the south wanted Texas annexed as a potential addition to the cotton empire and slavery; the north was opposed to annexation for the identical reason. Cass, as an empire builder, approved the adding of Texas to the United States; he was not overly disturbed about the slavery issue, feeling that the people of the new state would decide for themselves whether they wanted to be slave or free.

"Every day satisfies me more and more that a majority of the American people are in favor of annexation. As they are, the sooner it is effected the better." This statement put him solidly in the race.

When the Democratic convention opened on May 27, 1844, the only two rivals for the nomination were Lewis Cass, the rising star, and Martin Van Buren, the falling star. Martin Van Buren had been named by Jackson to succeed him in 1836, had served one term in the presidency from 1836 to 1840, and then had been defeated by General William Harrison, Cass's commanding officer in the War of 1812. Van Buren was the titular head of the Democratic party, the most ardent advocate of party regularity yet to appear on the American scene. Van Buren opposed the annexation of Texas because it would lead to war with Mexico, because it would add another potential slave state to the southern roster.

The voting on Cass and Van Buren is interesting:

Ballot:	1.	2.	3.	4.	5.	6.	7.
CASS	83	94	92	105	107	116	123
VAN BUREN	146	127	121	111	103	101	99

Van Buren had been a favorite on the first ballot as a gesture of party loyalty, but he had powerful adversaries and was sinking fast. As he fell, so Cass rose. There was no other competition. As Cass watched Van Buren's vote fall off, he had reason to believe that the nomination would be his in another four or five ballots. Since the Democratic party had been defeated only once in forty-four years, there was further reason for Cass to be convinced that he would be the next president.

That evening when the convention adjourned at the end of the seventh ballot Lewis Cass came his closest to being president, closer than the day, four years later, when he actually did receive the nomination. That evening in March 1844 Lewis Cass came within an inch of having his picture hung on schoolroom walls instead of fading into total obscurity. His ardent and optimistic backers had made one flagrant mistake, the kind that was to change a deal of American history in the following century: they let the convention adjourn that evening without nominating their man; they let the delegates go back to their hotels and begin to dicker and deal.

The following morning James K. Polk, who had not even been mentioned before in the balloting, received forty-four votes—out of nowhere! On the next ballot there was a stampede to Polk. The Democratic party, which had maintained a forty-four-year tradition of nominating only their best man, set up the first dark horse in American history, an obscure Tennessee governor whose backers had been lurking in the background waiting for Cass and Van Buren to stalemate each other.

Cass had authentic reason to be disappointed. Though he knew that a canvass of the Democratic voters in the country would have made him a ten-to-one choice over Polk, about whom the majority of Democrats were saying, "Who the devil is Polk?" and "Polk! Great God, what a nomination!" Cass got out and campaigned for his party's choice. His work in Michigan and the northwest helped elect the man who had cost him in the nomination.

Michigan sent Cass to the United States Senate, where he fought for expansion of empire on the American continent, became known as the champion of American rights and never unclenched his powerful fist against England. "His speeches were often too learned and too long; his cumbersome sentences were not always enlivening; but when he rose to speak on a subject in which he was interested he was always impressive. His large figure, his finely shaped head, his firm mouth and intelligent features bespoke earnestness, thoughtfulness and intellectual integrity." His speeches sounded like a chapter out of a book he had read in the prow

288

of an Indian canoe. The only ill effect of this reading in motion had been not upon his eyes but upon his tongue: like his brother general of the War of 1812, Winfield Scott, he had developed too pompous a vocabulary.

His comments on national and international subjects were published and distributed throughout the country, firmly entrenching him as the leading voice of the Democratic party. The Democrats were not very happy about President Polk; it soon became evident that Lewis Cass would be the next nominee.

Cass's major battle in the months preceding the 1848 convention was waged against the Wilmot Proviso, a proposed Federal law which would have made it illegal to introduce slavery into new territories. In his firm stand for Popular Sovereignty, from which Stephen A. Douglas was to draw his philosophy, he carried the approval of the south and parts of the west, but he fell into sharp disagreement with his own people of Michigan and the northwest who had grown up in the tradition of universal free men and free labor. Senator Cass no longer represented the people he had been elected to serve.

"It was hoped and expected by all the free north," said a fellow senator, "that he would give all his talent and influence to extend and secure to other territories that great ordinance of free labor, the practical advantages of which, social and political, he was fully aware."

Cass knew that no man who voted for the exclusion of slavery from the new territories had the barest chance of securing the Democratic nomination, yet there is ample evidence that he believed Popular Sovereignty to be the only compromise which could prevent war and bloodshed. He believed slavery to be a misfortune for the south but, having grown up with the institution, was more inured to it than the younger men just jumping into the breach. He was against the extension of slavery to free states, but he saw no legal reason why the Fugitive Slave Law should not be enforced, a judgment in which Chief Justice Taney was to uphold him a few years later. As a lawyer and a strict constructionist he felt that the Constitution had not conferred upon Congress the right to control the lives and possessions of the people who moved into the new territories.

"If the relation of master and servant may be regulated or annihilated," said Cass, "so may the relation of husband and wife, or parent and child, and of any other conditions which our institutions and the habits of our society recognize."

The proof of the fact that Cass's theory of Popular Sovereignty was the most popular compromise in the country was offered at the Democratic convention which met in Baltimore on May 22, 1848. Once again Van Buren sought the nomination, but Lewis Cass was nominated on the fourth ballot. The Democratic voters now had the nominee they had wanted four years before; Cass emerged with a happy smile on his face, Van Buren with blood in his eye.

To oppose Cass the Whigs selected General Zachary Taylor, victor of the Mexican War battle of Buena Vista. General Taylor was connected with no party, had never voted; unlike his commanding officer in the Mexican War, General Winfield Scott, he had never studied politics or taken social stands. His nomination was the work of the Whig leaders who needed a popular hero and could find him only in a military victor, just as they successfully had found one in General Harrison in 1840.

There were no major differences between the two parties: the Whigs were simply those unrelated dissidents who had fallen away from the Democratic party for a variety of reasons during its forty-eight years of power since the election of Jefferson. They were united on only one thing, their desire to kick out the Democrats; the only discernible principle was to be against everything being done by the Democrats: the war with Mexico, the subtreasury, the low tariff, the northern-boundary dispute with Great Britain. Actually the Whigs stood for so little they refused to draw up a platform.

The Democratic platform was little better: it did nothing but pat itself on the back for its allegedly superb accomplishments during Polk's four years of administration. Thus the voter had no choice of principles, only a choice between men. For this reason it was not a sectional or geographic election; each candidate won half of the southern states and half of the northern.

Nearly every biographer of the Also Rans maintains that his subject was defeated by the dirtiest and most unscrupulous campaign in American history; each in turn is right. To this tradition Cass, though he was one of the few men in public life who generated no ill will, was no exception:

"No means, fair or foul, were left unused to defeat General Cass. A course of political warfare, until then unknown in party politics, was adopted: his private character was slandered, and acts in his life which are generally considered as conferring honor and worthy of respect were turned against him and distorted into weapons of injury." The north attacked him because he would not declare against slavery in the new territories, the south attacked him because no northerner could be trusted to be truly sympathetic to slavery.

However Cass and the Democratic party were defeated by

290

the oldest and greatest living friend of the Democrats, Martin Van Buren, the man whose life had been built upon the rock of party solidarity and party regularity. Van Buren had burned for the nomination, but he had wanted it on a Free Soil platform. Neither his name nor his stand had received any support at the Democratic convention. Exactly one month later, on June 22, 1848, the Free Soil party met in convention and nominated Martin Van Buren. He knew that the Free Soilers had not the slightest chance of winning; he knew that his candidacy would split the Democratic vote and throw the election to the Whigs. Bitter and aging, Van Buren did not care; he loathed Lewis Cass and Popular Sovereignty with equal intensity; if he could not have the nomination on the platform of his choice, he would sunder the party whose leadership he had inherited from Andrew Jackson.

When the male citizens of the thirty states went to the polls there was every reason to believe that Cass would make a better president than Taylor: he had been a state legislator in Ohio, governor of the Michigan Territory, secretary of war, minister to France and senator from Michigan. This list of jobs in itself was no proof that Lewis Cass would make a good chief executive: a routine machine politician could build up as impressive a one. But Cass had a superb record of accomplishment and a complete grasp of the obligations of the executive. Taylor never had held public office, never had served as an administrator, had no executive experience outside the army. The country knew him only as a brave soldier. Was this enough to make a good president?

Up to this point the country had had good luck in the generals it had elected to the presidency: Washington and Jackson had served the office well; Harrison died only a month after being inducted, but not before manifesting a sense of what the job was about. The eight-year tragedy of Ulysses S. Grant was still in the future.

Taylor never had been overly bright; he had muddled through a routine career which included such fiascos as his inability to put an end to the Seminole War; his activities in the Mexican War had proved that he knew little about his own job, military science. During the Mexican War he had criticized the administration, disobeyed his commanding officer, sulked, fought for his own power over the interests of an American victory. Nevertheless he had won victories over the Mexicans at Palo Alto and Buena Vista. Until the advent of the movie star nothing was as powerfully publicized as military victory. The widely acclaiming press received by Taylor could not be duplicated by millions of dollars or months of campaign work. The emotional idolatry afforded to a military victor in 1848 was exactly the same as that heaped upon the head of General MacArthur almost a full century later for his defense of Bataan, followed by the immediate proposal that he be named as the Republican nominee for the presidency in 1944.

Cass won majorities in fifteen states to Taylor's fourteen. In New York, where Van Buren still wielded power, the Free Soilers took enough votes from the Democrats to swing the state to Taylor, and with it the thirty-six electoral votes necessary to win. Van Buren had crippled Cass throughout the nation by his public repudiation of him, many voters swinging to Taylor and the Whigs in distaste over the Democratic row. Had Van Buren acquiesced in the choice of the Democratic delegates, Cass would have taken a sizable majority of the states. He polled 1,220,544 votes to Taylor's 1,360,099, while Van Buren's 291,263 votes were almost entirely Democratic.

Once again a man and a party had come into power not because a majority of Americans wanted them, but because their opponents had committed political hara-kiri. Hell hath no fury like a woman scorned—unless it be a president scorned by his party for renomination.

5

Would Cass have made a better president than Taylor?

Lewis Cass reached the height of his value and accomplishment as governor of the Michigan Territory. Though he continued to render valuable service, nothing he was to do in his later years could equal the brilliance of his performance as an empire builder. He had fought at one and the same time hunger, privation, cold, neglect, lethargy, ignorance, the Indians, the British and indifference to self-government. As an executive he had had an iron will for accomplishment, energy and vision for his people and his land; at the same time he had been tactful, sensitive, loved. He had trained his people to govern themselves and had divested himself of his own power. He was well read and well educated; he had done scientific work in exploring the wilderness; he had built schools and churches and roads; he had turned the wilderness into a thriving American community with the best traditions of New England.

There was little that could be said against Cass: he had no humor, he was ponderous in speech and manner, he had made almost too much money out of Detroit real estate. He had been accused of being unwilling to make important decisions as secretary of war, of having been softened by six years of luxurious living in Paris. To offset these allegations, he had been valuable in public life for forty-two years; if he was no longer the bold and inexhaustible young man who had emerged from the wilderness in 1832, he had acquired certain experience to compensate: he was acquainted with the intricacies of Federal government, was trained in the diplomacy of foreign affairs.

His regime would have been serious, businesslike, characterized by integrity, tact and devotion to national interests. Though he had no creative imagination he was imbued with a love for the democratic traditions which would have kept him working tirelessly to expand the spheres of self-government. Though his doctrine of Popular Sovereignty would not have been able to settle the problem of slavery, any more than Stephen Douglas would be able to solve it with the same compromise twelve years later, Cass would have brought the full power of his manifold gifts to keep the country suspended in a peaceful solution.

No man ever walked into the White House with a hazier idea of what his duties and obligations were than General Zachary Taylor, or with less ability to fulfill them. As a civil administrator Cass's mind operated in terms of education; as a military leader Taylor's mind functioned in terms of force. He so ardently desired the admission of California and New Mexico to the Union that when the south objected on the grounds that they would be admitted as free states, Taylor threatened to lead troops into the field and hang every southerner who opposed their admission.

Taylor held office only sixteen months before he died. He was personally honest, he had a fund of common sense, he wanted to do the right thing, but there his virtues ended. Unable to understand his job, he leaned on others for advice as to how to be president. He was an uncultivated man who had read nothing, who understood little of international affairs, a provincial plodder who had spent the major portion of his life doing routine jobs in obscure army posts. He was an accident in the White House, put there through a single military victory which took place at exactly the opportune political moment.

Cass's vote combined with the bolting Van Buren ballots would have been a clear majority. The country had suffered the first of its many victimizings on the slavery issue; Lewis Cass was its first political casualty. In every instance among the Also Rans where a candidate has been soundly defeated he has been obliged to retire from public life. Lewis Cass came so close to being elected that he was obliged to remain in his country's service until his eightieth year. Recounting the many presidents who had served one term and then been retired to pasture—Van Buren, Polk, Pierce, Buchanan—Lewis Cass came to realize that although the presidency is the highest office in the land, it is not always the one in which a man can render the most continuous service to his country.

Taylor, the Whig, was inferior to Cass, the Democrat, in 1848 as Pierce, the Democrat, would be inferior to Scott, the Whig, in 1852. In both instances the inferior man won. In 1848 the voters elected the inexperienced army man over the experienced statesman, and made a mistake; at the next election they mended their ways by selecting an experienced statesman, Pierce, over the politically inexperienced General Scott, and again they made a mistake.

The task of the voter is indeed a hard one; political discernment is difficult to achieve; for the democracies the royal road to electoral wisdom has been staked out, but it has not yet been paved.

CHAPTER TWO

Horatio Seymour

HE IS THE ONLY Also Ran who literally was forced to run for the presidency. He alone could say with complete honesty, "I have not the slightest desire to occupy the White House; there is too much trouble and responsibility, and no peace."

Horatio Seymour was twenty-seven when his father, a wealthy banker and landowner, killed himself because he imagined he had been ruined by the panic of 1837. This suicide was one of the determining factors in Seymour's life: he resolved that he would live placidly, permitting nothing to distress him, that he would not allow himself to become moody, bitter, depressed, nervously ill. He did not have the magnificent nerve and gland structure of a Lewis Cass; he had to accomplish his result by sheer will power: a storm center of American politics for three decades, he faced some of the worst abuse of the century with serenity of soul. When his sister cried out in anguish:

"Why don't you do something about this? Why don't you deny the charges?" Horatio answered quietly:

"Time will take care of all that."

Time has: he emerges from the jungle of Civil War politics as one of the finest men to appear on the nineteenth-century scene. Edward Channing said of him, "If Horatio Seymour only had become a Republican he would have died a great American statesman." Seymour managed to become a statesman while remaining a Democrat.

But kindly as time has been in setting his record straight, it has not employed its best agents to make the facts known: for Horatio Seymour, like Lewis Cass, is slowly fading into the limbo of forgotten men. Few remember that he ran against Ulysses S. Grant when General Grant was at the height of his fame, that in spite of the disfranchisement of the south Seymour gave him a close race, carried New York State for the Democrats, trailed by only three hundred thousand out of nearly six million votes cast.

Seymour's most astonishing quality was his timelessness: the things he said in 1840 were being said in precisely the same language in 1940. He was a completely modern man: his lifelong educative campaign for local self-government and the need for the most talented men in each community to guide its destinies cannot be distinguished from the best work being done in that field today; he was one of the first of the modern criminologists, anticipating much of the prison reform and liberalizing of the criminal code of the twentieth century; the message with which he vetoed the Prohibition Law passed by both Houses of the New York legislature in 1854 is as concise and penetrating as the most effective writing done about the Eighteenth Amendment prior to its repeal by the American people.

Horatio Seymour would have felt perfectly at home in the United States of 1943; he would have been equally at home with the Constitution makers of 1786. No more dogged battler for the Bill of Rights or universal tolerance ever has ranged the American countryside: living in an era when the Know-Nothing anti-Catholic party was growing in strength, he extolled the great contribution being made to the state by the incoming Irish; in an era when the Native American party was sweeping the east, he hammered unceasingly at the important contributions made to the prosperity, the strength, the arts and the cultures of the country by the immigrant European. To an expatriate niece he wrote:

"What is the use of your staying any longer in Europe? All the world is coming here. You will find three million more of American people than there were when you left. All the European statesmen are failures; when a people wants to run away from their homes there is trouble brewing."

He feared and disliked the northern abolitionists, maintaining that the only legitimate place to work against slavery was in the states that had slavery; yet when a crowd tried to howl down the abolitionists at a public convention in Utica, Mayor Seymour exclaimed, "This convention has a perfect right to assemble here and discuss any subject they choose without molestation. I come here armed with no authority other than as a citizen of Utica, but I earnestly request the audience to be quiet."

The audience was quiet.

Horatio Seymour earned his hard-won infamy by his insistence that the Civil War be avoided at all costs and, once it had begun, his determination that President Lincoln must fight the war within constitutional limitations. Elected Democratic governor of New York in 1862, Seymour opposed Lincoln's suppression of the writ of habeas corpus, or the right to a public trial.

"Under no circumstances can the division of the Union be

296

conceded," he cried. "But I deny that this rebellion can suspend a single right of the citizens of the loyal states. I denounce the doctrine that civil war in the south takes away from the loyal north the benefits of one principle of civil liberty. The new and strange doctrine of Martial Law holds that the loyal north lost its constitutional rights when the south rebelled: loyalty is thus less secure than rebellion, for it stands without means to resist outrages or to resent tyranny."

For a man who wanted a placid life, Seymour took the long way round Robin's barn. His resolve had not been that he would be tranquil in balmy weather, but that he would remain calm in the midst of storm. If he had been afraid of a fight or of a disruption of his peaceful way of life it would have been simpler for him to sign the Prohibition Law after both Houses had passed it, easier for him to go along with the abolitionists among his neighbors, to abandon the Catholics and the immigrants to the attacks of the Know-Nothings and Native Americans, to approve the Republican management of the war. Then he would not have been called a tippler, drunkard, tool of the liquor interests, tool of the Pope, Copperhead, traitor. . . .

Seymour stood six feet tall with a slender and lithe figure, a man who liked to work in his hayfields or go on long camping trips in the Adirondacks. His face too was long and lean, an impression heightened by a growing baldness on the top of his head while abundant hair grew over his ears, flowing down into luxuriant sideburns. He had an attractive face, candid, clean-cut, likeable. His large hazel eyes had sparkle and magnetism, yet they were the eyes of the philosopher rather than the man of action; his nose was straight and forceful, he had the lean cheeks of the ascetic, with lines which curved in concentric circles from the inside corners of his eyes down to the jawbone and from the inside corners of his nostrils to the corners of his mouth. His mouth was full-lipped, his strong chin was holed in the center by a deep and circular dimple. His expression was sensitive and gentle; it did not cry out:

"Here am I!" but rather,

"Where are you?"

It was a face at once sensitive and hard-bitten, penetrating and gentle; it was the barbed placidity of the unconquerable fighter who may lose battles, even campaigns, but never the war against evil, stupidity, intolerance and hate. He had a graceful manner, was well read and cultivated in the arts, spoke concisely and to the point. The inner secret of the man, the essence which enabled him to carry out his youthful resolves until his death at seventy-five, was his wholeness: his face, his expression, his manner, his mind, his figure, his way of life were organically knit into an indigenous design. No split personality here, no enigma, contradiction, anomaly or torn allegiance. Neither success nor failure changed him, praise nor abuse: placidly but resolutely he went his way, the perfect embodiment of the American way of life for which he fought so valiantly.

Parker and Hughes had been reluctant to accept the presidential nomination; Horatio Seymour was grimly resolved to reject it: five times he expressly informed the Democratic party and its 1868 convention that he would not be and could not be their candidate. When at the end of his fifth impassioned plea he left the convention hall for a brief respite, the delegates nominated him with equally impassioned acclaim.

2

Horatio Seymour was born in 1810 at Pompey Hill in Onondaga County, New York, a tiny settlement where his father had built a country store at a crossroads in 1800. His grandfather was Major Moses Seymour, who fought in the Revolutionary War and established a three-generation traditon of serving in the New York legislature. Henry Seymour, Horatio's father, grew prosperous as his community developed, was elected clerk of the town meeting and then senator in the state legislature. Henry was able, affable, persuasive, capable in handling men.

Governor Clinton had begun work on the Erie Canal, the great project which was to transform millions of acres of wilderness into prosperous farm lands by providing transportation and an outlet for crops. Henry Seymour was appointed to the Canal Commission, moving with his wife and six children to Utica to build the stretch of "Clinton's ditch" between Utica and Rome. Thus the Erie Canal became a tradition in the Seymour family; their home stood on the bank of the canal, Horatio's thoughts never wandered far from it: when he was seventy-two he at last accomplished what he believed to be the culminating act of his career: the opening of the canal to free transportation. So great was his love of the canal that when he vetoed the Prohibition Law one commentator observed: "Political opponents might call him the champion of rum, but wiser men knew that Seymour was the best friend water ever had."

Though tremendous sums of money passed through Henry Seymour's hands he was conceded by everyone to be honest and ethical, "in all respects a correct businessman." He was rising rapidly in political circles; his chances of becoming governor appeared to be good. However Henry felt that ten years of service to his state were enough, that he should be allowed to retire to private business, which he enjoyed more than public life. He moved to New York City, became president of the Farmers' Loan and Trust Company, bought heavily in land and became rich. Then the panic of 1837 hit the country; banks failed, business houses closed down, Henry Seymour thought himself ruined. He returned to his home in Utica, brooded over his losses and shot himself.

Horatio's mother was Mary Forman, daughter of Colonel Jonathan Forman. She was a woman of beauty and character, raising six children, all of whom enjoyed successful lives. Her youngest daughter says of her, after the death of the father, "Doubtless our mother had cares, but I never felt them cloud the sunshine; there never seemed to be much money, but the household was exquisitely ordered, and we had every pleasure and comfort."

The tranquillity was due to the mother; for the comforts they could thank their brother Horatio, who, by prudent management, was able to rescue some part of the shattered family fortune.

Young Horatio had gone to the academy at Pompey Hill which his father had helped to build, moved to Oxford Academy at Utica when he was ten, spent several years in a military academy at Middletown, Connecticut, read law in the office of an attorney and been admitted to the bar when he was twenty-two.

Because his father still had been prominent politically, young Horatio was appointed military secretary to Governor Marcy. At the outset the job was little more than to be the bearer of confidential messages, but Governor Marcy became attached to the tall, lanky, quiet-spoken youth, gave him six years of training in the practical intricacies of New York politics, an invaluable heritage for a future governor.

When he was twenty-five Horatio married Mary Bleecker, daughter of a wealthy landowning Dutch family. Upon the death of her father Mary Seymour inherited vast stretches of land, including a considerable portion of Utica. The Seymour marriage was a happy one, lasting for fifty years, though its childlessness was a tragedy for Horatio, who was fond of having children about him.

At the end of six years in Albany, and after the death of his father, Seymour returned to Utica and to private life, undertaking the management of the combined properties of his wife and his father, a pursuit which kept him interested and well off and provided leisure for his studies. Like Lewis Cass, he loved books and knowledge. In his spare hours he read

New York history, writing papers and delivering lectures before educational societies on the contributions of various racial stocks, on the plant life and agricultural development of the state and the promise of its future.

"Eminently respectable, called rich in his time, well read and widely interested in the history and geography of his native state, always an orator well above the average of his day, Horatio Seymour moved about the streets of Utica a handsome figure, familiar to all men and famous for his grace of speech and the easy charm of his manner."

Thus he stood at the age of thirty, a country gentleman who might easily have become a wealthy dilettante and patrician. Maturing in an era when politics was the chief interest, sport and amusement of the people, when anger and violence ruled the temper of the times, Seymour as a mild man of peace found himself standing on the periphery of the whirlpool, deeply anxious lest the uncurbed passions destroy the democracy he loved so well. He was distressed at the way his neighbors fought and bickered over differences that could easily have been adjusted; he distrusted fanatics, haters, interferers, non-compromisers. Horatio Seymour had inherited the virus of politics from his father and grandfather; during his six years as military secretary to Governor Marcy he had become acquainted with the Democratic leaders of the state; above all, he loved the Democratic party and wanted it to be at peace with itself. Very soon it was learned that he had the quiet power to bring warring men and factions together, that he was able to persuade them to bury their differences in a common cause. He became a healer of wounds, binder of hurts, a psychological repairman and trouble shooter for his party.

"He was conciliatory and cultivated peace."

So rare in American politics was the man who cultivated peace, who had the skill to make it bloom, that Horatio Seymour, who wanted no public office, who asked only to be allowed to remain in private life and advise his party behind the scenes, became the leader of the Democrats, the catalytic force which held the battered segments together and kept it from destruction, the power of the loyal opposition to Lincoln and the Liberal Republicans on the waging of the war.

Seymour stood for the Assembly in 1842 because he wanted to help his party oust the Whigs from control of the state; he could not know that by this simple gesture of party loyalty he would be immersing himself in politics for forty years.

He was next elected mayor of Utica, a job his father had held only nine years before, and then re-elected to the Assembly, where he was appointed chairman of the Committee on Canals. For thirty-four-year-old Horatio this was the most important position in the land: it would enable him to carry on the work for the canal he had watched his father construct. Due to rising taxes, opposition to the further development of the canal was intense; Chairman Seymour brought in such a brilliant report on what the canal could do for the people and the state of New York that his bill passed both Houses, became the operating plan for the coming twenty years.

The Erie Canal had made his father an important personage in the state; the Canal Report now snatched the son out of his comfortable obscurity and made him a figure of national importance. A historian of the period pronounced it "one of the ablest and best-written documents ever presented to a legislative body." Up to this time he had been known among the Democratic leaders for his "kind, social nature and fascinating manner," his ability to nurse recalcitrants back to orthodoxy. The manner in which he guided his report through two unfriendly Houses indicated that Horatio Seymour had, in addition, "a shrewd, discerning mind, sound judgment, great familiarity with state affairs."

For his contribution he was elected Speaker of the Assembly, presiding over a session of such bitter warfare and lunges for power which could do no possible good for the public or the state that his worst suspicions about New York politics were confirmed. He refused to stand for the legislature in 1845, retiring to the sweet-smelling calm of his private life in Utica.

During this period of tranquillity the Seymours built their family home on the crest of a three-hundred-acre farm overlooking rolling fields and the town of Utica. Seymour planted with his own hands a pear orchard, English hawthorn along the road leading to the house, and many of the indigenous New York plants and flowers in which he was interested. His grandfather's Revolutionary War pistols were crossed over the fireplace in the spacious parlor, but the library was Horatio's favorite room, for here in the sanctuary of book-lined quiet he could study and write his articles on the history of New York. The Seymours were delightful hosts: there was good company, good food, good conversation. Into their library came the leaders of the state, the businessmen, newspapermen, politicians, for their home was in the center of the state and Seymour's mind was in the center of important events. He was happy and satisfied with his life as he had made it. He had no intention of ever going back into public office.

But men's lives are controlled more by an inner pattern than by their wishes: Seymour had run for his first office in 1842 in order to defeat the Whigs; in 1848 the Whigs once again were in control, and the Democratic leaders came to their Medicine Man urging him to bring peace to the warring factions within the Democrats that they might defeat the Whigs in 1850. This was a call Seymour could not refuse: he summoned all Democrats to a convention and, by dint of his tact, poise, good nature, logical persuasion and willingness to let others take the credit, succeeded in establishing peace between the radicals and the conservatives, the farmers and the city men, the landlords and the renters, the wets and the drys, the hunkers and the barn-burners—a task peculiarly built for a conciliatory man who cultivated peace.

He was rewarded for his successful operation by the nomination for the governorship in 1850. He refused to make campaign promises, telling the public that "a man should seek office on his character and person," not on catch-all promises which he probably would not be able to fulfill.

He was defeated by a bare two hundred and sixty votes out of half a million cast, running so far ahead of the Democratic ticket that his re-nomination in 1852 was assured. This time he carried the state for the Democrats, moving into the governor's office in Albany where only fourteen years before he had served as glorified messenger boy.

Horatio Seymour was not yet forty-three when he took the oath of office. He was "tall, lean, alert, with hazel eyes and a wide mouth. Friends always spoke of his charm, but his soft answers seldom turned away wrath." He was first of all a conscientious public servant, remaining at his desk every night to handle the mass of detail work. His military secretary reports that sometimes he would go into the governor's office at midnight and begin reading to Seymour the packet of mail that had arrived during the day.

He pushed through a bill authorizing a loan for ten millions to widen the Erie and build lateral canals, a debt which was repaid by increased tolls within nine years; he worked for the granting of free lands to settlers; he modernized the state prisons and the criminal code; he worked for progressive education, the founding of state historical societies, art galleries, agricultural and botanical societies. He was a good executive and a sound businessman; as had been said of his father, no one ever questioned the honesty of his management of the millions of state funds. His love of the intermixed races and religions of the state brought an era of good feeling.

Then he ran into the Maine Liquor Law, the prohibition

law which had been born in Maine and was in process of spreading through the states of the north. Seymour vetoed the bill on the ground that it was an invasion of local self-government, hence unconstitutional. His statement to the people of New York in 1854 was a brilliant prognosis of what would happen to a dry America three quarters of a century later:

"The idea pervades the bill that severe penalties will secure enforcement; but all experience shows that undue severity of laws defeats their execution. After the excitement which has enacted them passes away, no one feels disposed to enforce them, for no law can be sustained which goes beyond public feeling and sentiment. All experience shows that temperance, like other virtues, is not produced by lawmakers, but by the influences of education, morality and religion. Men may be persuaded—they cannot be compelled to adopt habits of temperance."

The remainder of his first administration could be called How To Make Enemies While Being a Good Governor. His veto of the prohibition law earned him the name of drunkard and panderer to the liquor interests, and the enmity of about a third of the state. When he invited a papal nuncio to dinner along with the Protestant clergy of the city he earned himself the title of panderer to the Pope, alienating the anti-Catholics who represented another large segment of the state.

There was nothing in the world Seymour wanted less than the renomination. "It is a very great sacrifice for me to be a candidate," he wrote to a friend. "To what end do I expose myself to the abuse and discomforts of a canvass which is to be bitter beyond all precedent?" Deep in his soul lay the muted cry, which he was too gentle and conscientious to utter: "For God's sake, leave me alone! I have had enough of your witches' brew!"

It was a filthy campaign. The Know-Nothing candidate ran on a platform of hatred and repression of the Catholics and immigrants; the Whig candidate endorsed the Prohibition Bill. Even with a fourth candidate, a rival Democrat, splitting Seymour's total, he lost by only a few hundred votes.

Having done as well by his party as any man could, Seymour said privately, "I am relieved to be in the minority, and out of power." When there was talk of his appointment to a Federal office he replied, "No appointment will be tendered to me, nor would I accept any office. I am 'discharged cured' of all ambition for official station. I could not be persuaded again to give up the comfort and respectability of private life."

But politics is a recurrent disease: there is no cure.

Relieved from the stringencies of both office and ambition, he was free to work for the cause he loved best: the friendly unity of his party, his state, his nation. He spent his years, his money and his talents flinging himself against what he called the three obsessions of the north: Abolitionism, Nativism, Prohibitionism. "He was not a Catholic, never drank, and believed slavery to be doomed," but he worked on the thesis that the Constitution protected the people from the "peculiar views" of segments of the citizenry. On one lecture he was described as "tall, immaculately dressed, with golden voice and large luminous eyes, right hand tucked into his tightly buttoned frock coat, facing a critical audience of poker-faced Yankees."

Slavery was the jagged rock against which Seymour dashed his lean and graceful life in the years to come. He took no moral stand against slavery because he believed that he had no right to take a stand against the way other people lived. He told his audiences that he resented agitation against slavery where it did not exist as causing more trouble than slavery itself. In part his feeling was based on his devotion to local self-government, but the major portion was based on economics: he was convinced that slavery would disappear in competition with free labor, that it would be too expensive for the south to maintain, that they would abandon it within a few years, even as New York had voluntarily abandoned it. He said:

"If the early settler wanted to buy beef, he must buy the whole ox—hide, horn and tails; then comes a time when he can procure a quarter; and at last, as population increases, he can go to market and purchase a beef steak, or any joint most pleasing to his taste. The same thing occurs in the case of labor: at first it may be necessary to take the whole man; then you can hire part of a man; and in due time you may be able to get so much of the time of a man as may just suit your purpose."

The only danger lay in the incendiary talk of the abolitionists, who were going to force emancipation on the south before it was ready. Such a war, which was useless and unnecessary, would destroy the Union and drown it in blood. If only the north would be patient, think in terms of peace; if only it would regard its southern brothers with good will, slavery would disappear and unity would be preserved.

To lecture audiences throughout the east and northwest he said, "The nation soon will be three-quarters free, the Congress two-thirds free. Force destroys those who use it; let us be patient, and we will find peaceful ways of settling our problem." So thought Horatio Seymour; so thought the northern Democrats.

Then Fort Sumter was fired upon. Seymour called for "unanimous support of President Lincoln! The Rebellion must be put down!"

He was put in charge of recruiting for his county; on several occasions he paid the expenses of the volunteers out of his own pocket. He felt convinced that the Republican party, as a purely sectional group, had helped bring on the war; as the opposition he would keep a hawk's eye on the policies of the administration, make sure that it kept within its constitutional bounds.

By 1862 the war was going badly for the Union, the Republicans in Washington were at each other's throat, and there was an upsurge of Democratic strength. Once again the party leaders came to Seymour: he was the only leader who had a chance to carry the state. "We know you do not want to run," they said, "but you must help us keep our party together. What restraint will there be left on the Republicans if the Democrats become too weak to raise their voice?"

There was no way for Seymour to hold out for his own peace and privacy in a war-torn country. "I did what I could to avoid the nomination," he said, "but I was forced on. In many respects it is very injurious to me to be nominated, but now that I am in the field I want a sharp, bitter fight. I want a strong compact party that can defy violence and keep the fanatics in check."

He stumped the state on the platform of "suppressing the Rebellion by all legitimate means, restoring the Union as it was, and the Constitution as it is." He employed a small army of men to distribute pamphlets and literature from house to house to persuade the voters that "a victory of the Democrats in New York would bring the government in Washington to its senses by reminding men that the Civil War was being waged to crush a revolution—not to change the social system of the states which insisted on trying to secede."

His case against the Lincoln administration was centered on two fronts: the suspension of the writ of habeas corpus, and the threatened Emancipation Proclamation. When loyal northerners were arrested by the military and imprisoned without trial for criticizing the administration's waging of the war, Seymour demanded to know why the north had to be warred upon by its own government, why its guaranteed rights and legal, constitutional government had to be destroyed.

"Liberty is born in war," he cried. "It does not die in war! I denounce the doctrine that Civil War in the south takes away from the loyal north the benefits of one principle of civil liberty!"

He fought the Emancipation Proclamation on the same grounds of unconstitutionality: "If it is true that slaves must be abolished to save this Union, then the people of the south should be allowed to withdraw themselves from that government which cannot give them the protection guaranteed by its terms."

Horatio Seymour's feeling for a moderate and constitutional war must have been shared by a considerable portion of the north, for he was elected the Democratic governor of New York. Despite his criticisms, he never uttered a hostile word against Lincoln, who was suffering a hailstorm of abuse from his own party members in Washington; nor did his loyalty to the Union waver in the midst of the chaos and confusion and defeat. He kept the New York volunteers well above their national quota; when Secretary of War Stanton wired for help on the eve of Gettysburg, Governor Seymour rushed more New York troops to the aid of General Meade. Both Lincoln and Stanton telegraphed their fervent thanks for his help in winning the battle of Gettysburg, which turned the tide of the war.

After Gettysburg, when it was clear that the south no longer could win, and before the Emancipation Proclamation could transform the southern rebellion into what he called a northern revolution, Seymour brought before the country his plan for a negotiated peace. He knew that in a war between countrymen a victory doubles the defeat for both sides; he felt it sufficient that the rebellion be put down, that an armistice in 1863 could finish the war without finishing the south.

At that very instant in New York City, just nine days after Gettysburg, there broke out draft riots, riots for which Governor Seymour was blamed: he had opposed the Draft Act as unconstitutional; he had criticized the administration's conduct of the war; he had been undermining the morale of the north by preaching the wisdom of a negotiated peace. Washington came to look upon him as the most detestable Copperhead at large.

On Monday, July 13, 1863, Governor Seymour was handed a telegram telling him of the riots. When he reached Manhattan he found that a mob had burned the headquarters of a draft official and a whole block of property at Forty-sixth Street and Third Avenue. Stores had been looted,

Negroes beaten, a Negro orphan asylum burned down. The rioters had clashed with the police, and between seventy and eighty persons had been killed. One company of militia could have quelled the riots in an hour, but Seymour had sent the militia to Pennsylvania to oppose General Lee.

Governor Seymour promptly declared the city to be in a state of insurrection. At the lunch hour, when workers from the neighboring office buildings collected on the steps of the City Hall and called for a speech, he addressed the crowd briefly, urging them to protect their fellow citizens as well as the property of the city.

His resolve to remain unperturbed amidst political tornado was put to the ultimate test: cartoons appeared in the opposition press in which the group of orderly working people on the steps of the City Hall became a filthy, drunken, murderous mob to whom Governor Seymour was accused of opening his speech by crying, "My friends!" Thus the moderate and peace-loving Horatio Seymour was presented to the country as a friend and abettor of rioters, one who encouraged their activities as a means of fomenting insurrection.

History presents no neater irony than the picture of precise, legal-minded, meticulous Horatio Seymour calling a mob of murderers "my friends!" yet the legend was perpetuated through the newspapers of the day, played an important role in defeating him for the presidency in 1868. That is why so much of the truth of American history remains obscured: every minute fact has been drowned in a blood bath of partisanship . . . a partisanship among supposed brothers which finally broke Seymour's iron will.

Discouraged, ill from the grief of being an opposition governor in times of war, heartbroken at the viciousness, destruction and killing, Seymour reached the lowest ebb of his life when he refused to be renominated for the governorship in 1864. He was certain that his two years in office had been hopeless and worthless: he had not succeeded in cooling passions, in healing the breach, in holding the war within constitutional bounds, in bringing peace to the country before victory made peace impossible. His health had been shattered, his business affairs had been neglected, he had given the best efforts of his heart and head to no avail.

Within one hour after receiving his flat refusal to run, the Democratic convention nominated him with wild acclaim. Once again he was trapped: to refuse after he had been nominated would be to strike a blow at his party, repudiate the things he had fought for during his two-year regime, particularly the need for a vigorous opposition. He was learning that it was easier to get into politics than to get out.

He campaigned on the platform of a negotiated peace, the return of the southern states to the Union with full rights, no revenge or reparations to be forced upon the defeated. In his one major speech he predicted to the letter the years of the locust that would be visited upon the south by a victorious war administration. "The honor of the north demands a conciliatory policy; the cry of no compromise is false in morals, it is treason to the spirit of the Constitution."

Though there were internal Democratic rows, though the Republican soldiers got ballots where the Democrats did not, he was defeated by less than one per cent of the vote cast.

"My enjoyment in the prospect of relief from the hard duties of this office is perfect," he wrote.

The one per cent that defeated Seymour voted against him because he had protested the unfairness of certain New York draft quotas. Immediately after the election the new governor succeeded in having President Lincoln lower the New York quotas on the basis of the statistical work done by former Governor Seymour; a by now thoroughly befuddled north was treated to the spectacle of a Copperhead Democratic ex-governor being thanked by a Republican state legislature for his good and loyal work for the people of New York!

The years following the end of the war were unhappy ones for Seymour, but he never stopped preaching the thesis upon which his life was founded: *force destroys those who use it!* "We have more to fear from the south if it accepts the doctrine of subjugation than we ever had to fear from its armed rebellion; we cannot enslave them without enslaving ourselves." As president of the Prison Congress he opposed the Delaware whipping post on the grounds that "the evil was not the harm done to the criminal, but to the onlookers."

Despite the fact that he had retired to private life and spent a considerable time in trying to mend his broken fortunes, he remained the outstanding and most icily penetrating critic of the Republican regime. From the viewpoint of a war-weary populace watching a venal senatorial clique attempt to impeach President Andrew Johnson and seize control of the national government, arch-critic Seymour made a valuable contribution.

From the viewpoint of the man who was resolved to remain in private life, he made a strategic error.

4

As early as November 1867 Horatio Seymour was named by the Democratic *Union* of Oneida County as the best possible candidate for the presidency in 1868. He promptly wrote to the editor, "I am not and cannot be a candidate for the presidency. In trying to uphold principles which I deem to be right, I can do battle with more vigor when I am not a candidate for official position."

When other editorials appeared naming him as the country's outstanding figure Seymour felt impelled to scotch the movement by exclaiming, "In my letter I meant what I said; and I am annoyed to have it looked upon by some as a strategic movement."

He went to the Democratic convention in New York City as a delegate and accepted the permanent chairmanship, thus eliminating himself as a potential candidate. His keynote speech was a ringing declaration for the return of constitutional government and a real peace. His choice for a candidate was Chief Justice Chase, who had presided with complete fairness over the impeachment trial of President Johnson; he had told this to the New York delegates only a few days before when he had denied them permission to present his name to the convention.

On the first ballot the convention was presented with the names of Andrew Johnson, Winfield Scott Hancock, Church, Pendleton and Hendricks. Seymour's name was not mentioned. On the fourth ballot the chairman of the North Carolina delegation rose and cast his nine votes for Horatio Seymour. This unexpected move caused "loud and enthusiastic cheering," but Seymour left his chair, advanced to the front of the platform and made his fourth refusal. "I must not be nominated by this Convention, as I could not accept the nomination if tendered. My own inclination prompted me to decline at the outset; my honor compels me to do so now. It is impossible, consistently with my position, to allow my name to be mentioned in this Convention against my protest. The clerk will proceed with the call."

For twenty-one ballots the opposing candidates were at loggerheads: the east was battling the west for control, the conservatives battling the radicals. The two leading candidates were determined that the other should not receive the nomination; because of the two-thirds rule of the convention it was apparent that a compromise candidate would have to be found. Seymour still was hoping it would be Chief Justice Chase, but on the twenty-second ballot the chairman of the Ohio delegation announced that "at the unanimous request and demand of the delegation I place Horatio Seymour in nomination with twenty-one votes—against his inclination, but no longer against his honor."

Seymour had to wait for the nine rousing cheers to die down before he could address the delegates and make his fifth refusal. "I have no terms in which to tell of my regret that my name has been brought before this convention. God knows that my life and all that I value most I would give for the good of my country, which I believe to be identified with that of the Democratic party . . ."

"Take the nomination, then!" cried someone from the floor.

". . . but when I said that I could not be a candidate, I *meant* it! I could not receive the nomination without placing not only myself but the Democratic party in a false position. God bless you for your kindness to me, but your candidate I cannot be."

Perspiring profusely from the intense heat, excited and over-wrought, Seymour left the platform to cool off and rest. No sooner had he left the hall than the Ohio chairman cried that his delegation would not accept Seymour's declination; Utah's chairman rose to say that Seymour was the man they had to have. While Horatio was waiting in the vestibule, mopping his brow, the convention nominated him unanimously, named a vice-presidential candidate in great haste, and shut up shop before Seymour could dash back into the hall and reject their offer still once again.

"The failure to insist on my declination of the nomination then," said Seymour in later years, "was the mistake of my life."

The 1868 campaign of Horatio Seymour versus Ulysses S. Grant was conducted vigorously; despite the fact that today not one American in a hundred could tell you who Grant's opponent was, the Republicans were fearful as late as October that they might be beaten. The Democrats were the disinherited party, Seymour had been called a traitor, a trouble-maker, the votes of thousands of southern Democrats would not be counted, yet everyone knew that Seymour, the man of charity and peace, would give the warrior Grant a hard race. Had he not defeated the Republican candidate for the governorship of New York, and that right in the middle of the Civil War?

The Liberal Republicans, who had tried to impeach President Johnson for his peaceful attitude toward the south, did their best to impeach Seymour before he ever set foot in Washington. Because his father had committed suicide, Horatio was accused of coming from an insane family. Henry Ward Beecher branded him a coward and a traitor by declaring him to be "a man who, through all the years of 1860 to 1868, studied how to help southern treason without incurring the risks and pains of overt and courageous treasonable acts."

Whittier, the gentle poet, abandoned the gentle Seymour in

310

favor of the warrior Grant. The voters were told that if they wanted to reopen the Civil War they needed only re-elect Horatio Seymour, spreading lurid tales of murder and massacre in the south to prove that the south needed the heavy foot of the conqueror on her neck. Despite the fervent thanks of Lincoln and Stanton for his quick dispatch of troops to Gettysburg, he was branded in the press as disloyal to the Union. The New York *Tribune* led the cartoon campaign with the picture of Seymour standing on the steps of the City Hall calling a mob of murderers "my friends"; other newspaper descriptions of the life and character of Horatio Seymour were staggering:

The New York *Post* called him "childless, scheming, not studious, selfish, stealthy, earnest of power, feeble, insincere, timid, closefisted, inept, too weak to be enterprising." The Hartford *Post* called him "almost as much of a corpse" as ex-President Buchanan, who had just died. "Seymour is a little creation; his face is an outlined wriggle; its expression is a dodge. He has a smooth tongue, feeble health, a constant fear of aberration. His art is to wheedle the vain, promise the ambitious, and charm the religious."

Small wonder that Horatio Seymour five times declined the scourge of the presidential nomination!

He answered none of the charges made against him, but went his quiet way, bringing in the hay during the hot summer days, making a few key speeches, indulging in no violence, no slander, no fraud. The bitterness and abuse heaped upon him seeped into history through the medium of the unrestrained newspaper and the partisan historian, never to be completely dislodged; his conduct of the campaign did his country and the institution of free elections great good, helped to keep alive the two-party system when the opposition was determined to remain the only party that could hold power.

Horatio Seymour polled 2,703,249 votes against 3,012,833 for Grant. If all the white men of the south had been permitted to vote, the election would have come very close to being a tie. Seymour conveyed his private attitude toward his defeat in one of the dry little jokes with which he expressed his deepest feelings. When someone commented that Chief Justice Chase would never be able to sleep peacefully until he got into the White House, Seymour replied, "Well, if Mr. Chase runs for president just once, and gets defeated, his ambition will be satisfied, I can assure you."

The presidential canvass and the defeat have been such a dreadful licking that few men have had the heart to ask for more.

It was not likely that Horatio Seymour could have defeated the man who, coming to power toward the end of the war, was being given credit for having won it. The closeness of the race startled the nation at the time, was forgotten by the succeeding generations, and now remains to startle each reader anew.

5

During the campaign Seymour had been called "a gentleman disguised as a Democrat." For the remaining eighteen years of his life he continued to act as a political gentleman and to prove that his being a Democrat was no disguise. Of one of the innumerable splits in the Democratic party he had commented, "We may forgive others, but the men who have left us will not forgive us." To the Democratic party he remained a wise and mellow senior statesman to the end of his days, but the Democrats who became Republicans in 1860 never forgave him for remaining loyal to the old party.

He helped Tilden break up the Tweed and Canal rings in New York, achieved his ambition to see the Erie Canal a free waterway, was instrumental in securing a majority of the national vote for Tilden in 1876, worked prodigiously for the election of Winfield Scott Hancock in 1880, and lived to enjoy the return of a Democrat to the White House, Grover Cleveland in 1884, the first Democratic regime since the election of Lincoln in 1860.

The placidity of his truly beautiful nature had been shattered during the years that he was governor of New York and during the months he had campaigned for the presidency. After his major defeat he succeeded in retiring to his country place, where he referred to himself as "an old humbug of a farmer," and found once again the serenity he valued so highly. For many years he regretted deeply having allowed himself to be jettisoned into the presidential race, but when he reached his seventies, when the thatch of hair above his ears had grown white, his eyes deeply luminous, he said, "I find that I could have done without my successes far better than without my failures."

Seymour's only modern biographer comments that "not even his enemies suggested that he would have failed so dismally in the great office as General Grant." When the bad blood of the election had been purified his former enemies gave him greater praise than his friends. Lincoln's secretary of the treasury, Hugh McCulloch, was to say, "No man in this country was better equipped for the presidency than Horatio Seymour"; Charles A. Dana, Lincoln's assistant

312

secretary of war, remarked of the alleged Copperhead, "Seymour stood firmly for preserving the integrity of the government and the unity of the country; amid all the changes of parties and policies, and under all the difficulties of tremendous and trying events, he was always a patriot, always a gentleman, and, above all, always an honest man."

The qualifications of Ulysses S. Grant for the office of the presidency and the inestimable tragedy of his eight years in the White House have been portrayed in the story of Horace Greeley. If the gap between the qualifications of Grant and Greeley, who had many idiosyncrasies and shortcomings, was of epic proportion, what must it have been between Grant and Seymour, who was one of the most intelligent, high-minded and able statesmen produced in America since the creators of the Constitution? It is an unbelievable fact that a free electorate could reject a Seymour for a military hero, and one of the most cogent arguments against the democratic form of government. In their magnificent wisdom the makers of the Constitution so protected the people that not even a hopelessly bad president could wreck the government—though a Grant could come mighty close.

Some historians find it better that Seymour was not elected because the Republicans would not have permitted him to carry out the duties of his office, would have set their armies to marching again. Seymour would have made a magnificent executive because he understood the function of an executive in a balanced-power form of government. The depth of his understanding of the commonwealth is best illustrated by his article in the *North American Review* answering the comment made by Gladstone in England that "the American Constitution is the most wonderful work ever struck off by the brain and purpose of man." Seymour replied that the Constitution was not and could not have been "struck off," that it had grown slowly in America from 1607, that "the compact of 1787 was the written record of political experience up to the time when it was made."

Seymour understood the political nature of his country and his people; like Lewis Cass, he was an ardent advocate of local self-government who by years of reiteration taught the nation that "the theory of self-government is not founded upon the idea that the people are necessarily virtuous and intelligent, but it attempts to distribute each particular power to those who have the greatest interest in its wise and faithful exercise."

In one of the country's most crucial periods he would have been a completely modern man in the White House, serving as the leader of drives for tolerance, for education, for the

313

furthering of the arts and the sciences. Grant filled the federal government with his relatives, flatterers and hangers-on. Seymour would have manned the government with the most able men the country afforded. Nor would he have indulged in grudges: when governor of New York in 1864, his secretary walked into his office as an army major was asking to be promoted to lieutenant colonel. The secretary drew Seymour aside, said, "That man was on my train coming from Washington. He publicly called you a traitor and abused you most unmercifully."

Seymour smiled, walked back to his desk and handed the major his promotion. To a stunned secretary he said, "The promotion was a meritorious one, it has been recommended by his senior officers. What he said of me does not enter the case at all."

The times might not have permitted Horatio Seymour to make his full contribution to the nation he loved so well. But neither time nor tide could have kept him from being one of the most farsighted and creative of American presidents. He would have been a militant crusader for the peaceful virtues of brotherhood and the development of the full genius of the American experiment. Under his leadership there would have been no Reconstruction Acts further to ravish the south; he was the most logical figure in the country to bind the wounds of the war and wipe out the bitterness, to reunite the two sections and restore workable economic and political relations.

A gentle soul, detesting hatred, force and strife, he took on some of the fiercest opponents to be found in any country's politics, never flinching, never giving up the battle, never running away, yet even in the turmoil and passion of the Civil War period he succeeded in remaining a statesman.

He was born a hundred years too late—or a hundred years too soon. He was a man of good will living in an era of ill will.

"The longer I live and the more I learn of men," he said, "the more I am disposed to think well of their hearts and poorly of their heads."

He died at the age of seventy-six, ripe with years and wisdom and good deeds.

It was left to the London *Times* to find that "Horatio Seymour was perhaps the best-loved man in America. No other American could so surely touch the chord of popular feeling and enthusiasm. His political career was full of self-abnegation. His private life was so beneficent and gracious that the whole country came to know about it and to take pride in it as exemplifying, at their very highest, the qualities of an American gentleman."

There would be no more politics for Horatio Seymour: at last he was discharged cured.

CHAPTER THREE

Alfred E. Smith

MANY OF HIS PREDECESSORS had come up from a rural lack-of-cash, but he was the first Also Ran to emerge from the poverty of the crowded city. He is also the first whose antecedents did not go back several generations in the American tradition.

The first political organization he ever joined was a Seymour Club; he became the fulfillment of Horatio Seymour's confidence in the Irish-American. No greater contrast between two men can be imagined, yet in essence Al Smith was the son for whom Seymour longed.

While Governor Smith was holding a Carnegie Hall audience with the clarity of his exposition on a governmental subject, a woman in one of the boxes murmured, "What a giant he would be if only he had a college education!" To this Smith would have replied laughingly, "But, madam, I have a degree. F.F.M. Fulton Fish Market."

He was plain and humble, but sensitive to any slight against his East Side origin. When he caused a furor in Albany society by refusing to accept a dinner invitation from a prominent family, he explained, "I have been in Albany for fifteen years. I have met all the members of that family socially a number of times. This is the first time they have invited me to their home. Governor Smith may be different from Assemblyman Smith to them, but not to me."

He grew up in the burning crucible of democracy, in the great welter of Irish, Italians, Poles, Russians, Slovaks, Greeks, Armenians, Rumanians who thronged the tenements of the East Side of New York. He knew less about the theory of democracy than either Lewis Cass or Horatio Seymour, both of them scholars, but he had seen a people's democracy at work; it became a deep-grained vision which was to enable him to accomplish as much for the people of his state as either Cass or Seymour.

"It would be difficult for me to conceive of any man being inaugurated Governor of New York with a deeper sense of responsibility," said Smith in 1918. "I was eager to demonstrate that no mistake had been made by the people of the state when they entrusted their government to a man who had come up from the lowest rung of the ladder to the highest position within their gift."

Therein lay the mainspring of his lifework: he must make good for the East Side, for all those who were still on the lowest rung, so that they too might have an opportunity to rise in the world. Though he was to be defeated for the presidency, he was victorious in a campaign of even greater importance: in proving to the nation that men from the lowest ranks of society can make important contributions to democracy.

"No man owes more to the state than I," said Al Smith. The converse was equally true: the state owed more to no man than to Alfred Emanuel Smith. He served as commanding general in a people's peaceful revolution, then doubled the accomplishment by making that revolution respectable. In a debate on the conservation of natural resources Governor Smith stated the essence of his political philosophy:

"The state is not made up of great industrial centers, great forest preserves, big cities and villages; the state, after all, is people, and if its people are not healthy, vigorous and happy in their work, the conservation of all the rest does not mean much."

As a child he had been open-faced, laughing and lovable; he carried this sunny personality into manhood, and even his political rivals were his friends. "I never oppose men," said Smith. "I oppose principles." He had a gift of cutting sarcasm: when he got through with a subject it might be lacerated with laughter, yet his opponent would have suffered no personal disfigurement. When, as an assemblyman, he was trying to put through the legislature a six-day work week and was asked by the fish canneries for an exception in their case, he replied:

"I have read carefully the commandment, 'Remember the Sabbath Day, to keep it Holy,' but I am unable to find any language in it that says, excepting the canneries."

Where other Also Rans had been actors, Smith was a theatrical producer. He dramatized government for the people, staged its inner processes and mathematical equations in such an interesting manner that more and more people came to see the spectacle. Because he himself had had so much trouble understanding the intricacies of legislation when he first went to Albany, he simplified and clarified the machinery of government, wrote the dialogue in such plain, inelegant English that the least citizen could follow it. He called in the best actors, directors, scene designers and costumers to be found in the state.

"The greatest contribution that a man can make to his own success in high elective office," he said, "is to surround himself with men who understand their business, have intelligence and are interested in the subject, but personally disinterested."

He had an astonishing fund of technical information that he could summon at will to buttress his arguments; when he spoke to the people of the state he did not lecture, he took them into his confidence and shared with them the problems of being a governor. His considerable genius for efficient and creative government was that he was able to awaken the interest of the people in what had previously been thought too technical. In a democracy this amounts to a miracle.

Al Smith believed in miracles; he had every right to: in Houston, Texas, in 1928 the Democratic national convention nominated the East Side orphan boy for the highest position in the land.

2

Alfred E. Smith was born on the third floor of a tenement on South Street on December 30, 1873. South Street runs alongside of the East River, where Alfred swam as a boy, played among the docks and watched the Brooklyn Bridge go up. Both his mother and father had been born on Water Street, just a few blocks from where their son was born; it was a workingman's district.

Alfred was named after his father, a strong-bodied man who drove high wooden trucks drawn by teams of horses through the streets of New York. The father owned two trucks and pairs of horses, and thus was able to make something more than a driver's wage. He was a hardy man who would go out in the coldest winter weather without an overcoat, a precedent carried on by the son who braved icy blasts of opposition without ample protective covering. Alfred's father had the contract for hauling the Democratic voting booths on election day; each year the son earned a few extra dollars by folding the ballots. On election night Alfred would fight with the other boys of the neighborhood to capture the voting booths for the victory bonfire. When he was eleven years old he marched in his first Democratic parade, carrying a kerosene torch on the end of a long stick and chanting, "James G. Blaine, James G. Blaine, Continental liar from the state of Maine!"

The older Smith was a hard-working man, gone from dawn to dark, with only Sundays to spend with his family. When Alfred was thirteen his father took ill and died. Catherine Mulvehill Smith, Alfred's mother, was a woman of spiritual strength and goodness. So important a part did she play in her son's life that when he was governor of the state he did not hesitate to kneel by her side and ask for her guidance in difficult problems.

The father's illness had dissipated the family's modest resources; through the helpfulness of their landlady Mrs. Smith was able to buy the stock and fixtures of a basement grocery and candy store. The mother kept the store; Alfred and his young sister attended the St. James Parochial School, where their mother and father had gone before them; after school the sister helped in the store while Alfred sold papers, and after supper Alfred waited on customers until closing time.

Work as hard as they might, Mrs. Smith could not earn enough from the small store to keep her family going. When Alfred was fourteen, and before he had been graduated from grammar school, he found it necessary to take a job for three dollars a week, running along the water front delivering messages to his employer's trucks. After a few months he got a better job as a handy boy in an oil business at eight dollars a week. By the time he was nineteen he had worked himself up to the position of assistant shipping clerk, but the needs of his family continued to grow; he had to give up this genteel work and search for a higher-paying job. He found it at the Fulton Fish Market, where he was to earn twelve dollars a week, a high wage for its day.

"The salary was large," commented Smith, "because the work was hard. I reported for work at four o'clock in the morning, at three o'clock on Fridays." The work was not only hard, it was rough and dirty and smelly: checking crates of fish as they came off the fishing boats, unpacking the crates, cutting open the fish, cleaning them, selling at the stall. Later, when the Assembly was discussing a prospective measure on the state's fish, Alfred said proudly, "I am the only member of this Assembly who can speak the fish language."

After three years in the fish market he secured a job as shipping clerk in a steam-pump works, and it was while working here that he took on his first political job. He was twenty-two years old when he secured his appointment as a process server for the Commissioner of Jurors through a friend, Henry Campbell, a prosperous grocer who had taken a liking to the boy. Bright-eyed, eager Alfred Smith had always had a winning way, was full of good spirits and geniality no matter how great the drudgery or the difficulties at hand. As a youngster he had been the mascot and buff of the neighboring firehouse, the most envied position among the kids of the neighborhood; before his father's death he had gathered the youngsters in the attic of the house on Water Street where he staged and acted in rough reproductions of the current plays; at the St. James School he had been champion reciter, winning medals for his renditions of *The Bells* and *'Twas the Night Before Christmas*. By the time he was fifteen he had become the leading actor of the club at the St. James parish, where he impersonated English lords in such plays as *Hazel Kirke*, produced melodramas, and kept the organization going by his resourcefulness and unfailing good humor. He always claimed that his first success was due to the fact that the people of the neighborhood knew him from his years of amateur theatricals.

During the six years that he worked for the Commissioner of Jurors, rising to be an investigator at a salary which made life comfortable for his mother and sister, he had nothing to do with Tammany Hall because he disliked the personality and ethics of the man who was in charge. However, in 1901 Tom Foley was elected leader of the district, and young Smith's political career began in earnest.

Tom Foley liked people, took a genuine interest in them; he was honest, loyal, a leader to be trusted and loved. Foley helped the people of his neighborhood when they needed help, gave them food when they were hungry, coal when they were cold, found them jobs when they were unemployed, and got their children out of trouble when they ran afoul of the law. In gratitude the people of the neighborhood voted for Foley's Democratic candidates on election day. Tom Foley called in Alfred Smith to be one of his young district leaders. He made Alfred work hard and attend to his duties, but in the process he imparted to the younger man his stern code of ethics: "Never get a swelled head at your own importance; never get out of touch with your constituents; never make a promise unless you keep it; and tell the truth."

Alfred liked politics because he liked people and people liked him. He was clean-tongued, social by nature, loyal and reliable. Folks of the neighborhood called him Al now, and his popularity was growing. In 1903 Tom Foley decided to run him for the State Assembly; Al confessed that when he saw his picture in the store windows he nearly burst with pride.

At the age of thirty Al Smith boarded a train for Albany to become a state legislator. In his grip was his first dress suit, bought for him by his friend Henry Campbell who had said, while walking him up to Brooks Brothers, "The old neighborhood must have as well-dressed an Assemblyman as the uptown folks have!" He knew that he was going to the Assembly under severe handicaps: he had never been out of the city before, how could he help make laws for the whole state? He had had no formal education, he was not a lawyer, he knew nothing about the procedure of a legislative body. He had only Tom Foley's advice to keep still until he had something to say. He was honest and anxious to do the right thing, but what was a young man just a few years out of the Fulton Fish Market going to do in the august halls where Horatio Seymour and Samuel Tilden had gone before him?

The Alfred E. Smith who stepped off the train at Albany and went searching for an inexpensive boardinghouse room was tall and slender, with the strong body of his truck-driving father. He had a good face, not handsome but attractive in its openness, with ruddy coloring; his eyes were light gray when he was laughing, but darkened when he became angry; he brushed his hair up stiff and abruptly from a not overly large forehead; his lids fell too low over his eyes, in particular the left, which sometimes appeared to be partly shut; he had a strong nose, a trifle on the large side, a well-modeled mouth, an undisguised East Side accent, and the actor's stentorian voice which, during the election, said Al, "I was told I could be heard a block away, over the rattle of the horsecars on Madison Avenue." He had married his childhood sweetheart, an Irish girl from the East Side, even as his father had before him, and he now had two children. He had given up a steady job for an extremely temporary one, and he had not the faintest idea of where the future was going to take him.

As a member of the minority party Smith was given a seat in the last row of the Chamber; three and a half months later he still had not been introduced to the Speaker! He could not make head or tail of the legislation; at night he took the printed material on the proposed bills to his hall bedroom and spent hours racking his brain over amendments to laws of which he had never heard. The only time he heard his own voice in the Assembly was when he was called upon to vote—and he voted the way Tom Foley told him to.

He was re-elected in 1904 and 1905; he still sat in the last row. Appointed to the committees on banks and forests, he mourned, "I have never seen a forest, and I have never been in a bank except to serve a jury notice."

The Annual Appropriation Bill, a document of some three hundred pages, was a technical matter settled between the heads of departments and the inner ring of the legislature. No one read any part of it except his own pork-barrel plank. Al Smith did not know that he was not expected to read this weighty document: during each session he read the volume from cover to cover, insisting upon knowing why every item was there and what justified the expenditure of that sum of money. His boardinghouse room was his college dormitory; in his three lonely years he trained himself to become a student of state legislation.

"I have a deep and abiding affection for the Assembly Chamber," said Smith when taking the oath of office as governor there. "It has been my high school and college; the very foundation of everything I attained was laid here."

He was given no chance by the opposition to show his knowledge, nor did he attempt to force himself upon the Assembly. By the end of the third term he was completely discouraged, believing that he could never understand what was going on or be of any service. Tom Foley offered him the job of superintendent of buildings for New York City, but his failure had made him mad. His Irish was up. "I just hated the idea that I should have to admit there was anything I could not understand." He decided to try the Assembly for one more year; that decision set his feet on the long winding road to the White House.

In his fourth term his chance came: Speaker Wadsworth made friends with the young man, appointed him a member of the Committee on Affairs of Cities and a member of the Special Committee on Revision of the Charter of Greater New York. If there was any one subject that Smith knew about, it was New York City. He was moved up from the last row and given a desk in the heart of the Assembly.

He was also making progress on another front: among the legislators themselves, particularly among the upstate representatives, who liked him for his simplicity and ready wit. He gave little parties for a half a dozen of them at a time where, over corned beef, cabbage and beer, they could talk politics and become better acquainted. Slowly, as his character and self-training began to emerge, he won the respect and love of the Assembly.

He spent the next eight years doing what he called "exposing the shine on the gold brick." He became the demon of the Appropriation Bill to whom the local boys, who were pledged to bring home a new road or a bridge over the creek, had to prove the necessity of their demands. In 1911 the Democrats secured a majority in the Assembly, and Al Smith, now thirty-eight, became the party floor leader and was appointed chairman of the Ways and Means Committee which prepared the state budget. It was no longer necessary for Tom Foley to tell him how to vote.

He was growing in ability and stature, but there seemed little reason to believe that he would ever be anything more than an honest and efficient state legislator. Then in March of

1911 a fire broke out in the Triangle Waist Factory in New York City in which a hundred and fifty girls were killed because there were no fire escapes. The factories of New York were under no supervision: they did not have to register when going into business, they employed women and children who worked nights and Sundays, at any wage the factory set, and there was no protection against fire, accident, industrial disease.

Al Smith spent months on a Factory Investigating Committee, visiting every remote part of the state, studying working conditions. He understood human nature, he was hard to fool, he had come from working people; just as he never grew away from his loyalty to the East Side, so he had not grown away from his love for the people who earned their bread by the rigors of manual labor. What he found in his investigations made him determine that the chaos and lack of responsibility in industry must cease, that the state must protect its people.

With his colleagues he set up a labor code which was to serve as a model for other states and in part for the national government. As majority leader and as Speaker of the Assembly from 1913 to 1915 he worked indefatigably, against powerful and unscrupulous lobbies, to secure registration of factories, with ample state investigators and supervision over fire hazards, sanitation, unguarded machinery, industrial disease, long hours, nightwork for women, Sunday work, work for children who had not first passed a doctor's examination. Tenement-house factories were banned; measures were passed protecting workmen in such dangerous occupations as tunneling; workmen's compensation was turned over to a state commission so that the injured workman would not be forced to deal individually with the insurance company. It was an emergence from the dark ages of the Industrial Revolution into the dawning light of a new and free world.

In 1915 Al Smith took part in the work of the Constitutional Convention which was attempting to modernize the machinery of state government. He studied every proposal to the bitter end, as he had during the three years in his solitary boardinghouse room when he was an obscure and unrecognized sitter in the last row. His knowledge of the Executive Budget, taxation, water power, home rule, the reorganization of state departments continued to amaze his colleagues and made him one of the most cogent debaters on the floor. He had not lost his East Side accent, his language was never polished or formal, but everything he had to say was sharply pointed and informed. When Chairman Elihu Root asked if someone would submit a report on the history of legislation to control public-service corporations, Smith volunteered.

"When can we have the report?" asked Chairman Root.

"Right now," replied Smith, plunging into a two-hour discussion in which he reviewed in detail the history of previous legislation on the subject. When he sat down he received an ovation. At the close of the Constitutional Convention, Chairman Root bestowed upon Smith an honorary degree from his alma mater:

"Of all the men in the Convention, Alfred E. Smith is the best-informed man on the business of the state of New York."

3

Mr. and Mrs. Al Smith now had five children, and it was no easy matter to live on the wages of a state legislator. Mrs. Smith did her own housework, had to shave the grocery bills to make both ends meet. After eleven years in the Assembly, Smith was nominated for the lucrative office of sheriff of New York City, being supported by the papers of all parties. The Republican *Tribune* said, "In the past ten years there has been no Republican, Progressive or Democrat in the state legislature who rendered as effective, useful, downright valuable service to this town as Alfred E. Smith." He served as sheriff for almost two years, received fifty thousand dollars as his half of the legitimate fees of the office, and was then elected president of the city's Board of Aldermen.

He had been elected for a four-year term, but at the end of only four months he had to resign because the Democrats had nominated him for governor. This nomination came about not only because he was the rising star of his party, but because he had made warm and devoted friends in every part of the state. When his campaign managers decided that no man who wore his hat on the back of his head could be elected governor, they asked him to please set the hat straight. Smith replied:

"The people of this state don't care how the outside of my skull looks. They want to know what's inside of it. If I've got to change the way I wear my hat, you can get another candidate."

Al Smith was a successful campaigner: audiences liked him for his humor, his forthrightness, the bluntness of his language, the honesty that shone in his eyes, for the warm personal contact he established with every last member of his audience; but mostly they took Al Smith to their bosoms because he was so patently one of them, seeming to serve no lobby or interest or party, but the whole state and all its people.

The Alfred E. Smith who stepped into the Governor's Mansion in 1919 was considerably different from the green young man who had been bought his first dress suit by a friendly grocer sixteen years before. The raw edges had been knocked off; he had become a meticulous dresser. "I feel spiffy when I'm dressed just right," he would grin when anyone complimented him on a new suit. He carried himself with dignity and poise; he had mixed with the best minds of the state and won their admiration; he had developed a mechanism of thinking and research which provided him with as keen a set of tools as any man of his day; in the early years he had voted as Tammany told him, now he told Tammany how to vote. His hair was gray at the temples, it had thinned and he had taken to parting it in the center; his face too had thinned; his complexion become more ruddy, his eyes more penetrating. Those who had been afraid that the crude and uncouth fishmonger from the East Side would disgrace the governor's chair soon found themselves admiring Al Smith for his quiet dignity, his force, his ability to make a swift and sure decision, his genius at public administration. They could not know that Governor Smith was saying to himself:

"Never will anybody be able to raise their head in this state and say that a man from the East Side of New York, that belonged to Tammany Hall, could not run the state."

In many ways Governor Smith followed the pattern of his predecessor, Charles Evans Hughes: the Smith children played on the lawn of the Governor's Mansion, and neighboring children were invited in for supper; his office was thrown open to the people because "it is the duty of the governor to let the people tell him their troubles." Men traveled to Albany from all parts of the state without an appointment, knowing that the governor would see them. He named his department heads without consideration of political party, choosing the best talent he could find. When an engineer to whom he offered the job of head of the Department of Roads answered, "But, Governor Smith, I know nothing of politics," Governor Smith replied, "That's one of the reasons I want to appoint you. We have had a good many political superintendents of highways, and now we want one who knows how to build roads."

His enthusiasm for good government brought into the service men and women who gave liberally of their time and talent and money. He set up a Reconstruction Committee to study the problems of the war, strengthened the state employment agencies, created an Industrial Commission to settle strikes, and organized a program of state-wide improvements. He faced a Republican majority in both Houses which was determined to defeat every measure he proposed. "The attitude of the Republican leaders toward me," commented Smith, "although most friendly in their personal relations, was that my election was some kind of an accident and that after two years I would never be heard of again. It seemed to them that it was not necessary to do anything I recommended."

When the legislature refused to grant funds for the work of his Reconstruction Committee, Governor Smith secured them through private donations; when the legislature opposed the committee's report in toto, the governor went directly to the people, lecturing to boards of trade, women's clubs, extolling the virtues and necessities of the new program; compulsory education for children, Americanization for foreigners, adult education, reorganization of the state government for the purposes of efficiency. Businessmen liked his ideas of economy; women liked his emphasis on education—and the fact that he had put women into key positions; large sections of the Republican voters of the state acceded to their governor's request, demanding of their legislators that they pass the committee's program. The now befuddled legislators passed it.

In consonance with his reform work, Governor Smith was broadminded and tolerant: he made it possible for local communities to enjoy Sunday baseball and motion pictures on the grounds that "those members of a community who oppose all recreation on Sunday have no right, in law or morals, where they constitute a minority, to impose their views upon a majority. Some form of relaxation on Sundays is most beneficial in the cases of that great mass of our people who during the six weekdays are employed in confining occupations." He vetoed the Lusk Bill, which provided for special police to check on teachers and the necessity of all teachers taking an oath of allegiance to the flag, with the statement, "The traditional abhorrence of a free people of all kinds of spies and secret police is valid and justified and calls for the disapproval of this measure."

He was defeated for re-election in 1920 by a narrow margin, the Harding and Republican landslide capturing all of the state offices, but in 1922 he received a four-hundred-thousand majority, the largest ever given to a governor of New York. He immersed himself in a constructive program which included the passing of rent laws to keep a hundred thousand New Yorkers from being evicted: he set up a Housing Commission which studied slum and tenement sections and made recommendations for clearance and rebuilding: he opened the civil service to women, secured twenty-two millions additional salary for the teachers of the state, set up children's courts, revoked censorship on motion pictures, secured appropriations for the rebuilding of state hospitals, insane asylums, prisons, put through a bill which enabled mothers to keep their children at home, with state aid, when the fathers had died, supervised the execution of ever-strengthened labor codes.

The elements in his progressive program seldom originated with him; when a problem presented itself he would call in the experts in the field to find the solution. From these counselors he accepted what he thought was valid, put the remedy into clear, simple terms and then fought for months and years to get his legislation through the two Houses. When he was completely blocked he would go to the people to sustain him; so effective was his first radio speech asking for support for his reform program that Albany was deluged with letters, telegrams and phone calls demanding of the obdurate legislators that they pass the governor's bills.

But if his reform measures did not originate with him, his business program did: he was determined to make the government of the state of New York an efficient and economic business organization. When he was re-elected for a third term in 1924 he forced through a bill for an Executive Budget, with the need and purpose of every dollar sworn to by department heads, reorganized the state's overlapping hundred and eighty-seven agencies into nineteen departments, set up a cabinet to integrate the state's business. He did not enable the state to spend less money than it did before, he spent millions more than his predecessors, but the money was assigned to a ten-year building program of schools, parks, hospitals and the preservation of the state's resources, including water power.

His mind never took on airs; in spite of his staggering program, most of which he effectuated in the years between 1911 and 1928, he remained a blunt, hardheaded businessman in government. "He just eats documents up. Messages and reports are his meat. Figures talk to him."

He was no profound social theorist, he sought to remedy effects rather than causes; he still rolled his cigar around in his mouth while pondering problems behind the governor's desk, a performance which did not delight women who were pleading a cause before him; and in the privacy of his few intimates he liked to throw off his starched bib and tucker

327

and loll in informal clothing and informal language over a bottle of beer.

In his crude and simple way he was a great man because he was giving wings to the flight of history.

4

Alfred E. Smith was first nominated for the presidency by an admirer at the Democratic convention of 1920, which finally named James M. Cox, but this was only a gesture designed for future use. During the years between 1920 and 1924, as Smith piled up his humanitarian reform plus business efficiency administrations, his name and his legend spread slowly to the south and the west. Laudatory articles were written about him in national magazines; clubs were formed to assist in his nomination; state conventions signified their intention of rallying to his name. When asked what he thought about all this, Smith glanced down at the mass of papers on his gubernatorial desk and replied:

"The man who would not have an ambition for that office would have a dead heart. But the man who used one office and neglected it in order to climb to a higher one was not deserving of the one he had."

Four years later he was placed in nomination by Franklin D. Roosevelt. Smith said, "Franklin D. Roosevelt was probably the most impressive figure in that convention." In his concluding line Roosevelt called Smith "the Happy Warrior."

In spite of the enthusiasm surrounding his name, Alfred E. Smith went into the 1924 convention with two strikes on him: he was a Catholic, and he was a wet. During his first campaign for the governorship certain circles had set out to defeat him on the sole grounds of his religion; the widespread innuendoes that if Smith were elected New York State would be governed from the Vatican in Rome unquestionably cost him votes.

During his years as governor Al Smith took a positive stand against any connection between church and state: on numerous occasions he had opposed and defeated the Catholic church. He fought with all the strength at his command when the church tried to force through censorship of motion pictures, saying in April of 1924, "Censorship in any form cannot be tolerated in a democratic government." He defeated the "Clean Books" bill which the church was backing, telling the people that "censorship is not in keeping with our ideas of liberty and of freedom of worship or freedom of speech." Though the church was fighting the Birth Control League, Governor Smith refused to obstruct birth-control legislation or propaganda. As severe a critic of Smith's short-comings as Henry F. Pringle says, after summing up Smith's weaknesses, "A close study of his career has convinced me that Al Smith has never been influenced in any act or any policy by the fact that he is a Roman Catholic."

Many southern delegations to the 1924 convention had been elected by the Ku Klux Klan; many of the delegates were Klan members. They cared nothing about Smith's record, abilities, tolerance or independence. Anti-Catholicism was a tenet of their fascistic faith, and they were out to defeat Smith at all costs. A newspaper called the *Fellowship Forum* was circulated among the delegates, repeating vicious slanders against the Catholic church. The religious conflict which rocked the four walls of Madison Square Garden in New York City in 1924 was a rehearsal for the struggle which was to reach the four borders of the nation in 1928.

The second count against him was that he was not a wholehearted prohibitionist. He openly expressed his regret that "the Eighteenth Amendment was not made permissive instead of mandatory." Though he insisted that the Eighteenth Amendment would have to be enforced as long as it was part of the Constitution, he approved a New York referendum which asked Congress for the right of New York State to modify the Eighteenth Amendment.

The New York Anti-Saloon League fired a barrage of telegrams to the Anti-Saloon leaders throughout the country instructing them to wire in turn to their delegates at the convention to continue their opposition to the wet candidate. Smith writes, "Wayne Wheeler, general counsel of the Anti-Saloon League, told me himself that he was at the convention for the purpose of keeping alive and active the forces of the Anti-Saloon League against my nomination." The *Outlook* commented, "That Rum and Romanism should enter the White House in the person of Alfred E. Smith seemed beyond possibility."

After two weeks of convention wrangling, Smith came to the conclusion that he could never be nominated, that the prolonged public squabble, being broadcast over the radio for the first time in history, was injuring the party's chances at the polls. He withdrew. When John W. Davis was named as the compromise candidate Smith went before the convention to assure them of his support.

"Mr. Davis," said Smith, "what can I do for you that will make the biggest contribution to your success?"

"Run for governor again," replied Davis.

"But I am anxious to retire from public life. I want to get back to work so that I can establish a business that I can leave to my children. Besides, I might carry the state, and you might not."

"Run for governor again," repeated Davis. "That is how you can help us the most."

Smith's prediction proved acute: he carried the state by more than a hundred thousand votes, but Davis lost it by almost a million. It was the first time in nearly a hundred years that the state of New York had elected the same man to the governorship three times; as a consequence, Smith broadened and deepened his progressive program. He was determined to retire in 1926; again the Democratic party leaders besieged him not to desert the cause, pointing out that if he did not run a Republican governor would be elected. Smith was not greatly impressed until he learned that the Republicans had nominated Ogden L. Mills, who had opposed his progressive and reform measures over the years. He knew that if he did not want his work destroyed he would have to run for a fourth time and defeat Mills. He won by more than a quarter of a million votes.

After this fourth impressive victory, and in the face of his unfading vigor for a modern state government and a modern economic civilization, there was no longer any doubt as to who was the leading Democrat of the country. The boom for his nomination became nationwide in 1927; mail poured into Albany; visitors reached the Governor's Mansion from every section of the country; the battery of newspapermen in Albany was increased; newspapers and magazine stories made legend of the Fulton Fish Market and the Brown Derby; his personality and his record became familiar to millions of Americans.

Then, on March 25, 1927, the Charles C. Marshall letter in the *Atlantic Monthly* raised the curtain on the tragedy of the election of 1928. Charles C. Marshall was a retired attorney whose hobby had always been church law. His purpose was constructive: to state in scholarly and refined fashion the full case to be found in Papal Church Law against the desirability of having a Catholic for president, and then to have these basic questions answered and the problems settled once and for all. The letter was restrained, studious, based on a knowledge of church history. The magazine released the letter to the press, and by the following morning literally millions of Americans were plunged into the religious controversy.

After praising Smith's record as governor and his personal character, Marshall posed the following problems: that the Catholic church believed all power not granted to the state to be left in the hands of the Catholic church, and consequently no other religion had a natural right to participate in the moral or religious affairs of the state; that the Catholic church believed itself the only true religion and did not grant tolerance to other religions; that the Catholics believed that in any conflict between the civil power and the secular power, "the jurisdiction of the church prevails and that of the State is excluded"; that the power of the Pope was considered to be superior to the sovereignty of the civil government; that it was the intent of the Catholic church to control education and marriage, to sweep all other religions into its fold; that the Catholic church had sometimes used armed intervention to force its demands upon the civil government.

For a full century the Catholic issue had been an important one in national elections; almost every presidential candidate had been accused of being a Catholic to alienate the anti-Catholic vote. But always the slander had been whispered, printed in sheets as scurrilous as they were anonymous. Alfred E. Smith was the first Catholic to be nominated for the presidency, and the problem was out in the open.

Smith's answer to Marshall in the *Atlantic Monthly* of the following month was sent in without a title, but the *Atlantic* called it "Governor Smith, Catholic and Patriot, Replies." In his letter Smith thanked Marshall for bringing the subject into the realm of dignified discussion, made a complete disclaimer of all the charges Marshall had levied, and commented, "So little are these matters the essence of my faith that I, a devout Catholic since childhood, never heard of them until I read your letter."

Smith had asked Father Duffy, beloved chaplain of the One Hundred and Sixty-Fifth Infantry during the World War, to help him with the refutations of Marshall's historical citations, for he was no student of church law. But the public was more interested in Smith's personal statement: the fact that his cabinet at Albany consisted of two Catholics, thirteen Protestants and one Jew, that his closest associate was "a Protestant, a Republican and a 32-degree Mason," that never in his eighteen years of office had any member of his church attempted to influence his administration, asked him to show special favor to Catholics or to discriminate against non-Catholics. He closed with the statement, "I believe that no tribunal of any church has any power to make any decree in the law of the land, other than to establish the status of its own communicants within its own church. I believe in the support of the public school as one of the cornerstones of American liberty. I recognize no power in the institution of my church to interfere with the operations of the Constitution of the United States or the enforcement of the law of the land. I believe in absolute freedom of conscience for all men, and in equality of all churches, all sects before the law as a matter of right."

"Would the Catholic church influence Smith as President?" asked Frank R. Kent in *Collier's.* "No more than the Baptist or Methodist church would."

Alfred E. Smith was nominated by the Democratic convention in Houston, Texas, because, as one politician put it, "the party is tired of finishing second in a two-horse race." The south, which had opposed him in 1924 because he was a Catholic and a wet, slowly swung into his camp when it was seen that no Democrat in the country could touch his political record or his chance of election. A Texas investigator reported that "the people of this state will vote as Democrats rather than Protestants or Prohibitionists." The name of "the Happy Warrior" now raced across the continent.

The Republicans nominated a man with an equally fine record; not since the Charles Evan Hughes-Woodrow Wilson election of 1916 had the voters an opportunity of choosing between two such first-rate men. Herbert Hoover was a mining engineer who had developed mines in the remotest parts of the earth and had skillfully reorganized and combined businesses which extended throughout the whole empire. In 1915 he had rescued some two hundred thousand Americans stranded in war-torn Europe, then turned in a great performance in feeding war-ravished Belgium and France, handling billions of dollars of international funds, managing an army of relief workers, accomplishing humanitarian miracles of diplomacy with hostile countries to save the lives of countless children and adults.

Hoover was a Quaker, a man of the most stringent honesty and ethics, public-spirited, with a reserved but deep personality. As secretary of commerce under Harding and Coolidge from 1921 to 1928 he had set up a new Division of Commercial Standards which greatly aided business, brought an engineer's training to the reorganization of the Bureau of Census, gave efficient supervision to the growth of such infant industries as radio and airplane manufacturing.

Thus democracy had arrived at one of the happier moments of its political pattern: the electorate could not lose, no matter which man it decided upon. Yet such was the irony of popular government that whichever man went into the White House would have a difficult time repairing the damage done in the days of the campaign.

The religious issue could be neither repressed nor confined to the high level of the Marshall-Smith letters. For pure virulence there was nothing in all American history to equal the whispering campaign inaugurated against Al Smith: he was building a tunnel which would connect with the Vatican; the Pope would set up his office in the White House; the Catholics would rule the country, and no one could hold office who was not a Catholic; Protestant children would be forced into Catholic schools; priests would flood the states and be in supreme command; Smith would set himself up at the head of a Catholic party which would supersede the old Democratic party!

A flood of letters, pamphlets and anonymous newspapers swept across the south, rehashing the worst libels against the Catholic church that had been circulated in the United States during the period of 1840–60. One Democratic chairman of North Carolina reported that the anti-Catholic literature that poured into the state must have cost at least half a million dollars. In addition Smith was accused of being a habitual drunkard, an illiterate, a rough, crude, uncouth tobacco-spitting bully of the East Side, a flunky of the corrupt Tammany of the Tweed days, an ignoramus who would disgrace the White House and make the United States the laughingstock of foreign ambassadors.

To offset this slander a group of Harvard professors issued a statement which read, "We support Governor Smith because of his power to reverse the present trend toward political apathy and arouse in the citizens of the United States an active intelligent interest and participation in their government."

The Republicans fought their campaign on the basis of the greatest prosperity the country had ever known, a chicken in every pot, two cars in every garage, every salesgirl and elevator boy cleaning up on the stock market. Their polite dissections of Alfred E. Smith in such magazines as the *Outlook* and *Independent* charged him with having a New York mind which was local rather than national in viewpoint, of having no experience in international affairs, of being unable to escape the influence of Tammany, of knowing nothing of such nationwide problems as agriculture.

Al Smith candidly admitted that he did not know as much about national affairs as he did the affairs of New York State, then set out to remedy the situation by boning up before taking to the road to give the nation its first view of the Brown Derby. "The Governor's train is the most marvelous publicity caravan ever set in motion. There are forty reporters, four newsreel cameramen, four still photographers, a radio announcer. A special car is carried on which, seated at a tremendously long and narrow mahogany table, the Governor

333

holds his conferences with the press. 'Well, gentlemen, throw the ball out and I'll kick it.' "

He opened his campaign at Omaha, Nebraska, with a speech on farm relief for which he had read widely and consulted the farm experts of the midwest; at Oklahoma City, where he perceived that religion was the major issue, he lashed out at an audience of thirty thousand spectators, excoriating the Ku Klux Klan and the Woman's Christian Temperance Union in some of the strongest language ever heard in a presidential contest. In Louisville, Kentucky, the police were so hostile he had to be protected by private detectives. He received his greatest ovation in Boston, where he attacked the corruption of the Harding regime, the big-business monopoly of government in the Coolidge regime, and presented his concept of an efficient, people's government.

"What kind of a president will I make?" replied Smith to a question; "the same kind as I made a governor."

As the campaign progressed it became evident that the Democratic solid south was being breached by the religious issue; this was doubly griping to Smith because the dry Catholics were solidly against him. He was advocating a modification of the Volstead Act which would enable each state to decide whether it wanted light wines and beer, but he was one election ahead of the country, and this stand made him a "wringing wet." In addition to accusing him of being a drunkard, the drys were charging him with being a tool of the liquor interests, of intending to bring back the saloon.

But the fundamental weakness of Al Smith's campaign was that in September and October of 1928 he was not able to convince the American people that their gaudy structure was in danger. What use to cry inefficiency in government to a people that was making more money than it ever had? What use to plead for reform and progressivism when there was little unemployment, when wages were high, jobs and consumer goods plentiful? What use to point out the waste and errors, blindness and partisanship of an administration to an electorate with a bank account?

On election day 14,626,803 Americans voted for Al Smith, while 20,812,912 voted for Hoover; a majority for Hoover of over 6,000,000. The electoral vote was also a smashing defeat: Smith received 87 votes to Hoover's 444. He had lost the traditionally Democratic states of Texas and North Carolina. He had also lost New York State by 125,000, a bitter pill for him to swallow.

Alfred E. Smith spent the next four years in private life, firmly believing that he would receive the Democratic nomination in 1932 and hand the crumbling Republican party as sound a thrashing as they had given him in 1928. When his old friend and advocate Franklin Roosevelt secured the nomination in 1932, Smith cried, "Treachery!" emerging in 1936 to assail President Roosevelt, urging the public in major campaign speeches to elect Alf Landon and put the Republicans back in national power. This defection becomes the more serious when one realizes how much of Franklin D. Roosevelt's political philosophy was based upon the record and accomplishment of Governor Smith.

Somewhere in Al Smith's character must have lain the seed of potential disgruntlement which turned him from the brown derby to the silk hat, from his love for the Democratic party's economic philosophy to the kind of wrecker who, like a Clay, works against his organization for the sake of personal vengeance. To millions of his baffled admirers throughout the country it seemed an unhappy ending to a brilliant career.

In 1920, when Davis had requested that he again run for governor of New York, Smith had replied, "I want to get back to work so that I can establish a business that I can leave to my children." He now became president of the Empire State Building, but to Alfred E. Smith even this tallest building in the world was dwarfed by the modest grandeur of the White House. Unlike Cass and Seymour, he was never to recover fully from the bitterness of defeat.

5

There were several reasons why the nation preferred Herbert Hoover over Alfred E. Smith in 1928: Hoover was a world traveler who knew every corner of his own land as well, whereas Smith had rarely been out of New York State. While Smith had never finished grammar school, never read any book except *The Life and Battles of John L. Sullivan,* knew nothing about the arts, and had no trade other than that of public official, Hoover was formally educated, a man of wide tastes and discernment, a creative mining engineer. Whereas Smith was feared as a radical, Hoover was trusted by the businessmen of the country who had approved his work as secretary of commerce. Hoover had proved himself to be a man of strength, courage and executive ability in his handling of the European relief work, whereas Smith's efforts had been confined to the bread-and-butter work of state politics.

The difference between the two men, however, was more basic: a fundamental difference of political philosophy. Hoover believed, sincerely and on the basis of his experience, that all prosperity in a nation sprang from business, and hence

335

business must be given its liberty, kept free from control, be allowed to run itself for its own best interests, which would in turn redound to the best interests of the whole people. Smith believed otherwise; he had watched business at close hand, he had seen what misery could befall a people left unprotected in its grasp. Hoover believed in *laissez faire,* Smith in social responsibility.

If the country had retained its prosperity for four years more, Hoover's philosophy would have been proved to be right, and the degree of prosperity would have been the judge of the voters' wisdom. But exactly a year after the election there came a complete and devastating collapse which Hoover inherited from the policies of Coolidge, and with the collapse of the country there came the collapse of Hoover's philosophy, and hence of his effectiveness.

For three devastating years the country was forced to struggle under the leadership of a man who was equipped to handle only prosperity, who believed that under the system of leaving things alone, with the local charitable agencies keeping the worst cases from starvation, the business cycle would complete itself and prosperity would return; who conscientiously believed that the creation of public projects and the responsibility of all the nation for the welfare of its least member would destroy the American way of life.

Alfred E. Smith knew how to handle public adversity and was temperamentally equipped to administer in times of stress as well as prosperity. He would have set on foot a gigantic program of reform and control, applying the brakes to the kind of frenzied finance he had protested against in his campaign. He would have formulated labor codes for the protection of the working people. He would have made the mechanics of government as clear and exciting to the people of the nation as he had made them to the people of his state.

He might not have been able wholly to avert the crash of November 1929 in the eight months that he would have been in office, but once the nation had been caught in its tragic plight he would have declared the people to be its greatest natural resource, that unless the people are happy and in good health no other wealth has any meaning. He would have set in motion a machine to protect the people with every last ounce of national wealth, thus protecting the American way of life as he envisaged it.

In November of 1928 Herbert Hoover seemed to the majority of voters to be the right man for the presidency. By November of 1929 the right man would appear to have been Alfred E. Smith. History had played a dirty trick on both of them—and on the nation as well.

CHAPTER FOUR

Alfred M. Landon

THEY CALLED HIM the poor man's Coolidge.

This was less than justice: he had a warm and lovable personality and could name nearly every Kansan as his friend.

His grandfather, a Methodist preacher, had been his first chum; from this companionship he developed a lifelong liking for clergymen. In the midst of one of his gubernatorial campaigns his irate manager exclaimed, "Alf wastes more time with preachers than any fellow I ever saw. He will settle back in his private office and chin with some plug preacher who doesn't control four votes, and let men who control blocs of counties cool their heels in the outer office." During the heat of the 1936 campaign the worst that the left-wing *Nation* could say about him was that he sounded like a second-rate Kansas clergyman.

Alfred's father was an oil prospector and promoter; thus Landon's character was compounded of equal parts of preacher and promoter, a happy combination which made it possible for him to accumulate almost a million dollars in the Kansas oil fields without making enemies or being charged with sharp practice.

He is the first plain businessman among the Also Rans: Greeley and Cox were newspaper editors; Parker and Hughes were judges; Scott, Fremont, McClellan and Hancock were soldiers; Clay and Bryan, Douglas and Blaine were political careerists; Cass was a frontiersman, Seymour a gentleman landlord, Tilden a corporation lawyer and Smith a government executive. A country whose greatest genius lay in its business brains was at last going to have the opportunity to elevate a businessman to the highest office in the land.

Landon was devoid of the gift of phrasemaking, yet he evolved one sentence which struck a tender chord in the breast of many a depression-harassed merchant: "I believe a man can be a liberal without being a spendthrift!" If he could have turned in a few more such sentences he might have offset the banality of the "Life, Liberty and Landon!" slogan with which the Republican party decided to sweep the country.

Landon was presented to the voters as "Frugal Alf, Kansas' Cash-and-Carry Governor," as one of Eddie Guest's "Just Folks," as an economical man who cringed at the sight of food left over on a plate, who wore his clothes until he came out at the knees and elbows, and who explained his miracle of balancing the Kansas budget by crying, "Don't spend what you haven't got!" *Harper's* said he "represented the mind of the middle class," while the Republican press reiterated that "Landon has just as good intentions as Roosevelt, and a head a whole lot better."

He called himself an everyday American, which carried the implication that Franklin D. Roosevelt was a week-end American. In order to give the country a rest from the ardors of watching the president's wife scurry unceasingly about the country, Mrs. Landon solemnly promised to remain invisible, not to emerge from the portals of the White House.

So complete and utter a contrast to Roosevelt did the Republicans desire that they even gloried in the fact that good, sweet, plain and honest Alf Landon was a trifle on the dullish side!

"A man who succeeded Roosevelt in 1936," said Landon, "would have a tough job, and would probably be the most unpopular president in history."

He was not only willing to be martyrized, but rushed out eagerly to embrace that awful fate.

2

Alfred Mossman Landon was born in his grandfather's parsonage on September 9, 1887, in West Middlesex, Pennsylvania. He attended Marietta Academy in Marietta, Ohio, where he played football until he broke his shoulder, was an average student, read the novels of Scott and G. A. Henty. There is no record of his having read a book after leaving the classroom; like so many of his predecessors in the family circle of Also Rans, he acquired his knowledge through his ears. *Harper's* observed, "He has a good mind, but no one ever accused him of being intellectual. His friends say that he gets most of his information by questioning those he comes in contact with, particularly those from outside his own intimate circle."

When the oil fields in southeastern Kansas were opened John Landon moved his family to Independence. For seventeen-year-old Alfred this was more than an accident, it was a gift of a benevolent fate, for he became the apotheosis of Kansas: he changed his name to Alf, began to talk through his nose with a midwest twang, later took to wearing his clothes with the farmer's disregard of elegance. If his family had remained in Pennsylvania or Ohio it is likely that Alfred Landon would have become what the newspapermen said he looked like during his brief spell under the political klieg lights: a clergyman, the owner of a hardware store, the president of a small-town bank.

In Kansas Alfred Landon cut quite a swath: he was considered a rich man's son, made the best fraternity at Kansas University, helped introduce the tuxedo to the campus, and cornered so much of the political power of the student body that he became known as "the Fox." The title fitted him about as well as their new tuxedos fitted the Kansas University students.

Landon graduated from the Kansas university law school without generating any liking for the law. He had a practical turn of mind; he liked figures and balancing books, as he had proved in college by balancing the budget of his fraternity house. He found a job as bookkeeper in an Independence bank at seventy-five dollars a month, but he had prospector's blood in his veins. From his first days in the bank he invested part of his wage in oil-drilling ventures; when at the end of three years he saw that his savings account contained three thousand dollars he quit his job, donned his old clothes and heavy boots and went into the oil field as a wildcatter.

"He was no swivel-chair executive: he got out and scrambled for leases; he swapped and traded and bartered; he stood in the middle of a dusty row of browned cornstalks and directed drilling operations; he got out his mud-daubed car in the middle of the night and drove like mad across two states to get on the ground of a newly discovered field."

Landon was called as unspectacular as a pair of bedroom slippers: he was as plain as the pair of oilman's boots in which he stumped the state in his first political campaign, as undramatic as Kansas corn. Alf Landon was a good guy, everyone said so. He was honest and sincere, spoke a simple if sometimes ungrammatic English and had friends in every corner of the state. Like Al Smith, he liked people and people liked him.

By 1929 he had boomed his oil fortune to something that passed as a reasonable facsimile of a million dollars by being "shrewd, calculating and gifted in his way." He had married in 1915 and had had a daughter, but his wife had died when the child was only a year old. During the World War Landon had left the daughter, Peggy, with her grandparents and secured a commission as a first lieutenant in the Chemical Warfare Division. The Armistice was signed while he was still in training; he returned to Kansas to resume his oil operations.

Alf Landon might have remained a good guy and a successful oil promoter for the rest of his days except for an appetite which not even his intimates suspected: he was personally ambitious. "I have never been out of politics," he said. He had enjoyed wielding political power at college; in 1912, when he was twenty-five, he had accompanied his father, who was a delegate, to the Bull Moose convention in Chicago. Here he became acquainted with William Allen White and ex-Senator Allen of Kansas and asked Allen's permission to organize his county for Theodore Roosevelt. Though the oilmen around Independence were opposed to Roosevelt, young Landon did such a good job that the Bull Moose party carried the county. As a reward, when Allen became governor of Kansas he invited Alf to become his secretary. One night, after listening to the governor make a speech, Landon commented:

"You know, you aren't doing this thing right."

"Didn't you like the speech?" demanded the governor.

"Oh, the speech was all right, but you should have stayed afterward and visited with those folks in the hall."

As a rehearsal for his first bid for public office, Landon managed the successful campaign of Clyde Reed for governor in 1928, making a survey of every remote corner of Kansas. In 1931 he entered the primary for the governorship. Dressed in a soft shirt, no tie, high-laced oil boots, accompanied by his twelve-year-old daughter, he made a cracker-barrel campaign, walking into crossroad stores, holding out his hand in his friendly fashion and saying, "I'm Alf Landon." Kansas people liked him because he discussed their problems but never mentioned politics or asked for votes.

He ran away from the field in the primary, and in the 1932 Democratic landslide managed to be the only Republican governor elected west of the Mississippi. He had made a wretched campaign speaker: his voice was a monotone, he stuttered, stammered, paused, backtracked, tied himself in knots—but after each meeting he stayed for an hour to shake hands and chat with the folks. The people of Kansas said, "We don't want a fancy talker; we want a plain and honest fellow who can run our state business-like."

Alf Landon gave the people of Kansas the kind of administration they had asked for: sound, economical, mildly progressive, tolerant, businesslike. He declared when he moved into the Governor's Mansion that he was going to "enlist with President Roosevelt for the duration of the war against depression," and called for an enlargement of the president's powers. Raymond Gram Swing, writing for the usually anti-Republican *Nation,* observed, "Landon is a gifted

340

executive who is not much less progressive in philosophy than Franklin D. Roosevelt."

Following the tradition of Al Smith, Landon announced, "In Kansas we insist that no teacher should be required to take an oath not required of any other citizen." Again like Al Smith, he kept the door of his office in the capitol in Topeka wide open; all who gathered in the anteroom could see the governor as he talked to those who had come before them. Few bothered with appointments: every man came when he liked and sat in line waiting his turn. When he had to leave his office Landon would stop in the anteroom and talk to those who were still sitting there. One interviewer watched as he talked to an old Negro who put an arm affectionately about Landon's shoulder, a gesture which the governor found as natural as did the colored man.

He proved to be a high-minded and hard-working administrator who set up a non-political budget for his state, achieved harmony among warring factions, created a research department to give the government accurate information, picked the best men he could find for the state jobs and gave them free rein in their departments. Even those Kansans who had voted against him began to praise Governor Landon for his tact, his honesty, his ability. He had no wilderness to subdue, as had Lewis Cass, no Civil War to hold within constitutional bounds, as had Horatio Seymour, no liberal revolution to engineer, as had Alfred E. Smith, yet within the limited confines of his agricultural state he met all problems that arose and settled them as ably and honestly as his predecessors.

Landon was the only Republican governor to be re-elected in 1934; this feat automatically made him one of the outstanding men of his party. He was mentioned for the presidency by the Kansas City *Journal Post* on the day following his re-election.

"We didn't do anything at first," said Landon. "We just sat back and it all happened."

In the fall of 1935 Alf Landon attended the American Legion convention at St. Louis where, to his astonishment, he found whole sections of the convention pledging themselves to the Landon-for-president movement. He returned to Kansas City in what was reported to have been a condition of shock, exclaiming to a friend, "Why, this thing is serious!" then paced the floor demanding of himself whether he was intelligent enough to be president.

Apparently the answer came back in the affirmative, for Alf Landon determined from that moment on that he was going to be the next president. When Kansas again balanced

341

its budget he took to the national air waves to tell the country about it. William Randolph Hearst clasped Landon to his politically amoral bosom, sending Damon Runyon to Topeka to write an article for *Cosmopolitan* magazine called "Horse and Buggy Governor," in which Runyon created another of his little fantasies on the subject of Why We Need an Unkempt President in the White House. Landon had been unknown outside of Kansas; after the Runyon article started national comment Hearst visited the governor in Topeka, then told the readers of his twenty-six newspapers that "I think Landon is marvelous!"

"After two and a half years of political pyrotechnics in Washington," wrote *Time*, "a quiet, undramatic family man who made nickel bets on baseball games and believed in running a government on a pay-as-you-go basis made spectacular popular copy."

Landon's opponents for the nomination appeared to be Herbert Hoover, Frank Knox, William E. Borah and Arthur Vandenberg, all of whom made important speeches and thrashed about in their respective ponds to attract attention. Landon refused all invitations to speak in the east and west: since he had never been in national politics he had neither enemies nor critics in the Republican party, and he had no intention of making any. He set up pre-convention offices in Topeka, Kansas City and New York, making middle-of-the-road speeches while his campaign manager, John D. Hamilton, successfully solicited funds in Wall Street.

Alf Landon had reached his most attractive period. He had married the daughter of the president of a Topeka bank, a romance allegedly engineered by his daughter Peggy, and had two small children. Mrs. Landon was a talented musician and charming hostess, so that the Landon home was a delightful one to enter. At forty-eight the governor's hair was thinning and silvering, but he had the healthy coloring of the man who has worked out of doors for many years. Though he was of medium build, only five feet eight inches, he had the wiry, nerveless inexhaustibility of a John C. Fremont. His reddish-brown eyes were alert and sparkling, the large pupils gazing at one with complete candor. He wore rimless spectacles, which further buttressed the impression of emotional stability, for no man who is not certain of his next move can afford to wear glasses that will break at an unexpected jar. Next to his eyes his most pleasing aspect was the sculptured carving of his head and chin, both of which were well formed, symmetrical and strong. His nose gave him slightly too large an opportunity to achieve the midwest twang, but his mouth was pleasant and friendly, and the words that came out of it denoted a man of good will. It was extremely difficult not to like him.

By the middle of February 1936 the Republicans were taking Alf Landon's nomination for granted. Newsmen sent from every large paper to interview Governor Landon wired back reports to the home folks that he was "sound . . . sensible . . . friendly . . . simple." For the over-rich food poisoning of a Franklin D. Roosevelt the Republicans were going to apply the bland antidote of an Alfred M. Landon: it was the desperate need of a party creating a candidate, a candidate diametrically opposed in appearance, personality, character, political philosophy and ambition to the man they were trying to defeat.

A continuous stream of Republican leaders flowed into the capitol at Topeka, one current from the east and the other from the west. Newspaper publicity pyramided as the convention neared. Landon and his photogenic family were photographed in every conceivable position except, as *Newsweek* commented acidly, "skinning the cat atop the state building." When the convention opened in Cleveland photographs of Landon at home, in the nursery, at his desk and with his dog flooded the delegates, while his favorite song, "Oh! Susanna," was played some eight hundred times! There was a current rage for the paintings of Vincent van Gogh, whose best-known canvas was a group of sunflowers; the state emblem of Kansas was also the sunflower, and Landon's manager seized the opportunity to dominate the convention with their emblem.

A European correspondent in Cleveland called the convention more of a carnival than a political gathering, and indeed it resembled nothing so closely as the American Legion convention at which Landon had received his first presidential shock. Whether it was the balancing of the budget, William Randolph Hearst, the sunflower in every buttonhole, "Oh! Susanna," the photographs, the lone Republican gubernatorial re-election of 1934 or the desperate need of his party, no one could tell, but Alf Landon of Kansas had no competition; he was nominated almost unanimously on the first ballot.

3

He had won his two elections in Kansas by dint of his ability to get out and meet the voters, to shake their hands, exchange a few friendly words, inspire them with confidence in his ability and integrity. It was physically impossible for him to shake the hands of fifty to sixty million American voters; his only direct contact had to be through the radio, but his voice on the air was monotonous, without any semblance of the warmth and humor and human quality of the man. Chairmen tried to anticipate Landon's poor speaking by telling audiences that he was no radio crooner, which drew laughter and a cheer but did not fully prepare the listener for the jerky, halting, almost dismal manner of his public speaking. The fine magnetism that drew people to Alf Landon vanished when he approached a microphone or loud-speaker; he became nervous, then formal, then cold, reading his speeches with his head buried in the manuscript. He took lessons from voice coaches; he improved somewhat as the campaign waxed hotter, but he developed no sense of vocal showmanship, could not think fast or wittily or graciously on his feet. Had his texts been revolutionary he might have fired his audience in spite of the poor delivery; as it was he received but scant applause even from Republican gatherings.

He was an energetic and confident campaigner; not for a moment did he doubt that he would be the next president. He made four national tours radiating in all directions from Topeka, ignoring Republican leaders of the Coolidge and Hoover administrations, taking with him two Kansas editors, a Kansas automobile salesman, a Kansas representative in Congress and ex-Governor Allen of Kansas. He made as many as twenty-eight short talks from the rear platform of his campaign train, working everyone around him into exhaustion. His dominant themes were:

The Democratic regime was hindering recovery: the industrialists' lack of confidence in Roosevelt was the greatest detriment, high taxes were injuring business, the administration was wasting vast sums of money and piling up a crushing national debt; the people were losing more and more of their rights by delegating them to the chief executive; Roosevelt was undermining the American form of government; the Democrats were using national funds to get themselves reelected.

In the first three of his tours Landon took a moderate tone, made many trenchant criticisms of New Deal failures. In his opening speech in Topeka, on a national hookup, he said, "Recovery has been set back again and again by careless thinking, unworkable laws and incompetent administration. The time has come to stop this fumbling with recovery." He dissected the NRA, criticized Roosevelt's plow-under economy of scarcity, documented the sharp rise in taxes, give irrefutable examples of waste, overlapping and bureaucracy in Washington, scored the administration for the still remaining high levels of unemployment. In Cleveland he spoke tellingly on the political corruption in the handling of relief. In Detroit he made a clear statement of the Republican ideology:

"No nation can continue half regimented and half free. National economic planning violates the basic ideals of the American system. The price of economic planning is the loss of economic freedom. Economic freedom and personal liberty go hand in hand."

In spite of the vigor of his attacks, Landon conducted his early campaign in such a gentlemanly fashion that when he met President Roosevelt at the Drouth Conference in Des Moines at the end of September, "each one had yet to speak a word in direct criticism of each other. The nominees met without embarrassment, conversed in warm good fellowship, parted with expressions of mutual admiration." Landon had every reason to believe that this method was bearing fruit, for a Gallup Poll taken on October nineteen among church members showed 51.3 per cent of the voters for Roosevelt, while 48.7 were for Landon. This was so close after the 1932 Republican debacle as to make a victory seem likely. The *Literary Digest* straw vote, which had accurately diagnosed the elections of 1920, 1924, 1928 and 1932, showed Landon leading with fifty-eight per cent of the votes on October tenth, while the same poll on October seventeenth gave him 1,004,086 votes to Roosevelt's 728,088.

Alf Landon made only two major errors in his early campaign: he antagonized labor by saying, "Roosevelt has the labor vote tied up anyway, so we might as well go after the employers"; in Milwaukee he made a spirited attack on the Social Security Law, basing his claims on material which he said came from an unpublished report of the Twentieth Century Fund. In his speech he also claimed that the Twentieth Century Fund was supported by a Filene Fund, which had withheld the unfavorable report because its publication would injure Roosevelt. Upon investigation it was learned that there was no Filene Fund, that he had based his speech not upon an accredited report, but upon the findings of one member of the Twentieth Century Fund whose material he had been allowed to see in the strictest confidence, and that his conclusions had been diametrically opposed to the conclusions in the analysis he had studied. This fiasco injured Landon considerably.

However, if he was making only a few errors in a long and difficult campaign, his followers were making the total add up. His campaign manager, John D. Hamilton, a pugnacious Fire Eater of the old-guard Republican school, was going about the country pouring bile and vituperation: Roosevelt was a wrecker and revolutionist, all liberals were enemies of the American way of life, the New Deal was destroying the country and its institutions, all labor leaders were wire-whiskered bolsheviki, the administration was dominated by communists.

"I'm running this show," said John Hamilton to Landon in public, and the public became frightened at what might happen if this brash, opportunistic, professional hater went to Washington in March 1937 and told the world, "I'm running this show!"

The high spot of the campaign was provided by the Landon First-Voters League which staged a show for college campuses. Professional models paraded with half of their gown cut away to show how much of its price had gone for taxes and how little was left for the money one had spent. At the end of the show a cute young thing, ostensibly naked, tripped out in a barrel with a placard with read, IF THE NEW DEAL WINS, while another beauty sauntered about in evening gown and white fur cape with a placard reading, IF THE NEW DEAL LOSES. This gaucherie was equaled in presidential elections only by the Belshazzar Feast given to James G. Blaine in the midst of the depression of 1887: from thirty to forty million Americans had lost their homes, their jobs, their security, were facing endless suffering and desperation, and the Republican managers were concerned only in terms of the fluff of expensive evening gowns for young women. It was as though a third of the nation had cried, "We haven't a shirt to our backs!" and the Republicans had answered, "Then why don't you wear your furs?"

In this same vein the *New Yorker* came out with a cartoon showing a rich old voluptuary kneeling beside a languorous beauty as he murmured, "And if Roosevelt is not re-elected, perhaps even a villa in Newport, my dear."

All this was unfair to Alf Landon, who was a progressive, who told his audiences that he favored large sections of the New Deal and only wanted to rid it of its excessive cost and its restraint on business. Raymond Gram Swing commented, "Landon is different from the use that his sponsors seek to make of him. He is no bitter partisan, and he would be no grim, reactionary crusader against the 'new tendencies.'" The Democrats jeered that "the Republicans promise they will do everything for the nation that the New Deal is doing, only they will do it cheaper."

Landon kept his coolness and held his temper through half of October, but the breaks were beginning to go against him: when he spoke outdoors in Detroit the weather was too cold for an audience to brave, when Roosevelt spoke there it was warm and balmy; when Landon drove through the streets of Chicago it rained pitchforks, but when Roosevelt drove through the sun shone brightly. Too many meetings were arranged for him, and he had to disappoint half of his audiences; his managers failed to get parade permits, his car would become lost in a procession, the streets along which he drove often were lined with silent or hostile crowds booing and calling out, "You're just another Hoover!" with nary a Republican in sight.

He had gone into the campaign facing gigantic obstacles: the country was in the midst of one of the most difficult and painful transitions of its history; the incumbent had been elected by an overwhelming majority only four years before; while he had not succeeded on all fronts, Roosevelt's administration had accomplished many things, had saved millions from starvation and eviction, saved thousands of homes and bank accounts and small businesses. Landon found himself in a difficult position: in 1936 he was charging that the New Deal was tearing down the American way of life, but from 1933 to 1935, when he had had no idea that he was going to become a presidential nominee, he had approved the New Deal and supported its program. He had not the heart to disavow its principal objectives: the youth movement, the CCC camps, the social conscience over hours and wages, abolition of child labor. He could build no alternative program because the only things he disapproved in the New Deal were its prodigality and waste.

Lastly, in entering the race against Franklin D. Roosevelt, with his warmth, his personal charm, disarming smile and humor, his geniality and sense of being a citizen of the world, Alf Landon was meeting one of the master campaigners of all times. On the radio, with his confiding voice, Roosevelt gathered the masses to his heart and made them part of him; on the stump he had a political aptness and genius of gesture. Everywhere he went the streets were jammed with wildly cheering crowds; no coliseum was large enough to hold all the people who wanted to hear him. Landon was met by scattered groups, indifference and hostility. It was apparent to everyone around him that the harder he worked, the more he spoke, the fewer votes he attracted.

And Alf Landon lost his temper. He started out on a fourth tour with blood in his eye. Gone was the courtesy, the temperate language, the charges based on economic waste, inefficiency and floundering. Alf Landon gave way to Alfred Mossman Landon, prophet of doom. He called his last tour "a battle to save our American system of government." "His attacks grew stern, then angry. As the campaign entered its final week not even John Hamilton had ever shouted blacker, more fearful prophecy of the doom in store for the United

States if Alf Landon should fail of election than Landon himself when he said at Baltimore, 'It is the essence of the New Deal that the Constitution must go in order to give men in Washington the power to make America over, to destroy the American way of life and establish a foreign way in its place. The profit motive is to be eliminated. Business as we know it is to disappear.' "

The Republican vice-presidential nominee, Frank Knox, toured the country crying, "Your life insurance and your savings accounts are already in danger." Landon topped this by exclaiming in Albuquerque, "Franklin D. Roosevelt proposes to destroy the right to elect your own representatives, to talk politics on street corners, to march in political parades, to attend the church of your faith, to be tried by jury, and to own property."

Landon suffered no personal attacks during the campaign; this was partly because there was nothing derogatory that could be conjured up about him, but largely because the Democratic managers had decided to give him the quiet brush-off. Independent journalists levied criticisms: Landon favored the dole rather than relief work because he was against the building of national projects with relief workers; he had opposed municipal ownership of power in Independence; he had called out the militia to help put down a strike against silicosis in southern Kansas; as an oil operator he was close to Standard Oil, and that was why Hearst had selected him. The charges were neither substantiated nor pressed: the Democrats concentrated on extolling Roosevelt's virtues.

If there was no vilification of Landon, who came out of the campaign with as clean a record as any of his more fortunate brothers among the Also Rans, the intensity of the attack on the other side was almost unprecedented. It appeared to be the Republican tactic to generate hatred for Roosevelt rather than enthusiasm for Landon: the basest slanders were circulated about the president's morals, sanity and integrity, while a whispering campaign of pornographic jokes deluged the Roosevelt family; the favorite appellation of the opposition was, "That s.o.b. in the White House!" One of the more popular cartoons of the campaign showed a group of fashionably dressed people standing outside a luxurious home saying, "Come along. We're going to the Trans-Lux to hiss Roosevelt." Bruce Bliven observed, "The hatred of President Roosevelt by a comparatively small but very vocal group is one of the natural phenomena of modern times. It is the more inexplicable because Mr. Roosevelt has done little or nothing to injure these individuals who hate him with such apoplectic fury."

Though Alf Landon of Kansas was having a difficult time convincing the people that Franklin Delano Roosevelt of Hyde Park was a communist who was attempting to destroy the American form of government, he was putting up a rip-roaring fight, and at length Roosevelt felt impelled to take to the stump. To Landon's charges Roosevelt replied, "I believe, I have always believed, and I always will believe in private enterprise as the backbone of economic well-being in the United States. It was this Administration which saved the system of private property, the system of free enterprise, after it had been dragged to the brink of ruin by these same leaders who try to scare you." To Landon's charge of extravagance Roosevelt told the nation, "True, we spent a lot of money, but we spent it for the conservation of human and material resources—we spent it for things which will repay their cost." To Landon's charge that he was a communist he replied, "Partisans will drag out red herrings to divert attention from the trail of their weakness. The most serious threat to our institutions comes from those who refuse to face the need for change. Liberalism becomes the protection for the farsighted conservative."

The first real break in the campaign took place when the New York *Times* came out for Roosevelt on the grounds that Landon had little to offer but a secondhand New Deal, that the traditional isolationism of the Republicans would injure the United States, that "commanding the confidence of the distressed masses, Roosevelt will provide insurance against radicalism of the sort which the United States had most to fear." This statement took the steam out of the Republican drive. The New York *Sun* countered with the statement of a prominent southerner who had never voted anything but a straight Democratic ticket: "I am going to vote the straight Democratic this year too, which means that I am going to vote for Landon."

The campaign trains of Landon and Roosevelt shuttled across the nation, crisscrossing each other at frequent points. The Roosevelt train was filled with confidence and joy; the Landon train was "grim and dour, filled with advisers troubled about where the money was coming from, worrying about campaign details that went askew. The only man on board whose morale was tiptop was Landon. Unsparing of his strength, resolute in his good cheer, confident of his election, the Republican nominee was battling his way forward against obvious odds and at each step improving his campaign technique."

As the voters went to the polls Landon placed his faith in the *Literary Digest* poll, which indicated a clear-cut Republican victory. The *Literary Digest* quoted Democratic National Chairman James Farley as having said during the 1932 campaign that the *Digest* polls could be relied upon to be accurate; John Hamilton commented that the *Digest* poll was an underestimate of Republican strength; and in 1936 James Farley predicted that Alf Landon would capture only two states, Maine and Vermont.

Alfred Mossman Landon received 16,679,583 votes, thirty-seven per cent of the popular vote; Roosevelt received 27,476,673, sixty per cent. Landon received only 8 electoral votes, one and a half per cent of the electoral total, the worst single defeat ever suffered by an Also Ran. William Allen White of Kansas said, "It was not an election the country has just undergone, but a political Johnstown flood." A new political adage was coined: as Maine goes, so goes Vermont; the *Literary Digest* went out of business; the Republicans tossed aside Alf Landon like a cheap coat that has shrunk in a rainstorm.

The *Nation* commented that "Roosevelt's smashing triumph left the country dazed and happy," but Alf Landon was dazed and bitterly unhappy. He could not understand his overwhelming defeat, nor did he like the idea of going down in history as the worst defeated of all presidential candidates. He had had a short national life and a merry one: transported with joy when nominated by the Cleveland convention in June, he had lived hectically, in the glare of the world's spotlight for almost five months, cheered and lauded, his every word and gesture commented upon. Now in November, crushed, blamed by the Republicans for their smashing defeat, unlikely to rise again to national power or importance, unwilling to take a minor Kansas position after having run for the most important office in the land, he retired to private life and to silence, rescued from oblivion only when President Roosevelt appointed him a delegate to the Lima Convention in 1938. Without the presidential nomination Alf Landon would probably have gone on to the United States Senate, where he would have represented Kansas ably for many years, a hardheaded businessman, who could have served as a balance wheel and done his country much good.

4

There have been periods in American history when Alf Landon would have made an excellent president: when the country was growing quietly, without stress or crisis or urgent need, when the world was dormant. He would have been an economical president, practical, hard to fool, honest, good-mannered, progressive and tolerant, inspiring confidence in business, bringing harmony to conflicting groups, unpretentious, seeking no power which the Constitution did not plainly grant him. Both his character and talents would have served his country best between 1880 and 1914.

When Alf Landon first was nominated investigators went among the people of Kansas asking, "Will he make a good president?" Some said, "Yes." Others said, "I don't know." All said he had earnestness and integrity of purpose, that he had no experience in national politics, so his talents must be taken on trust. "But then," said one man, "any president's talents must be taken on trust!"

In answer to the question, "Is Alf Landon big enough for the presidency?" William Allen White replied, "The impact of the job in the White House is tremendous. If a man has any latent subconscious powers they are aroused by the overwhelming responsibility. Few men fail to respond to this awful challenge. Taft rallied slowly, Harding failed . . . I am inclined to believe that Landon would rise to it. I don't know. No man knows. I don't think he knows. I think that is the reason he is modest. He stands in awe and fear of the terrible consequences of the failure to rise."

In 1936, with the country still floundering in a depression, with the Nazis about to set civilization on fire, with the people churned by revolutionary economic compulsions, Alf Landon might have found his experience as an oil promoter and governor of an inland agricultural state inadequate to achieve a peaceful transition which would have preserved all that was best in the American system. Landon was the first to admit that he was no student, that he was untrained in international politics, that he was a business executive and little more. Rightly or wrongly the American people blamed the collapse of their economy on the practical businessmen and voted for a social theorist who they believed could reconstruct their world according to the demands of the times. This was a task which Landon was vehement in disavowing. He said, in effect, "If you want a social visionary, count me out."

They counted him out.

BOOK EIGHT

Honest Wall Street Lawyers

I: JOHN W. DAVIS

II: WENDELL L. WILLKIE

*Wall Street money is reputed to be doubly tainted:
'tain't yours and 'tain't mine. Are Wall Street lawyers
similarly tainted?*

———◆———

CHAPTER ONE

John W. Davis

HIS FATHER WAS A DELEGATE to the Democratic convention of 1868 which nominated Horatio Seymour in New York City. He himself was a delegate to the Democratic convention of 1904 which nominated Alton B. Parker. Nominated by the Democrats in 1924 in New York City, John W. Davis completed the cycle begun by his father fifty-six years before. By one of those delightful coincidences which make all history contemporary, John W. Davis is closest in temperament and gifts to Horatio Seymour and Alton B. Parker.

In his rich and versatile nature he had every quality except anger; his friends considered this his greatest virtue, his critics his greatest weakness. He had watched his father grow angry in court and lose some of his effectiveness; like Horatio Seymour, he resolved that he would not allow his emotion to master or betray him. In one of his first cases he took indignant exception to the ruling of the court; the next morning he said to the judge:

"I was mad last night. I went back to the office to look up

cases to prove you were wrong. I found you were right. I wanted to tell you so."

He was one of those rare characters in American politics who received plaudits from Republican as well as Democrat. In 1910 the Republicans of his district in West Virginia informed the Democratic convention that they would bolt their party and vote for Davis if he were nominated for Congress; when he was appointed solicitor general in 1913 the Republicans in the House congratulated President Wilson on the wisdom of his choice; when he was nominated for president in 1924 the Republican press praised his character and career.

The liberal press, on the other hand, which for decades had been supporting the Democratic nominee, abandoned John W. Davis. The fact that he was a Wall Street lawyer was the handle by means of which the door of criticism could be thrown open; the real reason Davis lost the support of the progressive bloc was that for the first time since 1860 a third party, Robert M. La Follette's Progressives, had arisen to steal the Democratic fire. The Republicans found with glee that the criticisms of reaction and bondage to the financial interests, which could be charged against their own candidate Calvin Coolidge with greater truth than against any candidate since the formation of their party in 1856, were levied by the liberal press against John W. Davis because it was only from Davis that La Follette could hope to secure his votes.

John W. Davis never wanted to leave his home town; no man in the country seemed less likely to become a Wall Street lawyer. He had worked for Wall Street for only three years prior to his nomination, yet those three years proved a sufficiently long stick with which to beat his eleven-year record as an active and forceful liberal.

Throughout his growing years John W. Davis had imbibed as much political discussion as food at the family table; as an admirer of Thomas Jefferson he had never been anything but a Democrat. Though in his mind law and politics were inseparable bedfellows, he had no ambition to hold public office. He wanted to be a theorist in the science of politics, a behind-the-scene counselor to his party, as Horatio Seymour had been. His friends maintain that he was kicked into every office he ever held; in 1924 they did not kick him quite hard enough.

2

John William Davis was born in Clarksburg, West Virginia, on April 13, 1873. His mother had resolved that the child should be born on Thomas Jefferson's birthday; she succeeded in imposing her will upon nature, but a scant twenty minutes' delay and she would have been disappointed. That twenty minutes was important to Davis: he became one of the most ardent Jeffersonians of his times.

His mother, Anna Kennedy, had come from Baltimore where she had received her bachelor of arts from the Baltimore College for Women. Moving to Clarksburg in 1862, she became not merely an influence in the life of the town, but something like a natural force. She wrote poetry on women's rights, was a painter and a pianist, worked for women's suffrage several decades before it became fashionable, had a comfortable knowledge of French and German, read Latin and Greek. She was reading aloud the last chapter of Gibbon's *Decline and Fall of the Roman Empire* just a few moments before the birth of her son. The Davis house was filled with the best books the world had to offer: first young John read Mark Twain and Fenimore Cooper, then Hugo, Scott, Dumas, Dickens, then Stevenson, Poe, Browning, Shakespeare, then the political writings of Jefferson, Carlyle, Burke, Hume. Many of these books John's mother read to her five daughters and one son while they were growing up.

"Study was her life," said one of Mrs. Davis' daughters; another added, "She would let you argue your case without interruption. Then she would eat you up! By the time she got through there would be nothing left."

It was a gift which would enable John W. Davis to become one of the best legal minds in practice.

Davis' paternal grandfather, a saddler who looked enough like Andrew Jackson to double for him, moved to the pioneer outpost of Clarksburg in 1820. John's father was born in Clarksburg and grew up to be one of the two best lawyers in the town. As a loyal Unionist he was instrumental in separating his section from Virginia at the outbreak of the Civil War, helped found the new state of West Virginia and represented his district in Congress from 1871 to 1875. He was an impressive figure: over six feet, lean and wiry, with a handsome, alert face and burning eyes, a patriarchal beard and a tempestuous nature. He was a good attorney, of the rhetorical school, inclined to spout beautiful words which carried him afield.

John Davis loved his father devotedly but with wide-open eyes. From the time he was a child and accompanied his father on his political tours he made a dispassionate estimate of those qualities which he thought detracted from the older man's effectiveness. His parents' marriage was one of the happiest to be found in the countryside, but Mrs. Davis took one exception to her husband: the loquacity of his public utterances. She worked hard to counteract this tendency in her son, educating him in the rambling and comfortable Davis home of which one room had been set aside as a study for the children. In his English compositions she instructed John to "condense—condense, condense!"

"I want to make him positive, brief and concise," she said. John W. Davis' briefs before the United States Supreme Court were to be so logical and concise that Chief Justice White called upon President Wilson to urge on behalf of himself and his associates that Davis be appointed to fill a vacancy on the Supreme Court Bench. "The Court thinks so much of John Davis," smiled Chief Justice White, "that when he appears for the government the other side hardly gets 'due process of law.'"

John had a normal, happy childhood, swimming and sailing boats in the near-by creek, toting water from the spring for household uses, tending the horses and cows on the family farm. He studied in private tutoring academies in Clarksburg between the ages of ten and fourteen, then left home to begin his college preparatory work at Pantops Academy on a hill overlooking Jefferson's home at Monticello. At sixteen he entered Washington and Lee University at Lexington. Aside from a slightly more precise English than his fellow students, he was the average bright student. He played football, sang in the glee club, was secretary of the senior class, graduated in three years.

The panic of 1893 having reduced the Davis resources, nineteen-year-old John decided that he would earn the money for the rest of his education. For a year he tutored in a private family for twenty-five dollars a month and board; six years later he married one of the daughters he had been tutoring. He studied law as a clerk in his father's office for a year; when he was twenty-one his father backed his note for three hundred dollars which, added to his savings, would carry him through one year at law school. He graduated from Washington and Lee law college in a year, returned to Clarksburg and went into partnership with his father, a moment of great happiness for both men. His first case involved the recovery of a turkey gobbler and eighteen little turks; his average fee was one dollar.

After a year of practice he was offered a teaching job at the Washington and Lee law school, which he accepted in order to continue his studies. He was young to be teaching, only twenty-two, but he had the advantage of a clear, concise mind, the ability to digest large quantities of material and come up with its essence, to express himself in a sharp and illuminating English. His success came in equal measure from

355

his personality: quiet but pleasant, poised yet vigorous, one of those perfectly balanced, endearing natures that are so rare, even among the young. He was determined to succeed, yet he was never guilty of overweening ambition. He was tall and slender, but not as handsome as his father: he had his mother's high square forehead which gave his face a top-heavy appearance; eyes too old and mature for his face; a largish head which overshadowed the slender, elongated face; an overly aggressive chin which contradicted the gently inquiring expression of his face.

Davis' county had not elected a Democrat to the state legislature for almost twenty years; in 1898, with the Republicans quarreling among themselves, the Democrats saw their chance. They asked twenty-five-year-old Davis to run for the office. John's father, who had been soured by what he found in the postwar Congress of 1871–75, said, "John, don't let them nominate you. They are putting you up to be slaughtered. Besides, I want you to stick to the law and stay out of politics."

John informed the convention that he would not be a candidate. The delegates named him anyway, then adjourned the meeting while he was on his feet clamoring of the Chair to be heard, a replica of the Seymour nomination of 1868. Davis was elected by a majority of two hundred votes; though the legislative session lasted only six weeks, he did important work on the judiciary committee.

For the next twelve years he served as Democratic chairman of his county, refusing to run for public office even when offered the nomination for the governorship and for Congress. He was happy with his practice, was taking an increasing share of the work off the shoulders of his aging father. He spent most of his nights in his office, boning on briefs and books, for his wife had died only a year after their marriage, leaving him an infant daughter. His face, always mature, seemed old beyond his years; his hair was graying, his mouth had thinned with sorrow, his eyes had deepened, his mien was serious, sober, conscientious. Aside from riding his horse through the country there was little fun in his life.

John Davis built himself a diverse practice and an interesting one; his door, as his father's had been for half a century, was always left open, and people of all classes and walks of life came in with their problems. Just prior to his nomination in 1924 he stated his credo as an attorney:

"At no time have I confined my services to a single client, and in consequence I have been called upon to serve a great many different kinds of men. Since the law is a profession I conceive it to be the duty of the lawyer, just as it is the duty of the priest or the surgeon, to serve those who call on him."

He became counsel for the glass factories of the district, studying their industry in order to understand their problems; at the same time he served as counsel for the National Window Glass Workers' Union. He helped organize new companies, represented coal, gas and oil companies as well as the Miners' Union; neither labor nor management considered him prejudiced because he also represented the other side. He did his precise and impartial best with every problem, and that best came to be considered the finest to be had in the state. One of his associates of this period says of him, "He possessed a wonderful gift of analysis. He could grasp a case and put it in logical sequence. In his arguments he was concise and convincing; being reflective, he could see both sides of a case."

In 1910 he once again was abducted from his pleasant and profitable practice by a political ruse. Though the Democrats of the district had not elected a congressman for many years, the times were becoming increasingly progressive; they believed they had a chance if they put up their strongest candidate. One by one the committeemen called at the office of Davis and Davis; one by one they were turned down.

"You know I don't want John to enter politics," cried his father. "Knowing how I feel, why do you persist in this plan to nominate him?"

"Because he's the best man we've got and the only one we can elect."

When the convention met in Wheeling, John W. Davis went along to protect himself. The leaders emerged haggard from an all-night session to inform him that they were going to nominate him in spite of his opposition. Davis insisted that he would decline, but to a friend he commented, "I'm afraid that if I don't take it they'll say I laid down on my friends. I don't want any man to ever say that of me."

He telegraphed to his father for advice. His father wired back, "Do not yield to solicitations. Stand firm on declination." A few hours later his father wired again, "Say no and be firm."

The telegrams never reached John W. Davis. They were pocketed by an admirer who was determined to have Davis on the ticket. Davis was nominated by acclamation; again, as he had twelve years before, he jumped to his feet to decline, but the nominations were closed and he was half pushed, half dragged to the platform, one of his friends shouting in his ear:

"Now, damn you, accept this nomination!"

He accepted. He was also elected by a comfortable margin. He reached Washington at an opportune time, for the Democratic party was enjoying its first majority in sixteen years. Through friends who had watched his work in West Virginia he was appointed to the Judiciary Committee, where he helped prepare the final draft of the Clayton Anti-trust Act, wrote the anti-injunction plank of the act which would prevent the courts from enjoining workers from going on strike, and defended his plank before the committee with a brilliant constitutional study of American laws. He also prepared the anti-conspiracy clause, which would keep workers from being arrested for conspiring to strike, and the anti-contempt clause, which would prevent judges from jailing strikers or union leaders without trial by jury. In working for his portions of the bill he spoke several times before the House, short, concise, penetrating speeches which went a long way toward securing passage of the bill. As one of the managers of the impeachment trial of Federal Judge Archibald he was named to deliver the main charge before the house. In this address he struck fire from the rock of Jeffersonian democracy:

"No man can justly be considered fit for public office who does not realize the double duty resting upon him: to administer his trust with unflinching honesty, to so conduct himself that public confidence in his honesty will remain unshaken. The confidence of the people in the integrity of their officers is the foundation stone of all free government."

He was returned to Congress in 1913. He enjoyed his work, found it congenial. Yet his ambition lay in a different direction: he felt that his nature and his gifts fitted him for the quiet, non-partisan tasks of the Bench. There was a vacancy on the United States Circuit Court whose jurisdiction included the Virginias and the Carolinas; his fellow members on the Judiciary Committee urged President Wilson to appoint him, but the president passed him by. This was a sore disappointment to Davis, one of the major disappointments of his life. Shortly thereafter he was appointed solicitor general, which made him the most important trial lawyer in the country: he represented his government before the Supreme Court. His appointment came about in part because President Wilson had since become acquainted with Davis and developed an admiration for his personal qualities, His friendship with Wilson was to continue an important one up to the president's death: when Davis received the presidential nomination in 1924 Mrs. Wilson would wire him:

"I feel that in your hands the things that Mr. Wilson fought for will have a worthy champion."

The period of five years during which he served as solicitor general were the happiest since the death of his wife: he remarried, enjoyed a pleasant social life in Washington; his touch lightened, humor crept into his speech. It also developed into the period of his most intensive work: he personally tried more cases before the United States Supreme Court than any of his predecessors, arguing sixty-seven major cases in five years. His ability to handle great masses of material, extract the essence and state it with lucidity enabled him to turn in a first-rate job. In the Harvester Trust case his final argument was based upon thousands of pages of evidence, yet it took him only forty-five minutes to deliver it to the court. Small wonder the nine judges loved him!

Serving under a liberal president and administration, he was able to turn in a consistent record of progressivism, though he was sometimes defeated by the Supreme Court, as in the case of the Child Labor Amendment. He argued the constitutionality of the Adamson Act, which made the eight-hour day legal; he pled the right of the president to withdraw from public sale certain lands known to contain oil and mineral deposits; he tried the first steel-trust cases under the Clayton Anti-trust Act; he defended the constitutionality of the Interstate Commerce Act; in the Harvester Trust case he declared the Anti-trust Act to be "the deliberate effort of conservative, clear-thinking men to place some reasonable check on that liberty of combination which, if permitted to the 'logical extreme,' would in the end imperil liberty itself." He named as defendants in his suits most of the powerful bankers and industrialists of the nation, among them Morgan, Rockefeller, Carnegie, Frick, Schwab.

He was no quibbler at the law; as the *World's Work* said of him, "He was versed in the historical evolution of the law as an instrument for preserving the benefits of human society." He had once defined a natural lawyer as one who "knew the law and could get up and tell it." Davis had both the knowledge and the means of expression. At the solicitation of Chief Justice White, the president placed John W. Davis' name at the head of the list of eligibles for the Supreme Court.

In 1918 he was sent by Wilson to Switzerland to serve as American high commissioner for the exchange of war prisoners with Germany. While he was working in Switzerland, Walter Hines Page, ambassador to England, asked to be relieved of his post because of ill-health. The position was offered to Davis. He cabled to Secretary of State Lansing:

"Financial reasons alone would seem to be prohibitive. My resources are meager as you know."

Lansing cabled back, "Financial demand is between thirty and thirty-five thousand per annum. I know that it would be a great sacrifice, but unhesitatingly say that I feel it your duty to accept."

Davis checked his resources, saw that he had something over seventy thousand dollars in assets, enough to carry him to the end of Wilson's second term. He accepted the offer; when he returned to the United States in 1920 he would be broke.

The English had been fond of Ambassador Page. "At the announcement that the prize had been awarded to a certain John W. Davis of West Virginia, there was a faintly audible murmur of chagrin. Never was there a darker horse than he. The West Virginia lawyer was made to feel quite at ease; his inexperience was to be politely overlooked. To the surprise of high society, John W. Davis not only stepped onto the stage, but filled it. Handsome, suave, soft of voice, precise in phrase, dignified without assertion, well informed without pedantry, a lawyer without legalism, he appeared from the first day to the last as the complete diplomatist—easy, shrewd, sympathetic, candid."

The king of England said, "Mr. Davis is one of the most perfect gentlemen I have ever met." The king had no way of knowing that he was gazing upon the embodiment of Thomas Jefferson's conception of a true democrat.

His two years as ambassador were entirely successful: his habit of understatement made him a favorite after-dinner speaker, while his simplicity enabled him to unravel some of the highly knotted tape in the processes between Americans and the British government. In 1919 President Wilson called him to Versailles to help prepare the peace treaty. His work was a constant source of joy to the State Department.

When his ship left Southampton in March of 1921, after his Republican successor had been appointed, forty British destroyers escorted him down the Channel, whistles were blown, flags were dipped, and cheers came over the water from the British sailors. All this possibly heartened the forty-eight-year-old ex-congressman, ex-solicitor general, ex-ambassador, whose party was now out of power and who was himself out of a job, obliged to begin his life anew.

3

John W. Davis had come to a critical fork in the road: he could return to Clarksburg and resume the practice he had left behind ten years before, or he could accept the offer made to him by one of the most influential law firms in New York City, Stetson, Jennings and Russell, the one to which Grover Cleveland had belonged when he was re-elected to the presidency in 1892. Davis had little appetite to return to

Clarksburg; his mother and father were both dead, he could no longer enjoy the minor law the small town could afford him; he had been a member of the highest society of Washington and London and had acquired a taste for cultivated living, for the refinements of the world's great centers. He had grown used to the opera, the symphony, the theater, to the white tie and tails and the delightful accouterments of sophisticated living. He had not wanted to leave Clarksburg, but having been forced into the world of major politics and high society, he had outgrown his roots.

He accepted the offer of the New York firm and soon became its president, acting as counsel for J. P. Morgan and Company, the New York Telephone Company, the New York Rubber Exchange. He bought himself a spacious estate on Long Island and a town house in Manhattan. He tried to keep open the door of his office, as he had in Clarksburg, but it was no longer so easy: he was taking large retainer fees from important clients, there would be little time left for a delegation of glass blowers. In 1922, after only a year of active practice, he was elected president of the American Bar Association.

The Davis-for-president boom sprang from the same source that had precipitated him into the state legislature in 1898 and the Congress in 1911: his friends and admirers in West Virginia. When these enthusiasts mentioned him for the Democratic nomination in 1920, Mark Sullivan commented, "If an energetic group of Democratic leaders should get behind Mr. Davis, the movement to nominate him would go a long ways," while the New York *Times* praised him as a "great Democrat." His strength rose as high as seventy-six votes in the San Francisco convention which named James M. Cox, and his showing made him a strong contender for the next nomination.

In the winter of 1923 the Home-Town Davis-for-President Club undertook to tell the nation why John W. Davis should be its next president, and was doing such a rip-roaring job that Davis was embarrassed. When he returned to Clarksburg for a visit in the spring of 1924 he said to his oldest friend, the manager of the movement, "Clem Shaver, I feel obliged to protest against your activities."

"This is our affair," replied Shaver. "You're not responsible for what your fool friends do."

Davis' protest had been based on the early American conception that no man should seek the office of the presidency: certainly it was not based on indifference, for in his thoughtful book, *Party Government in the United States,* he writes, "The great prize of American politics is the presidency, the ultimate goal of all partisan effort the White House. Within proper limits it is a perfectly legitimate, indeed, a laudable ambition for every American. During his four-year term he is the most powerful figure in this country, and perhaps in the world."

There was only one charge that could be conjured against Davis: he was a Wall Street lawyer. He had given up a profitable law practice to serve in Congress; for five years he had served as solicitor general at ten thousand dollars a year when he could have earned twice that much in private practice; as ambassador to England he had exhausted his private resources in order to maintain American standards for which Congress refused to pay; as a lawyer in Clarksburg he had served the Miners' Union and the National Window Glass Workers' Union; as a member of the Judiciary Committee he had helped draft the Clayton Anti-trust Act and had personally written its most liberal labor planks; as solicitor general he had fought brilliantly and with the utmost courage on every liberal front. For only three years out of his professional career of twenty-five years had he been a Wall Street lawyer, yet he was being condemned by the liberal wing of the Democrats as unfit to represent their party.

In February of 1924 an admirer wrote to Davis asking him to abandon his Wall Street practice and return to Clarksburg, for such an act might insure his nomination. Davis replied, "If I were in the market for the goods you offer, I would not complain of the character of this consignment, although I notice you do not guarantee delivery. The price you put on them, however, is entirely too high. You offer me the chance to be the Democratic nominee for the presidency which carries with it more than a fair prospect of becoming president. In exchange, I am to abandon a law practice which is both pleasant and, within modest means, profitable; to throw o er honorable clients who offer me honest employment; and desert a group of professional colleagues who are able, upright and loyal.

"No one in my list of clients has ever controlled or ever fancied he could control my political conscience. The only limitation upon a right-thinking lawyer's independence is the duty which he owes to his clients, once selected, to serve them without the slightest thought of the effect such a service may have upon his own personal popularity or his political fortunes. If one surrenders his philosophy to win an office, what shall he live by after the office is won? Tell me that!"

Clem Shaver went to New York early in June 1924 to set up a Home-Town-for-Davis Club in the Waldorf Hotel. Davis' chances appeared remote: William G. McAdoo controlled half the delegates, while a full third had been pledged to Alfred E. Smith.

The Democratic convention did its best to lose the election before it had nominated a candidate. The platform committee wrangled for days, taking a weasel stand on the important issues, refusing to condemn the Ku Klux Klan or endorse the League of Nations. It was the first presidential convention to be broadcast over the radio, and for two weeks an interested, then amused, and finally disgusted electorate listened to the warring factions at each other's throats, until the people said, "If you are so torn between yourselves, you are not a safe party to have in power."

John W. Davis was placed in nomination by the West Virginia delegation, along with a host of other favorite sons. "The crowd was terribly weary," by the time Davis' name was mentioned, "but it stood up and made a decent amount of noise for five minutes." The first ballot showed:

McAdoo	431
Smith	241
Underwood	42
Davis	31

By mid-July the convention had taken seventy ballots, breaking the record set up by the 1860 convention in Charleston, which had cast fifty-seven ballots before the Secessionists bolted from Stephen Douglas' majority. The count now stood:

McAdoo	415
Smith	323
Davis	76

By July twenty-first, after watching the convention cast ninety-six ballots in the suffocating heat of a New York summer, McAdoo and Smith had to admit that they could not win. Both withdrew—but not to each other! Davis, who had been running third, captured their strength. He was nominated on the hundred and third ballot, and everybody prepared to go home, sick with fatigue and ill with the dissension and bitterness that had dominated the proceedings.

The jubilation in the Davis family reflected none of the despair of the convention itself. Mrs. Davis cried, "You've won! You're nominated!" Davis went to Madison Square Garden and essayed a peace talk:

"As a more or less interested bystander I cannot be ignorant of the fact that this convention has had its debates and its differences, and in the truly Democratic fashion has fought out its conflicts of opinion."

Davis' nomination was well received. *Outlook* called him a "sober-minded liberal, not a futile theorist." The Boston *Transcript* commented, "One thing most characteristic of him is straight thinking. He discerns the essential point unerringly, and never allows himself to be deflected." Walter Lippmann said in the *Atlantic Monthly,* "Davis' nomination was the result of confidence in his character rather than of studied agreement with his views." *Current Opinion* wrote, "Davis was born with both luck and brains. Part of his luck is that no one has said he didn't deserve his good fortune." Samuel Blythe in the traditionally Republican *Saturday Evening Post* poked fun at him because he dressed well and had the grand manner, but nevertheless called him "a great lawyer, efficient and experienced public servant, a cultivated and courteous gentleman, a well-born American." *Current History* summed up, "Affable, jolly, democratic, Davis has the rare gift of not thinking about himself when he is talking to anybody. A man of effortless courage, he never hesitated to give utterance to his own opinion whether it was popular or not, and he never gave the impression that it cost him anything."

If anyone could bring peace and unity to the shattered Democratic party it was John W. Davis, whom the press declared to be the outstanding personality of his party and the only effective antidote to the poisons generated at the convention. Yet he went into the campaign seriously handicapped: in addition to the disharmony of his party, the Democratic National Committee was poorly organized, with certain sections remaining disgruntled; the convention had nominated for vice-president Governor Charles W. Bryan of Nebraska on the grounds that he was a liberal and from the west: thousands would vote against John W. Davis because they thought William Jennings Bryan was his running mate! The Republicans were taking exclusive credit for the accelerated prosperity the country was enjoying.

However, his greatest trial was that a third party had arisen: Senator Robert La Follette of Wisconsin was leading a Progressive party which declared Davis and Coolidge to be as alike as the Gold Dust Twins! John W. Davis and the Democratic party, which had served as the liberal wing of American politics since the Civil War, were unceremoniously shoved aside; the liberals, progressives, radicals, the independents, the intellectuals, the farmers and the workers were lining up solidly behind La Follette in what was constituting the strongest third-party threat since the Fire Eaters split Stephen

Douglas' vote in 1860 and threw the election to Abraham Lincoln.

Davis was not responsible for the Democratic platform, which had been drawn several weeks before his nomination; he went about repudiating it by a vigorous denunciation of the Ku Klux Klan, a ringing support of the League of Nations, and a pledge of a liberal program for the benefit of the people which brought back the memory of his most effective work as solicitor general. His efforts did him little good; the left-wing press called him a Wall Street lawyer who in his unconscious motivations would be controlled by the financial interests he was now serving, condemned him as a false liberal because he had sat on the board of directors of the Santa Fe Railroad when that company had used a harsh injunction against its striking workers; because he had lived through the Red Hunts of 1921–23 without rising in anger, because as president of the American Bar Association he had said, "Increased solicitude for health and physical comfort of the individual has led men to think quite mistakenly of so-called 'human rights' as of something which can be divorced, either in practice or in legislation, from so-called 'rights of property.' " Burton K. Wheeler, vice-presidential nominee of the Progressives, sneered, "I am a Democrat, but not a Wall Street Democrat."

Davis bore up well under these attacks, urging the liberals and progressives not to throw their votes away on La Follette because that would help the Republican party. At no time did he attack La Follette or the Progressive program, for he appreciated the irony that he who was now being called "an honest and attractive conservative, but nonetheless a conservative" had implemented, by his work as solicitor general, the major portion of the Progressive program! He did not agree with La Follette's demand for the government ownership of the railroads, nor his insistence that the Supreme Court be denied the right to invalidate laws passed by the Congress, but for every other plank he had worked as hard and effectively as La Follette himself: abolition of the labor injunction and ratification of the Child Labor Law; the crushing of private monopoly and an end to the trusts; the lowering of the special-privilege tariff and the shifting of the tax burden to profits.

He reserved his fire for the Republicans, and white-hot fire it was. In his acceptance speech in Clarksburg he said, "I speak with restraint when I say that the Republican administration has brought forth corruption in high places, favoritism in legislation, impotence in government and a hot struggle for profit and advantage which has burdened us at home and humiliated us abroad. The time demands plain speaking!"

As a campaigner John W. Davis proved to be an expert surgeon, wielding a brilliant scalpel, covering thousands of miles across the width and breadth of the country, presenting the people with a lawyer's brief of plain speaking which laid bare Harding's ruinous program. "There will be no Falls, Daugherties, Gaston B. Means or Jess Smiths when the Democratic party gets into office." With the exception of a single remark in east St. Louis, where he told a crowd that a continuance of Republican policies might eventually lead to a social revolution, he indulged in no wild talk, made no charges that he could not substantiate. Nor did he try to smear Calvin Coolidge with the Harding brush:

"I make no charges against the honesty and integrity of the present occupant of the White House," he said. "I think no man truthfully can."

Davis' was a campaign at once energetic, truthful and well-bred; as the *World's Work* said, "Mr. Davis has tackled the issues with considerable vigor. His speeches have confirmed the impressions of his ability and his grasp on public questions." In spite of his skill, he found himself in the most embarrassing and anomalous position ever suffered by a candidate: the Republicans would not fight! Coolidge maintained an icy silence, while Dawes, the Republican candidate for vice-president, went about ignoring the Democratic nominee and inflaming the country against La Follette, warning the voters that the Progressives were the real danger, that if the Republicans did not win the Progressives would overthrow the existing form of government and cause a bloody revolution. Republican letters sent out in Pennsylvania said, "We have in La Follette and Wheeler a Lenin and Trotsky."

Thus Davis was forced to shadowbox! He got in some telling blows at his side-stepping opponents, but each time he struck hard the Republicans would murmur, "Go away, we're not fighting you. We're fighting La Follette. You're not important in this election. You're the third party that has no chance! By remaining quiet you can help us defeat the Reds."

Time magazine reiterated each week, "Cal Coolidge sat tight and held his peace." When the Republicans evolved their campaign slogan of "Keep cool with Coolidge," Davis finally blew up. "There are gentlemen in this country who believe that the greatest duty a public servant can perform is to keep cool! No one can deny that the chief characteristic of the present administration is silence. If scandals break out in the government, the way to treat them is—silence. If petted industries make extortionate profits under an extortionate tariff, the answer is—silence. If the League of Nations or foreign powers invite us into a conference on questions of world-wide importance, the answer is—silence! The Republican campaign is a vast, pervading and mysterious silence, broken only by Dawes warning the American people that under every bedstead lurks a Bolshevik ready to destroy them."

The policy of ignoring Davis and dragging the traditional red herring across the trail was a clever tactic: as the campaign progressed La Follette's strength appeared to grow while Davis' went down. This gave the Republicans new ammunition, for La Follette's real aim was alleged to be the securing of enough electoral votes to keep either the Republicans or the Democrats from gaining a majority, thus throwing the election into the Congress. If the House should be too evenly divided to give any of the three candidates a majority, the Senate would proceed to select a vice-president. Since the Senate had a Democratic majority which could not be overthrown by the 1924 election, it would unquestionably select Charles W. Bryan, who would automatically become president on March fourth. The Republicans made the most of this possibility by throwing a final scare into the electorate. Said the New York *Herald Tribune:*

> *A vote for La Follette is a vote for Bryan.*
> *A vote for Davis is a vote for Bryan.*
> *A vote for Coolidge is a vote for Coolidge.*

John W. Davis was not disturbed by these alarms, nor was he depressed by the *Literary Digest* polls which, by October eleventh, showed him trailing in third place:

COOLIDGE	808,340
LA FOLLETTE	352,178
DAVIS	275,674

He spoke as many as six times in one day, documented the scandals of Mellon and the aluminum trust, Dawes and his bank scandal in Chicago, and a host of other cases of special privilege for business at the expense of the consuming public. But the public couldn't be annoyed: they were making money, they were prosperous; they didn't care how much money was being embezzled as long as they were getting a share. In spite of the Harding scandals the lassitude which had defeated James M. Cox four years before was now engulfing John W. Davis.

His barbed thrusts finally goaded Coolidge into speech. A few days before the election he broke his tomblike silence to address the United States Chamber of Commerce on a national radio hookup. The fact that Coolidge chose to make his only public address before the Chamber of Commerce instead of speaking directly to the people is significant, as was his short talk the following day to representatives of forty-seven trades when he said, "This is a business country; it wants a business government."

The Republicans built up a four-million-dollar campaign fund against a million and a half for the Democrats, though Senator Borah, chairman of the Senate Investigating Committee, declared that thirty millions were spent on the election, more than a dollar for every vote cast.

John W. Davis presented a strong front to the very last moment. In his only arrogant statement of a long campaign he said, "It took longer to nominate me than any man ever named for the presidency, and it will take just one day, November 4, to elect me."

When the final result showed 15,725,016 votes for Coolidge, 8,386,503 for Davis and 4,822,856 for La Follette, he took the result with his usual urbanity, and went back to work. He had run third in thirteen states; he would fall into the limbo of such forgotten men as Lewis Cass, Horatio Seymour, Alton B. Parker. But like these predecessors he had fought a clean, intelligent fight for the two-party system.

In his book, *Party Government in the United States,* Davis wrote with his accustomed humor and clarity, "The attractions of public life lie in the interest and excitement it affords and, when one is successful, in the applause of one's fellows —a form of music to which no ear is deaf. Its one lasting reward is in the consciousness of duty done. To those who enter it with any other expectation, disappointment, disillusion and bitterness are as inevitable as the rising of tomorrow's sun. Do not forget that in this country political wounds are apt to be mortal and under the political mortality tables the expectation of public life is short."

The 1924 campaign proved mortal to Davis' political career. He had served for ten years, from congressman in 1911 through ambassador in 1921, and for five months as a presidential candidate. He was never to return to public life, contenting himself with his pleasant law practice, with occasional writings and speeches on legal and constitutional subjects. When, eight years later, his party was returned to power he hoped that at last his ambition would be fulfilled, that a Democratic president would appoint him to the Supreme Court of the United States as Charles Evans Hughes had been appointed fourteen years after his defeat for the presidency. He was still vigorous at sixty, but a younger generaion had arisen; though its philosophy was based in part on the work that John W. Davis had done, his time had passed; he was never to receive the appointment, never to be a judge.

4

What kind of president would John W. Davis have made? Were his gifts better fitted for the years of 1924–28 than those of Calvin Coolidge? The Baltimore *Sun* said, "In the White House he would be friendly, accessible, open to advice, gifted in counsel, skilled in finding formulas to solve difficult situations." Davis had strength and penetration, no one ever imposed upon him or fooled him, yet his dominant characteristic was his endearing personality. Nowhere in American history can one find such a shattering contrast between two human beings: warm, lovable, gracious John Davis, and Calvin Coolidge, the most glacial personality ever to appear on the American scene, frequently described by those about him as a "hatchet-faced sphinx." Coolidge was a kind man basically, sympathetic to the few intimates whom he trusted; but as William Allen White so ably documents in his *Puritan in Babylon,* he came into the White House a pathological case: cruel, frigid, distrustful, sour, loathing people and human contact.

Outlook magazine commented, "Mr. Davis is gracious in manner, dignified in bearing, has the gift of commending himself to common sense and of making the ideals he holds seem reasonable." Coolidge was as honest as Davis, he would allow no one to use him for his personal advantage, he guarded every last penny of government funds with as much zeal as he guarded his own. He was shrewd, had a granitelike kind of humor which he occasionally allowed to give off a spark, had the grim Yankee devotion to the rights and liberties of the individual, and no sharper trader for the government ever held office. But he had a brain which functioned without words; since words are the only means of communication between people, Coolidge maintained an Ice Age silence between himself and Washington.

In stating why he was going to vote for Davis, Walter Lippmann wrote, "He seems to me the only one of the three candidates whose mind actually deals with the postwar world." John W. Davis was Thomas Jefferson brought down to 1924; Calvin Coolidge was John Adams, living in 1796. In the *Puritan in Babylon* Republican White portrays him as a man who came out of the backwoods of Vermont a Yankee primitive, a full century behind his times. Coolidge neither liked nor understood the world in which he found himself; in the backwoods of Vermont he was a good neighbor, in Washington he was a misanthrope who froze the government. John W. Davis understood the modern world and loved it; he also loved people, had great sympathy for their struggle upward through the dark night of hardship and oppression. Everywhere he served, his warm, kindly personality opened new doors for human endeavor, shook the shackles of restraint, cold legalism and red tape. Davis had worked with Europeans and understood their problems; as president he would have done his best to strengthen the League of Nations and throw America's efforts on the side of peace; Coolidge knew nothing about Europe, was an isolationist in a period when the hearty co-operation of the United States was necessary to avert another world cataclysm.

But the great tragedy of Calvin Coolidge's regime lies neither in his clammishness nor his isolationism; it lies in a policy of letting things alone unequaled in the United States since the eighteenth century. When governmental experts came to him with figures which proved indisputably that the United States was heading for the financial crash which came in 1929, showed him how that crash and the resultant depression could be avoided by certain regulatory restrictions, Coolidge glared at them in icy loathing until the experts stuffed their papers into their brief cases and crept out of the room, crushed.

It was no accident that Coolidge made his one public speech of the campaign in the United States Chamber of Commerce building: for Coolidge this was a statement of his philosophy and his faith. It has been said of him by his own friends that while he was president the chief executive's offices were not in the White House, but across the street in the U.S. Chamber of Commerce building.

The financial interests of Massachusetts had helped Calvin Coolidge rise from an obscure ward heeler, petty opportunist and mediocre state legislator to the office of governor because in their wildest dreams they could not have conceived of anyone who would more completely serve them. This was not because they could bribe him or buy him; it was because in his primitive pioneer Vermont philosophy Coolidge was the perfect agent for their purposes. He believed, honestly and sincerely, that everything big business did was wise and sound and right; he would allow no restriction on its activities or attempt to control it in the alleged interests of the people. Change was abhorrent to him, he was repelled by the attempt of man to control his fate by political activity. He loathed all Democrats, good and bad; he detested their social legislation;

he yearned for the America that had existed prior to the advent of Thomas Jefferson.

Calvin Coolidge was an accident in the White House, put there by the death of Warren Harding; he could never have secured a presidential nomination on his own devices. A careful examination of his record shows him to be a mediocre mind. He willfully and stubbornly allowed the country to plunge into its shattering crash and depression; insofar as history can blame any one man for the years of misery and degradation suffered by the American people, Calvin Coolidge is that man.

No one fitted the needs of his country better between 1924 and 1928 than John W. Davis, a thoughtful liberal who would have listened to the experts and put a curb on wild speculation and the pyramiding of paper wealth. No man fitted the needs of the times worse than Calvin Coolidge. In 1796 Coolidge's blank check to business might have helped the country; in other periods prior to the Civil War his policy of being the least possible president might have done little harm; but only the malevolent fates could have brought to the White House in 1923 a stone-age reactionary, the one man in all the world who could do the utmost possible damage to the country by refusing to do anything at all.

The *Review of Reviews* said, "As a president of the United States John W. Davis will be ready to realize the requirements of the times and to meet them with new devices—but the wild radical and vain dreamer will find no support in him. The electorate may be certain that in Mr. Davis it will have a firm, able man at the head of its affairs."

John W. Davis would have faced the future as resolutely as Calvin Coolidge faced the past. A man who understood and approved big business, he would have encouraged its development and growth while protecting the people of the country from its excesses. A man of culture and refinement, he would have been a great educator in the White House, giving wings to the arts and sciences and the humanities. The best brains of the country would have been utilized in a co-operative effort of government; the democratic processes would have been extolled and implemented; the humble people would have felt that they had a father in Washington, even as they had felt it under Jefferson and Jackson and Lincoln. The worship of the golden calf, the crass and flinty materialism of the Coolidge era would have been replaced by spiritual and humanitarian principles which might have saved the American people from their hysterical scramble for money and more money and still more money which ended in bank-ruptcy and suicide, the morgues and the bread lines.

John W. Davis would have made the kind of president of whom Thomas Jefferson would have approved; Mr. Davis would have seen to that.

CHAPTER TWO

Wendell L. Willkie

WENDELL WILLKIE was one of the most puzzling and contradictory characters to appear in twentieth-century American politics. As with Henry Clay and William Jennings Bryan, it is difficult to begin a paragraph of praise without a note of censure creeping in; similarly it is difficult to write a line of censure without being obliged to temper it with praise.

Willkie was the most exciting young man to run for the presidency since William Jennings Bryan in the flower of his youth. Tens of thousands of women unwittingly voted for him to be their sweetheart rather than their president. He was eulogized by Raymond Moley as being "as literate as Winston Churchill and as full of driving energy as Theodore Roosevelt." He was called the Abe Lincoln of Wall Street, was likened to Will Rogers because he had never met a man he didn't like. Willkie would have been the first to laugh at these comparisons; he would have murmured, "I'm just an Indiana boy trying to get along in the world." The only crack that got under his skin was Secretary of the Interior Ickes' comment that "Wendell Willkie is just a simple barefoot Wall Street lawyer." Willkie countered, "I'm not a Wall Street lawyer; my office is on Pine Street, a full block away from Wall Street."

Was that far enough away to reassure the American voter?

Wendell L. Willkie and John W. Davis were two of the warmest and most lovable characters among the Also Rans. Both were small-town boys who became men of the world and consorted with kings; both were handsome, well built, with superb energy, inexhaustible dynamos who worked without strain or temper; both were fighting liberals who were raised by talented parents; both grew up in homes containing countless books and a love of learning; both left their home towns and tranquil lives reluctantly, were astonished to find that a chain of circumstances had made them Wall Street lawyers; both were men of personal honesty; both were intellectuals, cultivated in the arts, who spoke and wrote well; both achieved their considerable success on the basis of brains and character; both were Jeffersonian Democrats from

373

the first day they could distinguish between parties. Neither Willkie nor Davis was nominated by a machine; both had their campaigns handled by amateur enthusiasts instead of professional politicians.

When Wendell Willkie gave up his job as counsel for the Firestone Rubber Company, Mr. Firestone said to him, "Young man, I like you but I don't think you'll ever amount to much. No Democrat can ever amount to much." Willkie managed to stumble along pretty well under the burden, becoming president of the Commonwealth and Southern in 1933, at the same time that Franklin D. Roosevelt became president of the United States—and both at the same salary. Willkie got a kick out of saying, "Roosevelt and I took office at the same time, only my company is running at a profit while his company is running at a loss."

He liked to describe himself as "the best gadget salesman in the country." The gadget he sold easiest was Wendell Willkie; as with Davis, it was difficult not to like Willkie once you had met him. A supersalesman of power, he made an effective play upon the word when he said, "Power is just as destructive on Pennsylvania Avenue as it is on Wall Street." His outstanding thesis was, "In the prewar years we fought against the domination of the people by Big Business. We now face the domination of the people by Big Government. The liberal who fought against one kind of domination thirty-five years ago should find himself fighting against this new kind of domination today."

In the introduction to a 1940 campaign book called *This Is Wendell Willkie*, Stanley Walker said, "He is simply a big, two-fisted, Middle Western American who happens to be at the same time a scholar and a gentleman. In any gathering he is about as anonymous and inconspicuous as a buffalo bull in a herd of range cattle." It was the emanation of the buffalo bull which gathered seven tenths of his early volunteer workers from among housewives; similarly it was his incisive and articulate personality which made him a one-man social force.

He bears the distinction of being the lone Also Ran who, a few weeks after the election, was being patted enthusiastically on the back by his erstwhile opponents and kicked in the rear with equal enthusiasm by his erstwhile friends. A month before the election the Democrats were denying that Wendell Willkie had ever been a Democrat; a month after the election the Republicans were denying that he had ever been a Republican.

Just before the opening of the Republican convention in Philadelphia in June of 1940, Willkie commented, "I'm not running for anything, and I'm not running away from anything. But I would be a liar if I said I wouldn't like to be president or wouldn't accept a nomination." When the Willkie boom reached its height, just prior to his nomination, he said, "I would like to think it means I'm a hell of a fellow, but I think it means I represent a trend, or am ahead of a trend." Before the balloting began he observed, "I will be nominated on the sixth ballot."

He was nominated on the sixth ballot.

He was the first since the army generals to shoot into the presidential race without any political experience whatever. In the early days of his successful law practice in Ohio, when his friends had volunteered to send him to Congress, Wendell Willkie had replied, "No public office for me!" Fifteen years later the voters made him stand by his original decision.

2

Wendell L. Willkie was born in Elwood, Indiana, on February 18, 1892. His mother and father had been schoolteachers and were now practicing law together. The women on the Willkie side of the family long had been resolute characters: his grandmother had been a doctor, an aunt was a preacher, his mother was the first woman licensed by the Indiana bar. His father too was a strong character. Like so many of the Also Rans, Willkie's home was rich with the love of "larnin'," was reputed to contain sixty-seven hundred volumes. However, young Wendell never would have climbed so far nor so fast if he had not also inherited the wit to give his learning leaven.

His four grandparents had come from Germany during the Republican uprising and exodus of 1848. In his acceptance speech at Elwood almost a hundred years later their descendant said, "One of my grandfathers was exiled because of his religion; another was persecuted because he believed in the principles of the French Revolution; and still another was jailed for insisting on the right of free speech." No one could doubt that Wendell would stand squarely in the tradition of his forebears.

In 1892, when Wendell was born, the town of Elwood was enjoying an industrial boom due to the discovery of natural gas, and Herman Willkie was accumulating real estate and wealth. The following year the natural gas evaporated, and with it Herman Willkie's fortune. The Willkies were hardworking, conscientious, earning for their brood of four boys and two girls a modest, thrifty comfort. The six children were

375

lusty and rambunctious: Wendell grew to be six feet one, a solid two hundred and ten pounds.

"It was a harum-scarum, disputatious household. The boys in particular were full of high animal spirits. Herman Willkie had a habit of waking his brood by shouting quotations from the classics at them. The dinner table was a place for solid eating; it also resembled a somewhat daffy debating society in full cry."

Wendell graduated from the Elwood public schools and in 1909 entered the University of Indiana, where his two older brothers and sister Julia were in attendance. They lived together under Julia's housekeeping. Their various landlords complained that the Willkies made a shambles of every place they occupied and that it was hard to keep them from spitting tobacco juice on the mantelpiece. They were fast-talking, unpolished, unburdened by a superfluity of elegance or delicacy, but smart and likable as a family group. For the youngest of the Willkies the university was merely a continuation of the Elwood dinner table; he feasted on the important books of the age and at the same time was the spellbinder of the debating team.

"I had read everything I could get my hands on," said Willkie, "including *Das Kapital* by Karl Marx, and I was enormously impressed by it. I wondered why we did not have a course on socialism. A faculty member told me that he would conduct such a course if I could drum up ten students who were interested. I had to button nearly everyone in the university before I could get the ten. No wonder they thought of me as a socialist."

Like Alf Landon at the neighboring University of Kansas, for whom he would vote in 1936, Wendell Willkie became a campus politician. "Tall, thin and loquacious, with a loose-necked red sweater, a rampant forelock and a fine indifference to campus mores, he was known as champion of the underdog and spearhead of the unwashed. A rangy radical gadfly, he was consistently anti-administration—a characteristic which was not to grow weaker with the years—an astute and hard-working politician who was not the leader of the unwashed for nothing: he liked to negotiate and contrive and promote."

Willkie was "agin" nearly everything at the university: the fraternities, the faculty, the brand of thinking being done on the campus. The Willkie family had been known as the most emancipated in Elwood; Wendell was living up to the family tradition. Yet after three years of fighting the fraternities as a "barb," in his senior year he joined the Betas, the swankiest fraternity on the campus. In 1932 he was for the New Deal and President Roosevelt, but by 1936 he was "agin" everything being done in Washington. In 1929 he enjoyed calling himself a "La Follette liberal"; by 1940 he was a wholehearted Republican.

During the summer vacations he worked in the wheat fields of Minnesota, the oil fields of Texas, the cornfields of Iowa. He taught history and coached the track team at Coffeyville, Kansas, for a year, then returned to the University of Indiana, from which he was graduated in law in 1913. Now twenty-one, he went into his father's law firm and engaged in the usual small-town practice of Elwood. As with Davis, one of Willkie's first clients was a labor union.

When war broke out in 1917 Willkie enlisted in the army and became a lieutenant in the field artillery; he was sent to France, but hostilities ceased before he had a chance to see action. Returning to Elwood he worked with his father for a short time and then, finding the small-town practice too confining, moved on to Akron, Ohio. He entered the legal service of the Firestone Rubber Company and soon was earning five thousand dollars a year, establishing a reputation for himself in Akron as a smart lawyer and a good guy.

Once again Wendell Willkie, with his enormous energies and roving mind, found his work too restricted; though Firestone offered to double his salary he resigned his position and joined one of the leading law firms of Akron. The diversity of the new practice was refreshing, and before long he had tripled the business of his firm, which became Mather, Nesbitt and Willkie. His father had been known as a lynx in court, the son was more like a lion: his large frame had filled out, his eyes were bright and warm and quick, he was forceful and persuasive, his openfaced candor made people trust him and his wit helped them to like him.

He was still considered a roving gadfly, a non-conformist who stubbornly refused to buy an automobile or play golf with his fellow members of the country club. He fought the Ku Klux Klan during its rise in Ohio, championed liberal causes in public debate.

In 1917, before going to France, he had married Edith Wilk of Rushville, Indiana, proposing with his usual touch of humor: "Edith, how would you like to change that Wilk to Willkie?" The couple had one son, and lived with a solid and growing prosperity in Akron. Though he consistently refused to run for public office, he went to the Democratic convention in New York City in 1924 in an effort to get Al Smith nominated and attended the Chicago convention in 1932 in the interests of Newton D. Baker's candidacy. When Franklin D. Roosevelt received the nomination Willkie contributed one

377

hundred and fifty dollars to the campaign fund. By 1936 he was grousing:

"I wish I had that money back!"

During his high-school days young Wendell had liked to walk about saying, "Money is power." Soon he would be reversing this adage to read, "Power is money." The incident that started him on his way to power was the handling by his firm of the Ohio Edison business. Willkie reorganized their finances on an open and fair basis, and the Ohio Edison became known as a "reformed utility" in the wasteland of corrupt utilities, leading Senator Wheeler to comment that "if there had been no more abuses in other companies than in his, some of the strictures against holding companies would not have been put through." Through his contact with Ohio Edison and Northern Ohio Power and Light, Willkie became acquainted with the leading utility men in the country.

By 1929, ten years after he had come to Akron, he was one of the leaders of the Ohio bar, well known and well liked; since he had no yearning for politics or publicity it appeared that he would remain an able and intelligent midwest lawyer, backing the liberal causes of the day and growing decently rich among his law cases, his books and his friends.

But in 1929 Bernard Cobb was organizing a gigantic holding company of electric-light and -power distributors to operate from Michigan to Alabama. Believing Wendell L. Willkie to be one of the country's most effective young lawyers, he asked him to come to New York as corporation counsel for the newly formed Commonwealth and Southern. Willkie hesitated to leave Akron, where he was happy and comfortable, for the strange and vast New York whose high society and low finances he feared. Cobb offered to double his earnings for the past three years, and Willkie felt that he had no alternative but to accept.

Wendell Willkie was called into the one industry which became the center of an incipient revolution, the fork in the road between the capitalist and the social democratic society. Between the years of 1933 and 1940 he would be president of Commonwealth and Southern, associate with the Morgans and Whitneys, the Stettiniuses and Rockefellers, be photographed in white tie and tails, hobnobbing fraternally with the financial barons and industrial tycoons, become the most powerful voice of the opposition to government ownership and the controlled economy.

In 1929, at a meeting of power magnates during which Samuel Insull, arch-conspirator of the holding-company frauds, was lashing out at the "subversive" elements which were criticizing his methods of operation, bumptious young

378

Willkie insisted upon the right of people to speak their minds, even when it was criticism of the power companies they were uttering. Insull turned to Willkie and said:

"Young man, when you are older, you will know more."

It was this question of what Wendell Willkie had learned between the years 1933 and 1940 that would become the subject of such bitter dispute during the presidential election.

3

As counsel for the Commonwealth and Southern in 1929 Wendell Willkie, newly arrived on the scene, was in a difficult position; its stock had been issued at twenty-four dollars a share, so bloated that within a few months it had fallen to ten dollars, losing for its more than one million investors something like twenty-four million dollars. In 1940 candidate Willkie said, "I am very proud that I had nothing to do with the speculative orgies of the 1920s. I agree with the strictures about unloading on the public of common stocks beyond their true value." At the same moment the *New Republic* was saying in its special election issue, "Mr. Willkie was one of those responsible for the speculative orgy. It was that orgy which transformed him from a cracker-barrel Indiana liberal into a Wall Street insider as slick as they come." As counsel for Ohio Edison he had kept that company's finances honest and aboveboard; during the years he was president of Commonwealth and Southern no charge of manipulation was brought forth; yet as legal adviser to Commonwealth and Southern he must have known that the figures used for the evaluation were excessive.

Like Davis before him, Willkie did the job that was asked of him. He did not try to revolutionize the industry after taking his seat at the board table: John W. Davis did not restrain the Santa Fe from using an injunction against its employees; Wendell Willkie did not keep the Commonwealth and Southern from deceiving its investors.

Willkie lost most of his savings in the crash of 1929; the company for which he was counsel was on an ever-accelerating toboggan: its stock was down to two dollars a share, the sale of light and power was down to a critical minimum, the market for electrical appliances had disappeared. When Franklin D. Roosevelt was inaugurated president of the United States, Bernard Cobb resigned and Wendell Willkie was named president of the nearly bankrupt Commonwealth and Southern. Commonwealth and Southern had received monumental favors from the Republican regime during Cobb's tenure of office. Now all relations with the government were endangered. Wendell Willkie, like Davis, was one of the almost non-existent Democrats on Wall Street. He would be *persona grata* in Washington. As *Fortune* remarked about him:

"Find a public-utility officer who is a political liberal and you will have something almost as rare as a purple cow."

Cobb resigned because of mental ill-health. Willkie's promotion to the President's chair with the inauguration of Franklin D. Roosevelt seemed too pat to be coincidental, yet there was no one else on the board with anywhere near his qualifications.

Having been pushed upstairs, Willkie now staged one of the most heroic performances to be found in industrial history: he cut rates when everyone around him was saying that consumption had to increase before rates could be cut; he devised a bonus plan whereby the consumer could have an extra third of his consumption free if he would use a greater amount each month; he hired five hundred salesmen when salesmen were being laid off elsewhere, broadcasting them through his eleven states to sell electrical appliances on easy credit terms.

He did not rest behind his desk on Pine Street, but went on the road himself as a sort of supersalesman, instilling confidence in local power companies, pepping up appliance firms, spending as many as two hundred days a year in small towns across the face of the nation, making friends with merchants, newspapermen, consumers, selling them the idea that the more electricity they used the cheaper it would be, that they could raise their standard of living without increasing its cost. He was a friendly cuss with warm, sparkling eyes, a hearty and sincere handshake, a photographic memory and the gift of getting along with all people; a big, easygoing, shambling bear of a man with a lock of hair dangling over one eye, in rumpled clothes that had come off a Pullman hanger, a humorous fellow who said:

"It's an asset to my business to look like an Indiana farmer."

His plan worked: over a period of years he doubled the amount of power and light dispensed by his companies, quadrupled the sale of electrical appliances. He settled rate wars with fair compromises, refused to gamble in the stock of his companies or water that stock for quick profits in the market.

Not long after Willkie and Roosevelt assumed their separate presidencies the United States government went into the power-and-light business in the Tennessee Valley, began to compete with southern power companies and made evident its intention of buying out several privately owned lines.

Since Willkie's Alabama Power was the most seriously threatened he became the spokesman for the drive against public ownership of utilities. He accused the Tennessee Valley Authority of a number of unfair practices, charging that "the American people are paying more than half a billion dollars for eleven dams to supply power to one locality at less than cost. TVA enjoys privileges and exemptions which conceal the true cost of its power: exemption from taxes, exemption from depreciation charges, exemption from interest charges on capital on which TVA was built. The Tennessee Company, given these same privileges, would sell electricity at lower rates than the TVA."

Wendell Willkie figured that all was fair in love and economics. He had waged a great campaign to save his companies, he had them solidly on their feet, and he had no intention of letting the government wipe them out. He believed the government had started industrial warfare in which he had to defend himself as best he could. At the beginning he agreed to have his Alabama Company share with the government the electricity generated at the government constructed Muscle Shoals. When suit was brought against the Alabama Power Company by one of its stockholders to enjoin it from carrying out the agreement, it was reported by Willkie's company that the funds for the suit were being provided by the stockholders at twenty-five cents each. Upon investigation it was learned that the Edison Electrical Institute, of which Willkie was a director, was providing the necessary fifty thousand dollars. Willkie later claimed that at two Edison Institute meetings he voted against this appropriation, and when it was passed during his absence from a subsequent meeting, he resigned from the Institute.

His companies erected spite lines where they had refused to provide power before, tried to intimidate the residents from using government power, used every conceivable method to block the farmers' co-operative, to which they had refused to provide electricity before the entrance of the new lines; they blacklisted the Chattanooga *News,* which favored public ownership, and ran the newspaper out of business; placed misrepresenting newspaper advertisements against municipal ownership of light and power, purporting that they had been paid for by the local power companies when the money actually came from Willkie's office of the Commonwealth and Southern.

The purple cow was fading fast.

The TVA originally had offered to buy the Tennessee Power Company from Wendell L. Willkie for $55,000,000. Willkie had refused to accept the offer because he did not wish to give up a profitable company and because he believed the price to be too low. When the Supreme Court refused to declare the TVA unconstitutional Willkie reluctantly offered to sell the Tennessee Power Company for $100,000,000. The figure finally agreed upon was $79,600,000; by his years of fighting he had secured an additional $25,000,000 for his stockholders, a feat which became known as the "twenty-five-million-dollar Willkie shriek."

Willkie had talked hard and tough before the government committees when he was warned that he had better talk soft or it would be held against his company. However, though he fought to the hilt, he had managed to keep his good humor. When the nearly eighty-million-dollar check was passed, amid grinning reporters and grinding cameras, Wendell Willkie cracked to David Lilienthal, director of the TVA:

"Dave, this is a lot of money for a couple of Indiana boys to be throwing around."

The American people liked that remark: it indicated that all was forgiven, that peace had come to reign over the utilities, that Wendell Willkie had won a victory for his stockholders in certain respects and that he was being a good sport about those in which he had lost.

The battle he had put up earned him high praise in business circles. *Fortune* magazine gave him his first national recognition in May 1937 with a laudatory article and a series of exciting photographs. They said, "Wendell Willkie is the Mississippi Yankee, the clever bumpkin, the homespun, rail-splitting, cracker-barrel simplifier of national issues. He feels a dedication to the cause of private ownership; he knows all the arguments; they are persuasive on his tongue not because they are new but because he frames them intelligently and hence makes them sound new."

Three months later Willkie wrote an article for the *Atlantic Monthly* called "Political Power: The TVA," in which he stated forcibly the full case against government ownership of utilities. In January of 1938 he opposed Robert H. Jackson, assistant attorney general of the United States, on the Town Meeting of the Air; in the debate, staged before millions of radio listeners, Willkie sang a madrigal of the greatness of American production and what it had done for the standard of living of even the simplest people.

He was now writing and speaking often, developing an audience, sharpening his logic and his philosophy. In a commencement-day address at the University of Indiana he cried, "The true liberal will not tolerate executive or legislative domination." In an article in the *Saturday Evening Post* called "Idle Men, Idle Money," he stated the thesis of which so many businessmen had become convinced: "Four billion dollars are lying idle in the bank, money which industry needs desperately. The question is, can we cause our great reservoir of free capital to flow into the channels of industry? If we can, our democratic system will be preserved. If we cannot, then our democracy will vanish in the chaos of national bankruptcy."

For the *Atlantic Monthly* of June 1939 he wrote "Brace Up, America!" which was a stirring appeal to the American people to throw off the yoke of New Deal paternalism and return to the rugged individualism of their fathers. In Washington he spoke on "The New Fear," fear of government itself which had replaced the fear of depression. "We wanted to punish industry for past abuses and we wanted, quite rightly, to make certain that these abuses would not reoccur. However we don't want industry killed, not even in the interest of making it virtuous." *Reader's Digest* published his article called "The Faith That Is America," in which he charged the New Deal with being defeatist, of taking away freedom for the mirage of a planned security. Willkie saw himself as leading a mighty crusade for the preservation of American liberty.

"No duty has ever come to me in my life," he said, "even that in the service of my country, which has so appealed to my sense of social obligation, patriotism, and love of mankind as this, my obligation to say and do what I can for the preservation of public utilities privately owned."

This statement and the philosophy he built around it led directly to his nomination in Philadelphia in July 1940. Symbolically, as Senator Norris pointed out on the floor of the Senate, this placing of his obligation to fight for the private ownership of utilities above his obligation to fight for his country in time of war also led to his defeat.

Rounding the first curve, Willkie was picking up speed: through radio interviews, talks before civic forums, Rotary Clubs, advertising bureaus, Chambers of Commerce, through his magazine articles and his delightful performance on Information, Please, on which his warmth, humor and erudition shone through, his reputation was spreading. He engaged in a three-hour informal joust at the Harvard Club with Felix Frankfurter, coming off so well that word was flashed that at last an articulate businessman had appeared on the scene. Publishers came to him with offers to write books; invitations to speak poured in from all parts of the country. He had made himself one of the leaders of American thought.

But how does one in a thousand become The One?

It was a penetrating wisecrack that first got his name linked with the presidency. General Hugh S. Johnson wrote in his syndicated column that if Willkie were nominated he would make a powerful candidate and, if elected, a great president. Called on the long-distance telephone by a reporter who asked his reaction to this remark, Willkie retorted:

"If the government keeps on taking my business away at its present rate, I'll soon be out of work and looking for a job. Johnson's offer is the best I've had yet."

His little joke seemed so aptly the epitome of the government-versus-private-ownership controversy that he received two thousand invitations to speak on the day his reply was published in the papers. Perhaps attracted by the familiar aspect of the name, Willkie chose the Commonwealth Club of San Francisco at which to make his first preconvention speech, telling its members that the New Deal was hobbling industry in a skein of unnecessary regulations, that the American system would restore itself as it had always done if the government would let business alone.

"It was a clearly reasoned, restrained utterance which just happened to hit an unsounded keynote in the millions of people," wrote General Johnson in the *Saturday Evening Post* a few days before the meeting of the Republican convention. "In it there was nothing highbrow and nothing hateful. From complete political obscurity Willkie found himself a stellar attraction in record time. His immediate attitude was one of dizzy incredulity."

Willkie did not remain dizzy very long; in the April 1940 issue of *Fortune* he published a proclamation of faith called "We, the People" in which he reached his climax, made the most incisive and forceful statement of the existing opposition to the planned society, and catapulted himself into the nomination. He said, "This declaration will not interest those who regard the United States as a laboratory for social experiments, as a free-lunch counter or as an impoverished gold mine out of which they can still scrape a nugget or two for themselves. For the old American principle that government is a *liability* to be borne by the citizens for the sake of peace, order and security, the New Deal has substituted the notion that government is an *asset* without which none of us can survive."

He nailed his articles of faith on the door of the White House in the manner of Martin Luther nailing his ninety-five articles to the church door at Wittenberg:

Before the political platforms are written, we, the people, have a declaration and a petition to make:

In the decade beginning 1930 you have told us that our day is finished, that we can grow no more, and that the future cannot be the equal of the past. But we, the people, do not believe this, and we say to you: give up this vested interest that you have in depression, open your eyes to the future, help us to build a New World.

In this decade you have separated "business" and "industy" from the ordinary lives of the people and have applied against them a philosophy of hate and mistrust, but we, the people, say: business and industry are part of our daily lives; in hurting them you hurt us. Therefore abandon this attitude of hate and set our enterprises free.

Ringing as this declaration might be, it could have little effect upon a nomination by reaching only the *Fortune* audience. But shortly after its release the mother of Oren Root, Jr., laid a copy of the magazine on her son's desk. Young Root spent the night in a creative sweat; when morning came he had contrived a *modus operandi* for securing the nomination of Wendell L. Willkie by the Republican party. On a borrowed hundred and sixty dollars he had "We, the People" reprinted and distributed, along with a petition to be signed urging Willkie's nomination. When Root, who did not know Willkie, called on him at his office on Pine Street to tell him what he had done, Willkie declared that he had no chance of being nominated and wanted no political organization.

Undismayed, Root replied that his was no political organization, that it was a rising of the people; Willkie did not have to do anything about the movement, the movement simply would secure his nomination.

The first circulars having raised an immediate and enthusiastic response, Root took a leave of absence from his law firm and opened a Willkie-for-President office in his mother's apartment. Those who had signed the original petition sent out petitions of their own; when Root had no more funds with which to reprint "We, the People," Willkie admirers printed and mailed them at their own expense. One friend inserted a note in the personal column of a New York newspaper saying that Root needed money with which to continue his Willkie campaign; contributions began coming in at once, two hundred dollars a day. On the strength of this Root rented an empty store. The Willkie boom was on.

Twenty-five thousand Willkie buttons were printed as an experiment; soon eighty thousand were being distributed every day. Root inserted items in the personal columns of the newspapers in every important city, urging its residents to set up Willkie Clubs, which mushroomed with amazing spontaneity. In New York City a committee declaring itself to be spontaneous and unfinanced rented a hotel room and mailed out half a million pieces of campaign literature urging the nomination of Wendell Willkie. Willkie Clubs throughout the nation were operating at white heat, thousands of anonymous enthusiasts contributing their time and money and energies to the Willkie cause, securing more than three million signatures to the petition.

The movement was growing at such a terrific pace that Russell Davenport, managing editor of *Fortune*, also took a leave from his job to manage the campaign.

All this was bad news to the Republican politicians, to the senators, congressmen and old-line bosses who meant to nominate one of their own boys. It was sweet news to the bankers, industrialists and Wall Street brokers who saw in Willkie not a man they could control but one who would serve their purposes even more effectively because, like Calvin Coolidge, he believed in the pre-eminent fitness of business to rule the country. Thus from the beginning the Willkie movement was compounded of two parts: first the uprising of the unorganized public, second the businessmen and financiers, paced by their two magazines, *Fortune* and the *Saturday Evening Post*, for whom Wendell L. Willkie had become the most powerful spokesman in the land. How much the financial-industrial clique influenced and financed the amateur enthusiasts would become a matter of heated dispute during the campaign.

The Republican convention opened in Philadelphia in late June 1940, with Senator Robert A. Taft of Ohio leading the field. Wendell Willkie shattered precedent and all concept of good form by going to Philadelphia to make sure that the convention nominated him. He was the first since Horatio Seymour to be on the ground when the nominating was in process; Seymour had gone as a delegate to avoid the nomination, Willkie attended as a gadget salesman to sell himself, the ultimate electric appliance. Delegates pledged to other candidates cheered him as he walked down the street; when he entered a hotel lobby a crowd gathered around to hear him discuss the issues of the day. Wendell shook hands, kidded, made friends with hosts of strangers, met every question, every hostility in the open, with a warm broad smile, his big, friendly, stooping shoulders, his earnest purpose, his fast intelligence. He seemed to be saying:

"Look, boys, this is what I am, an Indiana farmer. No man owns or manages me. Anyone can step up and ask me a question and I'll give him an honest answer. I have nothing to hide, nothing to fear. No one speaks for me. I speak only for myself. I have no party organization, I have no powerful interests behind me. I make no deals, swaps, promises, I am simply a guy who would like to get the nomination because I think I can lick the Democrats and give you the kind of government you want and need."

The delegates liked him; the reporters liked him; the newspapers and magazines cried for his nomination; his rooters gathered from distant places. Excitement ran high; conferences were held behind locked doors; rumors sped like marathon runners through the streets and hotel lobbies. A kind of intestinal tremor shook Philadelphia and the nation.

To propositions which he received Willkie replied, "Tell them I didn't drop off the bush just yesterday."

The inner ring grew frantic, rushing into deals to stem the Willkie onrush. Forty congressmen and five senators signed a petition urging the delegates to work against Willkie's nomination; Senator McNary told the delegates that "the West will go against us if Mr. Willkie heads the ticket." He was accused by the Republican machine of being a tool of the money interests. The Committee on Foreign Affairs "modified overnight the position taken by their platform committee, set out to strengthen the isolationist commitment in the platform and bind the party to negative pledges so tightly that the Convention would not be able to nominate Willkie without repudiating their own platform."

But from the moment the nominations were opened the jammed and frenzied galleries set up a chant of "We want Willkie! We want Willkie!" When the chairman demanded that they watch their manners since they were guests one neophyte shouted:

"Guests hell! We're the People!"

The Democrats cried, "The galleries are packed! Willkie's promoters cornered the tickets and are staging this show to stampede the delegates!" The hoarse and feverish galleries snorted, "If we had tried to plan we couldn't have got to first base." When commentators called Willkie's nomination a spontaneous uprising the Democrats retorted, "Sure, a spontaneous uprising of the wealthy."

Wendell Willkie stood by watching the proceedings with a quiet smile on his face, a lock of hair dangling over one eye, his clothes rumpled from the heat and strain of being on the road. The pledges to favorite sons were dispensed with on the first five ballots and then, as he had predicted, Willkie was nominated on the sixth. It was the first time since the nomination of Charles Evans Hughes that the Republican voters had been able to dictate their choice; the amateurs, the general public went wild with joy; the professional politicians went home griped and muttering into their beards; analysts sighed publicly at the irony of Senator McNary's nomination for the vice-presidency after his prediction of the defeat of the party if Wendell Willkie were nominated.

Could an amateur win a presidential election?

5

Wendell Willkie entered the race with tremendous personal assets but shackled to his isolationist party; in addition he was embarrassed by the public embrace of the German-American Bund, the Italian Fascist organization, the American Communist party which was trying to prevent aid to Britain, Father Coughlin and his *Social Justice,* Joe McWilliams of Brooklyn, Mrs. Dilling. He detested the isolationism of such party leaders as Taft, Hoover, Dewey, Vandenberg, Fish, Martin, Nye and Johnson, yet he needed their support to win the election, and actively solicited that support.

On the domestic issues the campaign was a good deal like the Landon campaign of 1936, except that Willkie was a profounder exponent of his thesis, and the New Deal had had four more years in which to pile up attackable errors. His greatest selling point was the third-term issue, for President Roosevelt had decreed his own renomination to a lethargic Democratic convention. The Republicans charged that Franklin D. Roosevelt was trying to become a permanent dictator by overthrowing the traditional finality of a second term. Yards of literature were quoted from the Founding Fathers and the early presidents to prove that a third term was undemocratic, un-American and dangerous to the existing form of government. Many Democrats and most independents agreed with this dictum; in ordinary times they would have preferred a mediocre new man to an excellent president who had already served two terms. But the world was in flames, a crisis for the United States was imminent, and there was a question as to whether a country's danger did not throw out the third term as an issue. Willkie supporters pasted stickers on their cars reading NO THIRD TERMER; Roosevelt admirers retaliated with stickers reading BETTER A THIRD TERMER THAN A THIRD RATER.

Wendell L. Willkie went back to his home town of Elwood, Indiana, to make his acceptance speech on August 17, 1940. The lampposts were decorated with huge Willkie photographs; the streets were lined solid with shirt-sleeved men and women in white dresses and straw hats; hot-dog and lemonade stands were piled high with sustenance; Callaway Park was packed with two hundred thousand admirers who had journeyed from afar to hear the voice of the new prophet. Willkie rode through the town in the back seat of an open car, receiving an ovation usually accorded to conquering heroes. Throughout the country millions of pairs of ears were glued to the radios to hear the official opening of the campaign for which they had already worked so hard, and for which they had whipped themselves into a frenzy of expectation.

No speech could have satisfied them: when Willkie had finished his adherents felt let down, as though they had somehow been deceived, betrayed. It seemed that Wendell Willkie's bid for the presidency had died aborning, yet aside from this poor radio delivery there was little reason for his followers to feel depressed. He had stated simply the political philosophy that was in his heart:

"Party lines are down; nothing could make that clearer than the nomination by the Republicans of a liberal Democrat who changed his party affiliation because he found democracy in the Republican party and not in the New Deal. We go into this campaign as into a crusade. We shall fight the campaign on the basis of American liberty, not on the basis of hate, jealousy or personalities."

Even more than Landon before him, Wendell Willkie was in a difficult position: he approved of Roosevelt's foreign policy, and he appeared to approve of his domestic aims except for governmental waste and interference with business. Someone remarked that "every time Willkie opens his mouth he puts Roosevelt's words in it," while another wag said, "Willkie agreed with Roosevelt's entire program of social reform and felt that it was leading to disaster." The *Nation* remarked that Republican Willkie would have to stop running on the Democratic platform and record. Prior to the Elwood acceptance speech Bruce Barton, the Republican publicist, had announced that a survey showed Willkie leading with fifty-three per cent of the vote, but the press was not enthusiastic about the Elwood speech. John Chamberlain said in *Fortune*, "Elwood came and went, and no sound alternative to the New Deal emanated from the Willkie camp. All I got from that speech was an endorsement of the New Deal."

An early Gallup Poll showed Willkie running ahead of the Landon vote of four years before, but not enough to make an important difference: Roosevelt had a potential 453 electoral votes while Willkie appeared to have only 78. Along with the fact that he had been unable to show crucial differences of opinion between himself and Roosevelt, his most serious detriment appeared to be that he was a Wall Street lawyer. The politicians of his own party had smeared him with the tar of the money interests in an attempt to prevent his nomination, and the Democrats found their ammunition close at hand. The smear campaign that had been used against John W. Davis was put into motion against Willkie: his function as president of Commonwealth and Southern was labeled that of a stock fixer and money manipulator who robbed the innocent investor; he was accused of being a front man, a public-relations counsel whose job it was to build a good reputation for the privately owned utilities while the bankers who employed him were robbing the public; he was adjudged a crook and unscrupulous shyster who had tricked and robbed the government out of millions in the TVA deal.

Bruce Barton assured the public in *Collier's* that "Willkie's office is only a block away from Wall Street, but Wall Street has never felt that he really belonged." His act of throwing the bankers off the Board of Commonwealth and Southern was publicized, as were his pictures in a crumpled suit, for now it was even better for his business to look like an Indiana farmer than it had been in 1933. *American* magazine published an article by his secretary in which Willkie was portrayed as an informal and kindly cuss who telephoned with his feet on the desk; one of his campaign photographs that pictured him elegantly garbed in white tie and tails was deleted for fear of offending the great unwashed.

The Gallup Poll still showed him trailing hopelessly. Wendell Willkie thereupon treated the American public to the best knock-em-down-and-drag-em-out campaign since William Jennings Bryan had electrified the voters in 1896, lashing out at nearly everything Roosevelt did on both the domestic and international scenes. He surpassed Bryan's record by traveling thirty thousand miles on tour; like Bryan his magnificent energy and superb courage won the admiration of the reporters assigned to his campaign train. *Time* described it as "an extraordinary phenomenon almost certain to make a notable exhibit in the museum of political history."

With the reappearance of the hard-hitting Wendell Willkie of the TVA days his campaign was reborn and the results were immediately perceivable in a resurgence of enthusiasm on the part of the Willkie Clubs. Willkie was elated with the results of his first attacks; he saw that he must dish out fire and brimstone, repudiate everything the New Deal had done both at home and abroad if he hoped to win . . . and he figured that this gentle deception was not too high a price to pay for the presidency.

The close similarities between Wendell L. Willkie and John W. Davis melted down in the crucible heat of the election. Where Davis' utterances were consistent and logical to the bitter end, Willkie's were shot full of contradictions; where

Davis kept his balance and talked rationally, Willkie lost his head, hurled imprecations and dire threats of doom; where Davis was crystal clear, Willkie was confused; where Davis refused to truckle to the masses, Willkie indulged in the misleading demagoguery of telling the working people that he "had come up the hard way"; where Davis refused to compromise to garner votes, Willkie practiced opportunism; where Davis operated with a scalpel, Willkie laid about him with a bludgeon; where Davis insisted upon having the presidency on his own terms, Willkie was willing to pay almost any price to win.

This decision carried him within hailing distance of the White House; it also left a strange record for the historian to probe.

At Elwood he had said, "The New Deal does not distribute wealth, it distributes poverty!" He now addressed large and wildly excited audiences, preaching his philosophy. He announced, "It may be that the American people want to Sovietize or socialize American business. If they do, O.K., but I want to present the issue." In Cleveland he said, "New Dealers sabotage defense plans for fear some of their arbitrary powers might be taken away from them." At Wilkes-Barre he said, "The New Deal has approached the question of collective bargaining from a reactionary standpoint. It has created bad blood, it has created plenty of fights, but no jobs." In San Francisco he said, "I charge that this Administration has contributed to the downfall of American democracy. I charge that it must bear a direct share of the responsibility for the present war."

Thus Wendell L. Willkie traversed the nation, speaking with all his might and power to millions of people until his voice was hoarse and any other man would have been exhausted, crying, "Production! More production! Production creates wealth! Production creates jobs! I can get the factories back to their production! I can get the men back to their jobs! Production! More production! American prosperity was based on production! We will never be well and strong and powerful and rich again until we get back to production!"

If Willkie was not fighting with all his might, he was still following the Marquis of Queensberry rules: when Father Coughlin's *Social Justice* came out for his election Willkie publicly repudiated Coughlin for building his popularity on the spreading of religious differences; when someone in an Iowa audience booed the name of the Democratic vice-presidential nominee, Willkie protested by saying, "I recognize Henry Wallace as a fine gentleman and a scholar." When the professional Republicans came trailing back into camp wanting to take over the campaign, Willkie refused to deprive the Willkie Clubs of their management.

He received a tremendous press: seventy-eight per cent of the American newspapers were supporting his candidacy, with only nine per cent backing Roosevelt. Since sixty per cent of the papers had been for Landon in 1936, Willkie did not allow himself to become too encouraged by this support. But when the New York *Times* endorsed him as the second Republican candidate it had backed in sixty years, he felt that he had reached the turning point of the campaign. Within a few days his elation was dashed, for the Springfield *Republican* and the St. Louis *Post-Dispatch,* both of whom had backed Landon, took full-page advertisements in the New York *Times* to state why they could not support Wendell L. Willkie. The New York *Times* had postulated its fear of the third term; the *Post-Dispatch* replied, "Millions of citizens with great reluctance will overcome their opposition to a third term because the alternative—Mr. Willkie—is a poor alternative." The Springfield *Republican* said, "The promise held out in Willkie's behalf in Philadelphia of a statesmanship which would prove so commanding that it must cause him to be preferred to Roosevelt has not been fulfilled." Raymond Clapper, one of Willkie's earliest supporters, wrote, "If the Willkie administration in the White House functioned with no more unity, co-ordination and effectiveness than the Willkie administration in the campaign, then the government would be almost paralyzed."

Had he had more political experience Wendell Willkie might have avoided a number of critical errors, the most serious of which being his charge that President Roosevelt had promoted the Munich Pact, had telephoned to Hitler and Mussolini to sell Czechoslovakia down the river. This caused such an uproar that Willkie's press secretary was obliged to explain the next day that Mr. Willkie had misspoken, that "Mr. Willkie had meant to say that Mr. Roosevelt had urged a settlement at Munich, and the pact there agreed to sell Czechoslovakia down the river."

The public asked, "How could Mr. Willkie misspeak on so critical a matter?" Prognosticators said, "In that one sentence Willkie revealed such an abysmal ignorance of international politics that he has spelled his own defeat."

He accused Roosevelt with failing to arm and defend the United States despite the record that it was the overwhelming Republican vote against arming which had prevented Roosevelt from accumulating a store of strategic war materials, from fortifying Guam for fear of antagonizing Japan, from aiding Britain and the conquered peoples of Europe. Didn't Willkie know this record, hadn't he witnessed the isolationist tactics of his own convention? Or was he falsifying and concealing the facts to confuse the public, create spurious election issues?

He erred at a public banquet when he said, "If we are patient we will see the time when men like Tom Girdler are recognized as the true heroes of America." Willkie admired Girdler as a production genius who created jobs and wealth. It had been Tom Girdler who had led Little Steel's fight against the CIO unionization of the industry after the major plants had signed agreements, and the opposition press could bring forth one of the unhappiest pictures of twentieth-century America, that of the Chicago police caught in the act of beating steelworkers collected on the sward in front of Tom Girdler's Republic plant.

To make this statement look more frightening to the working people of the country, material was widely publicized from the La Follette Civil Liberties Committee findings which indicated that the various companies of Willkie's Commonwealth and Southern had spent thousands of dollars to hire Pinkerton labor spies, had purchased tear guns and shells, had intimidated their employees and discharged union organizers. It was on this record that the president of the United Automobile Workers declared Willkie to be "a streamlined version of Herbert Hoover—slicker, more clever and more charming, but underneath his synthetic build-up there is still the mind and outlook of a public-utilities manipulator and enemy of labor."

Willkie denied he had ever hired a labor spy and later brought forth evidence to prove that he had used the Pinkertons only as spotters on the new one-man streetcars. But any man who hires a Pinkerton, for any purpose whatever, becomes forever suspect with labor.

Wendell Willkie poured out an ocean of words, suiting the nature and sentiment of his remarks to the character of his audience. His mental energy was not able to keep up with his physical energy: since he was speaking to hundreds of groups, many of them diametrically opposed, it was inevitable that in his opportunism he must bog down in a welter of contradictions. To one group he declared, "The farmers are victims because they are forced to exist on what is virtually a dole"; to another he said, "I will not take away any of the benefits gained by agriculture during the past few years. I do not favor changing the present farm program unless a better one is gradually evolved." One day he would call Roosevelt a warmonger, the next day an appeaser. In the *Atlantic Monthly* he had denounced the Social Security and Wage and

Hour acts as indirect taxes on pay rolls which caused men to be thrown out of work; at Elwood he called for constant improvements in the Wage and Hour Act. He had always favored governmental regulation of the excesses of industry, had once thoroughly castigated the National Association of Manufacturers for not mending their monopolistic and predatory ways; he had credited the twelve-cent cotton of the AAA for keeping his southern companies profitable, yet *Newsweek* reported him as saying, "I predict again tonight that if the present administration is restored to power for a third term our democratic system will not outlast another four years."

Anyone addicted to the melancholy pursuit of checking campaign speeches once an election is over will be able to extend the list almost indefinitely. Willkie himself did not take the implications of these harangues too seriously; when confronted by one of his insupportable statements after the election he laughed and said, "Oh, that was just campaign oratory."

The Democratic campaign against Willkie was slow in getting started; in the beginning it did not appear that he would do much better than Landon. Charts were drawn to illustrate how the New Deal had rescued the financial and industrial structure after the Republicans had brought it to the brink of collapse in 1932, to indicate that 1940 production and profits were in many instances above the 1929 high. To Willkie's repeatedly hurled charge that Roosevelt had a vested interest in the depression, the Democrats replied with ridicule: apple vendors were suggested for the street corners to remind the people of the last Republican administration, of the years from 1930 to 1933; the New York *Post* ran a poem which summed up the sentiment of the Democrats who were asking, "Why do the rich people hate Roosevelt? He saved their money and he's making them richer than they ever were before."

> *I remember, I remember, the bread lines on my street.*
> *We had no money—and no jobs—and nothing much to eat.*
> *I remember, I remember, that I lost my House and Lot*
> *And in those troubled times there was—no chicken in my pot.*
>
> *All these I do remember, all these and plenty more,*
> *And yet I'm not a sorehead, but the thing that makes me sore*
> *Is looking at those dopey guys—for punishment what gluttons,*
> *With all the punishment they've had, they're wearing Willkie*
> *buttons.*

Willkie picked up momentum with each passing week; his rating in the Gallup Poll rose; hundreds of thousands of

Willkie pictures were framed in home and store windows; millions of Willkie buttons flooded the land; Willkie kits containing buttons, pamphlets, leaflets were broadcast through the Willkie Clubs; the "Women's Flying Squadrons" were indefatigable. At the height of the fever blonde cuties dressed in drive-in uniforms with brightly colored tight pants stood at the important intersections in Los Angeles flashing brilliant smiles to the motorists and attempting to insert Willkie photographs between the windshield and its wiper. The personable Mr. Willkie was being sold like soap. The Democrats charged the Republicans with flouting the Hatch Act by having big business and advertising agencies contribute not cash, which had to be accounted for, but materials and personal services worth many millions.

It was the first time since the Hughes-Wilson election of 1916 that a presidential contest entered its final weeks with no one able to tell who was going to win. The Democratic campaign was poorly financed, the local committees were dead on their feet from overconfidence; many of Roosevelt's former brain trusters, such as General Hugh Johnson and Raymond Moley, were cutting his regime into little pieces. In spite of the fact that Willkie's campaign was so badly organized that several of his important backers abandoned him on the grounds of inefficiency, it became evident to everyone that unless the Democrats did something drastic Wendell L. Willkie would be the next president. It was too late for the Democrats to do anything but play their ace of trumps.

Franklin D. Roosevelt once again took to the stump, making five speeches in five key cities. The passage of another four years had not dimmed the reassuring qualities of his magnificent voice, the incisiveness of his political gestures. His epitomizing of the Republican campaign in the figures of "Martin, Barton and Fish" was such a masterpiece of vocal ridicule that the listener could actually smell the fish. But more important, Franklin D. Roosevelt reviewed the accomplishments of the New Deal for the preceding four years, made a stirring statement of his conception of twentieth-century social responsibility.

The campaign of 1940 revealed how contemporaneous was all American history: no two elections resemble each other so closely as those of John Adams and Thomas Jefferson in 1800 and Wendell Willkie and Franklin D. Roosevelt in 1940. Jefferson was called the identical names, accused of the same sinister intentions by the Federalists as was Franklin D. Roosevelt by the Republicans: radical, revolutionist, dictator, rabble rouser, usurper of the Constitution, wrecker of the American form of government. The campaign literature, the slogans, the tempers, the fears, the threats, the issues could be transposed from one election to the other without anyone detecting the difference. Nor was there any fundamental difference between Adams' Federalism and Willkie's Republicanism; the man who had been raised as a Jeffersonian Democrat had abandoned his party and his master much as he had abandoned the unwashed "barbs" on the Indiana campus when the opportunity arose to join the aristocratic Beta fraternity.

As the campaign entered its final week business and social life were paralyzed. Nothing but the election was talked about; partisans on both sides went about with a hysterical glint in their eye. There was less crossing of party lines than Willkie had anticipated, for the election had turned into a class war in miniature, the worst the country had experienced since the Bryan-McKinley campaign of 1896. At the last moment John L. Lewis, president of the Congress of Industrial Organizations, tried to throw the support of organized labor to Willkie, confusing the campaign more than ever. And during this last week, intoxicated by his rising chance of success, Wendell Willkie lost both his head and his temper, began hurling threats of doom and damnation for the United States and its people in the calamitous event that Wendell L. Willkie were not elected.

A few days before the ballots were to be cast the *Atlantic Monthly* came out with two articles called "I Vote for Willkie" and "I Vote for Roosevelt." In the first John Hanes, former undersecretary of the treasury, listed twelve reasons why he was voting against Roosevelt but not one reason why he was voting for Willkie! In the second Dean James M. Landis of the Harvard Law School stated the reasons why he was voting for Roosevelt. This seemed to be the epitome of the campaign: people were voting for or against Franklin D. Roosevelt; Wendell Willkie was serving as a highly attractive decoy. Similarly hundreds of those who voted against Willkie were not voting against Mr. Willkie himself but against the party with which he had momentarily aligned himself. Only a few feared Wendell Willkie; many feared the Republican machine which had taken such vicious means to defeat him at the convention but which nevertheless would come into power if he won.

Election eve was tense and electric; feelings had run so high that for the first time in decades violence had flared. Willkie and his wife, sitting in the back seats of open cars, had had everything thrown at them from ripe tomatoes and bananas to stones and metal wastepaper baskets.

Roosevelt had been conceded a slight edge by the dopesters, but any last-minute break would put Wendell Willkie into the White House. The entire nation stood by its radio until midnight listening to the luminaries in both parties urge the faithful to elect their man and save the country from certain destruction.

By dinnertime the next day the Kansas City *Star*, which had been backing Willkie, acknowledged defeat. The final count was 27,243,466 votes for Roosevelt, 22,304,755 for Willkie. The electoral vote came out precisely as the earliest Gallup Poll had predicted it would just after Willkie's Elwood speech: Willkie 82 votes, Roosevelt 449. When she heard this result Mrs. Willkie cried:

"How could we lose? We tried so hard!"

Wendell Willkie received thousands of messages to keep up his work, but he took to the radio and in a heavy, tired voice instructed the faithful to disband the clubs that had been organized in his name, to give their full allegiance to their legally elected president. He had been shocked and deeply hurt by his defeat, but unlike Henry Clay he was a good loser in the best American tradition.

Wendell L. Willkie had dominated the campaign, winning every battle except the last.

6

What kind of president would Wendell Willkie have made?

At no time during the campaign was he the man he had been up to the moment of his nomination, nor any part of the man he would become in the years following his defeat. The canvas threw him, as it had thrown so many of his predecessors.

Wendell L. Willkie would have been courageous in the White House. He would have been independent, would have resisted the efforts of anyone to control him. He did not truly represent his party, yet in order to win he had strung along with the Republican party, and when he won he would have been obliged to put the political management of the country into the hands of the men who had formulated the Republican platform of isolationism.

With the Japanese attacking Pearl Harbor on December 7, 1941, and Germany and Italy declaring war on the United States a few days later, what would have been Wendell Willkie's capacity to serve his country as chief executive? As a producer of armaments he would have turned in a first-rate job; as an organizer of official Washington there is reason to believe he would have cut red tape, overlapping and bureaucracy. However, his knowledge of international affairs, his prescience for global strategy, his training in international diplomacy were considerably less than Roosevelt's. His background in these spheres was limited; he had had little experience in the past eleven years other than that of the businessman trying to keep his company afloat.

Willkie would have worked with all his considerable strength and skill to get production rolling, to end the strike of investment capital, to get idle money into industry and idle men into jobs. He had worked at business, got along well with businessmen, had stepped up production before. He would have freed business from the jurisdiction of extralegal commissions, given businessmen the confidence to go ahead on the basis that their profits would be guarded for them. Wendell Willkie would have been a businessman's president and a good one.

But try as hard as he might he would have had serious trouble making good on his promises. He was caught in a world revolution whose character of co-operative social security might have buried his concept of a production economy, made impossible his efforts to put the unemployed back to work because there was no buying power to consume the goods already produced. The Democrats claimed that Willkie's philosophy of production as the savior of the nation was a nineteenth-century conception, that only through the twentieth-century philosophy of consumption, with its co-operative imperatives, could the United States once again be swept onward with the tidal wave of contemporary forces.

The problem of Wendell Willkie is a problem of character. He was a man with a great potential for good and an equal potential for confusion and opportunism. In his heart he always wanted to do the brave and fine thing, but in time he found himself bored or at a disadvantage with the fine and the brave and rationalized himself into throwing them overboard for the immediate and advantageous. Like all opportunists he was dangerous because one could never tell whether the next opportunity which presented itself to him would be for good or evil, and it would be the opportunity that would determine his conduct rather than any rigorous set of ethical or spiritual values. No longer was he the radical gadfly of the unpressed clothes and unrepressed liberalism who had left Akron eleven years before. The Wendell L. Willkie who became president of Commonwealth and Southern in 1933 had spent the next eight years of his life without making one move for liberalism, without once raising his voice for progressivism. As Dean Landis said:

"Had Willkie been on Pennsylvania Avenue in those days

there would hardly have been a Bonneville, a TVA, and perhaps not even a National Labor Relations Board."

To this Willkie would have replied, "When I was president of Commonwealth and Southern I did everything I could find to do for my company. If I am elected president of the United States I will do everything there is to be done for my country."

To the business people and the more conservative elements in society, Wendell L. Willkie of Pine Street, New York, would have made a better president than "Wen" Willkie of Akron, Ohio. To the working people, the liberals, the independents, it seemed that Willkie of Akron would have made a better leader for the people.

Like John W. Davis, if Wendell L. Willkie had never left Akron he would not have been criticized and defeated as a Wall Street lawyer; but also like Davis, if he had never left his home town he probably never would have been nominated.

About half of the Republicans who voted for Wendell L. Willkie were glad, when war was thrust upon their country a year later, that the more experienced man in international affairs had been elected. The other half still believed that Wendell Willkie would have made the better president, even under war conditions.

His intellectual and political growth during the four years following his defeat are the most gratifying to be found among the entire history of the Also Rans, most of whom, with the exception of a Charles Evans Hughes, retired to the mixed blessings of oblivion. From the ashes of rejection he rose to become one of the country's greatest champions of liberalism, fighting for tolerance and the minority groups, wielding his considerable influence for the rights of people over the rights of property. His flight around the world brought American friendship and understanding not only to our Allies, but to remote lands, just as his valuable book, *One World,* brought a sense of international kinship to the people of the United States.

Wendell Willkie died in the midst of the 1944 campaign, died of a broken heart because he had nowhere to go, because he was a man alone. The Democratic party wanted him back, and President Roosevelt made a feeble overture, but Willkie could not bring himself to return to the party of his youth after he had fought it so intensely for eight years. The Republican party had been engulfed by Thomas E. Dewey, whose deep-freeze political economy and deep-freeze hatred of Willkie chilled the big, warmhearted fellow to his very marrow. There was no third party to which he could turn.

His tragic death shocked and grieved the people as had no death since that of his blood brother, Horace Greeley, who had died in the election of 1872. As with Greeley, all petty criticism fell away, and almost at once, instinctively, the people came to understand that a rare spirit had lived in their midst, a bright burning fire that had been extinguished, leaving the world a little colder and a little darker.

BOOK NINE

The Prosecution Rests!

I: THOMAS E. DEWEY

Why was he in such a blistering hurry? Where would he go to campaign after fifteen months in the White House?

———— ✦ ————

CHAPTER ONE

Thomas E. Dewey

OF THE FIVE Also Rans still alive, Thomas E. Dewey is the only one who has a chance to be renominated.

Only three candidates out of the twenty defeated for the presidency have been given a second chance to run: the curiosity about the new personality is gone, the novelty has worn off, the issues have changed. The electorate is fickle; it wants a new political romance with each election. Too many charges have been hurled by the opposition; the strength of the case against the candidate is known. Americans will root for the underdog at a prize fight or football game but not in a presidential race.

Dewey's grandfather was a founder of the Republican party in Wisconsin in 1854. The grandson inherited not only this fierce birth love, but his grandfather's political philosophy as well. Tom Dewey was also the youngest man to secure the Republican nomination since his grandfather helped nominate John C. Fremont in 1856. His detractors tried to laugh him off the political scene by calling him the Baby Prosecutor or the Boy Scout, and by shortening his nickname from Gangbuster to plain Buster when he ran for governor at the age of thirty-six.

But not since Henry Clay or William Jennings Bryan had a personable young man been bitten so hard by the swelling virus of presidentiasis. Like Clay and Bryan, he too would run three times to get into the White House; but also, like them, his chances are slim. Of twenty candidates defeated in their first try for the presidency, a scant three have been given a return match, and of these only one was successful: William H. Harrison in 1840.

Dewey's position in American history is secure as the most resourceful prosecutor of modern times. His fame rests not merely upon the consistent success of his prosecutions, but upon the creation of a *modus operandi* against organized racketeering which has served as a model to free other communities of their predatory gangs.

He is a champion in his own class, yet he is not content to be a lightweight; he knows that only the heavyweights can fill Yankee Stadium.

Tom Dewey's world, life and career are shipshape. He knows precisely where he is going, why and by what means. He has never yet failed to accomplish anything he set his heart on, though occasionally there have been annoying delays. Therefore he can't understand why fate should have made its champion a little fellow instead of a big one. Dewey is of average height, five feet eight, but he can bear no part of being average. His high-geared publicists never pass up an opportunity to tell the world that, in spite of his shortness, he is taller than Churchill, Stalin, yes, and Napoleon. He wears only single-breasted suits so that he will appear taller, refuses to be photographed standing when there are men about who would dwarf him, is alleged to sit on telephone books and to have had the ceiling in his Albany office lowered to increase his own stature. Jokes made by newspapermen about his height catch him on the sensitive side, as when they comment:

"Tom Dewey spent the night pacing up and down under his bed."

Like General George B. McClellan, his fellow Also Ran who was barely defeated by Abraham Lincoln during the war year of 1864, much of Tom Dewey's arbitrary and dictatorial conduct can best be understood in the psychoanalytical light of the short man who is determined to top his contemporaries.

The Also Ran he is most unlike is his immediate antecedent and alter ego, Wendell L. Willkie: Big, communicative, warmhearted, storytelling, laughter-evoking Wendell Willkie, who sat with his feet up on the desk, showing a hole in the sole of his shoe; who could electrify audiences and come close to winning a presidential election with no professional machine whatever.

When he was a child Tom Dewey's mother gave him a bicycle, but warned her only son that if he fell off even once, she would put the bike away for a year. Young Tom fell off almost immediately, and immediately the bike was stored in he Dewey cellar for a solid year. This stringent discipline taught Tom a lesson: he has never fallen off a bicycle since. He is a paragon of virtue in the tightest Sunday-school tradition, and in deadly earnest, but he could not be as dull as his press agents make him out to be: no man could be that dull and stay alive. Like his upstate New York neighbor, Alton B. Parker, who Also Ran against Theodore Roosevelt in 1904, he was known as a stuffed shirt, when actually his starched bosom was merely stuffed with virtue.

When a lady high in Republican ranks demanded, "How can you vote for a man who looks like the bridegroom on a wedding cake?" she failed to observe that Tom Dewey's right eyebrow is sometimes flurried, a hopefully human note in a face otherwise devoid of expression. It is a good face, clean-cut and healthy, and one gazes at it again and again, regretful that it is not more appealing. Smooth red cheeks, clear and penetrating brown eyes, wavy dark hair swept off a high brow, a retroussé nose and slightly indented chin, all these fine features would surely make him a handsome man were it not for the humorless and ministerial spirit which peers forth from behind his eyes.

In everything except the partisanship of politics Tom Dewey is a perfectionist. Therein lies much of his strength: he is so horrified by irregularity, waste, inefficiency or weakness that he becomes, in his deadly calm manner, a Jehovah leading a mighty crusade against evil. As a boy he insisted upon going to school with a sore throat because if he stayed away he would mar his perfect-attendance record. It would never have occurred to Tom Dewey that the real reason he should have stayed at home was so that he would not communicate his cold to his classmates.

In his four hundred pages of unrelentingly fulsome praise, published in the spring of 1940 to help Mr. Dewey secure the Republican presidential nomination, Rupert Hughes goes overboard only once in naming something about which Tom Dewey was passionate: his deep-freeze. In a sense this is symbolic: Dewey's mind is a refrigerated storage vault of facts and figures which can be taken out a week or a year later, thawed and digested. The chill emanating from his white porcelain front is greater than that of his two brother Also Rans who were reputed to be cold men: Samuel Tilden and Charles Evans Hughes.

Elected District Attorney of New York County at the age of thirty-five, with four years ahead in which to accomplish the gigantic reform task which during this campaign he had cried was so desperately needed, Tom Dewey after only nine months in office seized the first opportunity to move upward

403

on the political ladder. Defeated in the gubernatorial campaign by the incumbent Democrat, District Attorney Dewey threw his energies into the task on hand, but thirteen months later was once again out campaigning.

This time he was after the Republican nomination for the presidency. As early as December 6, 1939, he was speaking in Minneapolis against the New Deal, and attempting to seize the leadership of his party. He delivered partisan political speeches in Boston on January 23; Helena, February 10; Portland, Oregon, February 18; Lincoln, Nebraska, March 6; St. Louis, March 27; Indianapolis, April 15; Denver, April 23; Louisville, May 11. As Rupert Hughes proudly points out, in eleven days in February Tom Dewey covered seventy-five hundred miles, appeared on train platforms at forty-eight Western stations, made thirty-six impromptu speeches at stations and ten formal addresses, and shook hands with fifteen thousand voters. All this when he was drawing his salary as the District Attorney of New York County!

As a result of this intensive five months' canvass, Dewey entered the Republican convention in Philadelphia in June of 1940 as the favorite. But he was trampled underfoot by the Wendell Willkie stampede. He finished out the term of District Attorney and returned to private practice until the next political opportunity would come along, the gubernatorial election of 1942.

Since New York's citizenry had begun to suspect Mr. Dewey's job-hopping proclivities, he felt constrained to give them his solemn pledge during the campaign of 1942 that he would serve his full four years as governor. Yet in the winter of 1944, after he had been governor for only fifteen months, he set in motion, to secure himself the Republican nomination for the presidency, the most scientific political machine the country had seen since Samuel J. Tilden won a presidential majority in 1876 by sheer mathematical equations.

At the age of thirty-six Tom Dewey had been too impatient to fulfill his term and his promises as District Attorney. At the age of forty-two he was reluctant to fulfill his obligations as governor, or keep his solemn word to the people who voted for him. Thomas E. Dewey is a young man of courage, brains and high moral purpose, with one of the finest organizational talents abroad in his country.

He is also a young man in a hurry.

2

Thomas E. Dewey was born over his maternal grandfather's general store in Owosso, Michigan, on March 24, 1902, and was baptized in the Episcopal Church. His father was a six-foot West Pointer who hurt himself in an accident and had to leave the Army. Young Tom inherited his father's stiff military bearing, but he once jokingly told his mother that he could never forgive her for denying him his father's height. Tom says of his grandfather, "He thought advertising undignified, never allowed his name to appear in an advertisement." Like his father's height, this retiring nature was part of the family genes Tom did not inherit.

His father was a humble worker in the Republican vineyards. He stumped the state for the Republican candidates during the elections, worked in the auditor general's office in Lansing until 1905, after which he returned to Owosso to edit the Republican *Times,* which his father left him, and to serve as postmaster.

The Dewey family lived simply but comfortably on about eighteen hundred dollars a year. Tom says that his father had an extraordinary intellect and was a fine editor, yet the record indicates a mediocre career. Tom's brains seem to have come from his paternal grandfather who studied at Harvard, established newspapers, and helped to form the Republican party.

Being raised among editors and journalists served him in good stead. The many articles he wrote on the subjects of crime and racketeering were lucid, rigidly organized, penetrating in their analyses. Given the desire, he could have become a crusading journalist in the manner of a Lincoln Steffens.

He began selling the *Saturday Evening Post* and other magazines when he was eleven, and by the time he was thirteen he had some ten of the other boys of the village working for him, both as salesmen and as distributors of the Detroit *Daily News.* In what is set down by his biographer as the first eulogizing line about the youth, we read: "Every afternoon he met the four-fifteen train, divided a bundle among his employees, and sent them scurrying through the town hurling papers at front doorsteps." It is still possible to find forty-year-olds in Owosso who gripe about having gotten the short end of the deal from young Tom and who are hard pressed to figure out just how they became his employees.

Tom was a model student, industrious, in robust health. The more important part of his education was secured, as was that of his fellow Also Ran of 1868, Horatio Seymour, in the home of his parents, where all the Republican officials and enthusiasts stopped to discuss the issues of the day. These discussions were intelligent and hard-bitten, and they created a mold for most of Tom Dewey's subsequent political arguments.

In the summer of his sixteenth year, during World War I, he worked on a farm. The life was a little too much for his strength, but he did his job well and uncomplainingly. The post cards he wrote home to "Dear Folks" are full of a warm, boyish humor—the first and the last time that we can find him utilizing humor in the description of his lot. When he graduated from high school the yearbook versified under his picture:

> First in the Council Hall to steer the State
> And ever foremost in a tongue debate.

The truth of this doggerel was not to be fully perceived until he encountered such characters as Lucky Luciano, Waxey Gordon, Dixie Davis, Gurrah, Jimmy Hines. The only men who licked him in a debate were Governor Herbert Lehman of New York and Franklin D. Roosevelt.

During his high-school years he had sung in the church choir and minstrel shows; his major activity at the University of Michigan was as a member of the glee club, a soloist in the Ann Arbor Methodist Church, and in the college plays. He studied voice with the head of the music department and ended by winning the Michigan State Singing Contest. He also worked on the Michigan *Daily*. His singing helped him earn part of his way through college; his parents made up the balance.

After graduation from Michigan he went to the Chicago Musical College on a scholarship and worked in a cousin's law office. Wanting to follow in his grandfather's footsteps, he sent the Harvard Law School his Michigan grades, but Harvard turned him down. When his teacher at the Chicago Musical College went to New York, Tom Dewey decided to follow him and continue his vocal training while studying law at Columbia. It was this chance scholarship with Percy R. Stevens which brought Tom Dewey what has probably been his single greatest stroke of fortune: for here he met Frances Hutt, of an old southern family, who was paying for her tuition by working as Stevens' secretary. Frances Hutt was a lovely girl with a great deal of warmth and kindliness. She has given Tom Dewey a happy married life and two robust sons. There are some who feel that, if they must have a Dewey as president, they would prefer Frances Dewey.

While he was attending Columbia, Tom Dewey earned part of his expenses by singing at St. Matthew's and in a synagogue whose location he now claims to have forgotten. He was a routine student at law school, but he did a good job of editing the Legal Honor Society's magazine. He doubtless would have been a better student if he could have made up his mind whether he was to become a lawyer or a baritone at the Metropolitan Opera House. The fact that at the age of twenty-two Tom Dewey still had an idea that he might become an opera singer is the one inconsistent trait in an otherwise rigidly bourgeois character. His final abandonment of the musical career was determined by the logicalities of his nature: he developed a sore throat just before he was to participate in a concert, and this frightened him, for he realized that his vocal cords and not Tom Dewey would be the master of his fate.

Upon graduating from Columbia Law School he served his apprenticeship in various New York law offices, slowly increasing his income until by 1929 he was earning eight thousand dollars a year. He was practicing commercial law in his careful and thorough fashion, and there was every reason to believe that he would continue in this pleasant groove, working himself upward until he had a fifty-thousand-dollar-a-year income, a membership in several good New York clubs and a home at Great Neck.

However, there was one activity which indicated the potential of his future: he was serving in the humblest political position of the Tenth Assembly District, ringing doorbells and getting out the vote. By December of 1930 the heavy oaken door which leads to the political arena was swung open; if it had not been this particular opportunity, it would have been another, for the twenty-eight-year-old Dewey was surcharged with energy and ambition.

The incident which thrust him into the limelight was a meeting with a former assistant attorney general and district attorney of New York, George Z. Medalie. During a complicated lawsuit against his client, the Empire Trust Company, Dewey suggested that his firm call in Medalie to try the case in court. Young Dewey and the older Medalie stimulated each other, for both minds were fast and possessed of a high type of legal integrity.

When a short time later Medalie was appointed United States Attorney for the Southern District of New York, he offered Tom Dewey the post of Chief Assistant United States Attorney. Dewey accepted with alacrity, organized his office with sixty attorneys under him, and was off on his meteoric career.

He was almost too young to undertake such a responsible task, yet he handled it with the fullest administrative skill. As federal prosecuting attorney of Manhattan and all the land north to Albany, his job was one of the most difficult in the legal field. Here he developed his scientifically mathematical methods of bringing all types of offenders into court under such a mountainous load of evidence that almost no one could escape: the unromantic bookkeeper became virtually the chief of detectives, with account books and deposit slips replacing such more obvious forms of evidence as guns and bloodstains. George Medalie said of his young assistant:

"I dropped him in the cold water and let him swim out. He made a darned good job of it—so good a job that I relieved him of some of the administrative work and turned him loose on the racketeering field."

One of the more important aspects of Dewey's organizational talent was that he found top-notch assistants in every phase of scientific investigation, all the way from certified public accountants with a native gift for snaring mathematical discrepancies down to honest cops who knew the inside of New York rackets as no prosecutor could from the outside. He gave these men their head, he gave them his full confidence, and he was liberal in publicly praising their work.

The federal courts had rarely seen such speed and efficiency in the presentation of the government's case, nor anywhere near such a high record of convictions. Dewey and his staff never went into court until the case was airtight in their investigating files. If they were not positive of a conviction they stayed out of court and dug deeper into bank statements, account books, safe-deposit vaults, ledgers, vouchers, deposit slips, triple-entry fandangles.

His methods were a logical development of those which had been innovated by his temperamental counterpart among the Also Rans, icy-crag Charles Evans Hughes, who had utilized the implacabilities of mathematics to expose the corruption in the New York Gas Company and the New York Life Insurance Company some twenty-five years before. As a reward for his accomplishments Charles Evans Hughes had gone on to become Governor of New York State in 1906 and Republican candidate for the Presidency in 1916. Tom Dewey was certain that if history does not repeat itself, it does indulge in identical political patterns.

When George Medalie resigned, Tom Dewey was appointed to the post of United States Attorney. As United States Attorney he did his best work in the conviction of Waxey Gordon, the New York version of Al Capone, who had an income of approximately a million dollars a year from every type of organized depredation. Banks protected Gordon because of the gigantic size of his deposits, the police protected him and released his henchmen when they were arrested by Dewey's staff, witnesses went to jail for contempt rather than risk their lives by testifying against him. In the preparation of their case, Dewey's staff worked on Gordon's records for three years, checked one hundred thousand telephone calls to weave an unbreakable web around him and the men with whom he was doing business, developing to its highest pitch the "bulletproof witness—the impeachable, silent betrayer that racketeers cannot reach, cannot intimidate, cannot buy, cannot kill—the hidden bank account."

The spectacular conviction of Waxey Gordon and his ring took place in the incredible time of fifty-one minutes, after succeeding regimes of federal attorneys and New York district attorneys had refused to tangle with Gordon or had been bought off. This was important not only because it broke up this vulturous ring and sent its leaders to jail, but because it demonstrated both to the civilian world which was being preyed upon and to the gang world doing the preying that here was a man, and here was a method, which could eventually land all gangsters in prison.

3

Late in 1933, after two years as federal prosecutor, Tom Dewey was replaced by a Democrat. He returned to private practice with offices at 120 Broadway. There were clients and business immediately on hand. He gave about half of his time without charge to the Bar Association for the investigation and conviction of Judge Kunstler, who had been using his bench to amass a private fortune, and after the conviction wrote a first-rate report for the Association recommending a new procedure for the removal of crooked judges.

His income as Federal United States Attorney had been a modest one; now, through private practice, he was able to acquire some of the niceties of life: a spacious apartment in Manhattan for himself, his wife and his son, a summer home in Tuxedo Park, a small sailboat. His reputation in New York could have made him one of the most successful of the private legal practitioners, but his years of power and acclaim had washed out the less dramatic joys of money-making.

Then New York's investigating Grand Jury revolted against District Attorney William C. Dodge's apathy in his prosecution of organized crime, crying, "Every conceivable obstacle has been put in our path." The jury demanded that a special prosecutor be appointed. Governor Lehman, wanting to keep the appointment on a nonpartisan basis, submitted a list of such prominent Republicans as Charles Evans Hughes and George Z. Medalie; these men refused the offer and nominated Tom Dewey in their place.

Thomas E. Dewey was now a young man on his own; he

liked new brooms, new methods, new procedures, and above all he wanted no part of Tammany, the Democratic party, its equipment or personnel. He therefore turned a cold back on District Attorney Dodge and set up offices for himself on the fourteenth floor of the Woolworth Building, where he installed his staff and supervised the equipment so there could be no leaks in information. Then he issued a ringing statement to hearten the racketeer-dominated public: "Your businesses, your safety, and your daily lives are affected by criminal conditions in this city. There is today scarcely a business in New York which does not somehow pay its tribute to the underworld—a tribute levied by force and collected by fear. . . . In my opinion you can be freed from organized racketeering in this city. Those of you who have knowledge of criminal conditions owe it to yourselves and the people of this city to give this investigation your co-operation."

Dewey's work as special prosecutor in the district attorney's office broke sharply into two divisions. The first dealt with such criminal rings as those controlling organized prostitution and the numbers racket; the more important portion revolved around the rackets that had barnacled themselves to industries and were bleeding them white.

Dewey's approach to the organized prostitution ring was illustrative of his method in handling the many hundreds of big-time criminal cases. There had always been prostitution in New York, and except for random raids or street arrests it had been tolerated. Nor, as Tom Dewey agreed, would he have devoted the resources of the district attorney's office to this problem so long as it had remained in the free-enterprise category. However, one of gangland's overlords, Lucky Luciano, who had criminal rings operating in nearly every phase of the American underworld, decided that this was too lucrative a profession to remain in its unorganized state. He sent out his thugs to take over every house in New York City, and the pimps, runners, providers, madams and circuit bookers as well. By the time Dewey began his investigations Lucky Luciano controlled every prostitute in New York, each of whom paid him a substantial cut of her earnings and was moved about from house to house and county to county at his command.

It took a great many months to assemble full proof of this "compulsory prostitution" by means of which the men who bossed the racket could be convicted. With Tom Dewey's plans so highly perfected that no leak was possible, gigantic raids were staged, first on the gorillas who ran the racket and next upon the hundreds of prostitutes and madams operating the houses, all of whom were taken up in freight elevators to the fourteenth floor of the Woolworth Building, where the girls were made comfortable and then asked for information against the racketeers. The women refused to talk, knowing that they would be murdered if they did so. When they learned that every last one of their procurers also had been captured, that Lucky Luciano himself was in process of being arrested, and that the district attorney's office had both the will and the means to protect them, the women finally gave forth the wealth of evidence which crushed the ring and sent Luciano and his lieutenants to prison.

Dewey next utilized his talents to cleanse the business world of its leeches. Restaurant owners who did not pay tribute to the racketeers found stench bombs of butyric acid set off in their restaurants. Trucking concerns who refused to join the protective associations found that emery powder had been put into the crankcases of their trucks and the motors made useless. If cleaning and dyeing establishments refused to join, hoodlums broke into the store and slashed the hundreds of hanging garments to ribbons. If chicken dealers refused to buy, their coops were burned down. Those who protested were slugged or shot.

Tom Dewey broke these rackets, broke them by his courage, tenacity, and daring use of new techniques. He freed labor unions from the racketeers that were milking them dry; in conviction after conviction he sent up the bosses and henchmen whose protective societies had been terrorizing nearly every industry in the city. By exposure, by publicity, by giving courage to the oppressed businessman, and by obtaining almost unfailing convictions, Tom Dewey eliminated industrial racketeering from New York.

By this time he was a hero in his own country. Stories, novels, plays and motion pictures were spun about his work. It was almost impossible to pick up a newspaper or magazine without seeing his picture and the story of a new accomplishment. Every class and group in America admired him and gave him full credit for the job he was doing.

There were criticisms, of course, from the men he was pursuing, from his political opponents, from individuals who said he was not as fastidious of the civil liberties of those he was arresting as he might have been. He was accused of holding suspects incommunicado, of setting prohibitive bail, of whisking witnesses away to hiding spots where no one could find them, of jailing people on false Grand Jury subpoenas. He was accused of paying fabulous sums to prostitutes and madams to testify against Luciano and his henchmen because he needed the testimony; of wire tapping, spying, offering favors, trips to Europe, legal freedom to people who would buttress his cases in court. He was accused of caring more for convictions than justice, of being determined to maintain a one-hundred-per-cent batting average of convictions regardless of the ethics of criminal procedure, of choosing those cases which would do his career the most good. He was also charged with being not so assiduous in his prosecutions of wealthy men and their henchmen, such as Wall Street's Charles E. Mitchell, as he was of the maldoers in the poorer classes.

Aside from the accurate but not particularly nefarious charge that Thomas E. Dewey always kept his eye on his political career, very little of this holds up under rigid inspection: some few shady women seem to have profited by pulling his leg; wire tapping on characters like Luciano, Gurrah, Dixie Davis was almost unavoidable; and if Dewey sometimes went to great lengths to keep his witnesses where they could not be reached, this was necessary if they were not to be unceremoniously bumped off. Considering the complexities of the task he had undertaken, Tom Dewey turned in an entirely praiseworthy record. As a fitting reward he became the first Republican to defeat Tammany Hall's candidate for district attorney in twenty-one years, going into office with a triumphant majority.

New York's underworld had spent millions of dollars in its attempt to defeat him at the polls. The following year these same racketeers would spend even more millions to kick him upstairs to Albany.

4

As district attorney there was little change in his work. He secured the conviction of Dixie Davis, gangland's smartest mouthpiece, and arrested James J. Hines, the politician who was largely responsible for abasing the police force and the courts to the machinations of the underworld. When, after his staff had gathered the Hines evidence for countless months, the first Hines trial was declared a mistrial, Dewey showed his unbreakable spirit by saying to his group:

"Don't worry, boys, there will be another chance and we will win it."

His first attempt to become governor also got him thrown out of court; again he said, "Don't worry, boys, there will be another chance and we will win it." He was to make good on both promises.

At the end of September, nine months after he had been sworn in as district attorney, the Republicans held their State Convention in Saratoga. Dewey's steering committee, headed by Kenneth Simpson, had been working for months to secure him the nomination. When his name was put into nomination the Republican New York *Sun* reported that, "The Convention broke into one of the wildest demonstrations ever witnessed. The Republicans hadn't known any hour like this for twenty years. They had a new deal in politics; and they had a new leader."

Tom Dewey took the first train north. In his acceptance speech to the convention he gave a picture of what he conceived to be the function of a governmental executive. "Crime is wider than one county. A single district attorney is like a deep-sea diver fighting an octopus, one arm at a time. Crime is the product of social pressure and political cynicism. There are economic, social and political crimes as well as legal crimes."

He was going to become the *prosecuting governor* of New York State.

The Democratic incumbent, Herbert H. Lehman, was tired and ill; he had no desire to serve a third term. But there was no Democrat to replace him in electoral favor. If he did not run, Tom Dewey was certain to be elected. Every bigwig in the Democratic party from Franklin D. Roosevelt down urged Governor Lehman to run again, and reluctantly he consented.

The campaign was a heated one, with Dewey doing a superb job of exposing the corrupt Democratic machines in Albany, Buffalo and New York City, and Governor Lehman standing on his record as a progressive. In this, his first major political contest, Dewey encountered the impasse which was to become the road block in his 1944 drive for the presidency. He prosecuted Governor Lehman and the Democrats for their failure to operate more efficiently and on a wider scale those social reforms which the Democrats themselves had instituted, starting with Dewey's Also Ran companion, Alfred E. Smith. These reforms had been fought bitterly by the Republican legislature until the weight of public opinion silenced it: workmen's compensation, factory laws, slum clearance, unemployment insurance.

Tom Dewey, like his grandfather before him, shared the basic Republican belief that all planning should be done by private enterprise; that paternalism in government not only destroyed initiative and weakened the character of the people but would inevitably lead to a regimented state. What he said, in effect, was:

"We Republicans deplore this kind of legislation and governmental function, but since the people think they must

413

have it, we can do it on a wider scale, more perfectly, and with less waste."

Thomas E. Dewey's vigor, his honesty, his outstanding record as a prosecuting attorney, his fastidious appearance and melodious voice came within an inch of defeating Herbert Lehman. He frequently ran ahead, and the result was not decided until the very last moment, when New York City brought in its traditional Democratic majority. Because he had lost this contest for the second most important executive post in the United States by the astonishingly slim margin of sixty-four thousand votes, Dewey's defeat catapulted him to the uppermost rank of nationally important Republicans.

He once again returned to the district attorney's office, where his record for the next three years included the conviction of James J. Hines, the cleaning up of the ambulance chasers, the ring of loan sharks, and the indictment of Fritz Kuhn. His achievement of almost eighty per cent of court convictions led the *Harvard Law Review* to say in November 1939, under the title of "Streamlining the Indictment": "The recent revision and simplification by the District Attorney's office in New York County promises to be a significant step toward a more rational criminal procedure."

High praise indeed from a law college which had rejected him only twenty years before.

A year after he was defeated for governor, Tom Dewey was out campaigning again, this time for the Republican nomination for the presidency. He stumped every section of the country and published a book called *The Case against the New Deal*. His speeches and his book constitute a fiery denunciation of every thought and deed of the New Deal; every last Democrat is prosecuted in much the same tone and manner as Lucky Luciano, Dixie Davis, Lepke, Judges Kunstler and Manton. In this series of speeches is revealed Dewey's political philosophy:

The worst Republican is better in office than the best Democrat because the philosophy of the worst Republican is so natively good for the country that nothing he may do in the way of neglect or malfeasance of office can be as bad as the corroding influence of even an honest and well-meaning Democrat. The Republican party is the legal and hereditary party designed to govern the country, while the Democratic party is a combination of upstarts with neither legal rights nor legitimate claims. The country will always be governed by Republicans except in those rare periods when the electorate goes berserk.

As for the New Deal, it had created the depression of 1933–40 by its hostility to business; by its defeatist attitude toward business's ability to keep America prosperous, it had alienated the lifeblood of the country: investment capital. Industrial energy had been stifled by rising taxes, and investment capital discouraged from pouring into new plants; nor would industry improve its run-down machinery under Roosevelt. Government had gotten out of the hands of industry, the only group which could effectively run the country for the good of the whole.

One scans Thomas E. Dewey's manifest mind with the most high-powered lens and never finds the slightest intimation that he believes *the people* made America great, strong, prosperous; to Tom Dewey the people is neither Abraham Lincoln's great god nor Alexander Hamilton's great beast, but simply an inchoate mass, nonexistent except as so many pairs of hands and eyes to operate the omnipotent machinery of business. He was interested in the production rate of a coal mine, not in the miners who dug that coal; he was more concerned about the financial structure of a steel corporation than the structure of the men who worked before the blazing furnaces. Nowhere in this well-written and rigidly postulated panegyric of business does the observer stumble across the concepts of art or culture: the business machine has become an end in itself rather than an implement in the hands of mankind.

But his indictment of the ever-growing bureaucracy, overlapping, and waste in the operation of the New Deal was the best documented that had yet been presented to the public.

The first Gallup Poll taken in June of 1940 showed Tom Dewey leading with 67 per cent of the votes; Senator Vandenberg, 14 per cent; Senator Taft, 12 per cent; Wendell Willkie, 3 per cent. The first ballot at the Republican convention in Philadelphia in June of 1940 read: Dewey, 360 votes; Taft, 189; Willkie, 105. Dewey led on the first three ballots, but even during this time the convention hall was being rocked by cries of, "We want Willkie!", and Wendell L. Willkie was swept in on the sixth ballot. At this moment Tom Dewey made one of his few political jokes:

"I led on three ballots, but they were the wrong three."

He went out on the road to campaign for Willkie, speaking in White Plains, Pittsburgh, Peoria, Cleveland. His speeches were divided between attacks on the New Deal economy and the Democratic party's foreign policy: ". . . we know we cannot possibly remain strong and free unless we reject every entanglement in the affairs of Europe." He opposed Lend-Lease, praised Senator C. Wayland Brooks, the Chicago *Tribune's* bitter-end isolationist, spoke highly of Hiram Johnson, who had wrecked American participation in the first League

415

of Nations, and excommunicated Cabinet members Frank Knox and Henry L. Stimson from the Republican party on the grounds that they had always been interventionists.

Tom Dewey so embarrassed international-minded Wendell Willkie that Candidate Willkie had to ask him to subside because he was alienating the non-isolationist Republican vote. Willkie's campaign managers also complained that Mr. Dewey was not campaigning for their candidate's election in 1940, but for his own election in 1944: this caused a feud which would not end until four years later with Wendell Willkie's death and Thomas E. Dewey's defeat.

At the end of his four-year term as district attorney, Tom Dewey refused to run for re-election. He threw himself instead into the task of again securing the Republican nomination for the governorship. He was nominated at Saratoga in August 1942, at which time he told the convention, "You and I are not concerned here with 1944. This convention and the Republican campaign are concerned only with the winning of the war and with good government for the people of the state of New York for the next four years."

Confidence, which was running strong on the Republican tide, was heightened by the split in the Democratic party occasioned by James A. Farley's insistence that John J. Bennett be the Democratic nominee, when New Dealers and the labor vote wanted a more liberal candidate. America was now at war, and Mr. Dewey abandoned his isolationism; he was also beginning to approve the validity of certain kinds of social legislation. Such an important liberal as Dr. Alvin Johnson, director of the left-wing New School for Social Research, came out for Dewey in the New York *Times* by declaring that, "Dewey is a progressive who looks boldly to the future."

The 1942 campaign was as lethargic as the 1938 campaign had been dynamic. People were interested in waging the war. The independent voter said, "Dewey has been working so hard for the job and he wants it so bad, let's give him a chance to show what he can do." Campaign manager Herbert Brownell, Jr., predicted that his candidate would win by six hundred thousand votes. Tom Dewey did even better than that.

At the convention in Saratoga, Dewey had declared, "For my part let me say right now that I shall devote the next four years exclusively to the service of the people of the state of New York."

Astute political observers predicted, "If Dewey keeps that promise he will be elected to the presidency in 1948 on as great a tidal wave as swept Roosevelt into the White House in 1932."

Though the Republican party was hungering for patronage after its twenty years of starvation, Dewey had stated that he would be nonpartisan in his appointments, and he half fulfilled this promise: though he would appoint no Democrat, he did give positions to good men who had no party affiliation whatever—thus robbing a deserving Republican of a much-needed job. As prosecuting attorney he had disdained to draw racial or religious lines, utilizing the fine brains he could find in every religion and race. He continued this healthy attitude in Albany. Within a few months he built around him a crew of assistants, mostly his own age, who were competent in such fields as banking, finance, taxation. They were largely Wall Street men and their affiliates, well trained, agreeing entirely with Governor Dewey's political credo that business, and in particular big business, was the only force in America which could provide millions of jobs, prosperity, and happiness.

He was hard-working and conscientious. In the hottest weather he was always cool and flawlessly groomed, causing some of his perspiring assistants to observe that Governor Dewey carried his own self-generating refrigeration plant.

He was a strong governor in that portion of his work in which he had always been strong, as a prosecutor of crimes, as a corrector of legal evils. He investigated and cleaned up Creedmore and other mental hospitals which had fallen into serious neglect; his staff gathered evidence on the workmen's-compensation conspiracy between grafting politicians and unethical doctors; he cleaned up the state police, which was indulging in minor graft; and he exposed the machinations of the O'Connell machine in Albany.

On the positive or creative side of the ledger there was a less dramatic story to tell, despite the fact that he had a Republican legislature to work with, and hence every opportunity to put into effect whatever policies he thought desirable. He established a new State Department of Commerce, whose function it was to help manufacturers who wanted to operate in New York and to make things easier for industry. He set up a postwar reconstruction fund which was to safeguard the state surpluses against a potential depression, and alongside of it created a postwar planning commission to draw blueprints for proposed state hospitals and highways; the tax department simplified the tax forms and slightly decreased state taxes.

His opponents charged him with being the least possible

governor in the best possible manner. This was a partisan charge: the charge that is better grounded in demonstrable fact is that Tom Dewey set out to be big business's governor as the most direct way of being a good governor. For some thirty years the progressive trend in New York had been for the state government to use its offices to protect its people: minimum-wage laws, protection of women and children in industry, unemployment insurance, and the whole broad sweep of social security. Governor Dewey reversed this movement; social legislation stopped dead and, as the New York *Times* observed, "The entire trend was toward relaxation of the rules in favor of business enterprise."

Governor Dewey secured the passage of the Chamber of Commerce's Coudert-Mitchell Bill, which prevented minority stockholders from suing corporations in which they held stock, no matter what evidence they might have of manipulation. He opposed in the legislature a bill which would have controlled the private insurance companies, where many of the workmen's-compensation scandals had arisen, by giving the Superintendent of Insurance the right to revoke the license of any company engaging in fraud. He refused the small farmers' request for an investigation into the middleman's hogging of milk receipts because such an investigation might embarrass the gigantic Dairymen's League.

The governor's action in relation to workmen's compensation was not prompted by a disinterest in the honest functioning of the fund; it was motivated by his frank conviction that since insurance is big business, it should not be rigidly regulated or its freedom of action hampered. Nor was there anything insincere in his refusal to investigate the Dairymen's League; he believed that any embarrassment of big business would only result in stoppage of production, unemployment, depression, poverty for the people. Ergo, the best way to protect the people was to leave big business strictly alone. This philosophy he applied as well to the Coudert-Mitchell Bill.

Dewey's publicists claim for him the accomplishment of having balanced the state budget, with saving one hundred and sixty-three million dollars of state surplus. It was an effort to gild the lily: Dewey inherited eighty million dollars of surplus from Governor Lehman, credit for which he took by pushing back the state's fiscal year from July to April. The *New Republic's* special Dewey issue also points out that he came into the governorship at a time when war industries had sopped up unemployment and there were no relief millions to be spent, when wartime inflation had increased the state's income by many millions. While these observations were sound, they miss the essential fact that Tom Dewey would have balanced the budget even in the worst depression, just as his political blood brother, Herbert Hoover, had tried to do in Washington in 1930. His attitude toward human need versus the low-balanced budget was indicated by his cutting of school funds on the grounds that the war had caused total attendance to fall off—ignoring the fact that classrooms were overcrowded, that in war years the educational system had a greater responsibility than ever to the youth of the community.

His first year as governor highlighted several salient facts: Tom Dewey's organizational powers were sufficiently strong for him to hold the reins of state government securely in his hands. Little or no corruption, lassitude or inefficiency would be tolerated in the state bureaus or services; none of the taxpayers' money would be wasted; business and industry over all the land would be wooed by bright and secure promises to move to New York. No extension of the common man's economic heritage could be expected.

Most surprising of all, the governor who had been elected in a landslide, who was doing a good job within the narrow confines which his political heritage had set for him, and who had a Republican legislature to work with, was becoming the most personally disliked governor Albany had known.

The one sour note in the triumphant 1942 election had been uttered by Mrs. Kenneth Simpson, wife of the former Republican state chairman. She observed, "Dewey and his political advisers have succeeded in turning the Republican party in New York State into the most rigid and disciplinary machine the state of New York has seen since the days of Tom Platt."

It was soon an open scandal in Albany and New York City that Tom Dewey ran a merciless machine, was tyrannical in his methods, and was using his legislature as a rubber stamp. What he said was law, and the legislators would immediately make it so; legislation would originate in the governor's mansion and not in the halls of the legislature; his contact with the legislature would be devoted exclusively to his whips. His 1944 campaign biographer had to deal in double negatives when he wrote, "To say that he 'steam-rollered' the legislature, or 'had them under his thumb,' or 'bossed' them, seems, however, to be an unjustified straining of terms."

His legislature found him cold, hard, dictatorial, unsympathetic and unfriendly; they didn't like him as a person. The state government in Albany developed into a deep-freeze. One of New York's favorite jokes had been, "You really have to know Tom Dewey well in order to dislike him." This allegation was now hotly denied.

Tom Dewey had long enjoyed bad relations with the press. Newspapermen disliked him cordially, found him overbearing, opportunistic in making them work for his purposes, but always leaving them out on the limb for the material they published. They objected to the fact that Mr. Dewey looked down his nose at them, that a winter overcoat and heavy rubbers were needed at his press conferences.

In an attempt to set himself right with the press, Governor Dewey appointed James J. Haggerty, a former political writer of the New York *Times*, as his liaison officer. Haggerty served the boys food and drink and was himself well liked; frequently he would exclaim to reporters, "You will find the Governor changed!" but even with so conciliatory a contact man, the state's political reporters continued to dislike their governor.

Why should Tom Dewey have been so disliked? Why should part of Frances Hutt Dewey's job have been to kid her husband out of his grimness? He was happy with his wife and two fine sons; he had bought Dapplemere, a three-hundred-acre farm near the village of Pawling in Dutchess County. Here he had a beautiful home, enjoyed the animals and crops which were raised on his farm, played golf with his neighbors in the swank Quaker Hill Country Club. Though he was still paying off the mortgage on his thirty-thousand-dollar farm, certainly his future was secure, he had every reason to be cheerful, pleasant, warm natured, even lovable.

The answer lay in the irremediable nature of Thomas E. Dewey. He did not like people.

6

Very early in 1944 it became evident that the contest over the Republican presidential nomination would be between Thomas E. Dewey and Wendell L. Willkie. The future looked bright for the next Republican candidate: there were now twenty-six Republican governors, many of them elected in the Republican landslide of 1942, and these twenty-six governors ruled over a heavy majority of the American people.

Mr. Willkie had grown considerably in stature since his 1940 defeat: he had flown the world, made friends with the leaders of every nation, and had written a fine book, *One World*, which had conveyed the necessity of internationalism to previously unawakened Americans. He was also the titular head of the Republican party, with millions of devoted followers. Wendell Willkie believed Tom Dewey to be an isolationist and a tory in political economy; Willkie believed that

Tom Dewey represented the insular standpat Republicanism of Herbert Hoover, Robert Taft, John Hamilton, Colonel McCormick, Frank Gannett. Without any semblance of a machine Willkie took his one-man campaign to the public, trying to convince the Republican voters that their party could never and would never supplant the Democrats in Washington until they became a genuinely liberal and internationalist party. He took his fight to the Wisconsin primary, knowing Wisconsin as the home of the progressive movement in America. What he did not know was that the progressives were dead in Wisconsin—and he was roundly defeated.

This left Tom Dewey undisputed master in the field; but he was taking no chances. He set up his committee at the Hotel Roosevelt in New York: Herbert Brownell, tall, thin, emotionless corporation lawyer; J. Russel Sprague, National Committeeman, and Edwin F. Jaeckle, New York Republican Chairman. To this caucus room was summoned every Republican politician in America. In public Governor Dewey maintained silence on his political aspirations.

The Republican convention in Chicago, which opened on June 26, 1944, was one of the coldest, dullest and most colorless in American political history. There were no bands, no banners, no flowery speeches, no wild enthusiasms. Old-line delegates who had been going to conventions for years found themselves in a sea of strange faces. One of them groused, "If you've been a Republican for more than five years you're unwanted here."

The delegates' frustration was compounded of two elements: they were being used as robots to approve Tom Dewey, who had been sold to them as the only Republican with a chance to win; and they didn't believe the Republicans could win anyway. They were told that they had to nominate Dewey because the Gallup Poll had given him sixty-eight per cent of the support of the Republican voters.

The quartet of Dewey, Brownell, Sprague and Jaeckle also decided that they would give the vice-presidential nomination to the handsome and increasingly popular governor of California, Earl Warren, because he could bring in the Pacific Coast vote. They bestowed their accolade as a benign gift from above, and failed to ask Governor Warren if he were willing to run, failed to ask for his opinions in the framing of his party's platform. Nor did the Dewey committee bother to look up Governor Warren when it reached Chicago, to inform him of their decision.

The Republican platform was framed under the guidance of Dewey's board of strategy and Senator Robert A. Taft of Ohio, of whom Columnist Walter Lippmann said in the Republican *Herald-Tribune:* "He is probably more responsible than any other single man for leading the Republican party into blind alleys of dumb obstruction on the vital issues of our time." Tom Dewey decreed that Wendell Willkie, titular head of the Republican party, who had amassed twenty-two million votes in 1940 and still controlled some four million liberal Republican votes, was not only not to be consulted on what he thought should go into the platform, but was not to be allowed to speak at the convention. Dewey was afraid that Willkie would stampede the convention; it was also his revenge for the 1940 campaign slight.

The Dewey calculations were arrived at with mathematical precision; no one expected the slightest difficulty. The first blow fell when California's Earl Warren refused the nomination for the vice-presidency. Like New York's legislators, Warren could only have considered Tom Dewey's conduct highhanded and officious, realized how shabbily he would be relegated to the background as vice-president. To the public Warren gave as his reason for rejecting the vice-presidency the fact that he had faithfully promised the people of his state to serve his full four-year term. This was a roundhouse swing at Tom Dewey's jaw, for he pointed up for the voters the fact that he felt obliged to keep the identical promise Tom Dewey had blithely thrown overboard.

The second blow fell when the Republicans published their platform, and the conscientious portion of the press rose in a body to protest its vacillation, contradictions and refusal to face the international situation. The platform came out for high tariffs and for international free trade; for an international peace organization, but not a world state in which the nations intended forcibly to suppress aggression.

Thomas E. Dewey was nominated on the first ballot at the Chicago convention, nominated with less ostensible enthusiasm than any Republican candidate since Garfield. The delegates had agreed to vote for this man, and vote for him they did; but their electoral tongues were hanging out for tall, broad, genial John W. Bricker. The Republican nomination of Thomas E. Dewey was a marriage of convenience; no love was involved. John W. Bricker was given the consolation prize.

There had never been any question but that the Democrats would nominate Franklin D. Roosevelt for a fourth term. The rank and file of New Deal Democrats wanted Henry A. Wallace renominated as vice-president; Southern Democrats were against him because of his humanitarian views and his fight against the poll tax. The Democratic Chairman, Robert Hannegan, was the reverse of the shield of Herbert Brownell, and had equally as little to recommend him: a high-powered press agent who fought his greatest battles at the Stork Club, Hannegan conspired to have Wallace jettisoned in favor of the more conservative Senator Harry Truman, who had done a penetrating job of investigating war contracts and production. The liberal Democrats were as heartsick at having Truman replace Wallace as the liberal Republicans had been at Dewey's defeat of Willkie.

Tom Dewey had followed his long-established policy of conducting private polls to ascertain whether or not he could win the election in 1944. His informants told him that the country was tired after twelve years of Democratic control; that the idea of a fourth term for any candidate was repugnant; that Roosevelt and his administration had amassed millions of enemies on every possible front; that everyone was fatigued and entangled by the amounts of red tape emerging daily from Washington; that the people everywhere were saying it was time for a fresh administration; that they were frightened by this new kind of government by executive decree, which had robbed the Congress of its ruling powers; that the European war would be over by November of 1944, and the voters, turning away from war and the international scene, would want the governmental spending and regulation of the Democratic regimes sponged clean by the man who had accomplished a gang-busting task as District Attorney of New York County.

Thomas E. Dewey elected to run. He would move into the White House as the *prosecuting president* of the United States.

At long last he was in the ring against the man with the lovable smile, the hearty laugh and infectious humor, the man who had defeated three successive Republican candidates, who was one of the best-known figures in the world, with twelve years of penetrating thinking and irreplaceable experience on the international scene: the heavyweight champ.

7

There were striking parallels between the Thomas E. Dewey campaign and that of his two predecessors, Alfred M. Landon and Wendell L. Willkie. All three started their campaigns in a quiet and dignified manner, became very mad at about the middle of the contest at a Roosevelt stratagem, and began throwing haymakers. All three condemned the New Deal and then promised to retain it on a more efficient and economical basis. All three accused Roosevelt of violating the

Constitution, of changing the American form of government, of piling up crippling deficits, of continuing the depression, of obstructing industry, paralyzing initiative, of being defeatist about the future of the country, of leading America toward a totalitarian state.

The Republican speeches from the 1936, 1940 and 1944 campaigns could be stirred in a barrel and a reader would have difficulty telling them apart.

The election cycles were also similar: all three candidates left the nominating halls under heavy disadvantages; all three started cold and poorly and went deeper into the trough; all three finally hit their stride, gave the Democrats "October jitters" and forced them to get out and campaign. All three candidates believed just a week before election that they would win; all three were shocked at having been defeated.

Into the campaign of 1944, however, there were several new ingredients injected. The major difference was on the international scene: the candidate elected in 1944 would have to undertake the stupendous task of leading the world to a permanent peace organization with sufficient force at its command to outlaw war. Everyone agreed that with the swift advance in the destructive powers of armaments the human race was not likely to survive a World War III. The United States, along with Russia and Great Britain, would play the leading role in the success or failure of establishing an effective peace league. Therefore upon the shoulders of the man elected would rest the responsibility for the continuation or the destruction of the world!

The war was being waged successfully by the incumbent, and it was part of the American psychology not to change horses in midstream. Dewey was completely unknown in Europe, Asia and South America, all of which, except Germany, Japan and possibly Argentina, were hoping ardently for Mr. Roosevelt's re-election. Dewey's experience as a government executive was limited to fifteen months.

Major sections of the people were apathetic about the election because of their absorption in the war; others were disinterested because they believed Tom Dewey had so little chance of winning that it was a throw-away election. In the first week after the Republican convention there was hardly a Dewey vote to be found on the Westchester commuters' train, which had been solidly Republican within the memory of man. In restaurants, in theater lobbies, at social gatherings one heard the same comment:

"I've been a Republican all my life, but I just can't vote for Dewey."

An issue arose over the Armed Forces ballot. During the

Lincoln-McClellan contest of 1864 the troops had been given furloughs to go home and vote in person; since this was impossible with millions of Americans in the foxholes of Europe and far Pacific islands, it was agreed that the ballot had to be taken to the serviceman. The politicos assumed that a large majority of the servicemen would vote for their Commander-in-Chief, so that it behooved the Administration to make the Federal Ballot plan as simple as possible, and the opposition to make it as tough as possible. Under the Federal Ballot plan adopted by forty-four states, all the serviceman had to do was to go to headquarters, give the location of his home polling place, and cast his vote. Under Governor Dewey's New York State law the serviceman had to mail a request to Albany, after which a ballot was sent to where he had mailed the request from, and once he had received his ballot he could then vote. The ballot had to be back in New York three days before the election. This did not merely double the serviceman's difficulties in casting his vote, but multiplied them a hundredfold, making Governor Dewey's ballot the toughest to be used in the country.

On the home front both Dewey and his poll takers had underestimated the Congress of Industrial Organization's P.A.C. (Political Action Committee), which now plunged into the heart of the campaign with man-hours, money and a fighting spirit. Up to this moment no union official had been able to deliver the labor vote, and labor itself was too divided to be brought into any political movement as a whole. Labor in America had been traditionally nonpolitical; Samuel Gompers, long-time president of the American Federation of Labor, had kept the unions out of politics on the grounds that if they backed the wrong horse they would get kicked in the breadbasket. When John L. Lewis had ordered his United Mine Workers to vote for Wendell Willkie in 1940, some eighty per cent of them had made a grimace and quietly voted for Roosevelt.

The Political Action Committee was formed in July 1943, when the anti-labor sentiment of the country was reaching its peak, unfriendly legislation was passing the Congress, and the Republican press was playing up each strike for all its anti-union publicity value. The C.I.O. had come into existence under the Wagner Labor Act and President Roosevelt's ardent championing of labor's rights. C.I.O. leaders knew that in the cutback period after the war, with its attendant depression, every available force would be utilized to weaken the unions, repeal the legislation which protected them, and deprive them of their twelve-year gains.

Under the leadership of Sidney Hillman, who for thirty

years had been president of the successful Amalgamated Clothing Workers, the P.A.C. set out to help liberal prolabor candidates win in the primaries. Since their structure was loose and they were just cutting their political eye-teeth, they did not have much success in putting over the men they wanted. By the time the presidential election of 1944 came along, they were able to produce what *Time* magazine called, "The slickest political propaganda produced in the U.S. in a generation."

This propaganda machine was now set in full motion to defeat Tom Dewey and all other isolationist, conservative Republicans. Under the slogan of, "Love thy neighbor, and organize him," the P.A.C. sent tens of thousands of volunteer workers to ring the doorbells of labor in every county and hamlet in America, for it was universally agreed that a large vote would favor Roosevelt, a small vote, Dewey. They didn't wait for the workers to go to the registration booths, they took the booths inside the factories. Wives and children were made an integral part of the organization. Vast quantities of literature were skillfully written and distributed in an effort to educate the workers to the necessity of voting and to convince them that Roosevelt would use the nation's resources to maintain full employment after the war, that Dewey would maintain it only if the business cycle were propitious. There were election badges and radio broadcasts and printed throwaways—all the implements used by a major political party in its effort to win an election.

Tom Dewey had had his November victory figured in terms of mathematical probabilities, and here was Sidney Hillman and his P.A.C. jostling the equation. Something had to be done immediately, preferably in terms of counterattack. In politics there is always raw material at hand: during the Democratic convention's row over who was to be named vice-president, President Roosevelt was reported, by Arthur Krock of the New York *Times,* as having said to Bob Hannegan about a prospective vice-presidential candidate, "Clear everything with Sidney." The Republican steering committee believed that this phrase could be used as effectively as "Rum, Romanism and rebellion" had been used by the Democrats to alienate the Catholic vote and defeat Dewey's fellow Also Ran, James G. Blaine, in 1884.

Dewey had begun his campaign by declaring, "Anyone who injects a racial or religious issue into a political campaign is guilty of a disgraceful un-American act." However, the phrase "Clear everything with Sidney" became the crux of the Republican campaign. It was broadcast across the nation, repeated literally millions of times in the papers, magazines, at public meetings and on the air, the implication being that since Sidney is a Jewish name, a vote against Roosevelt was a vote against the Jews. The slogan was approved by Dewey and sparked by Herbert Brownell. The New York *Times* publicly rebuked the Republican National Committee for its distorted use of the phrase, but the committee spurned the *Times* injunction.

As a further use of the raw material huge posters were smeared across the face of the land: DEFEAT THE HILLMAN-BROWDER AXIS. Earl Browder was the head of the Communist party who recently had been pardoned by President Roosevelt after serving a prison sentence for falsifying his passport. Aside from the fact that a number of Communist party members had infiltrated government offices, there was no conceivable connection between Browder and President Roosevelt, except as it pleased certain Republicans to call the New Deal social legislation communistic. Before the end of the campaign fully two thirds of the Republican effort was being poured into a denunciation of Hillman and Browder.

But if Dewey pretended he was running against Hillman, Roosevelt returned the compliment by pretending that he was running against Herbert Hoover. While Dewey was pointing out the dangers of the future under Hillman, Roosevelt was portraying the dangers of the past under Hoover. While Brownell carried the torch against the Hillman-Browder Axis, Dewey stumped the country crying that Washington was being run by old, tired, and cynical men who hadn't the energy to terminate the war or build a prosperous postwar America. Against this backdrop he portrayed himself in the role of up-and-coming youth.

Starting on his first national tour, Governor Dewey told an audience in Pittsburgh that the United States simply could not face another period like the Roosevelt depression, and then convened in St. Louis with his twenty-four fellow Republican governors. His purposes were many: to indicate that the twenty-four governors were solidly behind him, to draw up a new platform to supersede the harshly criticized one from Chicago, to dispel the charges that he was a Herbert Hoover Old Guard Republican, and to strengthen the state political machines.

Through precise advance planning he achieved these results—but at a cost: bearing out the prophecy of Mrs. Simpson, he held the twenty-four governors under his schoolmasterish thumb, told them exactly what they must accomplish, what hours they must work and what their working methods must be. The conference ended with the governors agreeing on a mildly progressive platform. The storm did not break for several weeks, but when it did it was perhaps the most significant psychological element of the campaign.

The Republican National Committee wrote strong and abusive speeches for Republican governors Baldwin of Connecticut, Green of Illinois, and Warren of California, instructing them to give these speeches on the air. Brownell was so certain that the governors would obey like good robots that he gave copies to the press before the speeches even reached the governors. Governor Warren threw out half of the canned dynamite that had been sent him, but not in time to keep the Eastern papers from quoting him on the wrong script. The two other governors rebelled against these highhanded methods, revising the scripts to suit their own thinking. When shortly afterward Representative Dirksen of Illinois was handed a script for which he was called to task in Congress, Dirksen had to explain, "I like to be circumspect in my language . . ."

Chairman Brownell, faced with the proof of his arbitrary methods, remarked icily to the reporters, "Merely a matter of phraseology."

Within a few days another evidence of overorganization rose up to haunt Tom Dewey: Senator Taft of Ohio led the Congress to pass a Soldiers Vote Act which prevented the men in the Armed Forces from reading such books as *The Republic*, by Charles A. Beard, and *The Time for Decision*, by Sumner Welles, from seeing such motion pictures as *Wilson* and Fibber Magee's *Heavenly Days*, on the grounds that these books and pictures were Democratic propaganda which would influence the soldier vote. The nationwide outcry was tremendous: servicemen could get killed in their fight for freedom, but they could not have the freedom to choose their own books and pictures. And the Republicans had accused the Democrats of regimentation!

Despite these undercurrents of dissension, Tom Dewey began to hit his stride toward the middle of September. In Philadelphia, where he made his first big speech, he was "excited and a trifle nervous, for he had to overcome a widespread feeling that he was just a little man with a mustache." However, his radio manner was effective as he exclaimed:

"This is a campaign against an administration which was conceived in defeatism, which failed for eight straight years to restore our democratic economy, which has been the most wasteful, extravagant and incompetent administration in the history of the nation, and, worst of all, which has lost faith in the American people."

His campaign train moved to Louisville, back to Michigan,

then to Des Moines. His speeches were short, staccato, unemotional, talking facts and figures. When he wasn't speaking he sat at a table with his assistant, Elliot Bell, rewriting his speeches on the facts provided by telegraph from their research bureau in New York.

The majority of the sixty-three newspapermen assigned to the election special were Roosevelt men, few of whom confessed to any liking or respect for Tom Dewey. They found him cold, dull, formal; but before long they were fascinated by a new technique of campaigning which they could best describe as "metronomic precision." Everything had to be done in precisely the same fashion at every stop, until it began to look as though Dewey could operate only under automatisms: the train must not be one second early or one second late at the station; there must be a motorcade of twenty-five cars, no more or no less; the speaking rostrum must be an exact height; the introductions at meetings must be of precise length and say the prescribed things; his entrance must always be timed mathematically from the wings; certain political and business leaders were to be brought to his hotel suite, and no one else might appear.

Nothing was left to chance or even to individual management. The local Republicans had their orders, and they would do as they were told. There was no spontaneity, no conviviality, no enthusiasms, no drama, no excitement. Everything was tightly organized, including Dewey's prosecution of Roosevelt, for he now had his adversary in the political dock and was presenting to the Grand Jury the masses of evidence on bureaucracy, overlapping and inefficiency.

Because of his earnestness, his unrelenting labors, the reporters slowly came to respect Tom Dewey. When in a train wreck in Oregon Candidate Dewey showed his mettle by the unselfish manner in which he directed relief and helped everywhere, he began to make friends. A few of the reporters even changed their votes.

One of the major premises of Dewey's campaign was that the war would be practically over by Inauguration Day in January 1945, and that the new administration's two tasks would be to maintain full employment and peace abroad. A conference was opening at Dumbarton Oaks, just outside Washington, D.C., to be participated in by the Big Four, whose purpose it was to set up a preliminary structure for a world peace organization. The success of such a conference would diminish his charge that the Democrats were not capable of creating a postwar peace. To the public eagerly awaiting developments at Dumbarton Oaks, Dewey said, "I have been deeply disturbed by reports that it is planned to subject the nations of the world, great and small, permanently to the coercive powers of the four nations holding this conference."

Secretary of State Hull denied heatedly that the Dumbarton Oaks conference had any intention of suppressing minority groups or smaller nations, and ended with an invitation to Governor Dewey to come to Washington for further elucidation. Dewey chose to send his own prospective Secretary of State, John Foster Dulles. The Democrats were displeased with Secretary Hull, crying, "Dewey has been on the outside wistfully looking in. Now you have put him in a position where he can make a stir on the international scene." The Republicans groaned, "Why didn't Dewey go himself? By sending Mr. Dulles he conveys to the electorate that he doesn't know enough about international relations to tackle the discussion himself."

Dewey's strategy was sound: John Foster Dulles had worked for international peace since the Versailles Treaty, had been a secretary to the Second Hague Peace Conference, and an enthusiast of Woodrow Wilson's League of Nations. Though he was the wealthy president of the Wall Street legal firm of Sullivan and Cromwell, the worst the Democrats could find to say about him was that, like his potential boss, he had a cold, sour face and had long been known on Wall Street as Dull, Duller, Dulles.

In spite of Mr. Dulles' qualifications, Tom Dewey had a stroke of hard luck: John Dulles developed a bad foot at the worst possible moment. Photographs showed him hobbling along on crutches by the side of Secretary Hull. After so ardently telling the nation that they were governed by sick old men, Dewey now had his first officially designated representative appear in the light of a man who could hardly get around.

His campaign had been going so poorly that even the staunchest Republicans were down in the mouth. Now he began to get the breaks: Roosevelt's first radio talk, given from the bow of a destroyer tied alongside a Bremerton Navy wharf, was poorly organized and haltingly delivered. There were quarrels within the administration ranks, such as the one between Charles E. Wilson and Donald Nelson of the crucial War Production Board. The Allies started pounding at Germany from the east and west, and the war promised soon to be over. Major General Lewis B. Hershey, director of Selective Service, was reported as having said, "We can keep people in the Army about as cheaply as we can create an agency for them when they are out." Dewey used this bumbling quote to excellent effect, gaining the support of servicemen's wives with the promise that he would muster out the armed forces immediately upon cessation of hostilities. A

430

considerable portion of the Negro press came out in his behalf.

The Democrats could not seem to fight their way out of the hard crust of inertia in Washington, and the only effort they cared to make was the negative cry of "Don't change horses in midstream." Tom Dewey's own vigorous approach and detailed organizational work as he made his way across the depth and breadth of the country, replying triumphantly, "It's time for a change!" seemed to be accomplishing such important results that midway in the campaign the Gallup Poll was able to report that he could capture Michigan, Indiana, Ohio and Illinois if the election were to be held immediately. The professional gamblers' odds against him dropped from three to one, to two and a half to one because Dewey money broke into the open. Republicans were no longer saying that they could not vote for Dewey.

Chairman Brownell exclaimed in his New York office: "I'm going to have to hire a few pessimists to keep me from being too happy. If the reports coming in are true, Governor Dewey will be elected by a landslide."

Up to this moment President Roosevelt had preferred to remain in the role of Commander-in-Chief. Governor Dewey was heard to complain that Roosevelt was using his high office for political purposes, getting his picture on the front pages by going on an inspection tour of the Pacific or to a conference with Prime Minister Churchill at Quebec. But now Roosevelt's advisers warned him that young Dewey was coming up fast and that he had better throw his political hat into the ring and start swapping punches. This could mean only one thing: a radio address of the kind he had made at the close of the Landon and Willkie campaigns.

Franklin D. Roosevelt chose to open his fighting campaign before a dinner of the Teamsters Union in Washington. His supporters still were trembling over the poor speech from the Bremerton Navy Yards. But their fears were unfounded: the Old Master of the radio gave the most politically astute speech of his four campaigns: warm, lovable, ingratiating, confidential, full of a homely, tolerant humor, written with a piercing grasp of the 1944 world situation. He ridiculed the Republicans who love labor unions once very four years; he mocked Dewey's basic thesis of the "Roosevelt depression" by bringing back the tragic era of the soup kitchens and bread lines, the apple stands and the Hoovervilles of 1930 to 1933. He castigated Dewey for keeping the Federal Ballot from the servicemen, for using *Mein Kampf* methods in allocating still another million dollars on radio time to popularize the phrase "Clear everything with Sidney," and in climax he reviewed Dewey's indisputable record of isolationism. The high spot of the speech had nothing to do with politics, yet it was so effectively phrased and wistfully delivered that it helped stop the drift toward Thomas E. Dewey:

"The Republican leaders have not been content with attacks on me, on my wife, or on my sons—they now include my little dog Fala." This reference was to a charge that he had sent a battleship back to Alaska for his forgotten Scottie.

Tom Dewey didn't like this speech, and when thousands of telegrams began pouring in from disgruntled Republicans telling him to take off his kid gloves and start socking, he got mad. By the following day he had arranged for a national hookup and worked like a man possessed to write his angriest speech. For the first time the reporters saw a breakdown of his refrigerating apparatus, and when he went on the air with his broadcast from Oklahoma City, he struck out with unprecedented passion by placing the responsibility for America's unpreparedness on the shoulders of Roosevelt and the Democratic party. The Democratic National Committee ran circles around itself proving that Dewey had torn quotations from Truman and General Marshall out of their texts, and hence had falsified their meaning. It was a cry they were to repeat often and heatedly during the next few weeks.

And so Tom Dewey continued his cross-country junkets, promising San Francisco that he would retain the New Deal's social gains, "in an economic climate where business can grow and flourish," and in southern California promising the "Ham and Eggers" more and better social-security laws. There were no parades, no confetti, no cheering crowds through which to ride, and not much applause, but the audiences believed he stated the Republican case very well.

By mid-October he had awakened the electorate from its lethargy; he was being praised as crisp, vigorous, clear, precise, tough-minded, with a passion for neatness. The Gallup Poll showed him breathing down Roosevelt's neck; Democrats were saying, "Walk, do not Gallup, to the polls."

It is an infallible of presidential elections that during the last two weeks of the campaign the electorate is seized by a hysteria in which all of the repressed emotion on both sides suddenly blows its top. Base and dastardly charges that have been lurking just beneath the surface are brought out into the open; personal invective reaches new and unrepressed heights; logical reasoning and fair play are thrown overboard while the body politic is ravaged by a crisis which only a healthy organism could survive. The height of the fever was reached when the Republicans accused Roosevelt of plotting to become King of the United States, and the Democrats called Dewey the vilest name on the contemporary scene: Fascist.

In the home stretch the tide began to go against Tom Dewey. Military leaders predicted that the end of the war in Europe could not be hoped for until the middle of 1945 or later, or in the Pacific before 1947; it became clear to the electorate that the next presidency would be spent not in a postwar period but largely in a war-torn world. Governor Bricker lost votes for his ticket every time he made a speech, which was often; Dewey got so disgusted at pulling his running mate out of the soup that he avoided meeting Bricker for nine of the critical weeks of the campaign. Independent observers began to give Harry Truman the nod as the better of the two vice-presidential candidates. Though *Life* magazine made a heroic effort to "relegate isolationism to the museum alongside barnburner, locofoco and other mementos of our rich political past," Dewey's record of having opposed Lend-Lease and Aid to Britain, as well as his having bitterly attacked the State Department for recognizing Russia, in the process of which he had called Stalin some unforgettable names, became increasingly important to a public which was coming more and more to understand that we had to remain friends with Russia and England in order to outlaw war. Wendell L. Willkie died without approving his fellow Republican; immediately thereafter a number of Willkie's lieutenants disavowed Dewey and came out for Roosevelt. Writing in the *American Mercury*, Russell Davenport said, "Mr. Dewey played politics with foreign policy. He doffed and donned the cloak of internationalism at his own convenience and for his own purposes."

The propaganda that the president was incapacitated, actually on his deathbed, acted as a boomerang when Roosevelt, making a tour of New York City, sat in a downpouring rain with the water streaming off his face, waving his hand and smiling to the umbrella-roofed crowds, and coming out of the ordeal without even a sniffle. The cerebral hemorrhage which caused his sudden death on April 12, 1945, was, ironically, due to neither the infantile paralysis from which he had suffered so many years nor yet to any physical ailments anticipated by the Republican campaign charges.

When two weeks before the election the Gallup Poll gave Dewey almost a fifty-fifty chance to win, some of the Republican delegates began looking back at the Gallup preconvention figures with a jaundiced eye. Had the figures been rigged? Had they been sold a gold brick? The congressional investigation of Gallup Poll methods promised to be a bipartisan affair.

The *coup de grâce* was delivered on election eve, when Franklin D. Roosevelt read a beautiful prayer. Honest and intelligent voters, sitting before their radios on that night, sorely troubled by the conflicting claims of the two parties, wanting to do the right thing for their families and their country, heard the president say, "Almighty God . . . We commend to Thy overruling Providence the men and women of our forces . . . Guide . . . the nations of the world into the way of justice and truth and establish among them that peace . . . Make the whole people of this land equal to our high trust, reverent in the use of freedom . . . Make us ill content with the inequalities of opportunity which still prevail among us. . . ." The people listened, and their doubts were resolved. It would be Franklin D. Roosevelt for the fourth time.

And so it proved to be.

Thomas E. Dewey gathered 23,000,000 popular votes against 26,000,000 for Roosevelt, an extremely good showing for a young candidate trying to replace a Commander-in-Chief during a world war. However, his vote within the states did not show up so well: he won a majority in only ten states, giving him ninety-nine electoral votes, against thirty-eight states for Roosevelt, with a total of four hundred and thirty-two electoral votes. Along with him the electorate defeated nearly every last isolationist in the Congress—an inmistakable mandate to the administration not to fail in the creation of a peace league which would have guns as well as teeth.

When a reporter wished Tom Dewey better luck in 1948 he replied grimly: "I have no illusions about that."

It was the first time he had failed to say, "Don't worry, boys, there will be another chance and we will win it."

8

Would a prosecuting attorney make a good president?

The lawyers say no. The training and point of view of a prosecuting attorney is such that it slants the mental apparatus and outlook in the direction of pursuing criminals and evidence, developing courtroom technique, bringing in convictions. The prosecutor is trained to avoid the whole picture so that a single detail can be stressed.

Attorneys maintain that there is no prosecutor alive who does not look at life through the screen of, "You're guilty until proven innocent!", that convictions arise from this conviction. This is the worst possible training for anyone who has to deal with people, who must guide his countrymen instead of indicting them; it is the exact opposite of the patriarch who believes his people innocent until proven guilty, and even then does not send them to jail, but rather extends a helping hand.

There has never been a great man or a great mind who was a great prosecutor; those elements which make for greatness would make of a man a poor prosecutor. The great men have more frequently been the attorneys for the defense.

Given a free hand as Chief Prosecuting Attorney of World War II criminals, Tom Dewey might evolve a technique of international prosecution so infallible that potential evolvers of World War III would be a trifle dissuaded. He is also the logical successor to J. Edgar Hoover as head of the Federal Bureau of Investigation.

An examination of the record after the fury of the campaign died down indicated that Thomas E. Dewey was a trouble-shooting repairman, a filler-in of breaks and holes, washouts and slides on the political highway; that he was in no part the engineer whose job is to map new roads through the economic jungles of the future. By the time the results of the Crimean conference were announced the following February, a large portion of those who had voted for Mr. Dewey were saying publicly that they were glad they had been represented by Mr. Roosevelt at Yalta.

For all of the adulation of his campaign biography, Rupert Hughes missed Tom Dewey's basic passion, the one which frames his every thought and feeling: his unbounded enthusiasm and respect for business. Over and over again one heard Dewey cry, "Business gave us our living, our prosperity, our power, our progress. The genius of America is the genius of business. Give the government back to business, and we will once again become free, rich, powerful, great."

Nor was this an unrequited love: the list of contributors to his campaign fund reads like a roll call of the National Association of Manufacturers.

Thomas E. Dewey is, in the best and strongest sense of the term, a materialist. His materialism, which believes that people are created for business and production and the consumption of goods, and that the machine is the godhead, is not an unusual phenomenon in American life: it is an inheritance from the nineteenth-century industrial revolution in which the machine supplanted man. It is the jagged stone wall against which the artist, the writer, the intellectual, the idealist, the educator and the humanitarian has beaten out his brains since the opening of the twentieth century.

Dewey's supporters were intensely proud of the fact that he was the first presidential nominee to have been born in this century, and Stanley Walker gave his 1944 campaign biography the subtitle of *An American of This Century*. The exact opposite is true. Thomas E. Dewey was born out of his age; in political philosophy he stands shoulder to shoulder with his grandfather, who helped form his party eighty-eight years before.

It is the corollary of this materialism which makes him devoid of warmth and its inseparable companion, compassion. The president of one hundred and thirty-seven million humans should have a deep-seated and unshakable love for people. This human warmth emanating from the White House can do more to bind the people together, make them tolerant and happy, devoted to their government and their country than can a whole parcel of rigidly correct laws, aseptically administered. We have resources to spare, we have the means of corralling impingements on our personal liberty; but against the deep-freeze, against the lack of sympathy, tolerant amusement, and warm forebearance of our polyglot peoples there can be no corrective, no remedy. The heart of the people grows cold.

Tom Dewey would make the most efficient administrator of the *status quo* to be found in public life today. In this sense he would make half a good president, just as he made half a good governor. The bureaucratic waste and deadwood of the federal government would be struck by the efficiency typhoon it so sorely needs; administrative costs would be cut to a third; taxes would fall; we would have a minimum of government administered with mathematical precision. Businessmen would have their confidence restored, investment capital would come out of hibernation and, to the extent to which the business cycle can bring prosperity, the United States would enjoy prosperity. What can happen when the cycle hit its usual depression can only be guessed by Dewey's profound belief in letting business work these matters out for itself.

Two further embarrassing questions arise to plague Mr. Dewey: could anyone, no matter how efficient, maintain the *status quo* in a world gripped by revolution; and didn't he really prefer the *status quo ante* of Harding, Coolidge and Hoover? He gave no indication of understanding the nature of the upheaval through which the world was passing, or of the basic problem of our times: *how much freedom could we give up for how much security?* Didn't government need at its head someone who would make an enthusiastic attempt to build bridges across the transitional years, instead of looking back nostalgically at the good old days of the nineteenth century? Was it sufficient to have, in our sorely troubled times, a president who had a scientific mechanism of thinking, but no contemporary content of thought?

Tom Dewey rarely took a strong stand or committed himself on a major issue. The only program he offered the voters was a *return* to honest, businesslike government; it is impossible to find one paragraph in which he details what he would lead the country *forward to*. As Richard H. Rovere had pointed out in his "Man in the Blue Serge Suit" in *Harper's*, Tom Dewey was in the habit of using private pollsters to make sure that every opinion he was about to express would meet with the approval of the public.

While running for governor of New York, Dewey espoused the New Deal social legislation in order to attract the liberal vote, but once in office he not only stopped the entire program in its tracks, but began sniping at the more important security laws. During the presidential election he again publicly avowed the Democratic social program, but there is every reason to believe, from his writings and his record, that he detests this entire program as a weakener, a destroyer of initiative and character, and that by subtle sabotage he would do away with as much of the program as he conceivably could, until he was back at the governmental status of the McKinley regime.

The most dangerous characteristic implicit in Tom Dewey's record was that he was an imperious commander who ran his machine with icy disregard for anyone's wishes or consideration but his own. His methods were highhanded and dictatorial; anyone or anything that got in his way was steam-rollered out of existence. Conceiving himself as the savior of American government, he became St. George slaying the dragon of political and economic corruption. Not since William Jennings Bryan had the country seen so puritanical or fiercely moralistic a candidate aspire to the presidency. The charges that he would have been a dictator, circumventing civil liberties to achieve his ends, were insufficiently grounded; the worst he might have done was lead the country to governmental salvation with a ring through its nose.

His greatest weakness as president would have been on the international scene. During the election Gerald W. Johnson asked him in an *Atlantic Monthly* article, "What do you, as presidential candidate, offer me, as a voter, that Harding did not offer in 1920?" The answer was: very little. Tom Dewey grew up as a midwest isolationist: he hated European entanglements and believed they could be avoided; he fraternized with and approved of the worst dead-end isolationists within his party. Even knowing how desperately eager the American public was for an international organization, with all of the force and sovereignty necessary to prevent future wars, he could bring himself to give such a league only the barest lip service, and was castigated roundly by Wendell Willkie in *Collier's* for not understanding that the United States, like every other nation in the world, must give up some of its sovereignty in return for permanent peace.

As president Thomas E. Dewey would not be able to change his insular Americanism; before Pearl Harbor he cried for higher and higher walls around the country to keep war out—but are there walls high enough to keep out atomic bombs and jet-propelled planes?

Judged solely on the basis of his own qualifications, and without comparison with anyone else, it would be hard to conceive of anyone more temperamentally unfitted for the post of Chief Executive in the middle of the twentieth century.

He remains a highly lacquered nineteenth-century figurine who threw out his stocky chest to stem the onward-rushing tide of his times. As such, he served a salutary purpose: he forced history to question some of its less tenable postulates, he obliged the opposition to make secure its ground before moving forward. In this light he fulfilled his manifest destiny, not as a policy maker, visionary or leader, but as a policeman.

Transition

In the twenty-two years since the original Thomas E. Dewey chapter was written, five presidential races have been run. The first of these five was Mr. Dewey's second campaign against Harry S. Truman in 1948. The death of President Franklin D. Roosevelt in 1945 and the advent of Harry Truman to the White House appeared to bring about a sharp change in the country's political climate. Not all Democrats had thought Truman an inspired choice for the vice-presidency. However he achieved an orderly and intelligent take-over of the presidency. His decision to use the atom bomb put an end to World War II. He accomplished important results through the Truman Doctrine in 1947 which helped save Greece and Turkey for the free world; the Marshall Plan, also in 1947, for the United States' financing and rebuilding of Europe; the spectacular Berlin Airlift of 1948; yet he did not appear to be mounting any popular support for another term. The majority of the Congress, elected in 1946, was Republican and solidly against him. Most observers believed that the Republican nominee, whoever he might be, would score a smashing success in 1948.

Thomas E. Dewey had grown during his four additional years as governor of New York. His second campaign was better than his first, in terms of the political education of the country. Though he was widely accused of overconfidence by his own party, some of his thinking and expression during the campaign rose to the heights of statesmanship. All of the polls showed him so far in the lead as to make it impossible for Harry Truman ever to overtake him. All, that is, except one private pollster, Louis Bean, who did all of his own work, and brought back the unbelievable and unbelieved report that the majority of the American people were going to vote for President Truman.

Truman waged a vigorous slam-bang campaign, at last latching on to a phrase, "That Do-Nothing Congress!" which threw the blame for the three years of conflict onto the House and Senate. Thomas Dewey again faced criticism from the Republicans working with him. They complained of his coldness. He was still a loner. But he was going to be a winner, and so they kept their misgivings to themselves. On election eve *Life* came out with a full-page photo of Thomas E. Dewey bearing the legend: THE NEXT PRESIDENT TRAVELS BY FERRY BOAT ACROSS THE BROAD WATERS OF SAN FRANCISCO BAY. The Chicago *Tribune* carried an eight-column headline: DEWEY DEFEATS TRUMAN.

A majority of the American people, 24,104,030 to 21,971,004, thought otherwise. They had responded to Harry Truman's warmth. They were also astonished to find that he had won. Mr. Truman was not surprised.

Few expected anything new or startling out of Harry Truman during his second term. Again he confounded his most ardent supporters by developing a tremendous combination of strength and sagacity. He inaugurated NATO, our military alliance, the Point Four plan to assist underdeveloped nations, and threw our armed strength into Korea to support the United Nations' effort. When historian Arthur Schlesinger, Sr., of Harvard asked seventy-five historians to score the comparative achievements of all American presidents (*New York Times Magazine,* July 29, 1962), Harry S. Truman emerged with the rank of Near Great, with only Andrew Jackson, Theodore Roosevelt, and James K. Polk ahead of him in this category.

Thomas E. Dewey was influential in securing the nomination of Dwight D. Eisenhower in the 1952 Republican Convention. Doubtless he could have had an important cabinet post or ambassadorial appointment had he desired it. But during his years of public service he had made considerable financial sacrifice. He retired to private life, and to the practice of the law. Here he has remained.

The campaigns of 1952 and 1956 were dominated by the personalities of General Dwight D. Eisenhower and Governor Adlai E. Stevenson of Illinois. Both were genuinely reluctant candidates. General Eisenhower took considerable persuading. He had behind him the brilliant victories of World War II, and was the military idol of the nation. He had much to lose from a defeat. Nor was he convinced that he had the necessary economic or political training to fulfill the office of the presidency.

Governor Stevenson was determined, as little as a month before the Democratic Convention, that he would not be a candidate. He wished to serve for another full term as governor of Illinois, to gain background and experience. Stevenson could have avoided the draft by going to Europe for a vacation. But as fate would have it the Democrats met in Chicago in 1952. It was the duty of the governor of Illinois to open the convention and officially welcome the delegates. President Harry Truman wanted Stevenson, and Stevenson quoted from Matthew 26:42:

"If this cup may not pass away from me, except I drink it, Thy will be done."

General Eisenhower's major asset in the campaign, as indeed it proved to be in the White House, was his annealing nature. Part of his success as commander-in-chief in World War II derived from his rare talent for making people of differing ideas and conflicting personalities work together harmoniously. Governor Stevenson's outstanding talents, which brought joy to millions of literate Americans, were his erudition, his wit, his facility with words, his receptivity to ideas.

Governor Stevenson started fast, capturing the affection and admiration of large segments of the country. Although General Eisenhower had written General MacArthur's speeches in the Philippines, he started so slowly that by mid-September the Scripps-Howard papers announced he was "running like a dry creek." The Republicans immediately stepped up their campaign, calling on liberal writers not only to write the general's speeches, but attempting to get written a small pocket dictionary for him to carry so that he would be able to answer questions about economic problems when asked by reporters or audiences.

At the same moment someone in the Republican party coined the epithet "Egghead" to apply to Adlai Stevenson. To an America which has been anti-intellectual since July 4, 1826, the day on which two of the greatest Founding Fathers —Thomas Jefferson and John Adams—died, this derogatory term accomplished two simultaneous miracles: it persuaded a considerable portion of the American voters that Adlai Stevenson should be an object of derision because he was an eminently cultured and cultivated man; and it made acceptable General Eisenhower's tortured English and highly specialized, unintellectual training. Though Eisenhower's international military stature lent credence to his promise to keep the peace (a promise he fulfilled), in a sense the election became a contest between Western classical literature and Western stories. To so young and still pioneer a people, the Westerns quite naturally and logically won out, even as they do on our television tubes today.

In the process of losing, Adlai Stevenson proved to be as valuable an enunciator of ideas and ideals as any candidate since Horace Greeley. While Stevenson traveled the world, wrote books and articles on international affairs, even as Wendell L. Willkie had after his defeat in 1940, President Eisenhower gave the country an administration of good will,

441

binding up the political wounds incurred by twenty continuous years of emphatic Democratic administration.

In spite of his near-fatal heart attack, there never was any serious doubt about Eisenhower's re-election. The country enjoyed a warm, albeit soporific, affection for the president as a benevolent father figure, even those who had voted for Stevenson in 1956 because they believed Stevenson's inherent qualities would give the country a clearer and more profound leadership.

After his second defeat, in a campaign not quite as effective as the first, Adlai Stevenson returned to the private practice of the law, as had Thomas Dewey before him. It was not until October 1957, when the Russians launched their Sputnik, that the term Egghead did a reverse spin in the American mind, and came to denote those imperative qualities of education and intellectual discipline which might save us from being "buried" by the Communists. At this moment the true value and worth of Adlai Stevenson came into focus for the American people as a whole, and the word Egghead changed its status to that of a compliment instead of an insult. With the inauguration of John F. Kennedy to the presidency in 1961, Stevenson became the highly articulate and respected United States Ambassador to the United Nations, where he remained until his death in London in July 1965.

By one of the unfortunate twists of fate which happen to our political figures more often than to our military, by the time Professor Schlesinger, Sr., conducted his survey of the comparative status of American presidents in 1962, Dwight D. Eisenhower emerged next to last in the Average division, two scant positions from the Below Average category. Perhaps history, with its longer perspectives, will ameliorate this seemingly harsh judgment.

The presidential contest between Richard M. Nixon, vice-president under Eisenhower, and Senator John F. Kennedy in 1960 is one of the most psychologically fascinating in the entire American story. We are still too close to President Kennedy's assassination to make anything approaching an objective analysis of his three years in office.

It is also too early to write the chapter on Richard Nixon. Nixon is energetic, capable, and extraordinarily ambitious. At this moment he still has a chance for the Republican nomination in 1968. Should the draft for which he hopes fail to emerge that year, it is likely that he will begin planning his organization for 1972. Should he be nominated in 1968 or 1972, and elected, he will not be eligible for the nether role of Also-Ran hero in this book. But we can return to the campaign of 1960 in an effort to suggest the *ambiente* in which the contest was waged.

Vice-President Richard M. Nixon, after the 1960 nominations, had a considerable advantage. The political climate of 1960 seemed to indicate as clear-cut a victory for him as it had for Dewey in 1948. Due to his years in the Senate and eight years as vice-president, closer to the White House than anyone in our history, Nixon was known in the remotest hamlet in America. He had the important weapon of experience at the executive level.

Except to those interested in the excitements of off-year election politics, Senator John F. Kennedy of Massachusetts was largely unknown. Besides, there was the seemingly insuperable obstacle of his religion. Those who remembered the vicious campaign waged against Alfred E. Smith in 1928 because he was a Roman Catholic wondered if the country had matured sufficiently to live up to the mandate of its Constitution to judge a man on his merits.

Richard Nixon, like Thomas Dewey, is something of a loner. He does not work well inside his own organization. As the tempo of the campaign increased he grew fatigued from overwork, which his people could well have handled. Asperity took the place of his natural warmth and humor, followed by a certain confusion and separation from his supporters. He also had some bad luck: a knee injury which hospitalized him; an innovating T.V. debate which went disastrously against him; his resolution to go to Alaska to fulfill his early promise of speaking in all fifty states, lost him the closing dramatic hours for his appeal to the big city voters.

But in the last analysis Richard M. Nixon was actually defeated by John F. Kennedy's youth, vitality, wit, warmth, his knowledgeability, his courage in facing adversaries, as he did the clergymen of Houston when he enunciated his unshakable belief in the separation of church and state.

Kennedy waged a brilliant campaign, working very closely with his organization; and a more effective political organization this country has rarely known. He won by the narrowest of margins, 34,227,096 to 34,108,546.

As president, magnificently articulate John F. Kennedy infused the Western World with a new sense of purpose and hope. He was loved by people of all lands. His greatness will be assessed by the ages.

The nomination of Senator Barry M. Goldwater by the Republicans in 1964 was as gratifying a step toward political maturity as was the nomination and election of John F. Kennedy in 1960. For Mr. Goldwater was of Jewish origin: his grandparents, Michael and Sarah Nathan Goldwasser, settled in Arizona in 1860. True, his father had married a Protestant, and Barry himself had become a member of the Episcopal Church; but the Republicans who seized power for him in the state committees, those who managed his nomination and those who voted for him to be their president knew about his Jewish background. With his peculiar combination of talents and graces, Barry Goldwater laid the last ghost of religious intolerance, at least on an organized scale, in American politics. For this contribution the United States has reason to be grateful to him.

What was the man like who could gain control of the Republican organization and become the master of its party machinery, rendering futile the efforts of such widely known and experienced men as Governors Nelson Rockefeller, William Scranton, and George Romney?

Everything one knew about Barry Goldwater as a family man, citizen and public servant, right up to his suicidal rigidity in controlling the Republican Platform in San Francisco in July of 1964, was good. He was loyal to his friends, warmhearted, generous with money where there was need, and with help to his associates. He had an ingratiating personality, with humor, an openness of countenance and nature, a handsome sunburned glamour that perhaps arose from the majestic vistas of his native Arizona desert. A patriot of uncontested courage, he had flown C-47's in World War II and was at the time of his nomination a major-general in the United States Air Force Reserve.

He had other endearing qualities, particularly to those embattled Republicans in areas dominated by Democrats. He had won his own Senatorial nomination and election in his first try for national office in 1952. Over these years from 1952 to 1964 he was always available to travel hundreds or even thousands of miles to remote districts to make a supporting dinner speech, buoy lagging candidates, help them raise campaign funds. By the time the Republican primaries rolled around in 1964 it was said that the county and state chairmen owed more to Barry Goldwater than to all the other hopeful candidates put together. These local Republicans were eager to repay their debts in the only coin Senator Barry Goldwater desired: the Republican nomination for the presidency.

Yet their loyalty to him was based on a good deal more than gratitude: Senator Goldwater spoke for them as has no man since conservative Senator Robert A. Taft. What they liked most about Goldwater was his political philosophy. They agreed with his thinking: that the Federal government had become an octopus devouring people, rights, property, freedom. They agreed that what the Republicans needed was "a choice, not an echo." They affirmed that Senator Goldwater spoke for them as conservatives when he voted against civil rights and social legislation, when he declared against the infringement of states' rights, advocated the sale of the Tennessee Valley Authority, the putting of Social Security on a voluntary basis, the whittling away of matching Federal grants for state welfare work.

What was Senator Goldwater's political philosophy based on? In sharp contrast to the well-educated Senator Taft, who was known as Mr. Conservative during his many years of brilliant service in Washington, and who barely lost the Republican nomination for president to General Dwight D. Eisenhower in 1952, Barry Goldwater was a mediocre student, attended the University of Arizona for only a year, never completed any of the academic disciplines of economics, political science, law. Nor was he regarded as a particularly effective executive during his regime in the Goldwater family department store in Phoenix. He had done a modest amount of scattered reading but it would appear that his basic political beliefs arose out of his emotions, and a measure of self-interest as part inheritor of the Goldwater fortune. He was only sometimes articulate, and then frequently stated opinions which he spent months trying to retract. As he moved whirlwind-like about the country more and more articles, columns, speeches were written for him by people he knew little if at all, many of whom knew him equally little, did not understand his motivations, and expressed sentiments which he had later to repudiate. Goldwater commented publicly, "Hell, I have more writers than I can keep track of." A large part of the public had come to accept the necessity for speech writers, but only as men close to their principals, working along with them to express their beliefs. Senator Goldwater was not in control of the political convictions that were being presented under his name.

The story of Senator Goldwater's winning of the Republican nomination in July 1964 is implausible. He was defeated by Henry Cabot Lodge in the New Hampshire primary and by New York's Governor Rockefeller in Oregon's, nevertheless he controlled the Solid South. The issue finally came down to California; if popular Governor Rockefeller could take the state's eighty-six votes, he would be in good position to capture the nomination. The ground which Rockefeller had lost because of his divorce and subsequent remarriage the year before had seemed slowly and painfully to have been recaptured. Then, three days before the primary, the new Mrs. Rockefeller had a baby; the governor was shown on the television screens of the country as the rapturously happy new father. Thousands of the potential woman's vote went down the drain; and quite a few male votes with it. The effect in California was instant. Had the baby been born a week later, or had Governor Rockefeller stayed off television as the elated father, he might have won the California primary and the Republican nomination along with it. As it was, Senator Goldwater was victorious.

Now the moderates of the Republican party became frightened. In the period between the June second California primary and the coming July convention, the annual Governors' Conference was held in Cleveland. Frantic plans were made to "Stop Goldwater," and to launch Scranton or Romney as a unity candidate. The movement fell apart when former President Eisenhower reversed himself and, at the last minute, refused to approve anyone against Goldwater. The sole result of this conference, aside from the humiliation of the principals involved, was Governor Scranton's heroic albeit doomed tour to solidify anti-Goldwater sentiment into backing and votes.

It was a time for the gregarious, friendly Barry Goldwater to heal all wounds, close all breaches, reach out a generous hand to those who had opposed him. This is not only in the American tradition but, pragmatically, it is the only way to solidify a party behind a candidate and create the cohesive national force with which to win a national election.

Potential presidential nominee Goldwater did not see it that way. Nor did his jubilant and power-intoxicated proponents. This was to be their convention, the Republican Platform was to be theirs alone. Goldwater and his followers who had gained control of the Platform Committee allowed no tiny compromise, no participation by other segments of the party, no ameliorating changes which would have made the platform acceptable to the many temperaments in the Republican party. This dictatorship thoroughly frightened the other candidates and delegations, the press, radio and television commentators.

The convention in the Cow Palace in San Francisco was as alarming a convention as this country has known, dropping to an all-time low in democratic procedures: one by one important long-time Republican leaders and elected officials were humiliated in the arrogant refusal of the Goldwater delegates to consider their views. Governor Rockefeller himself was hissed and jeered when he appeared on the podium. The despotic spectacle culminated in Senator Goldwater's observation during his acceptance speech that:

"Extremism in the defense of liberty is no vice! . . . Moderation in the pursuit of justice is no virtue!"

These were not words that had been forced on Barry Goldwater unknowingly by a zealot who did not understand or represent the candidate. Senator Goldwater had worked over the lines many times. He simply never could see anything wrong with the concept or the statement, at the center of which lay a cancer which could destroy the United States government and the American way of life.

The enormous television audience was chilled to the marrow.

Barry Goldwater was certain that the election was already won, even as the nomination had been won. No man in American political history has been more wrong. The entire segment of Independents, representing between fifteen and twenty percent of the voters, fled from him as a potential tragedy to the American political system. Hundreds of thousands of Republicans, probably millions if one were to study the final figures, refused to countenance him and either voted for Democratic nominee, Lyndon B. Johnson, or simply abstained from voting. Presidential incumbent Johnson swept New England as well as seven out of eight political regions of the United States. Goldwater captured only seven states of the South, which turned to him because he had voted against the Civil Rights Bill, and his home state of Arizona by the bare margin of 50.4 percent of the votes cast.

Theodore White comments in *The Making of the President, 1964*, "The elections of 1964 left the Republican Party in desperate condition." Throughout the country first-rate Republican candidates, such as Robert Taft, Jr., in Ohio, and Charles Percy in Illinois, had been defeated by the flight of voters from Goldwater. Barry Goldwater was dismayed and staggered by the fact that he had received the smallest percentage (39 percent) of any presidential candidate in the history of American presidential elections; staggered that there was no hidden core of extreme conservatives waiting to rise to his call. The actual figures were 43,126,218 for Johnson; 27,174,898 for Goldwater.

It was clear by November 4, 1964, that the American people wanted a choice, but that Barry Goldwater could never be that choice. He might have made a better run if he had worked harmoniously with other candidates and sections of his party to write a moderate platform; if he had demanded of his followers even basic good manners and had controlled them instead of permitting the jeering of other Republican spokesmen; if he had chosen a moderate for vice-president instead of Congressman William Miller of New York, as reactionary as Goldwater himself.

But if he had done these things he would not have been Barry Goldwater. And the history of America might be very different indeed. As it was, President Johnson, inheritor of the office, Southerner, long-time majority leader of the U.S. Senate, was given an overwhelming majority of the vote, and what he considered as a mandate to use his enormous know-how and power in Congress to put into legislation the Democratic Party Platform.

It is interesting to speculate about the outcome had Governor Rockefeller, Scranton or Romney been nominated. Most observers feel they would have run a far closer race and would have helped elect many of the Republican candidates for Congress who were defeated in the Goldwater debacle; that President Johnson, with a smaller majority in the House and Senate, would have had rougher going to put through the legislation for his "Great Society." Might some of his far-reaching program have been delayed, watered down, or even defeated?

It is the guessing game of American politics.

Epilogue

THE SECOND HALF OF THIS STORY *indicates that the voters have been discerning in nine elections, derelict in four, with one contest a dead heat. The electorate appears to have used sound judgment in rejecting Rutherford B. Hayes for Samuel J. Tilden, Stephen A. Douglas in favor of Abraham Lincoln, James G. Blaine for Grover Cleveland, Alfred M. Landon, Wendell L. Willkie, and Thomas E. Dewey in favor of Franklin D. Roosevelt, Dewey in favor of Harry S. Truman, Richard M. Nixon in favor of John F. Kennedy, and Barry M. Goldwater in favor of Lyndon B. Johnson. However, even in elections where superiority was clear-cut, the decision has often been too close for comfort: Abraham Lincoln did not receive a majority of all votes cast, while Cleveland was able to defeat Blaine only by a few thousand margin which threw him New York's electoral vote. In the Alfred E. Smith-Herbert Hoover contest the voters had two good men to choose between. They were guilty of grievous errors in rejecting Lewis Cass for Zachary Taylor, Horatio Seymour for Ulysses S. Grant, John W. Davis for Calvin Coolidge, and Adlai E. Stevenson for Dwight D. Eisenhower, at least in the second election, 1956. Their first contest, in 1952, needs a longer time span for historical perspective in making a valid choice.*

In the first half of this book the electorate appears to have been either stupid or deceived in five elections and sagacious in three. In the latter half their ability to pick the superior man has risen at least to nine to four, a reversal of the odds. Only by the meagerest margin has democracy been able to prove that it has the discernment to choose the best man available for the most important office in the land.

The most numerous among the Also Rans were the generals, the governors, the politicos, four each of whom were defeated; the most numerous among the elected also came out of these three categories. Judges, lawyers and newspapermen come next, with two defeats each, while only one businessman is represented. No clergyman, doctor, scientist, inventor, explorer, naval officer, artist, writer, artisan or woman has been defeated because none has been nominated. Among our heroes two were Whigs, six were Republicans, eleven were Democrats. Most of them came from families of modest circumstances and had not only to pay for their own education but also to help their families while they were attending school. Many were teachers in their youth, and nearly all came from homes in which there was a love of learning and books. No one of them desired any form of government other than political democracy.

If these twenty-three men had been elected instead of defeated, would the course of American history have been altered greatly? Those historians who believe that men have little influence on the natural forces of history would say that their election would have changed very little, for men and their conduct are molded by the economic and political forces at play in their age. Those commentators who believe that men and tides of history interact upon each other would say that subtle changes would have taken place in American life which would be clearly demonstrable.

Throughout this story it has been evident that party lines have proven stronger than independent judgment; countless crimes against the welfare of the country and the best interests of the people have been committed in the name of partisanship. Popular government is thus faced with a dilemma: a two-party system is necessary to the functioning of a democracy, yet out of the two-party system has arisen a majority of the political ills of the nation. No political sulfa drugs have been evolved which could eradicate these election diseases.

The hundred and sixty-six years of elections have produced the following box scores:

Party	Candidate	Year	Win—Lose	
FEDERALIST	Washington	1788	1	
	Washington	1792	1	
	Adams	1796	1	
	Adams	1800		1
	Pinckney	1804		1
	Pinckney	1808		1
	Clinton	1812		1
	King	1816		1
			3	5

Party	Candidate	Year	Win—Lose	
DEMOCRATIC	Jefferson	1796		1
	Jefferson	1800	1	
	Jefferson	1804	1	
	Madison	1808	1	
	Madison	1812	1	
	Monroe	1816	1	
	Monroe	1820	1	
	Adams	1824	1	
	Jackson	1828	1	
	Jackson	1832	1	
	Van Buren	1836	1	
	Van Buren	1840		1
	Polk	1844	1	
	Cass	1848		1
	Pierce	1852	1	
	Buchanan	1856	1	
	Douglas	1860		1
	McClellan	1864		1
	Seymour	1868		1
	Greeley	1872		1
	Tilden	1876	Disputed	
	Hancock	1880		1
	Cleveland	1884	1	
	Cleveland	1888		1
	Cleveland	1892	1	
	Bryan	1896		1
	Bryan	1900		1
	Parker	1904		1
	Bryan	1908		1
	Wilson	1912	1	
	Wilson	1916	1	
	Cox	1920		1
	Davis	1924		1
	Smith	1928		1
	Roosevelt	1932	1	
	Roosevelt	1936	1	
	Roosevelt	1940	1	
	Roosevelt	1944	1	
	Truman	1948	1	
	Stevenson	1952		1
	Stevenson	1956		1
	Kennedy	1960	1	
	Johnson	1964	1	
			24	18
WHIG	Harrison	1836		1
	Harrison	1840	1	
	Clay	1844		1
	Taylor	1848	1	
	Scott	1852		1
			2	3

Party	Candidate	Year	Win—Lose	
REPUBLICAN	Fremont	1856		1
	Lincoln	1860	1	
	Lincoln	1864	1	
	Grant	1868	1	
	Grant	1872	1	
	Hayes	1876	Disputed	
	Garfield	1880	1	
	Blaine	1884		1
	Harrison	1888	1	
	Harrison	1892		1
	McKinley	1896	1	
	McKinley	1900	1	
	Roosevelt	1904	1	
	Taft	1908	1	
	Taft	1912		1
	Hughes	1916		1
	Harding	1920	1	
	Coolidge	1924	1	
	Hoover	1928	1	
	Hoover	1932		1
	Landon	1936		1
	Willkie	1940		1
	Dewey	1944		1
	Dewey	1948		1
	Eisenhower	1952	1	
	Eisenhower	1956	1	
	Nixon	1960		1
	Goldwater	1964		1
			15	12

Party	Win	Lose	Percentage
Democratic	24	18	.571
Republican	15	12	.556
Whig	2	3	.400
Federalist	3	5	.375

1776—*Federalist*—1816
1796—*Democratic*—?
1836—*Whig*—1856
1856—*Republican*—?

The results of this box score are interesting, yet it should be remembered that election results have to be measured qualitatively as well as quantitatively. A single victory of good judgment in time of crisis can atone for several election mistakes; conversely, one election error committed in a crucial hour can offset several wise victories in quieter years. Each man must set up for himself a qualitative box score on history.

No obscurity is so great as that which enchasms a defeated candidate for the presidency, not even that of the elected vice-president. There are only three ways to avoid this immersion: by retaining control over a political party, as Clay and Bryan succeeded in doing; by having established a reputation in an independent field, as had Greeley in journalism or Scott in military science; or by coming so close to victory, as had Hughes and Willkie, that they were able to "save face" and go forward in their work.

The story of presidential elections has not always been a pretty one: grievous wounds have been inflicted, dread diseases have been endemic. Yet for one hundred and seventy-six years the wounds have healed and the diseases have abated without killing the patient. That the American government has been able to sustain itself through forty-five major elections is one of the most promising performances in political history. Perhaps it is salutary that the body politic be ravaged at periodic intervals: it toughens, develops antibodies for the blood stream so that it cannot be killed off by the first adverse wind; although grown scarred and gnarled, democracy has developed the ability to withstand attack.

Every man interprets history according to his lights; the closer to the present the election lies, the stronger will be the divergence of opinion. The purpose of the biographer is to provoke rather than to persuade, and any difference of opinion which sends the reader back to the record will be salutary.

Source Notes

HORACE GREELEY

PAGE

13 "Fitness for president . . ." *Autobiography of Horace Greeley*, Ch. 8.

13 "Having loved . . . newspapers" *Autobiography of Horace Greeley*, Ch. 8.

14 "He chased rascals . . ." *Horace Greeley*, Don C. Seitz.

14 "His mind . . ." Julius Henri Browne quoted from Seitz.

15 "His nose . . ." Junius Henri Browne quoted from Seitz.

15 "I am drifting into a fight . . ." Seitz, p. 366.

17 "I am a beaten, broken . . ." Quoted by Seitz.

19 "Newspapers are, or ought to be . . ." *Autobiography of Horace Greeley*.

19 "His paper bristled . . ." Seitz.

20 "For forty years . . ." Seitz.

20 "We believe that . . ." *Tribune*, Aug. 13, 1853.

21 "A serious obstacle . . ." *Autobiography of Horace Greeley*, p. 154.

22 "The darkest day . . ." Seitz, p. 5.

24 "The cotton states . . ." *Horace Greeley and the Tribune in the Civil War*, R. R. Fahrney.

26 "At last a man . . ." John Bigelow.

26 Greeley's defense article, *Tribune*, May 23, 1867.

27 "The work of the convention . . ." *History of the Presidency*, Stanwood.

28 "I never saw . . ." Seitz, p. 380.

29 "For elevation of thought . . ." Seitz, p. 390.

30 "Grant's innocence . . ." *The Powers of the President*, Binkley.

31 "A fussy old man . . ." *A Man Named Grant*, Todd.

JAMES M. COX

33 "The power to take . . ." *Saturday Evening Post*, October 2, Vol. 193, Pt. 2, p. 10.

33 "When he goes fishing . . ." *Saturday Evening Post*.

33 "The same sort of admiration . . ." *Outlook*, Vol. 126, p. 193.

33 "He was forever reaching . . ." *Outlook*, Vol. 126.

34 "My friends are urging . . ." *Current Opinions*, Vol. 69, p. 85.

34 "I never talked . . ." *Outlook*, Vol. 126, p. 193 and fol.

34 "Coldly and absolutely . . ." *Outlook*, Vol. 126.

34 "A serious-minded man . . ." *Collier's*, quoted from *Literary Digest*, Vol. 66, p. 41.

35 "I can never remember the time . . ." *World's Work*, Vol. 41, p. 93.

36 "Cox was about the best reporter . . ." *Outlook*, Vol. 126, p. 40.

37 "The story of James M. Cox . . ." *Outlook*, Vol. 126.

41 "I sympathize with Jefferson's view . . ." *Forum*, Vol. 64, p. 151.

41 "A man of sturdy intellect . . ." "The Incredible Era," *The Life and Times of Warren G. Harding*, Adams.

43 "While it is true . . ." *Current Opinions*, Vol. 69, p. 139.
43 New York *World* and Tumulty quoted from *New Republic*, Vol. 23, p. 215.
43 New York *Globe*, San Francisco *Bulletin*, Syracuse *Herald*, New York *World* quoted from *Literary Digest*, Vol. 66, p. 12.
43 New York *Globe* quoted from *Literary Digest*, Vol. 66, p. 12.
44 Vox-populi jingle, quoted in "The Incredible Era," Conning Tower, Franklin P. Adams.
44 "It is a bitter disgrace . . ." *Forum*, Vol. 64, p. 151.
44 "I have no doubt . . ." *New Republic*, Vol. 23, p. 323.
46 "Harding stands for a kind . . ." *New Republic*, Vol. 23, p. 187.
48 "There is some hysteria . . ." *Saturday Evening Post*, October 2, Vol. 193, Pt. 2, p. 10.
Other sources consulted but not quoted directly: *The Independent*, Vol. 104, p. 3, *American Review of Reviews*, Vol. 62, p. 46; *The Bookman*, Vol. 52, p. 128.

HENRY CLAY

50 "I would rather be right . . ." *America's Silver Age*, Johnson, p. 42.
52 "An orphan boy . . ." *The Life of Henry Clay*, Van Deusen, pp. 5, 6.
53 "I never studied half enough . . ." McDowell Collection, Henry Clay to Henry Clay, Jr., April 19, 1829.
54 "Art of all arts . . ." Van Deusen, p. 9.
54 "Some superb instrument . . ." Van Deusen, p. 13.
55 "He fulfilled the popular conception . . ." *Henry Clay*, Mayo, Vol. 1.
58 General Glascock quote, *Autobiography of Horace Greeley*, pp. 103, 104.
59 "We are not legislating . . ." Van Deusen, p. 120.
62 "If an idea were taken up . . ." *Clay's Collected Letters*, Letter to J. S. Johnson, Sept. 19, 1824.
62 "When have I shown an avidity . . . ?" *Clay's Collected Letters*, Letter to Francis Brooks, Feb. 4, 1825.
62 "I think we are authorized . . ." *Clay's Collected Letters*, Letter to C. S. Johnson, July 23, 1831.
65 "Neither beautiful . . ." Van Deusen, p. 23.
67 "My friends . . ." *Henry Clay*, Carl Schurz, Vol. 2, pp. 180, 181.
67 "As to Jackson's veto measure . . ." Biddle to Clay, Aug. 1, 1832.
68 "The cause of Clay's failure . . ." *America's Silver Age*, Johnson.
68 "We are in the midst . . ." Van Deusen, p. 280.
69 "At the very beginning . . ." Van Deusen, p. 320.
70 "I am the most important man . . ." *Henry Clay*, Carl Schurz, Vol. 2, p. 181.
70 "Clay was far more concerned . . ." *Henry Clay and the Whig Party*, Poage, p. 47.
72 "Clay's resolutions were seized . . ." Johnson.
73 "Visiting all the important cities . . ." Schurz, Vol. 2, p. 241.
73 "As he read the death knell . . ." Van Deusen, p. 376.
73 "When the Whigs learned . . ." Schurz, Vol. 2, p. 266.
73 "The late blow . . ." Schurz, Vol. 2, p. 266.

WILLIAM JENNINGS BRYAN

77 "The Supreme Court is wrong . . ." *Bryan*, M. R. Werner, p. 4.

78 For the best physical descriptions of Bryan see *The Life of William J. Bryan,* Genevieve and John Herrick.

82 "They were like a trained choir," *The Memoirs of William J. Bryan,* edited by Mary Baird Bryan.

82 For the story of the convention see Werner, p. 73, and *Bryan: The Great Commoner,* J. C. Long.

86 For Bryan's description of the campaign see his *The First Battle, a Story of the Campaign of 1896.*

87 McKinley's canvass is described in *The Life of William McKinley,* Charles S. Olcott.

88 Dixon and Parkhurst are quoted from Werner, p. 86.

89 The story of Mark Hanna is well told in the biographies by Thomas Beer and Herbert Croly.

95 "A revolutionary change . . ." *Memoirs.*

96 For a good summation of Bryan's virtues see *William J. Bryan,* Wayne C. Williams.

98 "If events prove . . ." *Memoirs.*

ALTON B. PARKER

101 "The bank will meet its demands . . ." *World's Work,* Vol. 8, p. 4923.

101 "I hope you are not . . ." *Capital Stories about Famous Americans,* edited by Reverend Louis A. Banks, p. 2.

102 "As he develops . . ." *World's Work,* Vol. 8, p. 4923.

102 "An instinctive preference for cleanliness . . ." *Outlook,* Vol. 77, pp. 644, 646.

103 Eight-hour law, *Current Literature,* Vol. 36, p. 609.

103 "Presenting an average . . ." *Independent,* Vol. 56, p. 1111.

103 "There is no trick . . ." *Harper's Weekly,* Vol. 48, p. 664.

105 The reporter was James Creelman; the letter was reproduced in the *Review of Reviews,* Vol. 30, p. 131.

106 "One of the most exciting . . ." *America as a World Power,* Latané, Vol. 25, American National History Series.

107 "You made a contract . . ." *World's Work,* Vol. 8, p. 4923.

108 "You must run again . . ." *World's Work,* Vol. 8, p. 4923.

108 "Surrogate Parker . . ." *World's Work,* Vol. 8, p. 4923.

108 "Parker says he doesn't want the place . . ." *World's Work,* Vol. 8, p. 4923.

110 "I have no wish to be a candidate . . ." *World's Work,* Vol. 8, p. 4923.

111 "There will be . . ." *Harper's Weekly,* Vol. 48, pp. 1110–13.

111 "Only stupid people . . ." *Review of Reviews,* Vol. 30, p. 131.

111 The *Arena,* Vol. 32, p. 312.

111 The *Nation,* Vol. 77, p. 44.

112 "He would not gratuitously . . ." *Independent,* Vol. 56, p. 1111.

115 Parker on McKinley, *Review of Reviews,* Vol. 30, p. 131.

CHARLES EVANS HUGHES

117 "That is the strangest man . . ." *Literary Digest,* Vol. 52, p. 1860.

117 "I congratulate you . . ." *Literary Digest,* Vol. 52, p. 1860.

117 "You mustn't say that!" *World's Work,* Vol. 31, p. 412.

117 "I hope that, as a justice . . ." *Outlook,* Vol. 112, p. 602.

118 "Without mental reservation . . ." *Outlook,* Vol. 112, p. 602.

118 New York *World* and New York *Sun* quoted in *Literary Digest,* Vol. 51, p. 1272.

152 The Whig Platform, *A History of the Presidency*, Stanwood, Vol. 1, p. 252.
154 Scott's acceptance telegram, Elliott, p. 622.
155 "There never had been . . ." New York *Herald*, Aug. 17, 1852, quoted by Elliott from the Ohio State *Journal*, Nov. 20, 1852.
156 "A third-rate . . ." *Franklin Pierce*, Roy F. Nichols.
156 For portrait of Pierce see Nichols.
158 "Friend Winfield . . ." Scott's *Memoirs*, p. 7, note.

JOHN C. FREMONT

162 For the best account of Fremont's family background see *Fremont, Pathmarker of the West*, Allan Nevins, Vol. 1, Ch. 1.
163 For Fremont's relation with Nicollet see *Memoirs of the Life and Public Services of John C. Fremont*, John Bigelow.
165 "The discussions gave shape . . ." Nevins.
165 The account of Fremont's expeditions as written by himself will be found in *Memoirs of My Life*.
167 "Do not lose a day . . ." *Jessie Benton Fremont*, Catherine Coffin Phillips.
173 For the best accounts of the election see Nevins and *The Life of James Buchanan* by C. Ticknor Curtis, Vol. 2.
173 "A shallow, vain-glorious . . ." *A Man Unafraid*, Herbert Bashford and Harr Wagner.
174 "The election of Fremont . . ." Nevins.
174 "The campaign was full of personalities . . ." *Recollections of Elizabeth Benton Fremont*.
177 Criticisms of Fremont in St. Louis will be found in *John Charles Fremont*, Cardinal Leonidas Goodwin.

GEORGE B. McCLELLAN

181 "We are embarrassed . . ." *Abraham Lincoln*, Albert J. Beveridge, Vol. 1, p. 595; Myers, p. 33.
181 "The president is nothing more . . ." *General George B. McClellan*, Myers, p. 399.
182 McClellan's talk about making himself a dictator, Macartney.
182 "I find myself in a new . . ." Myers, p. 212.
183 "I have this moment received . . ." Myers, p. 293.
183 "Everything here . . ." Macartney, p. 85; Myers, p. 216.
183 "Any day may bring . . ." Myers, p. 289.
183 "I am tired of public life . . ." Macartney, p. 164.
184 McClellan's letters to his sister, Myers, p. 7.
185 "I am the only one . . ." Myers, p. 22.
186 McClellan asleep at Antietam, Macartney, p. 265.
186 "In the retreat . . ." Macartney, p. 195.
187 "Captain McClellan . . ." Myers, p. 28.
188 Confidence of Grant and Sherman, Macartney, p. 50; Grant on McClellan, Grant's *Memoirs*.
188 "McClellan's personal intercourse . . ." Myers, p. 191.
189 *George B. McClellan*, Eckenrode and Conrad, p. 27.
190 *General McClellan*, Michie, pp. 101, 103.
191 Comte de Paris suotation, Macartney, p. 97.
192 McClellan's sabotaging of Pope, Macartney, p. 220.
192 "Driblets," Macartney, p. 225.
192 Lincoln's telegram to McClellan, Macartney, p. 288.
192 "Lead us to Washington . . ." Macartney, p. 292.

WINFIELD SCOTT HANCOCK

SAMUEL J. TILDEN

STEPHEN A. DOUGLAS

JAMES G. BLAINE

271 "Pandemonium broke loose . . ." Muzzey, p. 281.
272 "United to rebuke . . ." Muzzey, p. 289.
272 "I oppose Blaine . . ." Muzzey, p. 297.
273 "Tell the truth!" *Grover Cleveland*, Nevins, p. 163.
274 For description of campaign see Muzzey, Chap. 12, Nevins, Chap. 11.
275 "The Democrats dream . . ." Muzzey, p. 314.
275 "Rum, Romanism and rebellion." Russell, p. 401.
276 "Elevated the standard of America . . ." Muzzey, p. 319.
276 "Toward Cleveland personally . . ." Muzzey, p. 325.
277 "What bitter discomfiture . . ." Muzzey, p. 7.
277 "Blaine was a phenomenon . . ." Russell, p. 3.

LEWIS CASS

278 "Basely to surrender . . ." *Lewis Cass*, Andrew C. McLaughlin, p. 78.
279 "The interests of the country . . ." McLaughlin, p. 338.
279 "I saw the Constitution born . . ." McLaughlin, p. 343.
279 "The people in the south . . ." Quoted from Lossing by McLaughlin, p. 339.
280 "A clever fellow . . ." McLaughlin, p. 37.
282 Cass as a commanding officer, *Sketch of the Life and Public Services of General Lewis Cass*, William T. Young.
283 "Oh, Major . . ." McLaughlin, p. 90.
283 "I never broke my word . . ." McLaughlin, p. 127; see *Life of Cass*, Young, for details of Cass's dealing with Indians.
284 "Of all purposes . . ." Quoted by McLaughlin, p. 123, from Michigan *Journal*.
284 "In proportion . . ." *Journal of the Legislative Council of Michigan for 1826*, McLaughlin, p. 122.
286 "He could be carried . . ." McLaughlin, p. 197–98.
287 "Every day satisfies me . . ." *Life and Times of Lewis Cass*, W. L. G. Smith.
288 "His speeches . . ." McLaughlin, p. 221.
289 "It was hoped . . ." McLaughlin, p. 230.
289 "If the relation . . ." McLaughlin, p. 232.
290 "No means, fair or foul . . .'" *Life of Cass*, Young.

HORATIO SEYMOUR

295 "I have not the slightest desire . . ." *Sketch of the Life of Horatio Seymour*, Alexander J. Wall.
296 "What is the use . . . ?" *Horatio Seymour*, Mitchell, p. 565.
296 "This convention has a perfect right . . ." Mitchell, p. 68.
296 "Under no circumstances . . ." Mitchell, p. 271, Wall, p. 24.
298 "Political opponents . . ." Mitchell, p. 20.
298 "In all respects . . ." Mitchell, p. 21.
299 "Doubtless our mother . . ." Wall, p. 65.
300 "Eminently respectable . . ." Mitchell, p. 57.
300 "He was conciliatory . . ." Mitchell, p. 74.
301 "One of the ablest . . ." Mitchell, p. 75.
301 Description of Seymour home, *Seymour and Blair*, David G. Croly.
302 "Tall, lean, alert . . ." Mitchell, p. 143.
302 Military secretary's report, Wall, p. 73.
303 "The idea pervades the bill . . ." Wall, p. 20.
303 "It is a very great sacrifice . . ." Mitchell, p. 164.